Contents

About the author

I have broad experience in what is perhaps a narrow field, having worked in the private EFL sector all my working life, as teacher, director of studies, school director and teacher-trainer, now in Spain (where I live), but previously in Egypt and with short stints in the UK and my native New Zealand. Teacher education has always been my special interest and was the subject of my MA dissertation at the University of Reading.

Recently, I have been moderating a busy internet discussion group. To give you a flavour of that group, here is recent posting of mine:

> Let me put it on record, though, that I really don't believe 'there is only one way to teach'. Even ignoring the truism that there are of course as many ways to teach as there are teachers, the variables of context, learner, teacher, and language (i.e. what role language is playing in the immediate teaching–learning moment) suggest that any notion of effectiveness is going to be elusive, slippery, ephemeral, and problematic. But better, I suggest, an approach that embraces the elusive, slippery, ephemeral and problematic than one that attempts to pre-empt it or circumvent it, as in the traditional coursebook and its one-mcnugget-a-day, faux-scientific, text-as-pretext, learner-as-consumer, kind of methodology.

Scott Thornbury

Thanks

... to my editorial team: Jill Florent, Adrian Underhill, Penny Hands and Anna Cowper. Huge thanks, also, to Felicity O'Dell, Jonathan Marks, and Alan Pulverness, whose insightful reports helped shape (and correct) the work in progress, and to Brian Brennan, John Field, Ben Goldstein, John Gray and Carol Read, who generously contributed expertise from their respective fields. (But only the author is to blame for any residual errors in the text). Finally, this book would never have materialized had it not been for the inspiration and enthusiasm of David Riley, to whom I owe a tremendous debt.

Dedication

P is for Piet.

About the series

Macmillan Books for Teachers

Welcome to the Macmillan Books for Teachers series. These books are for you if you are a trainee teacher, practising teacher or teacher trainer. They help you to:
- develop your skills and confidence
- reflect on what you do and why you do it
- inform your practice with theory
- improve your practice
- become the best teacher you can be

The handbooks are written from a humanistic and student-centred perspective. They offer:
- practical techniques and ideas for classroom activities
- key insights into relevant background theory
- ways to apply techniques and insights in your work

The authors are teachers and trainers. We take a 'learning as you go' approach in sharing our experience with you. We help you reflect on ways you can facilitate learning, and bring your personal strengths to your work. We offer you insights from research into language and language learning and suggest ways of using these insights in your classroom. You can also go to http://www.onestopenglish.com and ask the authors for advice.

We encourage you to experiment and to develop variety and choice, so that you can understand the how and why of your work. We hope you will develop confidence in your own teaching and in your ability to respond creatively to new situations.

Adrian Underhill

Titles in the Series

Introduction

This is a book for teachers of English as a foreign or second language. It is for those who are involved in training or development, whether pre-service or in-service, and whether informal or as part of a certificated training course. Training and development involves not just the acquisition of new skills and techniques but also a specialized *language* to talk about them and to make sense of how other professionals talk about them. Specialized language – called *jargon* by outsiders, but *terminology* by those who use it – is the *discourse* of any particular group of professionals. It facilitates communication within the group, and it identifies individuals as belonging to the group. Professional training and development, therefore, means becoming a member of a discourse community, and becoming comfortable with its language. This book aims to help you to do that.

Learning the terminology of language teaching also means understanding the concepts represented by these terms and understanding how they are interrelated. So, this book is more than just a glossary or a dictionary. It is also an encyclopaedia, where each entry provides a short summary of the major issues, debates and practical implications associated with each concept, as well as making connections between related concepts. You can check the meaning of terms that are new to you. You can also gain a more wide-ranging understanding of a specific topic of interest by reading around a topic and following up its network of cross-references.

The topic areas covered in this book are those that inform the professional skills of a language teacher. These divide into three main fields: *language*, *learning* and *teaching*. This means that you will find an entry on *modal verbs* alongside an entry on *motivation* alongside one on *mixed ability*. For convenience, these fields have been subdivided into the following categories:

Language-related topics:
- *discourse*, including *pragmatics*
- *functions*, including *notions*
- *grammar*
- *linguistics*
- *phonology*
- *sociolinguistics*
- *vocabulary*

Learning-related topics:
- *psychology*, including *psycholinguistics*
- *SLA* (*second language acquisition*)

Teaching-related topics:
- *methodology*
- *professional (development)*
- *testing*

These categories are used as labels to classify each of the 376 entries. The entries themselves have been chosen because their headwords figure prominently in the syllabuses of training courses, or in the indexes and glossaries of the standard reference books for teachers. The list of entries includes terms that are central to language teaching, such as *listening* and *assessment*, as well as topics that are easily confused, such as *inductive* and *deductive learning*. It also includes others that, in our field, have a specialized use, such as *scaffolding* and *task*. You will not, however, find biographical information about individual scholars and writers, such as Noam Chomsky or Diane Larsen-Freeman. Instead, you will find references to the contributions that these individuals have made to their particular field, under the appropriate headings (such as *mentalism* and *grammaring*). There is an index at the back which includes all the terms and names that are used in the entries, and which do not have their own entry. Entries are also cross-referenced using an arrow sign (→).

Every effort has been made to keep the entries non-technical and readable, even to users with little or no specialist knowledge. Bibliographical information has been kept to an absolute minimum. For users who are interested in following up particular areas in more detail, there is a list of further reading on page 256, where useful resources (both print and web-based) are included under the twelve main topic headings used to label the entries.

A

ability FUNCTION

The most common ways of expressing the notions of ability and inability are: (1) lexically, using the adjectives *able/unable (to)*, *(in)capable(of)* and verbs such as *to manage (to do something)*, *to succeed (in doing something)* and *to enable/help/assist/empower*, etc *someone to do something*; (2) grammatically, using the **modal verbs** *can/can't* and *could/couldn't*:

> *Scientists are now able to measure these changes much more accurately.*
> *He is incapable of singing in tune.*
> *On a clear day you can see forever.*
> *You can't take it with you.*

Can is limited to present contexts and general truths, but for a future ability *be able to* is used: *One day we'll be able to live on the moon.* In the past tense, both *could* and *be able to* are used to talk about general abilities, but only *be able to* is used to talk about achieving something on a particular occasion:

> *She could/was able to speak fluent Chinese when she was younger.*
> *The door was locked but Jeff was able to open it with his credit card.*

Can and *could* also express **permission** and **possibility**.

Good contexts for teaching the language of ability include: talking about skills, eg in a job interview; talking about past achievements and difficulties that were surmounted (eg in a holiday narrative); making excuses (for things you can't, or couldn't, do) and describing what particular animals are capable of.

academic writing → **English for special purposes**

accent PHONOLOGY

A person's accent is the way their pronunciation reveals their social and/or geographical background. Someone from New Zealand, for example, typically speaks with a New Zealand accent, which nowadays means that *shear* and *share* are both pronounced *shear*. But within New Zealand there will be differences in accent according to factors such as social class and educational background. The same applies anywhere. It is a common misconception that some people speak with 'no accent'. What this usually means is that they speak with an accent that is the listener's own accent, or that they speak a standard variety – that is, one that is not closely identified with a particular region. **Received Pronunciation** (RP) is considered a prestigious British standard accent, although fewer and fewer British people actually speak it. Learners of English may aspire to speak with a **Standard English** accent, but few achieve this, nor is it necessary for **intelligibility**. Worse, the adoption of an alien accent may threaten the speaker's sense of **identity**, since, from childhood, a person's accent is an important marker of who they are.

Traditionally, the teaching of **pronunciation** has focused on *accent reduction*, ie, reducing the learner's first language accent in favour of a Standard English one. Now that English is taught increasingly as an international language (→ **English as an international language**), an alternative approach, called *accent addition* is gaining favour, both on practical and ethical grounds. This approach recommends that only those features that promote mutual intelligibility between speakers of English – irrespective of their L1 – should be 'added' to the speaker's L1 accent (→ **phonological core**).

acculturation SLA

Acculturation is the process by which a person integrates into a particular culture. Some researchers have claimed that success in second language learning has a lot to do with the learner's degree of acculturation into the second language culture. For example, John Schumann tracked the development of one Spanish-speaking adult learner in the USA, called Alberto, whose English had effectively fossilized (→ **fossilization**). Schumann identified features of Alberto's **interlanguage**, such as the absence of **articles**. Some of these features closely matched aspects of pidgin languages, that is, languages that originally developed for trading purposes and which have a reduced grammar and vocabulary. He argued that this 'pidginized' nature of Alberto's interlanguage was due to his social isolation and his lack of any apparent desire or need to acculturate. The acculturation hypothesis was one of the first theories of SLA that attempted to prioritize social factors over purely cognitive ones, and, although ignored for a number of years, it has now been partly rehabilitated under the name **socialization**.

accuracy SLA

Accuracy is the extent to which a learner's use of a second language conforms to the rules of the language. This is usually measured in terms of *grammatical* accuracy. For example, *What means this?* or *I no understand* are inaccurate according to standard usage. It is also possible to talk about accuracy of **vocabulary** use (eg *She sent us a lot of homework*, for *She set us …*), and of **pronunciation** as well (*Where do you leave?* for *Where do you live?*). Because accuracy is relatively easy to test, it is often used as a measure of a learner's progress (→ **testing**).

Accuracy is often contrasted with **fluency**, ie, the capacity to be communicative in real-time conditions. Accuracy was once thought to be a precondition for fluency. Different **methods** of teaching – such as the **audiolingual method** – and different **lesson designs** (eg **PPP**) are based on this assumption. But to withhold fluency activities until the learners are accurate is now considered unrealistic. Nor does an 'accuracy first' approach reflect the way people learn languages naturally. Research into the **order of acquisition** of grammatical structures suggests that accuracy may be 'late-acquired'. Certainly it is the case that you learn to be fluent in your first language long before you are accurate in it.

There is often a trade-off between accuracy and fluency: if you focus on one, the other suffers, and vice versa. What's more, accuracy can vary according to **task** factors, such as the amount of time the speaker has for planning while speaking. The more time you give learners, the more accurate they are likely to be. At issue, too, are the standards by which accuracy is measured. For learners of **English as an international language**, in particular, native-speaker standards of English may no longer be applicable.

Classroom activities that target accuracy traditionally include **drills** and grammar **exercises**. There are grounds to believe, though, that the most effective incentive to improving accuracy is receiving negative **feedback**. That means getting clear messages as to when an **error** has occurred, as well as some guidance as to how to correct it (→ **correction**).

achievement test TESTING

Achievement tests are designed to test what learners have learned (or *achieved*) over a week, month, term or entire course. Thus, they differ from **proficiency** tests, which measure overall ability, irrespective of the teaching process. Achievement test items target the specific components of the **syllabus** (such as grammar items), although they may also test the overall **goals** of the course (where these have been specified), such as the learners' communicative performance (→ **competence**). While traditional achievement tests consist largely of grammar and vocabulary exercise-types, more innovative forms of achievement testing include asking learners to assemble and present **portfolios**. The choice of test type has important implications in terms of washback, ie, the effect on teaching. And, since achievement tests are directly related to the content of the teaching programme, they provide feedback on the teaching-learning process, and are therefore useful data for course **evaluation**. There are good reasons, then, why the design and implementation of these tests should not be left solely to administrators, but should involve teachers themselves (→ **testing**).

acquisition → **language acquisition**

action research METHODOLOGY

Action research is a form of teacher-driven research, the twin goals of which are to improve classroom practice, and to 'empower' teachers, ie, to give them greater control over their working lives. Action research is typically motivated less by the desire to answer the 'big' questions (such as *How do people learn?*) than by the need to solve a specific teaching problem in the local context. (*Why are my learners having difficulty with this kind of activity?*) It involves cycles of action and **reflection**. Having identified a problem, the teacher, either alone, or in collaboration with colleagues, follows an experiential learning cycle of *planning* ⇨ *acting* ⇨ *observing* ⇨ *reflecting*, which in turn leads to another research cycle. Action research is sometimes thought to lack the rigour of academic research. It can be made more rigorous by collecting data from different sources, or by the use of more than one data-gathering tool. For example, to investigate how coursebooks are being used in a school, a questionnaire could be distributed to teachers. The findings of this questionnaire could then be checked against the results of a survey of student opinions, or by classroom observation, or by both.

active (voice) → **passive**

activity METHODOLOGY

An activity is a general term to describe what learners are required to do, using the target language, at any one stage in the course of a lesson, and can include anything from **exercises** and **drills** (where the focus is primarily on the manipulation of the forms of the language) to **tasks** and **project work** (where the emphasis is on creating meaningful interaction or meaningful texts). Activities can involve any one of the four language **skills**, or a combination of these – such as listening and speaking, or reading and writing. They can also be organized so that learners are doing the activity individually, or in pairs or in groups or as a whole class (→ **classroom interaction**). *Activity-based learning*, in which the focus is entirely on projects, games and arts and crafts, is, arguably, better suited to the learning styles of **young learners** than is a more traditional, knowledge-based teaching approach.

activity-based learning → **activity**

adjacency pair → **conversation analysis**

adjective GRAMMAR

An adjective is a 'describing' word, like *old, expensive* or *boring*. Many adjectives are formed from nouns or verbs by the addition of **affixes**, as in *careful, useless, undrinkable*. Compound adjectives such as *broad-shouldered* or *top secret* are formed from two words, while others such as *interesting* or *shocked* are derived from **participles**.

An adjective typically has the following properties:

- It can go both before a noun, and after a **linking verb** (such as the verb *to be*): *a boring film; The film was boring* (compare *a horror film*, but not *★The film was horror. Horror* is a noun, not an adjective → **modifier**).
- It can be modified by an adverb, like *very* or *rather*: *a very boring film* (but not *★a very horror film*).
- It can appear as a comparative or superlative: *The film was more boring than the book*; *the oldest building in the street* (but not *★The most horror film …*).

When adjectives precede a noun, as in *the pink panther* or *it's a wonderful life*, they are said to be *attributive*. When they follow a linking verb, as in *life is beautiful* or *the king is alive*, they are being used in a *predicative* way. Sometimes adjectives can be used as nouns, with the definite **article**: *the good, the bad* and *the ugly*; *the spy who came in from the cold*.

Adjectives can be either *gradable* or *non-gradable*. Gradable adjectives – like *good* or *cold* – are adjectives that describe qualities that exist to different degrees, as in *quite good, very cold*. These contrast with non-gradable adjectives, such as *perfect* or *freezing*. Something is either *perfect* or it is not: you cannot say that it is *a bit perfect*, or *extremely perfect*. You can only say that it is *completely perfect* or *absolutely perfect*.

If more than one adjective precedes a noun, the usual order is:

determiner	adjectives					noun
	evaluation	size	age	colour	defining	
a	*lovely*	*little*	*antique*		*Chinese*	*vase*
three		*enormous*		*red*	*plastic*	*roses*

Adjectives are often taught in the following **lexical sets**: to describe people (*tall, slim, attractive*, etc); to describe places (*busy, peaceful, industrial*, etc); to describe the weather (*cold, rainy, mild*, etc); to describe clothes (*red, woollen, tight*, etc) and accommodation (*cheap, sunny, quiet*, etc); and to evaluate experiences (*exciting, dull, delicious*, etc). Texts in which adjectives occur frequently are typically descriptive, and may have a persuasive purpose, especially if the adjectives are strongly evaluative (→ **appraisal**), as in this extract from a brochure[1] (the adjectives are underlined):

The idyllic and unspoilt Greek island of Skyros is the home of two unique holiday communities, Atsitsa and the Skyros Centre. A holiday at either

[1] *Skyros '96*, Skyros, Eastcliff Road, Shanklin, Isle of Wight POS7 6AA

centre is a <u>delightful</u> combination of sun, sea, and <u>spectacular</u> Aegean scenery and <u>delicious</u> food. More than this, it offers the <u>stimulating</u> company of <u>like-minded</u> people and <u>fascinating</u> courses taught by a staff team that includes <u>world famous</u> tutors and authors.

adjunct → **adverbial**

adolescents, teaching METHODOLOGY

Adolescence is an ideal time to learn a second language, according to the research evidence (→ **age**). Adolescents tend to outperform adults, and to progress more rapidly than younger learners, at least to begin with. They do better at grammar than either older or younger learners, although, unlike many younger learners, they do not usually achieve a native-like pronunciation (→ **young learners**). Working against these positive cognitive findings, however, are a number of negative affective factors (→ **affect**) including acute self-consciousness. Adolescence is a period of rapid change, both physical and mental, and one in which the search for a personal **identity** is uppermost. In order to nurture the development of this identity, teaching should provide adolescents with opportunities to take some control of, and responsibility for, their own learning. At the same time, situations that may threaten their vulnerable sense of self-esteem should be avoided. Activities which enable them to express themselves in constructive ways and thereby assert their individuality, but without exposing them to the ridicule of their peers, are recommended. Asking teenagers to perform, without rehearsal, a coursebook roleplay in front of the class is potentially disastrous. But asking them to collaborate on choosing a scenario of their own, to script and rehearse it, and then to record it, with the addition of sound effects, as if it were a radio play, is likely to work much better.

advanced learner METHODOLOGY

An advanced learner is one who matches the description of a *proficient user* (levels C1 and C2) according to the **Common European Framework (CEF)**, and is thus distinguished from an *independent user* (levels B1 and B2) and a *basic user* (levels A1 and A2). Here is the way the CEF describes the C1 band[2]:

> Can understand a wide range of demanding, longer texts, and recognise implicit meaning. Can express him/herself fluently and spontaneously without much obvious searching for expressions. Can use language flexibly and effectively for social, academic and professional purposes. Can produce clear, well-structured, detailed text on complex subjects, showing controlled use of organisational patterns, connectors and cohesive devices.

The proficiency of advanced learners may be due to prolonged instruction, or prolonged exposure, or (more likely) a combination of both. This means that no two advanced learners will be the same, nor have the same needs. Some advanced learners will be communicatively fully effective, but may need fine-tuning in order to improve their **accuracy**. Others will demonstrate exceptional grammatical accuracy, but may lack conversational **fluency**. For the teacher of advanced learners this can pose a dilemma. But on the plus side, advanced learners are – by definition – successful learners, and probably largely self-directed, with a clear idea of their needs, and the ability to express these needs in

[2] *Common European Framework of Reference for Languages: Learning, Teaching, Assessment,* Council of Europe, 2001, p 24.

terms of learning objectives. This makes them ideal candidates for a negotiated **syllabus**, whereby the learners themselves are given some say in choosing the goals and content (including the materials) of their course (→ **beginner**; → **intermediate learner**).

adverb GRAMMAR

Adverbs are members of a **word class** that is so large and mixed that it is often said 'If in doubt about a word, classify it as an adverb.' The easiest adverbs to recognize are those words formed from adjectives by the addition of -*ly*, like *slowly* and *totally*, and which either describe the circumstances of an action (*Time passed slowly*), or which precede a word or phrase to express degree (*I was totally exhausted*). There are some common adverbs that take the same form as their adjective equivalent: *She's a hard worker.* (*hard* = adjective). *She works hard.* (*hard* = adverb). Other examples are *fast, late, early, high* and *loud*.

Like adjectives, many adverbs have comparative and superlative forms: *She drove more slowly. They sang the loudest* (→ **comparison**). Adverbs can also be premodified by other adverbs: *She drove very slowly.* When an adverb forms the head of a **phrase** (as in *much more slowly; very slowly indeed*, etc), the combination is called an *adverb phrase*. This is *not* the same as an **adverbial**, although both single-word adverbs and adverb phrases often function as adverbials in sentences:

subject	verb	adverbial
She	*drove*	*slowly* (= adverb)
She	*drove*	*more slowly than ever* (= adverb phrase)
She	*drove*	*to the shops* (= prepositional phrase)

The kinds of circumstantial meanings conveyed by adverbs include *manner* (*She drove slowly*); *place* (*They ran outside*); *time* (*We arrive tomorrow*); and *frequency* (*It often rains*). Adverbs of *degree* serve to modify the meaning of the word they precede, either by intensifying it (as in *absolutely fabulous*), or by reducing it (as in *fairly crowded*). Some adverbs have a *focusing* function, that is, they focus attention on one part of the clause: *It was only five o'clock. She can also sing.* Some adverbs stand apart from their associated clause or sentence, either because they have a linking function: *Eventually, the bus came*; or because they express the speaker's attitude (or *stance*) to what is being said: *Maybe he is busy. Frankly, I am fed up.*

Adverbs can take one (or more) of three positions in a sentence: *initial* (*Suddenly it started raining*); *mid* (*It suddenly started raining*) and *end*: (*It started raining suddenly*). While there is considerable flexibility allowed (most adverbs can stand in mid-position, for example), many adverbs are limited in terms of which of these positions they can take. And adverbs never go between the verb and its object: *⋆He plays often football.*

Because of the important meanings they convey (such as time, place and frequency) as well as their commenting and linking functions, adverbs appear early in teaching syllabuses, although they tend to be labelled, not as adverbs, but as *time expressions* or *linkers*, for example. Only adverbs of manner and of frequency are dealt with as adverbs in their own right.

adverbial GRAMMAR

An adverbial is one of the five possible elements in a **clause** or **sentence**. It functions like an **adverb** in that (1) it contributes circumstantial information to the clause or sentence, or (2) it serves to comment on what is being expressed, or (3) it links clauses or sentences to some other component of the text:

circumstance   *comment*   *link*

In winter,   generally speaking, it freezes.   As a result, the pipes burst.

Adverbials can consist of a single word (*She phoned yesterday*), or a phrase (*She phoned on Tuesday*) or a clause (called an *adverbial clause*: *She phoned when she heard the news*).

The most common way of forming adverbials are (1) adverbs and adverb phrases: *She ran fast. She ran faster than the others*); (2) **prepositional phrases**: *She ran up the stairs*; (3) some **noun phrases**: *She didn't run this morning*; and (4) clauses: *As soon as she heard the explosion, she ran*. Note that a sentence can consist of several adverbials, and in several different positions: *As soon as she heard the explosion, she quickly ran up the stairs*.

All the above examples demonstrate the way that adverbials function as part of the internal structure of the sentence: in this respect they are called *adjuncts*. But some adverbials act as if they stood apart from the sentence, and were commenting on it: *Not surprisingly, the shops were closed. It was not cheap, to put it mildly*. These adverbials are called *disjuncts*. They often express the speaker's attitude, or *stance*. There is a third class of adverbials, called *conjuncts*, that link clauses, sentences, and whole paragraphs: … *All in all, it was a real bargain*. … *On the other hand, the service was excellent* (→ **linker**).

Where there is more than one adverbial at the end of a sentence, the preferred order is represented by the letters M P T, where M stands for *manner* (or *movement*), P stands for *place* and T stands for *time*: *She ran quickly* (M) *up the stairs* (P) *when she heard the explosion* (T).

Adverbials are seldom labelled as such in language teaching materials, and their importance is therefore often overlooked. Yet they present an enormous challenge to learners, not least because many adverbials are formulaic (→ **formulaic language**) and therefore have to be learned from scratch, as it were (*from scratch* and *as it were* being two typical examples).

advising, giving advice FUNCTION

Common ways of expressing the **function** of giving advice involve the use of the **modal verbs** *should* and *ought to*, as in *You should take it easy. You ought to phone your mum*. The same verbs can be used to ask for advice: *What should I do? What do you think I ought to do? Must* (in its stressed form) is used to make strong recommendations and **suggestions**: *You must try Jan's cake. It's delicious*. Other ways of expressing advice include:

had better. *You'd better take a taxi.*
if I were you: *I wouldn't mention it to her, if I were you.*

plus, more formally, the use of the words *advice/advise*:

My advice to you is to join a gym. / I'd advise you to join a gym.

Often the response to a request for advice is for the speaker simply to narrate what he or she did in similar circumstances:

~ *What should we see when we're in Barcelona?*
~ *What we did was we took a tour on the tourist bus ...*

Topics that are good for teaching advice include: health and fitness, travel, relationships, decorating and educational or career choices.

affect PSYCHOLOGY

Affect (stressed on the first syllable) is the general word for emotion or feelings. The *affective factors* that positively or negatively influence language learning are emotional states such as pleasure and anxiety. Affective factors are often contrasted with cognitive factors such as intelligence and **learning style**. It is a key principle in **humanistic teaching** that instruction should focus not only on thinking but also on feeling. Indeed, humanistic teachers believe that feeling good about learning (called *positive affect*) is a precondition for learning. One way of achieving positive affect is to reduce the level of stress in the classroom, by, for example, building a supportive classroom **dynamic**, and by avoiding teaching behaviours – such as **correction** – that might be considered judgmental. Even some cognitive accounts of second language acquisition foreground affective factors. Stephen Krashen, for example, hypothesized the existence of what he called the *affective filter*, which acts to control the amount and quality of **input** learners receive. Learners with a low affective filter are emotionally well-disposed to processing input, but those whose filter is set high, because of stress, anxiety, or negative **attitudes**, will not process the input so effectively, and this will slow down or even block their rate of acquisition. There is also evidence to suggest that strong emotional associations with a word improve the word's chances of being stored in **memory**, a finding which argues for activities that encourage learners to make personal associations with new vocabulary.

affective filter → **affect**

affirmative → **negation**

affix, affixation VOCABULARY

An affix is an element that is added to a word and which changes its meaning. Affixes that are added to the beginning of a word are called *prefixes* (the *pre-* of *prefix* is a good example) and one that is added to the end of a word, such as *-ation* in *affixation*, is called a *suffix*. Affixes can change a word into an **antonym** (or *opposite*), as in *like* ➪ *unlike*, or *like* ➪ *dislike*, or from one **word class** to another as in *like* (= adjective) ➪ *likeness* (= noun) or ➪ *liken* (verb). Affixes can also have a grammatical function, as in the case of *-(e)d*, which adds past tense meaning to regular verbs: *add* ➪ *added*. The process of forming words by adding affixes is called *affixation* and is extremely productive in English (→ **word formation**). Knowledge of the form and meaning of the most common affixes in English is a useful tool for unlocking the meaning of many words that might otherwise be unfamiliar.

Some common affixes in English are:

	affix	meaning	added to	example
prefix	*in-* *im-* *il-* *un-*	not	adjectives	*insane* *impure* *illiterate* *unclear*
	mis-	wrongly	verbs	*mislead*
	sub-	beneath	nouns, adjectives, verbs	*subway*
	re-	again, back	verbs	*rewrite*
suffix	*-ship*	status, condition	nouns	*friendship*
	-ify	causative	adjectives and nouns	*simplify, beautify*
	-ise, -ize	process	nouns, adjectives	*nationalize*
	-ish	somewhat	adjectives	*warmish*
	-ation	state, action	verbs	*exploration*
	-er, -or	actor	verbs	*teacher, actor*
	-able/-ible	ability	verbs	*drinkable*
	-ly	in the manner	adjectives	*slowly*

affordance LINGUISTICS

An affordance is a particular property of the environment that is potentially useful to an organism. A leaf, for example, *affords* food for some creatures, shade for others, or building material for still others. It's the same leaf, but its affordances differ, depending on how it is regarded, and by whom. The term has been borrowed from ecology to describe the language learning opportunities that exist in the learner's linguistic 'environment'. It captures the way that language learning emerges out of meaningful activity, and it is used in preference to the term **input**, which has mechanistic, information-processing, associations (→ **sociocultural learning theory**). It is argued that one way of increasing learning affordances is to provide learners with a learning environment that prioritizes meaningful activity. Similarly, when learners receive feedback on *what* they are saying (rather than simply *how* they are saying it) they are more likely to perceive and use language affordances:

> **Student** I am live in new apartment.
> **Teacher** Tell us about it.
> **Student** Well, it's very nice. It's near …

affricate → **consonant**

age SLA

The precise relationship between age and second language learning remains unresolved and controversial, despite a good deal of research into the issue. It is still not clear what the best age to begin learning a second language is, or even whether there *is* a best age. (There may simply be 'best conditions'). Nor is it clear whether, and how, the process is different in children compared to adults. Clearly, there are cognitive, conceptual and maturity differences between children and adults that do make a difference in the learning process (→ **young learners**). However, with regard to grammar, research suggests that the acquisition process is largely unaffected by age. That is to say, both children and adults go through the same stages (→ **order of acquisition**). The rate of acquisition, and the ultimate level of success, varies, though. In formal (ie, classroom) contexts, **adolescent** and adult learners appear to do better on all linguistic measures (including pronunciation). But, in the long term, and with continued exposure, children are likely to become more native-like, and (with rare exceptions) only children are capable of acquiring a native **accent** in informal (ie, non-classroom) learning contexts. 'The younger, the better' is an argument that has encouraged many education authorities to introduce second language learning into the school curriculum at an early age, even at the pre-school stage in some countries (→ **primary**). However, the results and benefits of this are still inconclusive.

agency METHODOLOGY

If you have agency you have control of your own actions, including your mental activity. Learners are said to have agency if they are in control of their own learning. The notion of agency comes from **critical pedagogy**. Advocates of critical pedagogy draw a contrast between, on the one hand, traditional teaching approaches, where the learner is the *object* of the teaching process, and, on the other, progressive approaches, where the learner is viewed as the *subject* of the learning process. In this role, learners are encouraged to take initiative, solve problems, and discover things for themselves (→ **learner-centred instruction**). A 'sense of agency' has also been identified as a factor that contributes to **motivation**. Learners who feel they are responsible for their own actions are likely to go further. And they do not need to be rewarded or praised: they can take credit for their own success. On the other hand, learners who feel that learning is out of their control, and who depend on the approval of the teacher, may languish in a state of 'learned helplessness'.

agreeing/disagreeing FUNCTION

The functions of agreeing and disagreeing are ways of responding to statements of **opinion**, and to **suggestions**. They are commonly realized lexically, most literally by the verbs *agree* and *disagree*, as in *Yes, I agree (with you)* or *I (totally) disagree*. Other agreement expressions include *You're right*; *Good idea*; *I know*; and *I think so (too)*. Strong agreement can be expressed by *absolutely* and *exactly*. Mild agreement, on the other hand, is often signalled by verbs like *suppose* and *guess*, as in *I suppose so*; *I guess that's true*, or with *modal verbs*, as in *That may be true*; *You could be right*.

Disagreeing with someone poses a threat to their *face* (→ **politeness**), so it is often softened (or *mitigated*) by the use of **discourse markers** such as *Yes, but* ... or *I take your point, but* ... – often an indication that the speaker has not taken the point at all!

Teaching learners a set of expressions for agreeing and disagreeing is particularly useful as preparation for **discussions** and debates. These expressions can be displayed on the classroom wall for ready reference.

aids METHODOLOGY

Teaching rarely occurs without the use of some form of teaching aid, even if this is nothing more than a blackboard and chalk (or a whiteboard and felt-tipped pens). With the advent of the **direct method**, where translation and explanation were replaced with demonstration and illustration, the need for visual aids, including wall charts and flashcards, became a priority, especially for the teaching of vocabulary. And even better than pictures of things were the real things themselves (called *realia*, pronounced /riːælɪə/). Nowadays charts have largely been replaced with projections from either an overhead projector (OHP) using overhead transparencies (OHTs), or a data projector, which projects prepared presentations directly from a computer. *Interactive whiteboards* are becoming increasingly popular in institutions that can afford them. These permit the projection and manipulation of digitalized teaching content, both original and published. Materials are available in most classrooms (→ **materials**), whether mediated by the more traditional audio and video tape players, or by digital means, using CD and DVD players. Computers are increasingly used in many schools and classrooms as an aid to learning (→ **computer-assisted language learning**) and as a means for putting learners in contact with other learners and teachers (→ **computer-mediated communication**). For **young learners**, where learning through activity and play is encouraged (→ **language play**), classroom aids may include a variety of games, including card games and board games, and materials for creative language work, such as coloured pens, scissors, paste, etc. The best 'aids' to learning, of course, are the students themselves, with all the wealth of experience and knowledge (including language knowledge) that they bring to the classroom.

aim → **lesson plan**

allophone → **phoneme**

ALTE (Association of Language Testers of Europe) → **Common European Framework**

alveolar → **consonant**

American English SOCIOLINGUISTICS

Despite Bernard Shaw's quip that Britain and the United States were 'two countries divided by a common language', the differences between the two varieties of English are relatively few, compared to their similarities. The main areas of divergence between standard American English (AmE) and standard British English (BrE) fall into these categories:

1. *Pronunciation*: apart from easily recognized differences in voice quality, such as nasal drawl (→ **paralinguistics**), AmE has fewer vowel **phonemes** than BrE

(sixteen vs twenty). This is partly because AmE lacks the **diphthongs** /ɪə/, /ɛə/, /ʊə/, as in *sheer, share, sure*, using instead the combinations /ɪr/, /ɛr/, /ʊr/. Moreover, where BrE has the sound /ɒ/, as in *cot* or *dog*, AmE uses either /ɑː/ or /ɔː/ (so that *cot* and *caught* sound identical). The **consonant** distinctions are the same in both varieties, but with some differences in articulation so that, for example, when the sounds /t/ and /d/ occur between vowels they are 'flapped' so that *latter* and *ladder* sound the same. Apart from these general tendencies there are many words which are either sounded or stressed differently in the two varieties, *tomato* being the most celebrated. Others include: *pasta, data, vase* and *advertisement*.

2. *Spelling*: The tendency, in AmE, to simplify and regularize spelling results in *program* (as opposed to BrE *programme*), *dialog* (*dialogue*), *traveler* (*traveller*) and *plow* (*plough*). Moreover, somewhat arbitrary distinctions in BrE, such as *practice* (noun) and *practise* (verb), have been collapsed in AmE (*practice* for both noun and verb). And certain word endings that are variable in BrE, such as *-or* (*anchor*) and *-our* (*colour*), have been regularized in AmE (both *anchor* and *color*).

3. *Lexis*: It is in the area of vocabulary choice that differences are most often noted, and which most affect teaching decisions. Lexical differences vary from (1) those words for which there is no equivalent in the other variety, such as BrE *backbencher* or *giro*, and AmE *ballpark* and *dime*; (2) words that occur exclusively in one or the other variety, but which have a synonym in the other variety, like AmE *elevator, streetcar* and *liquor store*, and BrE *lift, tram* and *off-licence*; (3) those that occur in both varieties, but with different meanings, such as *subway* (which in Britain is an underpass, but in the US is the underground train system); other examples are *college, vest* and *bill*; and (4) those, like *flat* and *apartment*, that are used in both varieties, but with different frequency or connotation (*flat* being more common in BrE, *apartment* more common in AmE).

4. *Grammar*: The main grammatical differences that have implications on the teaching of English include (1) the AmE preference for the past simple over the present perfect with *just, already* and *yet*, as in *Did you have brunch yet?* (AmE); (2) the form of some past tense verbs, where AmE uses *-ed* for the past of *learn, spell, burn, dream*, etc (cf. BrE *learnt, spelt, burnt, dreamt*), and where AmE has retained some irregular past tense forms such as *dove* (BrE *dived*) and *pled* (BrE *pleaded*); (3) *get* has two past participles in AmE, *got* and *gotten*, each with a different meaning: *I've got that book at home* vs *I've just gotten a new book*; (4) AmE prefers to use collective nouns (*the government, the team*) in the singular, whereas BrE allows *the government are ...*; (5) the disappearance, in AmE, of the forms *shall/shan't* and their replacement with *will/won't*.

For teachers, the decision as to which variety to teach will depend on the local cultural context (for example, students in Argentina tend to opt for British English while those in Brazil prefer American English, on the whole); the learners' needs (eg they may be planning to study in one or the other country, or they may be preparing for public **examinations** in one or the other variety); the **materials** available, (note that many ELT publishers produce textbooks in both varieties); and, finally, the teacher's own variety, which, all other factors being equal, may be the most practical option. (Depending on the context, of course, the choice may not be between American and British English, but between other varieties of English, such as Australian, Canadian, Singapore or Indian English, or, just as probably, **English as an international language**.)

anaphora → **reference**

antonym VOCABULARY

An antonym is a word which is opposite in meaning to another one, as *hot* is to *cold*, or *alive* to *dead*. This relation of oppositeness (or antonymy) has different senses, however. *Hot* and *cold* are gradable opposites in that they occupy different points along a scale of *hotness* and *coldness*, so that something can be *very hot* or *rather cold*, for example. *Alive* and *dead* are not gradable in this way. Something is either *alive* or *dead* (but not, normally, *very alive* or *rather dead*). These non-gradable opposites are called *complementaries*. Other examples are *male* and *female*, and *married* and *single*. A third kind of oppositeness is where there is a reciprocal relationship, such as *buy* and *sell*, or *lend* and *borrow*, so that the reverse of *He lent me the book* is *I borrowed the book from him*. This relation is called *converseness*. Note, also, that a word can have different antonyms, according to context. The opposite of *dry* might be *wet*, when referring to the weather or to hair, but *sweet* if referring to wine. Likewise, the opposite of *single* can be either *double* or *married*.

apologizing FUNCTION

By far the most common way of performing the **function** of apologizing – at least in spoken English – is simply saying *sorry*. Variations include *I'm sorry*; *I'm very/terribly/awfully sorry*; *I'm so sorry*. The expressions *pardon (me)* and *excuse me* are generally used to apologize for mildly impolite behaviour, such as yawning, or for asking someone to repeat something they have just said, as in *Pardon? Excuse me?* The verb *apologize* and the noun *apology* are used almost only in writing, or for official announcements: *Please accept my sincerest apologies …*; *We apologize for any inconvenience this may cause*. The sentence starter *I'm afraid …* is used to apologize for having to give potentially unwelcome news, such as when refusing a request or invitation: *I'm afraid I can't. I'm busy*. (This last example also demonstrates the way that apologies are often accompanied by an excuse.) Common ways of responding to – and deflecting – an apology are: *That's OK*; *Never mind*; and *Don't worry about it*.

apostrophe → **punctuation**

applied linguistics LINGUISTICS

This is the branch of **linguistics** that is concerned with the application of linguistic theory to solving language-related problems in the real world. It encompasses such fields as *language planning* (ie, planning and implementing national or regional language policies, such as the maintenance of minority languages), *speech therapy*, *lexicography* (eg dictionary writing), *translation studies*, *forensic linguistics* (ie, solving crimes using linguistic evidence) and second language teaching and learning. In reality, it is with the last of these areas that applied linguists are most concerned, and a degree course in applied linguistics will focus on such subject areas as grammar and phonology, second language acquisition, literacy studies, curriculum design, and testing and assessment.

appraisal LINGUISTICS

Appraisal (also called *stance*) is the way speakers and writers use language to express their personal attitude to what is being said or written. Appraisal language is one of the main ways that language's interpersonal **function** is realized, and accounts for the fact that **conversation** – largely interpersonal in its purpose – is rich in appraisal language, as this extract demonstrates:[3]

<S 01>   Well I've had my article accepted too so that was <u>good</u>. Last week.
<S 02>   Mm.
<S 03>   <u>Great</u>.
<S 04>   <u>That's great</u>!

Three categories of appraisal have been described: *affect* (the expression of personal feelings, such as pleasure and satisfaction, and their opposites), *judgment* (the expression of social values and social esteem), and *appreciation* (the expression of **opinions**). All three categories are expressed either lexically or grammatically, or through the use of **paralinguistic** devices, such as **intonation** and voice quality.

Appraisal language at the word level includes a range of expressive devices such as the use of highly coloured **adjectives** (*stunning*, *awful*, *hideous*, *amazing*, etc) which are in turn frequently intensified by the use of **adverbs** such as *incredibly*, *totally*, *really*, *just*, etc. Another way appraisal language is realized is through the use of verbs that express likes and dislikes, such as *hate*, *adore*, *loathe*, *love*, etc. Grammatically, appraisal is often expressed using *stance adverbials*, such as *hopefully*, *incredibly*, *unfortunately*, etc, and through the use of constructions of the type:

I think <u>it's awful how</u> some people treat animals.
I <u>doubt if</u> it will be as busy as you think.

Later in the same conversation referred to above, the speakers use more appraisal language:

<S 01>   And I I wrote it um … when I spoke to the editor I said I'll write it. If you don't <u>like</u> it you've got every right to not accept it.
<S 05>   Right.
<S 02>   Mm.
<S 01>   because he was <u>very worried</u> about taking on someone who was new. Um but he <u>liked</u> it so that's
<S 06>   Oh <u>that's great</u>.
<S 53>   <u>Good.</u>
<S 04>   <u>That's wonderful.</u>
<S 06>   Well <u>hopefully</u> he might get you to do something else.
<S 01>   Yeah yeah.

Positive appraisal language is frequent in certain kinds of written texts, particularly advertising. It is also noticeably absent from many learners' spoken and written language, which suggests that it may need to be given more prominence in syllabuses.

approach → **method**

appropriacy, appropriateness SOCIOLINGUISTICS

If you use language *appropriately*, you use it in a way that is suitable for the context, including the cultural context, and in a way which meets the

---

[3] OZTALK: Macquarie University/UTS Spoken Language Corpus.

expectations of the people you are communicating with. Learners need to know not only how to be accurate (→ **accuracy**) in the target language, but also how to be appropriate. Appropriacy is an aspect of what is called *sociolinguistic competence* which in turn is a component of a speaker's overall **communicative competence**, defined by the linguist Dell Hymes as the knowledge 'when to speak, when not, and as to what to talk about with whom, when, where, in what manner'.[4] The Japanese student, for example, who attached the following note to her application to do a Spanish course at a school in Barcelona, used an inappropriate **style** to express the urgency of her request:

> Dear Sirs/Madams,
> I'm so harry because I may leave Japan at the end of January. I'm gonna stop by N.Y. and go to España. Please get busy!

Activities designed to sensitize learners to appropriacy include: contrasting two dialogues, one in which a speaker is accurate but inappropriate, and the other in which these qualities are reversed; asking learners to spot the inappropriate sentence or utterance in a text; roleplaying different scenarios, where the relationship between the speakers is different each time.

appropriation SLA

If you *appropriate* something, you make it your own. If you appropriate a skill, you gain ownership of the skill by first doing it with someone who is more skilled than you are until you can control (or regulate) the skill yourself. This is the principle underlying the notion of *appropriation*, which is a key concept in **sociocultural learning theory**. A good example of appropriation at work is the way an older child will teach a younger one the rules of a game, by both talking and walking the child through it, until the younger one has got the hang of it.

It is argued that learning a second language involves the same stages of teacher- and self-regulation. The term *appropriation* captures the idea that language is not simply a behaviour that is conditioned through repeated practice, but that it is one of collaborative construction, in which skills are transferred in socially-situated activity.

Classroom activities that promote appropriation are ones in which learners collaborate on a task, such as transcribing a *dictogloss* (→ **dictation**), each contributing their own strengths to the task, or when the teacher first performs a task – such as a roleplay – with selected learners, before the learners go on to perform it among themselves.

aptitude PSYCHOLOGY

Your aptitude is your innate talent or predisposition for language learning. Recent research suggests that an aptitude for language learning comprises at least three distinct abilities: *auditory ability*, *linguistic ability* and *memory ability*. The first of these is what is popularly known as 'having a good ear', but more technically means having the capacity to analyse foreign sounds in such a way that they can be later recalled. Linguistic ability is, essentially, the ability to discern patterns in input, and to infer rules from these patterns. A learner with this ability should be able to identify the 'odd one out' in these sentences:

[4] Hymes, D. 1972. On communicative competence, in Pride, J. and Holmes, J. (eds) *Sociolinguistics: Selected Readings* (Harmondsworth: Penguin Books) p 277.

1. *I hadn't met her before.*
2. *We had the kitchen painted.*
3. *Had it been raining when you arrived?*
4. *Where had I left my keys?*
5. *When we got there, the film had already started.*

(The answer is 2, an example of **causative** *have*; all the others are instances of *have* being used as an auxiliary verb to construct the past **perfect**.)

Finally, memory ability involves not just the ability to store items in long-term **memory**, but to retrieve them quickly and efficiently.

The bad news is that aptitude is probably immune to training. However, a weakness in one area (such as linguistic ability) can be compensated for by exploiting abilities in another (such as memory). *Language aptitude tests* are designed to predict success in language learning. But a learner's aptitude might not be realized if the nature of the learning situation does not allow their innate abilities to flourish, or if they are not motivated. Aptitude, then, is only one of several factors that predicts success in second language learning. Other factors include **learning style** and **motivation**.

ARC (authentic-restricted-clarification) → **lesson design**

article GRAMMAR

The two articles in English are *the* and *a/an*, and they belong to the **word class** of **determiners**. They go before a **noun** and tell us simply whether the thing that is referred to is, or can be, identified (*definite*), or if it is not (yet) identified (*indefinite*). In this short extract, the articles are highlighted:

This is a[1] true story. It happened to the[2] cousin of a[3] friend of mine. There was a[4] girl and she was babysitting. The[5] parents had gone to a[6] party, and had left the[7] girl in charge of their baby boy. At one point in the[8] evening the[9] mother phoned to see if everything was all right and the[10] babysitter said, 'Oh fine. Everything's great. The[11] turkey's in the[12] oven.' 'Turkey? What turkey …?' …

The use of the indefinite article *a* in examples 1, 3, 4 and 6 signals that the noun that follows it is not identifiable, because it is one of several (1 and 3), or because this is the first time it has been mentioned (4 and 6). By contrast, the nouns that follow *the* are identified in the text, or can be identified by reference to the knowledge that the reader and writer share. Thus (2) is not just any cousin but the cousin of a friend (the identification comes forward in the text). In (7) *the girl* is identifiable as being the girl previously mentioned (the identification comes back in the text), as is also the case with (10) *the babysitter. The parents* (5) and *the mother* (9) are not identifiable by direct reference either back or forward in the text, but by reference to what both reader and writer know about 'babysitting' (their babysitting **schema**). Babysitting involves parents, and parents implies mothers. Likewise *the oven* (12) belongs to the speaker's and the listener's shared world. But when the girl mentions *the turkey* (11) the mother is confused, since she has no referent for the shared knowledge implied by *the*. Hence her question: *What turkey?*

The indefinite article *a/an* is only used with singular, countable nouns (→ **noun**). So there is also a 'third', invisible, article in English, which occurs when a plural noun or a singular uncountable noun has indefinite reference, as in *[Ø] Apples are* *good for you but [Ø] sugar is not*, where [Ø] represents what is called the *zero article*. Thus, the full article system can be represented like this:

		countable	uncountable
singular	definite	*the girl*	*the sugar*
	indefinite	*a girl*	*Ø sugar*
plural	definite	*the parents*	
	indefinite	*Ø parents*	

The articles are among the most frequent words in English, but perhaps the most difficult to explain to learners. This is partly because the notion of definiteness, interacting with the notion of countability, is very abstract. But it is also because articles have very many idiomatic uses which resist easy categorization. Compare *He plays* <u>*the*</u> *guitar, He's playing* <u>*a*</u> *guitar, He played Ø lead guitar*. The article system is perhaps best approached through the analysis of texts, as in the example above.

articulator PHONOLOGY

The articulators are those parts of the mouth, throat and nose that are used to produce (or to *articulate*) speech. A flow of air from the lungs passes through the larynx, and into the vocal tract, whose shape is modified by the articulators in order to create the forty-four different **phonemes** (the **vowel** and **consonant** sounds) of Standard English. The main articulators are shown in the diagram:

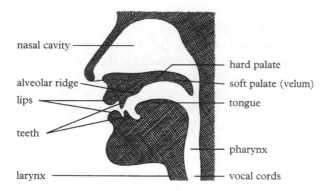

aspect GRAMMAR

The aspect of a **verb phrase** is the way the speaker's 'view' of an event is expressed by the verb phrase, regardless of the time of the event itself. (The time of the event relates to **tense**). Aspect is concerned with the internal nature of the event, eg, whether it has duration or not, whether it is completed or not, whether it is repetitive or not, or whether it is connected to the time of speaking (*speech time*) or not.

There are two aspects in English: the **progressive** (also called *continuous*) and the **perfect**. Both aspects are formed by a combination of **auxiliary verbs** and **participles**. In the case of progressive aspect, these are the auxiliary verb *be* and the present participle. In the case of perfect aspect, the combination consists of the auxiliary verb *have* and the past participle. The auxiliary verbs can be marked for tense, and the two aspects can be combined. The following grid represents all the possible combinations of tense and aspect (ignoring combinations with **modal verbs**):

	[no aspect]	perfect	progressive	perfect + progressive
present	*they work*	*they have worked*	*they are working*	*they have been working*
past	*they worked*	*they had worked*	*they were working*	*they had been working*

The names of these forms combine first the tense, and then the aspect (or combination of aspects). So, *They have worked* is an instance of the present perfect. *They had been working* is an instance of the past perfect progressive. Note that these different combinations are often misleadingly called 'tenses', as if the differences between them had to do solely with time. In fact they are combinations of two quite different but interlocking systems: tense and aspect.

Teaching aspect is not easy, partly because systems of aspect vary from language to language (in those languages that have them), and partly because such concepts as duration and completion are abstract, often subjective, and difficult to explain. More successful are approaches that focus on the typical contexts that aspect is used in (such as talking about experience, in the case of the present perfect, or description, in the case of the progressive). Also effective are approaches that associate these forms with the kinds of words and expressions that commonly co-occur with them, such as *ever, yet, already, for ages*, etc (in the case of the perfect), or ...*when X happened* (in the case of the progressive).

assessment TESTING

Assessment refers to the different ways of collecting information about a learner's progress and achievement. One of these ways is by **testing** the learner, but testing and assessment are not necessarily the same thing. Assessment may include informal procedures such as those carried out by the teacher in the course of a lesson. Teachers, for example, can assess their learners by listening to what they say in pairwork, and collecting examples of error for subsequent feedback. Assessment may take place at certain key points in a course, such as half-way through and at the end, or it may be ongoing, in which case it is known as *continuous assessment*. One mode of assessment that has received attention recently is *self-assessment*. The ability to assess one's own progress is seen as crucial in the development of **autonomy** as a learner. Research shows that learners usually need to be trained in self-assessment skills, but once trained, they can accurately assess their own progress. The accuracy of self-assessment increases when learners are given clear descriptors of language ability to use. The **Common European Framework** provides such descriptors in the form of *can do* statements, e.g. *I can express myself fluently and spontaneously without much obvious searching for expressions.*[5] However, research suggests that learners find it easier to say what they *can't* do, rather than what they can do.

Assessment is also distinguished from **evaluation**, which is concerned with evaluating the effectiveness of the overall course or programme, rather than the progress of individual learners on it.

[5] *Common European Framework of Reference for Languages: Learning, Teaching, Assessment,* Council of Europe, 2001, p 24.

assimilation → **connected speech**

associations, teachers' PROFESSIONAL

Most countries and regions have professional, non-governmental, associations for teachers of English. These function as a network system, putting practising teachers in touch with one another, and raising the profile of the profession generally. Membership normally entails an annual fee, in return for which members may attend national and/or regional conferences and workshops, as well as receive a newsletter or magazine. These associations may also function as lobby groups, representing the interests of English teachers and students to the relevant government authorities. Some work to represent the interests of teachers as employees, and hence are more like trade unions. Many local associations are affiliated to an international teachers' association, the largest of which is TESOL (the international association of *Teachers of English to Speakers of Other Languages*), whose headquarters are in the USA, and which has over 20 000 members worldwide. The stated aim of TESOL is 'to develop the expertise of its members … to help them foster effective communication in diverse settings while respecting individuals' language rights'. With its headquarters in the UK, IATEFL (the *International Association of Teachers of English as a Foreign Language*) rivals TESOL in terms of influence, although not in membership size. Both organizations run annual conferences and are involved in the publication of scholarly journals, newsletters, and conference proceedings. IATEFL co-ordinates the activities of a number of special interest groups (SIGs), such as those for teachers involved in teaching business English or young learners, or for teachers interested in global issues, or the teaching of pronunciation. Each of these SIGs produces its own newsletter and organizes special-interest conferences or workshops.

attention PSYCHOLOGY

If you pay attention to something, you direct mental effort at it, while ignoring other things. Consider the way in which at a noisy party you are able to focus on the voice of the person you are speaking to, and ignore others. Some degree of attention is said to be a pre-requisite for learning. Claims, therefore, that you can learn a language in your sleep are probably unfounded. The notion that learning requires attention has led to the established view that it is necessary for a language learner to *notice* the form taken by an utterance in order to acquire the grammar that it contains (→ **noticing**). However, recent findings have led some researchers to conclude that we are capable of learning some aspects of language implicitly (→ **usage-based acquisition**).

Another important finding with regard to attention is that it is limited in capacity. The effect is to restrict the amount of mental effort which can be allocated to a given task. If the task, or combination of tasks, demands too much attention, then you cannot perform them satisfactorily. This happens when, for example, a learner is required to perform a speaking task without sufficient planning time. The learner's mental resources are focused on getting meaning across, but with the result that there is no remaining attention available to devote to accuracy. Your *attention span* is the extent to which you can sustain attention on a task over a period of time. Young learners have shorter attention spans than adults, in general, and teachers need to take this into account when planning lessons.

Factors that serve to focus attention and to ensure more reliable recall include interest, humour, relevance, and the sense that what is happening is connected to what has just happened and to what is about to happen (called *contingency*). Personal and emotional factors can both lower the amount of attention that somebody has available to give, and reduce their attention span. These factors include tiredness, boredom, anxiety or a preference for a different teaching style. One of the teacher's most important **classroom management** roles is capturing, maintaining, and directing, the attention of learners. Typically, teachers get learners' attention by using their names, using eye-contact and gesture, using 'framing' language (such as 'Right, now …'), and by changes in the volume, pitch and pace of their speaking voice. And, to focus learners' attention on a selected feature of language, they can write it on the board, ask questions about it, or ask students to repeat it.

attitude PSYCHOLOGY

Your attitude to language learning is the way you feel about it. Learners may have positive or negative attitudes towards language learning in general, or towards the target language and its speakers and culture, or towards the teacher and the other learners, or towards the materials, the methodology, and the learning situation. These attitudes are important in determining their overall **motivation** and ultimate success. But success can also be the cause – not just the effect – of having positive attitudes. For example, the satisfaction gained from having successfully communicated in the target language can be a powerful incentive to continue learning. By the same token, negative attitudes can be reinforced by the experience of failure. Teachers can positively influence attitudes, by creating a supportive classroom **dynamic**, by 'accentuating the positive', and by helping their learners experience communicative success, eg by **scaffolding** their attempts to communicate.

Teachers' attitudes to their learners can also contribute to the success or failure of the learning process. For example, teachers who have been told that their students are 'high achievers' (even if they are not) tend to get the kind of results associated with high achievement.

audiolingual method, audiolingualism METHODOLOGY

This is a language teaching method that became widespread in the 1950s and 1960s, especially in the United States, and whose most distinctive feature was the drilling of sentence patterns. The audiolingual method claimed to have transformed language teaching from an art into a science. It was derived from a view of language that was based around sentence structure, and from a view of learning that emphasized habit-formation (→ **behaviourism**). As in the **direct method**, spoken language was prioritized; translation and the use of **metalanguage** were discouraged; and **accuracy** was considered to be a precondition for **fluency**. Errors were regarded as potentially 'contagious', so learners were given few opportunities to make them. A typical audiolingual lesson began with the repetition and memorization of a scripted dialogue, followed by pattern-practice **drills** – which might then be practised in a language laboratory.

In its favour, audiolingualism generated an impressive variety of controlled **practice** activities. And, undoubtedly, many learners made significant progress using this method – as learners tend to do if they are motivated enough. However, audiolingualism received a mortal blow when, in the early 1960s, the linguist Noam Chomsky argued persuasively that sentences are not learned by imitation and repetition, but are created afresh from an innate rule-based competence (→ **mentalism**). Nevertheless, the legacy of audiolingualism, in its form called *programmed learning*, survives in many mail-order and 'multi-media' computer-based language courses. It also survives in the belief that 'practice makes perfect' (→ **repetition**), and that language learning is best achieved through the strict application of scientific principles.

auditory learner → **learning style**

authenticity LINGUISTICS

A classroom text is authentic if it was originally written for a non-classroom audience. A newspaper article or a pop song are thus considered authentic, whereas a coursebook drill or dialogue are not. The notion of authenticity was originally introduced to distinguish between artificially simplified texts and unmodified 'real' texts. With the advent of the **communicative approach**, inauthentic texts were felt to be inadequate, either as models for language use, or as preparation for real-life reading and listening. This view was reinforced by the demand for courses designed to teach **English for special purposes** (ESP). Accordingly, authentic texts and semi-authentic texts (that is texts that look like authentic texts but which have been adapted in some way) started finding their way into ELT materials. In order to make these ungraded texts accessible to learners, an approach based on the principle 'grade the task, not the text' was developed. Thus, reading and listening tasks that require only a very general understanding of the text, such as skimming, scanning, and listening for gist, became identified with authentic materials (→ **reading**; → **listening**).

A related development – the use of authentic data for compiling dictionaries and grammars – has been driven by developments in **corpus** linguistics. The term 'real English' has become a popular way of marketing reference materials. Finally, the term 'authentic' has been used to characterize a quality of **classroom interaction** – one which reflects the structures of real talk as opposed to traditional classroom talk. Advocates of this kind of authenticity reject conventional exchanges of the type:

> **Teacher** *Have I a nose on my face?*
> **Student** *Yes, you have.*
> **Teacher** *Good.*

in favour of genuinely communicative exchanges about the sort of things learners might talk about outside the classroom (→ **teacher talk**). Not only is authentic interaction more communicative, it is argued, but it offers more **affordances** for learning.

However, there has been a backlash against the authenticity movement. The fact that classroom texts, grammar and dictionary citations, and classroom interactions are artificial (by the standards of non-classroom contexts) may actually be based on good sense. Learning a language (or anything, for that matter) requires that the content of instruction should be modified in ways that make it more accessible to learners.

automaticity PSYCHOLOGY

If you can perform a task automatically, you can do it without having to focus attention on it. In this way, you free your limited attentional resources for more demanding activities (→ **attention**). Somebody who is a novice in a skill has to perform a task step by step, and to focus on each step. As novices become more expert, they simplify the process. They combine (or *chunk*) the steps and set up associations that link one step with another. As a result, they develop a procedure for doing the task and, after using this procedure many times, they no longer have to concentrate on what they are doing. In the case of driving a car, for example, you learn to chunk the individual stages of gear-changing or of indicating, so you can concentrate on negotiating heavy traffic or bad weather. In language speaking terms, this automatization process means being able to draw on a set of internalized procedures in order to construct spoken utterances under the pressure of time. It is supported by the fact that language that is frequently encountered becomes stored in the mind in chunks instead of having to be assembled freshly each time a particular sequence is used (→ **formulaic language**). Without stored language plus the routines for retrieving it, you would have to assemble each utterance slowly and consciously, word by word, at the obvious expense of **fluency**. Automaticity, however, does not mean a sacrifice of **accuracy**. When chunks of language are produced in a pre-assembled form, the speaker has much less chance of making mistakes.

One way of developing automaticity in the classroom is to manipulate the features of a speaking **task**, eg by providing some planning time (but not too much), or reducing the time available to perform the task (the shorter the time, the greater the need to automate performance). Another is through task **repetition**. For example, learners tell an anecdote to a partner, then change partners and re-tell the anecdote, and so on. Each re-telling should show gains in automaticity.

autonomy PSYCHOLOGY

Autonomy is your capacity to take responsibility for, and control of, your own learning, either in an institutional context, or completely independent of a teacher or institution. It is also called *self-directed learning*, and it has been advocated as a way of addressing the fact that many – particularly adult – learners have individual **needs** and **learning styles** that are not always easily accommodated in a classroom situation. Autonomous learning assumes that the learner has well-developed **learning strategies**, and the development of such strategies is the aim of **learner training**. Giving learners some say in the choice and management of classroom activities is a step in the direction of autonomy (→ **learner-centred instruction**). Making resources available for individualized learning, such as in a self-access centre, is another. Critics of the autonomy movement argue that the notion of *self-directed learning* is – for many learners – a contradiction in terms. If they were autonomous, they would not have enrolled for a language course in the first place. However, all learners will at some stage need to function independently of their teacher and classmates.

auxiliary verb GRAMMAR

Auxiliary verbs are verbs, like *be* and *can*, that have a grammatical function. They therefore contrast with **lexical verbs**, such as *go, eat, steal*, etc. There are two types in English: the primary auxiliaries *be, do,* and *have*; and the secondary, or

modal, auxiliaries, such as *will, would, may, might,* etc. The primary auxiliaries serve to express **aspect** and voice (ie, active and **passive**). For example:

> *Someone <u>has</u> stolen my bike* (= perfect aspect)
> *My bike <u>was</u> stolen.* (= passive voice)
> (cf *Someone stole my bike.*)

The primary auxiliaries change their form according to **tense**, **number** and **person**:

> *Someone <u>had</u> stolen my bike.* (= past tense)
> *Both my bikes <u>were</u> stolen.* (= plural)
> *Someone <u>has</u> stolen my bike.* (= third person)

Auxiliary verbs can occur in combination, as in *My bike <u>has been</u> stolen* and *My bike <u>must have been</u> stolen*, but only the first auxiliary is the *operator*. The operator is the verb that performs the following functions:

- **negation**, using *not*: *My bike was <u>not</u>* (or *wasn't*) *stolen.*
- **inversion** with the subject to form questions: *<u>Has</u> someone stolen my bike?*
- **emphasis**: the operator can be stressed to emphasize that a clause is positive: *My bike WAS stolen.*
- **ellipsis**: the operator can stand in for a whole clause: *My bike wasn't stolen but my helmet <u>was</u>.*
- (related to the above) the operator can form **question tags**: *My bike was stolen, <u>wasn't it?</u>*

In a sentence where there is no auxiliary verb (such as *Someone stole my bike*), the above operations are performed using the *dummy operator* 'do/did':

> *Ben <u>didn't</u> steal my bike.* (= negation)
> *<u>Did</u> someone steal my bike?* (= inversion)
> *Someone <u>DID</u> steal my bike!* (= emphasis)
> *Who stole my bike? Ben <u>did</u>.* (= ellipsis)
> *Someone stole my bike, <u>didn't they?</u>* (= question tag)

Note that auxiliaries often have unstressed (or *weak* → **weak form**) and stressed (or *strong*) forms: *My bike was* [/wəz/] *stolen. (No, it wasn't). I'm telling you it WAS!* [/wɒz/]. Alternatively, they can be contracted: *My bike's been stolen* (→ **contraction**).

Not being a highly inflected language, English relies on the auxiliary system to do a lot of its 'grammar work'. To many learners, the system seems somewhat obscure, especially the use of the dummy operator. It is not helped by the fact that auxiliaries are often unstressed or contracted, and therefore difficult to spot. Teachers need to make a special effort to help learners **notice** them. Teaching the term *auxiliary verb* (or 'helping verb') at an early stage can help.

awareness-raising → **consciousness-raising**

back-channelling → **conversation analysis**; → **listening**

background knowledge → **comprehension**

backshift → **reported speech**; → **conditional**

backwash → **testing**

base form → **verb**

beginner METHODOLOGY

In theory, a beginner learner has zero knowledge of the target language, and hence has to learn it from scratch. In fact, it's unlikely that there are many learners these days who have had no exposure to English at all, given its global spread. Their own language may include words that have been borrowed from English, or that are **cognates**, ie, words that derive from the same root, such as German *Buch* (book) and French *papier* (paper). There may also be some grammatical features in common. This means that many beginners have some 'passive knowledge' of English and are better classified not as *real beginners*, but as *false beginners*.

Beyond that, there is some debate as to what beginners need most. Traditionally, they were given a grounding in basic grammar structures, while vocabulary input was deliberately limited. The **communicative approach**, in promoting the ability to cope in real-life situations with minimal means, prioritized the teaching of functional language, such as ways of asking for directions, shopping, or telling the time (→ **function**). At the same time, the tight hold on vocabulary was relaxed, as was the insistence on grammatical accuracy. Proponents of a **lexical approach** urge the teaching of a core vocabulary of, say, a 1000 high frequency words and *chunks* (→ **formulaic language**), as soon as possible. A core vocabulary, they argue, is both communicatively useful and also the raw material out of which the learner's grammar will emerge. A more cautious approach might combine a mix of grammar, functional language, and vocabulary, until the learner's more specific needs and abilities become apparent.

Beginners are usually distinguished from **elementary** students, who may already have had some classroom instruction. The two levels correspond more or less with the A1 and A2 bands of *basic user* according to the **Common European Framework**.

behaviourism, behaviourist learning theory PSYCHOLOGY

Behaviourism is the psychological theory, popular in the mid-twentieth century, that viewed learning as a form of habit formation. According to behaviourism, habits are formed when the learner's responses to external stimuli are positively reinforced. So, the learner who answers *Yes, I am* to the question *Are you a student?*, and gets an approving nod from the teacher, is more likely to answer the same way when next asked the same – or a similar – question. To behaviourist psychologists, language was just another kind of behaviour, and it could be conditioned in much the same way that seals could be trained to jump through hoops. The language teaching method that is associated with behaviourism is called **audiolingualism**. In this method, the stimulus–response–reinforcement cycle was realized through pattern practice **drills**. Use of the learner's L1 was discouraged, since it might lead to bad habits. **Errors** were avoided for the same reason.

Behaviourist theory rejected any role, in learning, for mental processes such as thought and reasoning. With the revival of **mentalism**, which re-affirmed the role of these processes, support for behaviourist theory declined, and, along with it, audiolingual teaching methods. Behaviourist thinking persists, though, in the widespread belief that mistakes are 'bad', that the use of the L1 causes errors, and that language learning can be scientifically programmed in short, incremental, steps. Current **second language acquisition** research disputes these claims.

bilabial → **consonant**

bilingual → **bilingualism**

bilingualism SLA

Bilingualism is the use of two languages, either by an individual, or by a social group; *multilingualism* is the use of more than two. Bilingual users of English speak English as their **second language** alongside one or more other languages. This does not mean that they speak both (or all) languages equally proficiently: even an elementary student is bilingual in a sense. Bilingualism was once seen as a handicap, rather than as a resource, for second language learners, since – according to **behaviourist learning theory** – the first language *interfered* with the second. Accordingly, the two languages were kept separate. Similar attitudes persist with regard to the raising of children bilingually: that is, that both languages will suffer. The evidence suggests that, on the contrary and all things being equal, bilingual children have several cognitive advantages over monolingual ones. However, a distinction is made between *additive* bilingualism, in which the second language is added to the first without threatening the speaker's first language identity, and *subtractive* bilingualism, in which the second language replaces the first (which is often a minority language), thereby threatening the speaker's first language identity.

Nevertheless, monolingualism is the exception rather than the norm: according to some estimates, over seventy per cent of the people in the world are bi- or multilingual. And most language learning is conducted in bilingual settings. A *bilingual* school is one where instruction is provided in both the child's first language and another, usually more dominant, one. Some of the curriculum content may be taught in one language and some in the other. Or both languages may co-exist in the same class, where, for example, the teacher uses the second language but the learners are allowed to use their first. Bilingual schools can help keep alive minority languages, while providing a transition into the use of a dominant one, such as English.

More recently, the term *plurilingualism* has been coined, to characterize a less compartmentalized and more fluid kind of language use. Plurilingual users draw on their skills in any number of languages to achieve effective communication in a particular situation. Plurilingualism is one of the goals of the **Common European Framework**.

blend → **word formation**

blended learning → **computer-mediated communication**

bottom-up processing → **comprehension**; → **listening**; → **reading**; → **schema**

business English METHODOLOGY

A form of ESP (**English for special purposes**), business English is distinguished from general English by its more specialized vocabulary and its more narrowly defined field, (eg banking, trade, manufacturing, etc). Teaching business English also involves coaching learners in such business-related skills as speaking on the phone, giving presentations, conducting meetings and negotiations, not to mention socializing and making small talk. Sensitivity to different **registers** of English (formal and informal) is also important, as is the ability to read and write the specialized kinds of texts (or **genres**) associated with business. In order to equip learners with the skills to cope with the kinds of cultural differences that might affect business communication in a global context, the teaching of *intercultural awareness* (or *intercultural competence*) is now a standard feature of business English materials. Most business English students already have some general English background, at least to intermediate level. They may be aiming to sit a public **examination** specifically in business English, such as one of those offered by City and Guilds, London (previously Pitmans). Business English classes are typically small, often **one-to-one**, and may take place on site, ie, at the student's place of work. Generally it is felt that, while a business background may not be essential, teachers of business English need specialized training.

CAE (Certificate in Advanced English) → **examination**

CALL → **computer-assisted language learning**

causative GRAMMAR

The causative is the name sometimes given in coursebooks to the form of passive construction *have/get* + noun phrase + *-ed*, as in:

> *Michael had his nose straightened.*
> *We're getting the kitchen re-painted.*

The construction is used when someone causes something – typically a service – to be done by someone else. It is more common in spoken than in written English. The same construction is sometimes used to talk about experiences, where no cause is implied, as in: *I had my bike stolen – again!*

'Causative' also describes verbs that are used to talk about people causing events to happen, as in *She started the fire. He felled the tree*. (But not *The fire started*. Or *The tree fell*.)

CEF → **Common European Framework**

children, teaching → **young learners, teaching**

Chomsky, Noam → **mentalism**; → **universal grammar**

choral drill → **drill**

chunk → **formulaic language**

classroom dynamics → **dynamics, group, class**

classroom interaction METHODOLOGY

Classroom interaction is the general term for what goes on between the people in the classroom, particularly when it involves language. In traditional classrooms, most interaction is initiated by the teacher (→ **teacher talk**), and learners either respond individually, or in unison. Teacher-centred interaction of this kind is associated with *transmissive* teaching, such as a lecture or presentation, where the teacher *transmits* the content of the lesson to the learners. In order to increase the amount of student involvement and interaction, teacher–learner interaction is often combined with **pairwork** and **groupwork**, where learners interact among themselves in pairs or small groups. Other kinds of interaction include *mingling* or *milling* (→ **pairwork**). Pairwork and groupwork are associated with a more **learner-centred** approach. Rather than passively receiving the lesson content, the learners are actively engaged in using language and discovering things for themselves. The value of pairwork and groupwork has been reinforced by the belief that **interaction** facilitates language learning. Some would go as far as to say that it is *all* that is required.

The potential for classroom interaction is obviously constrained by such factors as the number of students, the size of the room, the furniture, and the purpose or type of activity. Not all activities lend themselves to pairwork or groupwork. Some activities, such as reading, are best done as *individual work*. On the other hand, listening activities (such as listening to an audio recording, or to the teacher) favour a *whole class* format, as do grammar presentations. The whole class is also an appropriate form of organization when reviewing the results of an activity, as, for example, when spokespersons from each group are reporting on the results of a discussion or survey.

The success of any classroom interaction will also depend on the extent to which the learners know what they are meant to be doing and why, which in turn depends on how clearly and efficiently the interaction has been set up (→ **classroom management**). Pair- and groupwork can be a complete waste of time if learners are neither properly prepared for it, nor sure of its purpose or outcome.

Finally, the success of pair- and groupwork will depend on the kind of group **dynamics** that have been established. Do the students know one another? Are they happy working together? Do they mind working without constant teacher supervision? Establishing a productive classroom dynamic may involve making decisions as to who works with whom. It may also mean deliberately staging the introduction of different kinds of interactions, starting off with the more controlled, teacher-led interactions before, over time, allowing learners to work in pairs and finally in groups.

classroom management METHODOLOGY

In order to ensure the best use of the available time and resources, one of the teacher's key roles is the management of learning. Classroom management refers to this organizational and directive function. While a certain amount of planning is possible, most classroom management decisions are made 'in flight', and in response to such immediate factors as the need to maintain the lesson flow, or to vary the pace, or to provide opportunities for **classroom interaction**, or to draw attention to a feature of the language. Management is particularly important in large and diverse classes (→ **mixed ability**), and in lessons where the focus is on activities, such as **tasks**, as opposed to more lecture-type lesson formats.

The successful setting up of an activity or task depends on giving clear **instructions**. Once set up, the task needs to be monitored by the teacher to ensure that the learners are *on task*, ie, doing what they have been instructed to do. Monitoring may also involve providing learners with **feedback** on what they are saying or writing, as well as being available in a consultant role to answer questions, eg about unfamiliar vocabulary. The post-task stage usually involves some kind of *wrap-up*, such as getting individuals to comment on, or summarize, their group's performance of the task, as well as some teacher feedback on the task, such as the correction of any **errors** that were noted.

Teachers can short-cut the setting up stage, if the activity is one that is familiar to learners. Experienced teachers are often able to manage their classes fluidly through the regular use of **routines**. Many teachers, for example, have a 'beginning of lesson' routine, which may involve learners, in pairs, checking the homework from the last lesson, or asking and answering questions about the weekend. For **young learners** in particular, familiarity with classroom routines can save the teacher a great deal of organizational time and effort.

clause GRAMMAR

Clauses are to **sentences** what branches are to trees. That is, they are the largest grammatical unit smaller than the whole sentence. Looked at another way, words are grouped into **phrases**, the phrases form the components of clauses, and one or more clauses comprise a sentence. In the following extract the clauses are in brackets. Notice that some clauses are embedded in other clauses:

[Jan opened the door] and [we went in]. [When we were inside] [the door closed behind us]. [A woman [who had been sitting at a desk [writing]] came forward] and [greeted us]. [To be honest], [I don't remember [what she said]], but [I do remember [that I wanted to leave]]. [If the door hadn't been closed], [I would have].

A simple definition of a clause is any group of words that includes a verb. (For exceptions, see below). Most clauses also contain a **subject** as well. Other clause elements, identified by the function, are: **objects** (O), **complements** (C), and **adverbials** (A). The following (single sentence) clauses illustrate different combinations of these elements:

SV: *The door opened.*
SVC: *The door was open.*
SVO: *Jan opened the door.*
SVA: *The door opened slowly.*
SVOA: *Jan opened the door with a key.*
SVOO: *Jan gave the door a push.*
SVOC: *Jan found the door open.*

Depending on the verb, a clause can be *finite* or *non-finite*. A finite clause contains a **finite verb**, ie, one that is marked for tense and agrees with its subject:

When the door opens, you can go in.

A non-finite clause is one that has a **participle** or an **infinitive** as its verb:

Having opened the door, we went in.
The door being open, we went in.
To open the door, use the key.

Occasionally, the verb can be left out, to form a verbless clause:

Once inside, we took a look around. = Once we were inside …

Clauses can be linked to one another using **conjunctions**. When two or more clauses of equal rank are linked, they are called *co-ordinate clauses*: [*Jan opened the door*] *and* [*we went in*]. When one clause outranks another because it contains the main idea of the sentence, it is called the *main clause*, and the clause it outranks is called a *subordinate clause*:

[*The door closed behind us*] = main clause [*when we were inside*] = subordinate clause (→ **subordination**).

There are three main kinds of subordinate clause:

- adverbial clause: [*when we were inside*]; [*if the door hadn't been closed*]
- relative clause: *a woman* [*who had been sitting at a desk*]
- reported clause: *I don't remember* [*what she said*].

Adverbial clauses function as sentence **adverbials**, ie, they form the A element of SVA and SVOA structures. They have a variety of different meanings: there are clauses of *time*, of *place*, of *purpose*, of *result*, and *conditional* and *comparative* clauses. **Relative clauses** provide more information about nouns.

Reported clauses are usually the object of verbs of speaking or thinking, and are either *that*-clauses or *wh*-clauses, or begin with *to*-infinitive:

> She told me *that it was locked.*
> I wondered *who she was.*
> They asked me *to sit down.*

Clauses that stand 'outside' the main part of the sentence, and express the speaker's *stance* are called *comment clauses*: [*To be honest*], [*I don't remember what she said*].

Faulty clause structure accounts for a great many of the errors learners make, particularly in writing. For example:

> * *The last weekend in my family has passed something very horrible.*
> * *I would like that you could stay here.*
> * *It wasn't me the only one who went.*
> * *My friend suggested me if I would like to go to Madrid for a weekend.*
> * *The agency said me it wasn't their problem.*
> * *I want to explain you something about the tour.*

Part of the problem is that learners are not familiar with the way that the choice of verb (eg *suggest*, *say*, *explain*) determines the clause structure. Verbs take different patterns (→ **verb pattern**), and learners prefer to transfer verb patterns from their first language. Another problem is not knowing how clauses can be combined to make *complex* and *compound* sentences (→ **complex sentence**).

cleft sentence GRAMMAR

In order to foreground one element in a **sentence** in relation to others, the sentence can be split in two: the result is a *cleft sentence*. For example, in the sentence *Dorothy gave Toto a bone*, depending on the emphasis required, the sentence can be re-arranged in at least three ways, using two verbs instead of the original one:

1. *It was Dorothy who gave Toto a bone.*
2. *It was Toto who Dorothy gave a bone to.*
3. *It was a bone that Dorothy gave Toto.*

In each case the information that is being emphasized is that which follows the first verb in the sentence (in this case *was*). In order to focus on the action, rather than the agents, a fourth organization is also possible (sometimes called a *pseudo-cleft sentence*):

4. *What Dorothy did was give Toto a bone.*

It's important to remember that these arrangements are not arbitrary but respond to the demands of the context. For example, only one of sentences 1–3 logically completes this text: *People said that I gave Toto a bone. They are wrong. It was Dorothy who gave Toto a bone.*

CLIL → **content and language integrated learning**

clipping → **word formation**

cloze test TESTING

A cloze test is a text in which every *n*th word (say, fifth, sixth or seventh) is removed and replaced with a space so that (1)_____ looks something like this. Cloze (2) _____ were originally designed to test (3) _____ skill of reading, but they (4) _____ very popular in the 1970s (5) _____ 1980s as they were thought to test the learners' general **competence**, not just their knowledge of individual grammar and vocabulary items. This is because learners need to process the text at various levels (vocabulary, grammar, discourse) in order to fill in the spaces. These claims were shown to be somewhat exaggerated, but nevertheless cloze tests are still popular, partly thanks to the fact that they are very easy to construct and to score. (Two systems of scoring are used: Either the scorer accepts only the exact word that was used in the original text, or he/she accepts any acceptable word. Thus, the answer to (4) above is *became*, but *proved* would be acceptable). A less random version of this kind of test (but not technically a cloze test) is the *gap fill*. In a gap-fill exercise the word that is removed is not the one that happens to occur at a regular interval, but one that has been chosen for a particular reason, eg, because it belongs to a particular **word class** (such as verbs, articles or prepositions) which the tester wants to focus on.

cluster → **consonant**

code-switching → **communication strategy**

cognate VOCABULARY

Cognates (or *cognate words*) are words which have the same or very similar forms in two languages. This is because the words derive from a source that was once common to both. In these two short translations of the same text, one in German and the other in Finnish, words that are clearly cognates in English are underlined:

Sehr geehrter Kunde, als Anlage <u>finden</u> Sie die <u>Namen</u> <u>und</u> <u>Adressen</u> der jeweiligen HP Gesellschaft, die <u>in</u> Ihrem <u>Land</u> die HP Hersteller<u>garantie</u> gewähren.

Hyvä asiakkaamme, oheisesta luettelosta löydätte yhteystiedot valmistajan takuusta vastaavaan HP:n edustajaan maassanne.

This example demonstrates that some languages share more cognates with English than do others.

A word that looks like a cognate, but in fact has quite a different meaning, is called a *false friend*. To be *embarrassed* in English is not the same thing as to be *embarazada* (ie, 'pregnant') in Spanish. And the English word *actually* is a false friend for speakers of several languages, including French and Polish, since its equivalent means 'nowadays' or 'at the moment'. Nevertheless, there are many more cognates in languages (like French, Italian, German and Dutch) that are related to English, than there are false friends, and these cognates offer learners of English a handy bridgehead into understanding texts, even as **beginners**.

cognitive learning theory PSYCHOLOGY

Cognitive comes from *cognition* which refers to the way in which the mind handles and stores knowledge. Learning theories that are described as *cognitive* draw upon ideas from cognitive psychology, the branch of psychology that deals with perception and thinking. The cognitive psychologist Piaget first proposed the view that language develops out of the child's thoughts and growing awareness of the world. This is at variance with the view that language is 'hard-wired' in the brain, and that the capacity to learn languages is something we are born with (→ **mentalism**; → **universal grammar**). A later version of cognitive learning theory suggests that the child acquires language by forming and testing hypotheses about the adult language it hears around it.

In a learning context, the cognitive tradition argues that learning a foreign language is essentially no different from acquiring other kinds of skill such as playing the guitar or driving a car. Both involve the acquisition of expertise. This demands mental effort and lots of practice before the component sub-skills become automatic. According to one theory of expertise, learning proceeds from conscious mental activity to subconscious, automatic processing (→ **automaticity**). Cognitive models of language learning replaced earlier **behaviourist** models, which were solely concerned with observable behaviours and not with internal, mental processes. Cognitive theory was used to justify a return to rule-based learning, but one where learners were encouraged to test hypotheses by working the rules out for themselves. For a short time, this was called the *cognitve-code method*. More recently, the importance that cognitive theory attaches to achieving automaticity, and hence **fluency**, has been used to justify **task-based learning**. However, cognitive models have been criticized as being mechanistic, and for ignoring social and affective factors.

cognitive style → **learning style**

coherence DISCOURSE

If a **text** is *coherent*, it makes sense. The following text lacks coherence:

> If there is a fault with the toilet please call extn 1071. Place in water halfway up basin. That's where all that salty water comes from.

It lacks coherence because it is difficult to see how the sentences relate, despite some shared elements (*toilet*, *basin*, *water*). They do not relate to each other, nor does the whole text relate to anything in our background knowledge of the world. Furthermore, the text does not resemble any kind of text we are familiar with (unsurprisingly, since the three sentences were taken out of three different texts). The following text, however, is more coherent:

We want you to be delighted with this facility. If there is a fault with the toilet please call extn 1071 on the nearest white courtesy phone.

We now recognize the text as belonging to the type: *public notices*. The language and organization of the text are appropriate, especially when we know that the text was written to be read in an airport restroom. Moreover, the two sentences of the text have a logical relation: you could put the **linker** *so* between them, for example. And the word *facility* belongs to a similar topic area as the word *toilet*.

Likewise the following text makes sense:

Of course. That's where all that salty water comes from. *Len Clarke, Uxbridge, Middx.*

… when we discover it is the (humorous) answer to this question (in a newspaper column[1]):

QUESTION: Do fish sweat?

Coherence, then, is achieved when (among other things) a text follows certain textual conventions, when it is relevant to its context, when it is relevant to other texts (a property called *intertextuality*), when its sentences have a logical relation, and when there is a consistent topic. It can also help if there are clear links between its parts – when, in other words, it is *cohesive*. But coherence is not the same as **cohesion**. A text can be coherent even if there are few if any explicit links between its sentences, as in this short text:

Remove carton. Pierce film. Place in water halfway up basin. Top up as necessary.

Context clues (the text appears on the packaging of a Christmas pudding) plus familiarity with this kind of text (cooking instructions) helps the reader make sense of the text in the absence of pronouns (eg *it*) and linkers (eg *then*). By the same token, the nonsense text that we began this entry with has elements of cohesion (*toilet, basin, water, water*) but it is not coherent.

Coherence, then, is less a property of texts than of the relation between the text and its context, and between the writer and reader (or speaker and listener). If writers or speakers make too many unchecked assumptions about the state of their readers' or listeners' knowledge, they are likely to come across as incoherent, irrespective of the degree of organization or cohesion they build into their texts. This has implications in the teaching of **writing**: a focus on teaching **linkers** and text organization in the absence of any clear idea of who the reader will be, or what purpose the text will serve, may be a case of putting the cart before the horse.

cohesion DISCOURSE

If a text is *cohesive*, its elements are connected. Cohesion is the use of grammatical and lexical means to achieve connected **text**, either spoken or written. Unlike **coherence**, which different readers or listeners may experience to varying degrees, cohesion is a stable property of texts. And, while cohesion may help make a text coherent, it cannot guarantee it. The main *cohesive devices* in English are these:

- lexical:
  - repetition of words, or words from the same word family (eg *coherent, cohesive, cohesion*) or use of synonyms

[1] Harker, J. 1994 *Notes and Queries* (5), (Fourth Estate) p110.

- use of general words (like *the place, the girl, the facility*) to refer to something more specific that is mentioned elsewhere
- use of words from the same thematic field (eg *texts, readers, written*)
- **substitution** of previously mentioned words with *one/ones*
- **ellipsis** of previously mentioned words (ie, leaving a word out because it can be recovered from the previous text).

- grammatical:
  - **reference** devices, especially **pronouns** (*it* *may help* ...) and some **determiners** (eg *this, that*)
  - **substitution** of previously mentioned clause elements, with *do/does*, or *so/not*
  - **ellipsis** of clause elements
  - **linkers** such as *therefore, what's more, then*
  - **parallelism**, ic, sentences that 'echo' the structure of previous sentences

In the following genuine text,[2] the cohesive devices are identified:

> Could you imagine being a 222-car family? Sounds crazy. But[1] in Singapore it[2] happens. There[3] they have a big pool of cars[4]. Honda cars[5]. And[6] everyone shares them[7]. You use one[8] when you need it[9]. [10]Drop it[11] off when you don't[12,13]. We call it[14] the Intelligent Community Vehicle[15] System. It's[16] like one big happy car[17] sharing[18] family[19]. Perhaps one day we'll make it[20] happen here. Do you believe in the power of dreams[21]?

1. linker
2. back reference (to *being a 222-car family*)
3. back reference (to *Singapore*)
4. repetition (*222-car*)
5. repetition
6. linker
7. back reference (*cars*)
8. substitution (*a car*)
9. back reference (*one*)
10. ellipsis (*You*)
11. back reference (*one*)
12. ellipsis (*need it*)
13. parallelism
14. back reference (to everything that has been described so far)
15. general word (for *cars*)
16. as 14
17. repetition
18. partial repetition (of *shares*)
19. repetition
20. as 14
21. word thematically related to *imagine* in first sentence

Typical ways of focusing on cohesion in the classroom include: joining pairs of sentences with an appropriate linker; adding the linkers to a text; choosing the best way of continuing a sentence; identifying pronoun *referents* (ie, the things that the pronouns refer to); identifying chains of words that belong to the same thematic area; inserting sentences into a text; and deleting 'rogue' sentences from a text. It is important to remember, though, that cohesion doesn't make a text *coherent*, although it might help.

[2] Honda advertisement, *The Observer Sport Monthly*, 59. January 2005, back cover.

collocation VOCABULARY

If two words *collocate*, they frequently occur together. The relation between the words may be grammatical, as when certain verbs collocate with particular prepositions, such as *depend on, account for, abstain from,* or when a verb, like *make, take,* or *do,* collocates with a noun, as in *make an arrangement, take advantage, do the shopping.* The collocation may also be lexical, as when two **content words** regularly co-occur, as in *a broad hint, a narrow escape* (but not *a wide hint* or *a tight escape*). The strength of the collocation can vary: *a broad street* or *a narrow path* are weak collocations, since both elements can co-occur with lots of other words: *a broad river, a busy street,* etc. *Broad hint* and *narrow escape* are stronger. Stronger still are combinations where one element rarely occurs without the other, as in *moot point, slim pickings* and *scot free.* Strongest of all are those where both elements never or rarely occur without the other, such as *dire straits* and *spick and span.* These have acquired the frozen status of *fixed expressions* (→ **formulaic language**).

Unsurprisingly, learners lack intuitions as to which words go with which, and this accounts for many errors, such as *You can completely enjoy it* (instead of *thoroughly*), *On Saturday we made shopping* (instead of *went*), and *We went the incorrect way* (for *wrong*). Using texts to highlight particular collocations, and teaching new words in association with their most frequent collocations are two ways of approaching the problem. Nowadays learners' dictionaries also include useful collocational information, such as this entry from the *Macmillan English Dictionary for Advanced Learners*:

Words frequently used with **wrong**	
adverbs	badly, disastrously, dreadfully, horribly, seriously, terribly **1**
	completely, entirely, hopelessly, plainly, quite, totally, wholly **2**

Common European Framework (CEF) TESTING

To give it its full name, the Common European Framework of Reference for Languages is the result of many years' research and consultation by the Council of Europe (representing over forty countries). It is intended to provide a common basis for language education in such areas as **curriculum** design, methodology and **assessment**. One of its achievements has been to devise a comprehensive description of the components of language **proficiency** at all levels and across a range of skills. (An example can be seen in the entry in this book on **advanced learners**). Another achievement is its promotion of the notion of *plurilingualism* (→ **bilingualism**). A third has been the impetus it has given different examining bodies to compare and align their proficiency measures (→ **examination**). Here, for example, is how the CEF levels correlate, in broad terms, with those of ALTE (the Association of Language Testers of Europe) and Cambridge ESOL (English for Speakers of Other Languages).

CEF		ALTE Levels	Cambridge ESOL 'main suite' examinations
Proficient user	C2	5	Certificate of Proficiency in English (CPE)
	C1	4	Certificate in Advanced English (CAE)
Independent user	B2	3	First Certificate in English (FCE)
	B1	2	Preliminary English Test (PET)
Basic user	A2	1	Key English Test (KET)
	A1	Breakthrough	

Aligning teaching materials, including coursebooks, and examinations to CEF standards has now become common practice across Europe. Another important development has been the introduction of user **portfolios** which contain an individualized record of a user's language achievements, in terms of what he or she *can do*, as defined according to CEF descriptors.

communication strategy SLA

Communication strategies are ways that learners get round the fact that they may not know how to say something. Most communication strategies are directed at filling in the gaps in the learner's vocabulary knowledge. Some commonly encountered communication strategies are:

- paraphrase: such as *a small bed for a sick person* to mean *stretcher*.
- word coinage: such as *drummist* for *drummer*.
- foreignizing a word: such as turning Spanish *emocionado* (*'deeply moved'*) into the English-sounding *emotionated*.
- approximation: such as saying *two-floor bus* for *double-decker bus*.
- using an all-purpose word, such as *stuff, thing, make, do*.
- language-switching: borrowing a word or expression from their first language (also called *code-switching*)
- paralinguistics: using gesture and mime to convey the intended meaning.
- appealing for help, eg by saying *I don't know what it's called in English*.

All of the above are labelled *achievement strategies*, in that they help the speakers achieve their intended message. But the speaker might decide that the message is simply not achievable, by whatever means. Then they might adopt what is called an *avoidance strategy*, such as abandoning the message altogether, or replacing the original message with one that is less ambitious. For example, if a learner wanted to express the idea *If I'd known you were coming I'd have baked a cake*, they might instead use the less grammatically complex construction: *You came. You didn't tell me. So I didn't bake a cake*.

Learners can be trained to use communication strategies effectively. But some researchers have raised doubts about the wisdom of doing this. There are documented cases of learners who have come to rely too heavily on the use of their *strategic competence* at the expense of developing their *linguistic competence*, such as knowledge of vocabulary and grammar (→ **competence**). This failure to develop linguistic competence can lead to the eventual closing down (or **fossilization**) of their language development. Nevertheless, if combined with ongoing instruction, any risks associated with strategy training seem minor compared with the potential gains in fluency and confidence.

communicative activity METHODOLOGY

A communicative activity is one in which real communication occurs. Communicative activities belong to that generation of classroom **activities** that emerged in response to the need for a more **communicative approach** in the teaching of second languages. (In their more evolved form as **tasks**, communicative activities are central to **task-based learning**). They attempt to import into a practice activity the key features of 'real-life' communication. These are

- *purposefulness*: speakers are motivated by a communicative goal (such as getting information, making a request, giving instructions) and not simply by the need to display the correct use of language for its own sake
- *reciprocity*: to achieve a purpose, speakers need to interact, and there is as much need to listen as to speak
- *negotiation*: following from the above, they may need to check and **repair** the communication in order to be understood by each other
- *unpredictability*: neither the process, nor the outcome, nor the language used in the exchange, is entirely predictable
- *heterogeneity*: participants can use any communicative means at their disposal; in other words, they are not restricted to the use of a pre-specified grammar item.

And, in the case of spoken language in particular:

- *synchronicity*: the exchange takes place in real time

The best known communicative activity is the *information gap* activity. Here, the information necessary to complete the task is either in the possession of just one of the participants, or distributed among them. In order to achieve the goal of the task, therefore, the learners have to share the information that they have. For example, in a *describe-and-draw* activity, one student has a picture which is hidden from his or her partner. The task is for that student to describe the picture so that the partner can accurately draw it. In a *spot-the-difference* task, both students of a pair have pictures (or texts) that are the same apart from some minor details. The goal is to identify these differences. In a *jigsaw activity*, each member of a group has different information. One might have a bus timetable, another a map, and another a list of hotels. They have to share this information in order to plan a weekend break together.

Information gap activities have been criticized on the grounds that they lack **authenticity**. Nor are information gap activities always as productive as might be wished: unsupervised, learners may resort to **communication strategies** in order to simplify the task. A more exploitable information gap, arguably, is the one that exists between the learners themselves, ie, what they don't know – but might like to know – about one another (→ **personalization**).

communicative approach METHODOLOGY

Also known as *communicative language teaching* (*CLT*), the communicative approach is an umbrella term used to describe a major shift in emphasis in language teaching that occurred in Europe in the 1970s. Essentially, the shift was away from teaching language systems (such as vocabulary and grammar) in isolation to teaching people how these systems are used in real communication. Put another way, there was a shift from viewing *linguistic competence* alone as being the goal of language learning, and replacing it with the notion of

communicative competence. This entailed a major re-think of syllabus design, materials, classroom practice and testing. Early attempts to define syllabus goals in communicative terms resulted in the *functional–notional syllabus*. This either supplemented, or replaced, the traditional grammar syllabus with items such as *asking for information, ability, apologizing*, etc. The emphasis on real-life language use ushered in the widespread use of authentic materials ($\rightarrow$ **authenticity**). Interactive **communicative activities**, such as *information-gap tasks*, became a standard part of teachers' repertoires. Test designers, too, responded to the challenge, and traditional grammar tests gave way to tests of overall ability in the four **skills**, including tests of oral performance. The new emphasis on the communicative purposes of language also meant recognizing that these purposes might be different for different learners. This encouraged the development both of **needs analysis** and of special courses designed to meet these needs, ie, **English for special purposes** (ESP).

Quite soon, two distinct schools of thought emerged as to how communicative theory should be realized in practice. There were those that argued that communication should come first, and that 'you learn a language *by* using it'. This *strong* form of CLT led to the development of **task-based learning**, with its emphasis on 'deep-end' communication. In contrast, proponents of a *weak* CLT argued that 'you learn a language *and then* you use it'. According to this 'shallow-end' view, you need to learn the language systems and then put them to communicative use. That is, you start off doing controlled, language-focused activities, and then graduate to more meaning-focused activities, before doing purely communicative ones. It is the weak form of CLT that has prevailed, and this is now standard practice in many parts of the (western) world. Resistance to CLT in some contexts is justified on the grounds that it might not be appropriate in cultures where theoretical knowledge is valued more highly than practical skills.

communicative competence LINGUISTICS

Communicative competence is what you know in order to be able to communicate effectively. First proposed by Dell Hymes, the term contrasts with Noam Chomsky's much narrower conceptualization of **competence** (now known as *linguistic competence*), which is the knowledge that enables the creation of well-formed sentences. There is more to communication than well-formed sentences. As Hymes put it, there is also knowing 'when to speak, when not, … what to talk about with whom, when, where, and in what manner'. Thus, Hymes introduced the notion of **appropriacy** into the argument. This broader conception of competence suggested the need to re-define the goals of language teaching, and to design a methodology to match. Thus, the notion of communicative competence fuelled the development of the **communicative approach** ($\rightarrow$ **usage and use**).

community language learning (CLL) METHODOLOGY

Also called *counseling learning*, CLL is a teaching method that was developed by Charles Curran in the 1970s in the United States. It falls within the **humanistic** tradition. Based on principles derived from counselling therapy, the method places the learners (or *clients*) at centre stage, allowing them the responsibility of deciding the content of the lesson. The teacher (or *knower*) adopts a largely consultant role. Its best-known technique involves the learners, seated in a circle, having a conversation (about whatever they want to). They consult with the teacher-knower, who is outside the circle, to help formulate each utterance – by translation, if need be. The conversation is audio-recorded, utterance by utterance. It is then played back, translated, transcribed on to the board, and read aloud. The teacher-knower may then draw attention to any grammar or vocabulary features that are considered useful. At all times the learners' own meanings and feelings are positively valued.

As a method, CLL is not widely practised, but its core activity – the group-generated conversation – has become a much used (and often highly productive) classroom technique within more conventional classroom settings.

comparative adjective → **adjective**

comparison FUNCTION

The most common way of making comparisons in English is to use comparative forms of **adjectives** or **adverbs**, which may or may not be followed by a **phrase** or **clause** beginning with *than*: *Poznan is nice but Krakow is more beautiful. Cairo is bigger than Alexandria. An antelope can run faster than a lion. Prague was less crowded than we expected.*

To make equal comparisons, *as … as* is used: *The film was just as good as the book.* To negate an equal comparison, use *not as … as*: *Alexandria is not as big as Cairo.*

When comparing more than two things, *superlative* forms are used: *This is the best restaurant in town; it is also the most expensive. Of her books, this one is rated the most highly.*

Generative contexts for teaching and practising the language of comparison include: comparing places (as in many of the above examples); recommending restaurants, hotels, shops, methods of transport, etc; evaluating consumer products, such as cars, computers, clothes, etc; talking about what different animals can do; talking about records and achievements (for superlatives). Advertisements are good places to look for examples in context.

competence LINGUISTICS

Competence is what we intuitively know about a language in order to be able to use it. It is the kind of internalized knowledge that allows us to distinguish well-formed from ill-formed sentences, such as *This is the book that I lost it* and *This is the book that I lost*, even if we can't say what the rule is. It is also the knowledge that allows us to appreciate the ambiguity of a sentence like *I don't like annoying students*, or *Kate showed Jane a photo of herself.* According to Noam Chomsky, competence contrasts with *performance*, which is the way that competence is realized, with all its 'imperfections', in actual speech or writing. More recently, the distinction between competence and performance has been re-labelled as the difference between *I-language* (internalized language) and *E-language* (the way this internalized language is put to use externally).

In the past, the focus of both teaching and testing has been on competence – on teaching and testing the idealized system, regardless of how it is used in 'live talk'. But in the real world language users are judged, not on their competence, but on how well they perform. As many teachers know, there is often a big gap between what learners *know* and what they can *do*. Shouldn't teaching and testing be directed at performance, then, rather than competence? One response to this question has been to broaden the notion of competence to embrace **communicative competence**. Another has been to argue that the descriptions of language which inform teaching should be based not on grammarians' intuitions about I-language but on real instances of E-language. This has been one of the arguments in favour of the use of **corpus** data to inform grammars, dictionaries, and classroom materials. The I versus E distinction also underlies many staffroom discussions, of the type: should I teach *Who did you give it to?* (because that's what I say) or *To whom did you give it?* (because that's what the grammar says)?

competency METHODOLOGY

A competency is a specific practical skill. *Competency-based* teaching, training and testing developed out of the need to upgrade the work-related skills of adults, and the idea has been adopted in language and literacy programmes. Competency-based teaching starts with an analysis of the specific skills needed to do a job, or to pursue a field of study, or to survive as a tourist, for example. These skills (sometimes called *key competencies*) form the basis of the course design, and are the goals of classroom instruction and testing. Competencies are often expressed in the form of *can do* statements, as in these examples (from the Association of Language Testers in Europe (ALTE) work statements summary[3]):

ALTE Level	Listening/Speaking	Reading	Writing
ALTE Level 3	CAN take and pass on most messages that are likely to require attention during a normal working day	CAN understand most correspondence, reports and factual product literature he/she is likely to come across	CAN deal with all routine requests for goods and services

Critics of a competency-based approach to course design say that it represents a rather narrow view of what language proficiency really is. On the other hand, its practical focus makes it a popular approach to teaching **English for Special Purposes (ESP)**.

complement GRAMMAR

The complement of a **sentence** or **clause** is the clause element that follows **linking verbs**, such as *be* and *seem*, and which provides further information about the **subject**: *My brother is <u>a nurse</u>.* (Compare this with *My brother married a nurse*, where *a nurse* is the **object** of the verb). Also:

> *She seems <u>tired</u>.*
> *The news proved to be <u>false</u>.*
> *What you see is <u>what you get</u>.*
> *Tony looks <u>like his father</u>.*

---

[3] in *Common European Framework of Reference for Languages: Learning, Teaching, Assessment*, Council of Europe, 2001, p 251.

A further distinction is made between complements of the subject (as in the above examples) and complements of the object, where the complement adds more information about the **object**: *They call me Trinity. Some like it hot.*

complexity SLA

A learner's language is complex if it uses structures more typical of advanced learners than of lower level learners. A learner may be both accurate and fluent, but if their output consists of very simple sentences, they cannot really be said to be advanced. Factors that are taken into account when assessing complexity include:

- the amount of **subordination**, including the use of **complex sentences**
- the use of pronouns for back **reference**
- the proportion of **lexical verbs** to **linking verbs**: the more of the former, the more complex
- the proportion of **content words** to **function words**: the more of the former, the more complex
- the frequency of use of **conjunctions**

In the following two transcripts of learners recounting shopping experiences,[4] the second shows greater complexity on all counts (but only the subordinate clauses have been underlined):

(1) Two months ago I went sightseeing in London with my friend. We went to Trafalgar Square and around here around there, we walked and by accident we saw a market and my friend wanted to see clothes and we went to market and we saw bag and clothes, and she wanted to buy clothes, and she found her favourite clothes and I also wanted to buy her similar clothes, we tried to try to wear the clothes. I thought at the time I thought that clothes suit me but shop assistant said cost down if we bought two clothes it cost down. […]

(2) My story was that at Christmas I wanted to buy a present, and I wanted to buy a walkman, so I went to a shop in Ealing and I chose the walkman, but I didn't notice that it didn't have autoreverse and … things like this, so I wanted to replace it, so I went to the shop again, and I asked to the sales assistants to give it back. He didn't know what to do so he called the manager. It was a lady, so when she came she said that it was impossible because she suggested that I used this walkman, and I didn't use it so she said that the box was opened, but it had to be opened, because when they sell something they have to check that it is inside.

Complexity has been shown to vary according to **task** difficulty. Certain kinds of task, such as open-ended tasks (ie, tasks where there is no predetermined solution), or tasks involving narration, produce more complex language than others. Allowing students time to plan the task also increases the complexity of the language they produce: ten minutes seems to be optimal. And having students repeat a task also shows gains in complexity.

complex sentence GRAMMAR

A complex sentence is one that contains a main **clause** and one or more subordinate clauses. (The relation between the two clauses is called **subordination**.)

[4] Research data collected by Gairns and Redman for *natural English* (OUP)

This is the house [= main clause] *that Jack built* [= subordinate clause].
Jack and Jill went up the hill [= main clause] *to fetch a pail of water* [= subordinate clause].

Compare this with a *compound sentence*, which contains only co-ordinate clauses. (The relation between the two clauses is called *co-ordination*):

Jack fell down and *broke his crown*.
He put in his thumb and *pulled out a plum*.

compounding → **word formation**

compound sentence → **complex sentence**

comprehensible input → **input**

comprehension PSYCHOLOGY

Comprehension is the process of understanding speech or writing. It results from an interaction between different kinds of knowledge. At one level there is linguistic knowledge, such as a knowledge of words, including how they are spelt and pronounced, and a knowledge of grammar. Attending to these features is called *bottom-up processing*. At a higher level there is knowledge of different text types and styles, as well as knowledge that is not linguistic at all, such as knowledge of the situational and cultural context, and background knowledge about the topic (→ **schema**). Using these higher-level clues to make sense of a text is called *top-down processing*. In order to comprehend a text (whether spoken or written), successful listeners and readers are able to draw on all these types of knowledge at the same time. Sometimes, higher level knowledge can compensate for lack of lower level knowledge. For example, a degree of comprehension of the following text is possible, even without a knowledge of Czech (the language the text is written in):

George W. Bush je prezidentem Spojených států amerických. Byl zvolen roku 2000 a převzal úřad po Billu Clintonovi. Byl znovu zvolen roku 2004. Narodil se ve roce 1946. Jeho ženou je Laura Bushová. Mají dvě dcery, Jennu a Barbaru.

If you don't speak Czech but you understood the gist of that text, you were probably using top-down processes in order to access knowledge of the topic and the text type. These top-down processes would have been triggered by certain recognizable names and words. This suggests that teachers can make reading and listening easier by choosing texts that are about topics that are familiar to their learners. On the other hand, if learners are exposed only to texts that are about things they know, they may over-rely on intelligent guesswork, at the expense of developing their ability at bottom-up processing.

Comprehension also involves different psychological operations, including *perception*, *recognition* and *inferencing*. For example, you might hear a word (ie, perceive it), but not recognize it. You might, however, be able to guess what it means from the context (ie, make an inference). Learners experience problems with comprehension due to a failure in one or more of these operations. Either they don't perceive items correctly (perhaps because of the influence of their first language), or they don't recognize items (because they are not yet part of their internalized knowledge). Finally, they may not have the confidence to make intelligent guesses (often because they are over-dependent on bottom-up processing, and tend to focus on one word at a time). Teachers can assist at the level of perception by, for example, reading a text aloud so that the learners can match the form of the words with their sound. At the level of recognition, teachers can help by pre-teaching vocabulary in advance of reading or listening. And at the level of inferencing, they can help by asking learners to predict what a text is about before they read or hear it, on the basis of its title or an accompanying illustration (→ **listening**; → **reading**).

Does comprehension contribute to language learning, or is it just evidence of successful language learning? Many researchers argue that it does contribute, and that without comprehension there is no learning. Stephen Krashen has gone so far as to say that *comprehensible input* is the *only* condition necessary for language acquisition to occur (→ **input**). Others, however, have pointed out that it might be *lack* of understanding, or *mis*understanding, that acts as an incentive for learners to re-evaluate and restructure their current level of competence.

comprehension questions METHODOLOGY

Comprehension questions are often used in conjunction with reading or listening texts. These include *multiple choice* questions, *yes-no* questions, *wh-* questions (ie, questions beginning *where, who, when ...?* etc), true/false statements, statements to correct, or a choice of summaries of the text to choose from. In theory, the purpose of comprehension questions is to check learners' understanding of a text, either spoken or written. More often than not, though, they are simply a test of learners' ability to recall the text, ie, they are a test of **memory**, rather than of **comprehension**. This is especially the case if the questions are not given to the learners until *after* reading, or listening to, the text. The difficulty is increased if the questions themselves are long or wordy.

An alternative, more helpful approach, is to set questions in *advance* of listening or reading, and which learners answer *while* reading or listening. These can act to focus learners' attention during the task, and can be staged from initial *gist*-checking questions to questions requiring more intensive processing of the text. Because this kind of questioning is designed to support the *process* of reading or listening, the questions might better be called *comprehending questions* (→ **listening**; → **reading**).

computer-assisted language learning (CALL) METHODOLOGY

Computer-assisted language learning, or CALL, is one of a number of names to describe the way that computers are used to complement (although not necessarily to replace) classroom instruction. CALL is just one aspect of TELL, or *technology-enhanced language learning*.

The earliest CALL programs were written for mainframe computers in the 1950s and 1960s. They reflected both the limitations of computers at the time, as well as the prevailing **behaviourist** approach. In *programmed instruction*, for example, information would be presented in short steps, each step being tested by mechanical exercises, before the next step was presented. Quite soon, however, the potential of computers to offer **games** and simulations was being exploited. Simulations offer learners options (such as ways of continuing a dialogue), the choice of one of which determines the next set of options, and so on.

Since the advent of microcomputers in the early 1980s, the availability of language teaching software for both classroom and private use has grown enormously. It has not always been able to keep pace, however, with technological innovations, nor with developments in learning theory. There is still a tendency to focus on the more mechanical aspects of language learning, such as *gap-filling* and answering *multiple choice questions*, even though these are now enhanced by the use of sound, animation, and full-motion video.

The more imaginative exploitations of computers have included the creation of *interactive multimedia environments* which provide opportunities for problem-solving in the target language; word-processing software which allows learners to create and proof-read their own texts, and automated reading 'coaches' that monitor the learner reading aloud and provide helpful feedback. Speech-recognition software is widely used for pronunciation practice, and programs have been devised that, by responding to written input, simulate human–human interaction. Prototype programs that respond to *spoken* input have also been developed. However, 'intelligent' CALL must await developments in artificial intelligence (AI).

Of perhaps more immediate usefulness has been the use of networked computers to provide opportunities for teacher–learner, and learner–learner interaction (→ **computer-mediated communication**). Also, the internet allows learners to access English language texts to suit any interest or need, to use search engines to locate specific words or phrases, to access on-line corpora (→ **corpus**), dictionaries and grammar references, and to obtain information in order to complete tasks and projects (→ **webquests**). Interactive whiteboards allow on-line and other digitally-stored information to be displayed and manipulated in full view of the class. For teachers, there is now a wide range of authoring software available, much of it downloadable from the internet, which allows them to create their own exercises, games, and puzzles.

computer-mediated communication (CMC) METHODOLOGY

CMC, also known as *on-line communication*, is the use of networked computers in order to communicate. It is becoming increasingly popular as a means both of tutoring language learners, and of setting up opportunities for learner–learner interaction (→ **computer-assisted language learning**). CMC is either *synchronous*, where people communicate in real time using chat or discussion software; or *asynchronous*, where the communication is delayed, such as when people are exchanging emails, or posting on message boards, or reading and responding to web logs (*blogs*). In both synchronous and asynchronous CMC, the interaction can be one-to-one, one-to-many, or many-to-many. CMC now offers the possibility of teachers and learners interacting in virtual classrooms (or *virtual learning environments* (*VLEs*)) using specialized software. Web cameras and *video conferencing* can enhance the interaction in a virtual classroom.

The potential for CMC to supplement, or even replace, face-to-face interaction is now the focus of a great deal of research. It has been found, for example, that CMC allows a more balanced participation than in traditional classroom settings, that its language displays greater **complexity** and lexical density than that of face-to-face conversation, and that it is possible to create all the conditions for communicative interaction (→ **communicative activity**). Moreover, learners' experience of instructional CMC can help prepare them to use CMC in academic and professional settings.

CMC is often used to supplement face-to-face instruction in what is called *blended* (or *hybrid*) *learning* situations. For example, learners attend scheduled classes, but between classes participate in on-line discussions, collaborate on projects, or maintain email contact with their teacher.

concept question METHODOLOGY

A concept question is a question designed to check or to guide learners' understanding of the meaning of a new word or grammar item. Asking concept questions allows teachers to monitor their students' understanding without having to resort to **translation** or to the rather unreliable question *Do you understand?* Concept questions are designed to isolate the core meanings of the item. For example, if the teacher has introduced the structure *must have* [+ past participle], as in *I must have left my umbrella on the bus*, the learners' grasp of the concept can be checked by asking these questions:

> *Did I leave my umbrella on the bus?* [Expected answer: *Maybe. Maybe not.*]
> *Is it certain?* [No]
> *Is it a strong possibility?* [Yes]

Note that the question *Must I have left my umbrella on the bus?* is inappropriate, since it uses the structure whose meaning the concept questions are aiming to check. The concept questions for a vocabulary item, such as *sand*, might be:

> *What colour is it?* [Expected answer: *Yellow, white,* etc]
> *Where can you find it?* [*By the sea, in the desert,* etc]

Concept questions, especially about grammar concepts, can be difficult to formulate in a way that is clear to learners. But they can be an effective tool in gauging learners' initial understanding of a new item. They need to be used in conjunction with other ways of checking learning, such as verifying the learners' ability to use the target item to formulate original sentences about their own, shared, world (→ **meaning**).

concord GRAMMAR

Concord (also called *agreement*) is the name given to the grammatical relationship whereby the form of one word requires a corresponding form in another. In English, this is the case with **subjects** and the verbs that follow them, as in *I + am, you + are, Jan + is, Robin + has, Jan and Robin + have,* etc. The most troublesome concord rule in English is the *third person -s* in present tense verbs, as in *it works*, a rule that for most learners defies all logic, and (as researchers have shown) is late-acquired (→ **order of acquisition**). As compensation, adjectives in English do not have to agree with their nouns, which is not the case in languages such as Spanish or German.

concordance LINGUISTICS

A concordance is a list of words in a text, or in a **corpus**, along with each word's immediate context. It functions like an index and is a convenient way in which corpus information can be made available for study. Concordances can show, for example, the typical **collocations** of selected words. Here, for example, is a concordance of all the instances of the word *corpus* that occur in the entry in this book under *corpus*, arranged so that *corpus* is the *node word* of the concordance:

```
1                                    A corpus (plural corpora) is a c
2     the case of both the COBUILD corpus and the British Nationa
3     rpus and the British National Corpus (BNC)). There are also
4     ts can, in theory, comprise a corpus,although, for general
5     , the more representative the corpus,the better. The use of
6     e structure and use is called corpus linguistics, and has le
7     n invented ones. One way that corpus information is often pr
```

Even from this limited information, it can be seen that the word *corpus* is singular, countable, and that it can function as a *noun modifier* (items 6 and 7). Concordances used to be compiled by hand, but now software programs (called *concordancers*) can process texts rapidly, and there are a number of websites that provide an instant concordance of any submitted text.

conditional GRAMMAR

Conditional sentences express imaginary or hypothetical situations (→ **hypothetical meaning**). They usually contain a **modal verb**, eg *would*: *It would be awful to be famous. I would never eat kangaroo meat.* Conditional sentences often consist of a main **clause** and a conditional clause, ie, a subordinate clause typically beginning with *if* or *unless*: *If it rains, we'll eat inside. If I had known you were coming, I would have baked a cake. I'll make some coffee, unless you prefer tea.* The conditional clause expresses the condition on which the situation described in the main clause depends.

Conditions can be classified as *real* or *unreal*. A real condition is one that can possibly be fulfilled, either now or in the future. An unreal condition is one that the speaker regards as unlikely or impossible, whether in the past, present, or future.

Real: *If it rains* (as it might), *we'll eat inside.*
         I'll make some coffee, unless you prefer tea (as you might).
Unreal: *If I had the car now* (but I don't), *I'd give you a lift.*
         If I had known (but I didn't), *I would have baked a cake.*

With future reference, the difference between a real and an unreal condition may be slight, given that the future is inherently uncertain. A speaker might equally say:

I'll be surprised if Felicity passes her driving test. (= real)
I'd be surprised if Felicity passed her driving test. (= unreal)

In the first instance, the speaker implies a greater degree of likelihood

The verb forms in unreal conditions are *back-shifted*. That is, for present or future reference, the past tense is used in the *if*-clause: *If I had the car now* … For past reference, the past perfect form is used in the *if*-clause: *If I had known* …
For teaching purposes, conditional sentences are usually classified into three types:

- *first conditional* or present simple + *will*: *If it rains, we'll eat inside.* (ie, a real condition)
- *second conditional* or past simple + *would*: *If I had the car now, I'd give you a lift.* (ie, an unreal condition, with present or future reference)

- *third conditional* or past perfect + *would have*: *If I had known, I would have baked a cake.* (ie, an unreal condition, with past reference)

A fourth type, called the *zero conditional*, accounts for sentences where both verbs are in the present. It is used for stating general truths: *If you heat ice, it melts.*

This way of classifying conditionals is convenient for the purposes of syllabus design, but it does not cover all the combinations possible. (Sometimes these are bundled together under the heading *mixed conditionals*). For example:

> *If you're going to behave like that, you can go to your room.*
> *If she hadn't been delayed, she'd be here by now.*
> *If it didn't rain we would usually eat on the terrace.*
> *If you would like to wait here, I'll go and see if the manager is available.*

Other **conjunctions** that introduce conditional clauses include *provided (that)*, *so long as*, *as long as*, and *on condition that*.

Contexts in which conditional sentences are likely to occur, and which are therefore useful for teaching purposes, include:

- *first conditional*: making promises, giving warnings, and making threats; giving advice, eg about travel or career
- *second conditional*: wishing, imagining, fantasizing, eg about travel, wealth or global concerns; hypothetical scenarios (as in *If you found a $100 in the street, would you (a) keep it; (b) … etc*)
- *third conditional*: regrets, lucky escapes, coincidences; re-imagining history and biography (*If Kennedy hadn't been shot …*).

conjunct → **linker**

conjunction GRAMMAR

Conjunctions are members of a **word class** whose function is to join together words, phrases, clauses and sentences (→ **linker**). There are two types of conjunction: *co-ordinating* and *subordinating*. Co-ordinating conjunctions, such as *and* and *but* join equivalent units, such as two **clauses** of equal rank:

> *The cat will mew, <u>and</u> dog will have his day.*
> *O, banish me my lord, <u>but</u> kill me not.*
> *And so he goes to heaven, and <u>so</u> am I revenged.*

Subordinating conjunctions, such as *if*, *because* and *when*, join a subordinate clause to a main clause (→ **subordination**):

> *No longer mourn for me <u>when</u> I am dead.*
> *<u>If</u> music be the food of love, play on.*
> *<u>As</u> Caesar loved me, I weep for him.*
> *<u>Because</u> I love you, I will let you know.*

The number of conjunctions in a text is one measure of the text's **complexity**.

connected speech PHONOLOGY

Connected speech refers to the way that speech sounds are produced as part of a continuous sequence, rather than in isolation. This affects their production in the following ways:

- *assimilation*: This happens when a sound is modified by a neighbouring sound, such as when the final /n/ of *green* is followed by a /p/, and is pronounced /m/ as in *Green Park*: /griːm pɑːk/.
- *elision*: This happens when a sound is omitted, because another, similar, sound follows. This is common when two *plosive* sounds occur together, as in *I walked to work*, where *walked to* is pronounced /wɔːktə/. Similarly, *baked beans* is pronounced /beɪkbiːnz/.
- *liaison*. This is where a sound is introduced at word boundaries, especially after words ending in a vowel, as in *law and order*, where a /r/ sound (called an *intrusive r*) is inserted between *law* and *and*: /lɔːrənɔːdə/.
- *juncture*: This is the pausing (or lack of pausing) at the boundary between two sounds, which accounts for the difference between *ice cream* and *I scream*, or between *Gladly the cross I'd bear* and *Gladly, the cross-eyed bear*.

These effects, some of which alter the 'dictionary' pronunciation of words, can cause learners problems, particularly in understanding natural speech. There is normally no difference, for example, between *I walk to work* and *I walked to work*. And *I can't come* may sound like *I can come*. Learners, therefore, need practice in decoding short stretches of natural speech. Recordings are good for this. Simply asking learners to write down what they hear (as in a **dictation**), and playing and re-playing a few lines of a dialogue, is good ear-training. Another technique is to dictate sentences and ask learners to say how many words there are in each one. It is probably of less use for learners to practise *producing* the effects of connected speech, since they are not necessarily an aid to intelligibility, especially when speaking to other non-native speakers. Even native speakers 'disconnect' their speech when they are taking pains to be understood, such as over a difficult phone line, or when talking to foreigners.

connectionism PSYCHOLOGY

Connectionism is a way of using computers to model the way that the brain processes and learns information, including language. Connectionist models are based upon the way that the brain's neural networks function by being massively interconnected.

Information that is fed into the system triggers activity that is rapidly distributed throughout the network by a process called *spreading activation*. Over time the connections in the network are strengthened or weakened according to how frequently they are used, and according to whether the output from the system is correct or not. In this way, connections are established and the network 'learns': strong, weak, zero and negative associations are built up in the form of connection strengths. The kind of connection that might be established is one between the stem of a verb (eg *take*) and its inflected forms (*takes*, *took*). Activity that gives rise to wrong answers (eg linking *take* to *taked*) leads to a weakening of the connection involved.

In other cognitive models of learning, rules are generalized from the input and are stored abstractly in long-term memory. However, a connectionist model stores the traces of thousands of previous occurrences. The model behaves *as if* it were rule-governed, but there are no rules, only traces of activity. This rule-*like* behaviour is what is termed an *emergent property* of such systems, which are said to be *self-organizing*. In this sense, the way language emerges as patterned behaviour is regarded as similar to the way other complex, adaptive systems develop.

Connectionism belongs to what are called **usage-based** accounts of language acquisition. It does not presuppose any innate language-learning faculty (→ **universal grammar**) nor any rule-learning and rule-using (→ **cognitive learning theory**). Instead, it assumes we are mentally predisposed to look for associations between elements and create links between them, in response to frequently encountered patterns of usage.

Researchers have successfully used computerized connectionist models to simulate the learning of some language 'rules', such as past tense formation in English. But the claim that *all* learning happens like this is hotly debated. To proponents of a **mentalist** position, who view language learning as innately rule-governed, the idea that learning is driven by patterns in the input sounds suspiciously like **behaviourism**.

connotation VOCABULARY

The connotations of a word are its good, bad, humorous, old-fashioned, or other, associations. These co-exist with its core meaning, or *denotation*. Words like *propaganda* or *collaborator*, for example, have negative connotations in English, although their **cognate** forms in other languages are not necessarily so loaded. To describe a man as a *cad and a bounder*, or as *dashing* and *gallant*, evokes old-fashioned, even comical, associations. Part of knowing a word is knowing the associations it triggers in its users. Since many of these associations are culturally determined, they can prove elusive to learners.

consciousness-raising (CR) PSYCHOLOGY

Consciousness-raising describes the way that learners become aware, or are made aware, of features of the language they are learning. The term belongs to **cognitive learning theory**, which claims a central role for conscious mental operations in learning. At the very least, it is argued, learners need to *notice* features of the **input** (→ **noticing**), if these features are to become intake. For example, they need to notice that the past tense ending of regular verbs is *-ed*. Helping learners to notice such things is what used to be called **presentation**. But the term consciousness-raising (or *awareness-raising*) is now preferred, since it credits the learners with some active role in the process of learning, whereas presentation does not. Moreover, presentation is associated with the **PPP** model, which is directed at immediate output on the part of the learner. There is some evidence, though, that learners first need to pay attention to the input without the pressure of instant production.

Of course, teachers can highlight input features but this is no guarantee that learners will notice them. So it may be better to talk about the things that teachers do that have *CR potential*. These include: enhancing the input in some way so as to make certain items more salient (→ **input**); asking learners to infer rules from examples (→ **inductive learning**); asking them to compare their own output with that of more proficient users of the target language (what is called 'noticing the gap'); problematizing the input, ie, forcing them to notice distinctions that they had previously ignored; and *pushed output*, where they are forced to 'notice the holes' in the present state of their language knowledge (→ **output hypothesis**).

consonant PHONOLOGY

Consonant sounds are made when the airflow from the lungs is obstructed in some way by the **articulators**. (Compare this to **vowels**, which are not obstructed). Consonants are classified in terms of the *place* where the obstruction occurs; the *manner* (or type) of obstruction; and whether or not the sound is *voiced* (→ **voiced sound**). In English, the place of airflow obstruction can be anywhere from the *glottis* (the aperture between the vocal cords) which produces a *glottal* sound like /h/, all the way to the lips, to produce a *bilabial* sound, like /b/. The majority of English consonants are formed in the area around the teeth, including the tooth ridge (*alveolar ridge*), and the part of the hard palate just behind that.

The *manner* of obstruction for most consonants produces either a 'popping' effect or a 'buzzing' one. Popping sounds, like /p/, /t/, and /k/ are called *plosives*, and are formed by a build-up and sudden release of the airflow. Buzzing and hissing sounds, like /f/, /z/, /θ/ (as in *thin*) and /ʃ/ (as in *shin)*, are formed by the friction caused by constricting the flow of air, and are called *fricatives*. Some sounds, like /tʃ/ and /dʒ/ (as in *char* and *jar*) combine both a plosive and a fricative effect, and are called *affricates*. *Nasal* sounds are so called because they are produced by diverting the airflow through the nose. There are three nasal consonants in English: /m/, /n/ and /ŋ/ (as in *sing*). Finally, there are four consonants where the airflow is hardly obstructed at all: /w/, /r/, /l/ and /j/ (as in *you*). These are called *approximants* (/l/ is also called a *lateral*).

So, the sound /t/, as in *top*, is *alveolar*, *plosive* and *non-voiced* (or *voiceless*). Its 'sister' consonant /d/ is also an alveolar plosive, the only difference being that it is voiced.

In English, there are twenty-four consonant sounds. Note that there is not a one-to-one relationship between the consonant *sounds* and those letters of the alphabet that are also called consonants. The spoken consonants are displayed in this chart, in their **phonemic script** form, according to their place and their manner of articulation. Where there is a pair, the first in the pair is non-voiced/voiceless, and the second is voiced.

Manner of articulation	Place of articulation							
	Bilabial	Labiodental	Dental	Alveolar	Palato-alveolar (Post-alveolar)	Palatal	Velar	Glottal
Plosive	p b			t d			k g	
Fricative		f v	θ ð	s z	ʃ ʒ			h
Affricate					tʃ dʒ			
Nasal	m			n			ŋ	
Lateral				l				
Approximant (or semi-vowel)	w				r	j		

Roach, P. 1991 *English Phonetics and Phonology* (CUP) p 62.

Consonant sounds carry a greater share of the informational load of spoken language than do vowels. You can prove this by taking the vowels out of a sentence: t s nt dffclt t rcnstrct th wrds. U i ou a_e e o-o-a ou, i i i-o-i-e (= but if you take the consonants out, it is impossible). This is good news for learners, since the consonant sounds in English match those of other languages relatively closely. The vowel system, on the other hand, is much more idiosyncratic. Even among native speakers, the pronunciation of vowel sounds displays much greater regional difference than does the pronunciation of consonants. Probably the most difficult consonant sound for learners of English is /θ/, as in *three* and *breath*. Happily, its mispronunciation is seldom if ever a cause of communication breakdown amongst non-native users of English (→ **phonological core**).

consonant cluster PHONOLOGY

English pronunciation permits sequences of two or more consonants at the beginning or end of syllables, and these are called consonant clusters. For example, the word *straight* has a three-consonant cluster to begin with (/str/), but ends with a single consonant (/t/) – despite what the spelling might suggest. On the other hand, the word *sixths* ends with a four-consonant cluster: /ksθs/. Different languages permit different lengths and combinations of cluster (The technical term for the way sounds can combine in a particular language is called *phonotactics*.) This can cause acute problems for learners. Even native speakers of English reduce most complex final clusters, so that *texts* rhymes with *sex*, for example. Learners frequently simplify clusters by adding or inserting a vowel, so that Spanish speakers, for example, tend to say *Escott walkéd* (/escɒt wɔːkɪd/) for *Scott walked*. Reduction of initial consonant clusters (as in /pɒdʌk/ for *product*) can jeopardize intelligibility, and hence this is a pronunciation feature that is targeted in the teaching of the **phonological core**.

constructivism PSYCHOLOGY

Constructivism is a theory of learning that claims that individuals actively construct knowledge, rather than passively receiving it. They do this by filtering and organizing their experience so as to match their existing knowledge (or mental representations) of the world. If there is a mismatch between their experience and their existing mental representations, they restructure the latter to accommodate the new information. According to this view, different individuals who are exposed to the same experiences will each construct a different and unique reality.

The view of the learner as an individual, actively constructing personal meaning, has obvious implications for language teaching. For a start, it suggests that such passive learning procedures as imitation and rote learning may play only a minor role, if any. Furthermore, by viewing the learners as individuals, each with a unique set of mental representations and their own learning strategies, constructivism supports the case for **learner-centred instruction**, and for learners discovering how the language works for themselves (→ **experiential learning**). Finally, since learning is the construction of personal meaning, constructivism underscores the argument for **personalization**.

Key figures in the development of constructivism include the cognitive psychologists Jean Piaget and Jerome Bruner. Constructivist learning theory contrasts with **behaviourist** theory, and is therefore ideologically aligned with both **cognitive learning theory** and **mentalism**. In asserting the importance of the individual, constructivism is also closely affiliated to *humanism* (→ **humanistic approaches**). A form of constructivism which emphasizes the dynamic interplay between individuals and their social context is called *social constructivism*, and shares many of the principles of **sociocultural learning theory**.

content and language integrated learning METHODOLOGY

Teaching a subject, such as geography, natural science, or history, *through* English, to learners whose first language is not English, is known as content and language integrated learning (CLIL). It is also known as content-based teaching. CLIL belongs firmly in the tradition of the strong form of the **communicative approach**, in that there is no predetermined language syllabus. Instead, instruction is organized solely around the content. It is also closely related to **immersion** teaching, whereby learners in a situation of *additive bilingualism* (→ **bilingualism**) take all or some of their school subjects in a second language. Immersion teaching has been shown to be effective in some contexts, such as Canada. Here, English-speaking children receive content instruction in French, with no detriment to their English nor to their subject knowledge, and with impressive gains in French. Content and language integrated learning instruction probably works best where teachers are adept not only at teaching the subject matter, but also at addressing their learners' language needs, such as being able to modify their own classroom language, and to provide 'in flight' assistance when necessary.

content-based learning → **content and language integrated learning**

content word VOCABULARY

Also known as *lexical words*, content words are the main carriers of meaning in written and spoken texts. They belong to four main **word classes**: nouns, verbs, adjectives, and adverbs. Content words are the words that remain when you write texts that are dense in information, such as headlines, text-messages and lecture notes. For example: RAIL STRIKE TALKS COLLAPSE (for *The talks about the rail strike have collapsed*). They contrast with **function words** (such as *the*, *about*, *have*), which have a grammatical function but little or no easily definable 'dictionary meaning'. The proportion of content words to function words in a text is a measure of the text's *lexical density*. The lexical density of information texts (such as this one) is much higher than in casual conversation, for example.

context LINGUISTICS

The context of a language item is its adjacent language items. In the absence of context, it is often impossible to assign exact meaning to an item. A sentence like *Ben takes the bus to work*, for example, could have past, present, or future reference, depending on the context:

I know this chap called Ben. One day *Ben takes the bus to work*, and just as …
Most days *Ben takes the bus to work*, but sometimes he rides his bike …
If *Ben takes the bus to work* tomorrow, he'll be late, because there's a strike …

Likewise, a sentence like *You use it like this* is meaningless in the absence of a context. By the same token, a word or sentence in one context can have a very different meaning in another. The sign *NO BICYCLES* in a public park means something different to *NO BICYCLES* outside a bicycle rental shop. It is sometimes necessary to distinguish between different kinds of context. On the one hand, there is the context of the accompanying **text**, sometimes called the *co-text*. The co-text of this sentence, for example, includes the sentences that precede and follow it, as well as the paragraph of which it forms a part. It is the co-text that offers clues as to the meaning of unfamiliar vocabulary in a text. The *situational* context (also *context of situation*, *context of use*), on the other hand, is the physical and temporal setting in which an instance of language use occurs. The typical context for the spoken question *Are you being served?* is in a shop, for example. Both co-text and context influence the production and interpretation of language. **Discourse analysis** studies the relationship between language and co-text, including the way that sentences or utterances are connected (→ **cohesion**). **Pragmatics** studies the relationship between language and its contexts of use, including the way meaning can be inferred by reference to context factors.

Various theories have been proposed in order to account for the ways that language choices are determined by contextual factors. One of the best known of these is Michael Halliday's **systemic functional linguistics**. Halliday distinguishes three variables in any context that systematically impact on language choices and which, together, determine a text's **register**:

- the *field*: what the language is being used to talk about, and for what purposes
- the *tenor*: the participants in the language event, and their relationship
- the *mode*: how language is being used in the exchange, eg is it written or spoken?

For example, this short text shows the influence of all three factors:

  Do u fancy film either 2nite or 2moro? Call me.

The field is 'making arrangements about leisure activities', hence the use of words like *film*, *2nite* (tonight), *2moro* (tomorrow). The tenor is one of familiarity and equality (accounting for the informal *fancy* and the imperative: *call me*); and the mode is that of a written text message, which explains its brevity, its use of abbreviated forms (*u, 2nite*) and the absence of salutations. A change in any of these contextual factors is likely to have a significant effect on the text.

Language learners, it is argued, need to know how these contextual factors correlate with language choices in order to produce language that is appropriate to the context (→ **appropriacy**). One way of doing this is to ask them to make changes to a text (such as the text message above) that take into account adjustments to the field, tenor, or mode.

continuous → **progressive**; → **aspect**

continuous assessment → **assessment**

contraction GRAMMAR

A contraction (or *contracted form*) happens when you reduce a **function** word (like *not*) and attach it to an adjacent word (like *is*) to form one word (*isn't*). Contractions are most common in spoken language and in informal written language. The most common contractions are formed either by joining a subject pronoun and an **auxiliary** (including **modal** auxiliary) verb (*I'm, they'll, we'd*), or by joining an auxiliary verb and *not*: *wasn't, mustn't, can't*. Contractions for auxiliary verbs are not used where the auxiliary is stressed, as in *Are you busy? Yes, I am. Can you tell us where she is?* Note that in Standard English there is no form **amn't* (for *am not*). The contracted form of *am not I?* is *aren't I?* as in *Aren't I clever!*

contrastive analysis (CA) SLA

Contrastive analysis refers to the way that the linguistic systems of two languages are compared and contrasted. It used to be thought that a comparison between a learner's first language and a second language would predict the errors that a learner would make learning the latter: the greater the difference, the more likely an error. The underlying assumption was the **behaviourist** one, that errors occur as a result of *interference* when the learner transfers first language habits into the second. In fact, **error** analyses of learners' **interlanguage** show that many errors that might be predicted on the basis of contrastive analysis do not occur. Others that are not predicted *do* occur. Spanish-speaking learners, for example, seldom if ever say **Juan it saw*, although this is the standard word order in Spanish: *Juan lo vio*. On the other hand, Spanish-speaking learners do say **María working*, despite the fact that a similar structure to the English present continuous exists in Spanish: *María está trabajando*. For these reasons, many errors are now attributed to *developmental* causes. That is, they occur as a result of the way interlanguage develops naturally, irrespective of the learner's first language (→ **order of acquisition**). Moreover, there are many ways that learners draw on their first language as a resource, suggesting that **transfer** can have positive as well as negative outcomes. CA's most successful predictions are in the area of **phonology**, where the influence of the first language is more in evidence than it is in grammar learning. *False friends* (→ **cognate**), as when a Polish speaker says *actually* to mean *now*, or when a Spanish speaker says *career* to mean *course (of study)*, are instances of negative transfer at the level of vocabulary.

controlled practice → **practice**

conversation METHODOLOGY

Conversation is informal talk between one or more people. Most learners identify the ability to participate in conversations as a desirable language-learning goal, but opinions differ as to how this goal should be met. There are currently two schools of thought: the *direct* approach, and the *indirect* approach. The former argues that the characteristic features of conversation, as identified in **conversation analysis**, should be taught explicitly and in isolation, before being integrated into freer practice activities. These features include specific *conversational gambits*, such as those used for opening and closing conversations, or for *turn-taking*, as well as ways of performing specific speech acts, such as agreeing and disagreeing. Other possible items for inclusion in a conversation syllabus might include the use of **discourse markers**, the language of **politeness**, **appraisal** language (that is, ways speakers express their judgments and evaluations), **vague language**, **pause fillers**, etc. The *indirect* approach, on the other hand, argues that conversation is best learned by *having conversations*. Accordingly, the conversation syllabus might consist of a list of *topics* to talk about (such as the weather, holidays, politics, the family), or of *situations* where conversations are likely to occur (introductions, eating out, small talk at the workplace, telephoning, etc). Specific features of conversation might be introduced as the need arises.

Of course, in reality, a blend of both the direct and the indirect approaches probably works best. Just as important, arguably, is that the quality of classroom talk (including **teacher talk**) is frequently conversational in style. In fact, proponents of **sociocultural learning theory** argue that conversation is the ideal context for learning, since it provides learning **affordances**, including opportunities to take risks with language, within a familiar and secure framework (→ **scaffolding**). Some commentators have gone so far as to recommend that the process of learning should be like one 'long conversation'.

conversation analysis (CA) DISCOURSE

Conversation analysis is concerned with describing the structure of conversational interaction, including the sequential organization of talk and the ways that speakers repair communication problems. From a CA point of view, the basic unit of talk is the *turn*: speakers take turns when they talk, avoiding either long silences or speaking at the same time. The way this is managed is called *turn-taking*. The occurrence of two consecutive turns, where the first turn determines the second, such as a question and an answer, or a request and an acceptance, is called an *adjacency pair*. Other features identified by CA include *conversational openings* and *closings*, *back-channelling* (ie, the verbal signals given by the listener to indicate interest, attention, surprise, etc), and **repair** strategies – either *self-repair* or *other-repair*.

CA has provided useful tools for describing conversational structure but is limited in that it divorces conversation from its **context**. A related field, *interactional sociolinguistics*, has attempted to redress this imbalance, by situating talk in its social contexts. In a similar vein, a **systemic functional** approach aims to relate the features of casual conversation, such as the frequent use of **appraisal** language, to conversation's main function, the establishing and maintaining of social ties. Meanwhile, **discourse analysis** has investigated the features of conversation that distinguish it from other spoken and written genres, including the effects of production in real-time. These include: repetitions, filled pauses, false starts, incomplete utterances, non-standard forms, **vague language**, and the use of **discourse markers** to signal the speaker's intentions. Some of the characteristic features of conversation have been identified in this short authentic extract[5]. (The symbol ⌊ indicates an overlapping turn):

<Speaker 1>   That eggplant is gorgeous[1]

<Speaker 2>   I did it sort of[2] um[3] you know[4] you drain it for a long time then you[5] I rinsed it then[6] I dried it then I fried it

<Speaker 1>   ⌊[7]Must have took[8] forever

<Speaker 2>   then I sprinkled lemon juice on it put it in the fridge.

<Speaker 3>   The eggplant?[9]

<Speaker 2>   Delicious. Yeah.[10]

<Speaker 4>   Did you put salt on it first? To draw the[11]

<Speaker 2>   No[12] I didn't actually.[13] It doesn't seem to have made any difference.

[5] OZTALK: Macquarie University/UTS Spoken Language Corpus.

1. appraisal language
2. vague language
3. filled pause
4. discourse marker (appealing to shared knowledge)
5. false start
6. linker
7. ellipsis (omission of elements)
8. non-standard form
9. clarification request
10. response (9 and 10 form an adjacency pair)
11. incomplete utterance
12. response (second part of adjacency pair)
13. discourse marker (hedging)

co-operative principle DISCOURSE

The co-operative principle is the principle that speakers try to co-operate with one another. When people take part in conversations they do so on the assumption that the other speakers will observe certain unstated 'rules'. If, for instance, you were to ask someone the way to the station, you would be justifiably surprised if (a) they gave you the directions but didn't tell you that the station had been closed for the last five years; (b) they gave you directions which turned out to be knowingly false; (c) they didn't give you directions, but talked about the poor state of the train service; (d) they gave you the directions but in the reverse order. In any of these cases, you might judge them as having been unco-operative.

The co-operative principle was first articulated by the philosopher H.P. Grice, and consists of four 'maxims', which are:

1. *maxim of quantity*: Make your contribution just as informative as required.
2. *maxim of quality*: Make your contribution one that is true.
3. *maxim of relation*: Make your contribution relevant.
4. *maxim of manner*. Avoid obscurity and ambiguity. Be brief and orderly.

In the example situation above (about the station) the speakers are violating each of these maxims respectively. This is unusual. Without the shared belief in a co-operative principle, we would be compelled to ask, after any utterance, *Is that all? Is that true? What has that got to do with it?* and *Can you be any clearer?* The fact that this only happens in exceptional circumstances, such as in a court of law, suggests that, for day to day purposes, Grice's maxims apply.

The co-operative principle has been criticized as being culturally biased. Learners from other cultural backgrounds may have different views as to what constitutes being informative, truthful, relevant or clear. Nevertheless, the theory has had an important influence on **pragmatics**, since it goes some way to explaining how it is that speakers are able to make sense of responses such as the following:

A   How do you like my new dress?
B   Well, the *colour's* very striking.

Because B seems to be giving less information than A might expect (B is *flouting* Grice's first maxim), A can only assume that this is deliberate, and therefore she must now look for an alternative interpretation of B's response, eg that B *doesn't* like the dress. (This is called conversational *implicature*). In other words, it is possible to infer from what *has* been said what has *not* been said.

Other critics have argued that all Grice's maxims can be subsumed under the one they regard as the most important, which is: *Make your contribution relevant.*

co-ordination → **complex sentence**; → **conjunction**; → **spoken grammar**

copular verb → **linking verb**

corpus LINGUISTICS

A corpus (plural *corpora*) is a collection of actually occurring texts (either spoken or written), stored and accessed by means of computers, and useful for investigating language use. Corpora can vary in size from fewer than a million words to several hundreds of millions (as in the case of both the COBUILD corpus and the British National Corpus (BNC)). There are also specialized corpora, such as collections of teenager talk, of casual conversation, and of learner English. In fact, any collection of texts can, in theory, comprise a corpus, although, for general English purposes, the more representative the corpus, the better. The use of corpora for researching language structure and use is called *corpus linguistics*, and has led to the development of grammars and dictionaries that claim to be more reliable than their forbears, in that they are based on attested (ie, real) data. **Dictionaries**, for example, can now present the different meanings of a word according to their relative **frequency**, and can include the most commonly occurring **collocations** of a word, as well as using authentic examples, rather than invented ones. One way that corpus information is often presented is in the form of a **concordance** (a list of words, along with each word's immediate context).

Corpus linguistics has been criticized on the grounds that the information it reveals relates only to language performance. This information cannot be used to make claims about language **competence**, that is, the way that language is stored and organized in the mind. Therefore corpus information, while intensely interesting for grammarians and lexicographers, may be of only marginal interest to learners. Nevertheless, the availability, now, of corpus and concordancing software on the internet is a useful tool for teachers, especially when it comes to checking hunches, such as whether people really say *I'm going to go to the shops* (rather than *I'm going to the shops*) or *She mustn't have known ...* (rather than *She can't have known ...*) or *me and my sister ...* (rather the *my sister and I ...*).

correction METHODOLOGY

Correction is a form of **feedback**, when the teacher or another student provides the correct version of an error, either spoken or written. The amount and type of correction favoured by teachers is closely related to the teacher's attitude to **error**, which is in turn influenced by the teacher's theory of language learning. Where mistakes are seen as evidence of bad habits, they need to be corrected overtly and fast, as in the following exchange:

Student My brother is a good cooker.
Teacher (1) Not cooker, *cook*.

On the other hand, where mistakes are viewed as a natural stage in the development of the learner's **interlanguage**, and where learners are credited with having the capacity to work things out for themselves, teachers may use a variety of strategies to elicit *peer-correction* or *self-correction*. Here are some alternative ways of dealing with the mistake *My brother is a good cooker.*

(2) No. Try again.
(3) My brother is a good …?
(4) A *cooker* is the thing. The person is a …?
(5) Good thinking: add *-er* to the verb, like *teacher, worker,* but this is an exception.
(6) He's a good cooker, is he? Is he gas or electric?

Some teachers feel that correction of any sort is de-motivating for the learner, and that feedback should be given only when learners get something right (*positive feedback*). Moreover, it seems that correction does not have any long-term effect on the **order of acquisition** of grammar structures. However, second language acquisition research suggests that lack of negative feedback may be a contributing factor to **fossilization** (→ **error**). Even if corrections have little *direct* effect on acquisition, correction may nevertheless serve to remind learners to take **accuracy** seriously. And attention to accuracy (also called a **focus on form**) is claimed to be a necessary condition for interlanguage development. The question as to when best to correct is also disputed. Conventional wisdom suggests that teachers shouldn't interrupt their learners in **fluency** activities. However, there is an argument that the most effective correction may be the correction learners get when they are in what is called 'real operating conditions', that is, when they are focused on communicating. Here, for example,[6] is a teacher 'nudging' students towards accuracy in the context of real communication:

Learner 1 On Sunday what did you do?
Learner 2 Oh, er I stayed in home.
Teacher At home.
Learner 2 On Sunday I stayed at home and watched the Wimbledon Final. What did you do on Sunday?
Learner 1 On morning
Teacher In the morning
Learner 1 In the morning I took a bus …

To encourage self-correction of written work, the use of *correction codes* is widely advocated. Errors are coded in the margin according to such criteria as *wrong word, spelling mistake, missing word,* etc. While this is common practice, there is in fact no evidence that correction of this type has any long-term effect, either on learners' **writing** skills or on their grammar. Again, this suggests that delayed feedback may be less effective than immediate feedback.

co-text → **context**; → **text**

countable noun → **noun**

coursebook → **materials**; → **method**

course design METHODOLOGY

Course design means both the design of a language teaching programme, or of specific materials to be used on a programme, or both. Detailed course design is seldom undertaken in general English teaching contexts, where the choice of a coursebook is often the only major planning decision. However, for learners of ESP (**English for special purposes**), course directors are often called upon to create customized courses.

[6] in Seedhouse, P. 1997. *Combining form and meaning* ELT Journal: 51/4: 342.

The stages of course design include: **needs analysis**, ie, assessing what the learners' particular language needs are; goal setting, ie, defining the overall objectives of the programme, in relation the learners' needs; **syllabus** design, ie, the drawing up of a sequenced list of course content items, consistent with the course goals, and which teachers can use as the basis for planning their classes (→ **lesson plan**); **materials** choice, ie, selecting or producing resources, such as a coursebook, to support the learning process; **assessment** instruments, ie, ways of testing learners at different stages of the programme; and **evaluation** procedures, ie, ways of evaluating the overall success of the programme from the point of view of the different stakeholders.

If the course requires specialist skills, some kind of teacher training may also be necessary.

critical pedagogy METHODOLOGY

Critical pedagogy has roots in progressive education (and is sometimes also called *transformative education*). It gained particular prominence through the work of the Brazilian educator Paulo Freire, whose experience teaching illiterate adults informed his widely read book, *Pedagogy of the Oppressed* (1970). Freire contrasted traditional models of education, that treat learners as empty vessels to be filled by the all-knowing teacher, with a 'problem-posing', liberating form of education, based on equality, dialogue, and hope.

Critical pedagogy assumes first of all that education can never be purely disinterested or neutral. Instead, it either functions to maintain the status quo (and thus serves the power structures in a society), or it works to *change* the status quo – by challenging, critiquing, resisting, or subverting those power structures. It is this latter set of functions that is the domain of critical pedagogy.

Critical pedagogy in language teaching has been influenced by such diverse schools of thought as **humanism** (with its emphasis on engaging the 'whole learner'), the learner **autonomy** movement (with its concern for empowering learners to become self-directed learners); literacy training (as a means of providing minority groups with access to the discourses of power); critical discourse analysis (which studies how ideology is encoded in texts); identity politics, including feminism and queer theory; and cultural studies, including such concepts as **identity**, multiculturalism and *plurilingualism*. Also influential have been writings on postcolonialism and linguistic imperialism (which critique the global spread of English and the uses to which it is put). The net effect of all these different influences is the message that the teaching of English is neither value-free nor ideologically neutral.

Some ways in which teachers and course designers have interpreted critical pedagogy in ELT include: negotiating the content and goals of courses with the learners; using locally produced materials rather than 'globalized' coursebooks (→ **Dogme ELT**); personalizing the instructional content; encouraging authentic language use, rather than language display; challenging stereotypes in classroom materials; encouraging the use of non-sexist and non-racist language; and developing the skill of *critical reading*, ie, learning how to identify the ideological sub-text of texts.

Cuisenaire rods → **form, highlighting**; → **Silent Way, the**

Most definitions of culture distinguish between capital-C *Culture* and small-c *culture*. The former refers to those highly valued activities and artefacts related to the arts, as in the term *Ministry of Culture*. The latter refers to the beliefs, values, traditions, and practices shared by a particular community, as in the expression *people of different cultures*. It is in terms of this latter sense that questions about the role of culture in language teaching are generally framed, such as:

- What is the relation between language and culture, and to what extent do languages express cultural values?

It is generally recognized that languages are a mix of universal concepts and of others that are more culturally specific. It is the presence of the latter that explains why speakers of one language may perceive the world and remember events differently from speakers of another language. A strong version of the belief that language determines thought is known as the Sapir–Whorf hypothesis (after the two anthropological linguists who formulated it). Nowadays, the claims of *linguistic determinism* – that, for example, if you have no word for *blue* in your language, you will not be able to see blue – are largely discredited. Otherwise, any kind of cross-cultural communication (including reading novels in translation) would break down constantly. And learners seem relatively adept at making conceptual adjustments when compelled to. The fact that German, French and Spanish have two verbs for the one English verb *to know* is less of a problem for English-speaking learners of these languages than sorting out the more pragmatic issue of when to use *du* or *Sie* (or *tu/vous*, or *tu/Usted*).

- Does learning a second language involve learning a new set of cultural values?

It does not mean replacing a new set of values with another. But it does mean becoming sensitive to different **connotations** of words due, for example, to differing social, economic, historical and geographic factors, such as the fact that the Spanish *suburbios* has a negative connotation that English *suburbs* does not have. And it will also require learning how speakers of the language 'do things' with language, particularly the more ritualized and interpersonal behaviours associated with greeting, complimenting, thanking, offering and refusing, etc. Some writers have argued that sociocultural knowledge also extends to the learning of a different conversational style and different **paralinguistic** behaviours, such as the use of gesture. More usefully, it may also mean learning a set of strategies to adopt when confronted with situations where cultural differences might put successful communication at risk (see below).

- Does teaching a second language involve teaching the culture of the community that speaks that language? And if so, is there any longer a homogeneous English culture?

Where a language is closely associated with a particular people, region, and culture, as is the case with Japanese, Catalan or Maori, there is a strong case for teaching aspects of the local culture (both capital-C and small-c). This is especially the case if the learners' **motivation** is an integrative one, eg if they plan to travel or settle in the target culture. In the case of English, however, which is no longer associated with one particular culture, and which is now used more for instrumental, rather than integrative, purposes (→ **English as an**

international language), the argument for including cultural content – especially of the capital-C variety – is hard to sustain. The globalization of English is reflected in coursebook texts, which tend to cover a wide range of themes that are chosen less for the values they convey than their general interest and exploitability. However, where learners' needs are clearly integrative – as in the case of learners of English as a second language (→ **English as a foreign language**) – then cultural content will be very important, so long as the target culture is clearly specified.

- How do cultural factors impact on methodology? How, and to what extent, should methodology adapt to take account of local cultural practices?

The appropriacy of importing 'western' teaching approaches, such as the **communicative approach**, into contexts where the values enshrined in that approach may not apply has been the subject of recent debate. Unfortunately, the debate has led to a considerable amount of cultural stereotyping, of the type: 'Asian [sic] students don't like working in groups' or 'Polish students like grammar'. Nevertheless, any teaching method that is not sensitive to the expectations and traditions of the local context is less likely to succeed than one that is. At the same time, teachers should not be made to feel unnecessarily constrained by cultural factors. Classrooms are 'small cultures' that happen to be nested within larger ones. They have a life of their own, and, given time and the development of a good rapport between teacher and learners, anything is possible.

- Is there such a thing as *intercultural competence*, analogous to **communicative competence**, and, if so, how is it fostered?

Intercultural competence, meaning the ability to negotiate cultural contact and difference in a second (or third or fourth, etc) language, is now recognized as being an important component of overall communicative competence, and features prominently in the **Common European Framework**, for example. It does not mean, though, simply learning a list of 'dos and don'ts' about the target culture, but rather (to quote from the CEF):

- the ability to bring the culture of origin and the foreign culture into relation with each other;
- cultural sensitivity and the ability to identify and use a variety of strategies for contact with those from other cultures;
- the capacity to fulfil the role of cultural intermediary between one's own culture and the foreign culture and to deal effectively with intercultural misunderstanding and conflict situations;
- the ability to overcome stereotyped relationships.

How these worthy aims are to be realized and tested in the language classroom is less clear, however. One possible approach might be to roleplay situations in which cultural misunderstandings might occur, such as those involving greetings, invitations, requests, compliments, and apologies.

curriculum METHODOLOGY

The curriculum of an educational organization refers to the whole complex of ideological, social and administrative factors which contribute to the planning of its teaching programmes. A curriculum embodies at least four different kinds of decisions:

1. decisions about the objectives or goals of the programme
2. decisions about the content – from these decisions the **syllabus** will be derived
3. decisions about the method of instruction
4. decisions about how the programme is evaluated (→ **evaluation**)

The terms *curriculum* and *syllabus* are often used interchangeably, but it is useful to distinguish between them. The curriculum is concerned with beliefs, values and theory (all of which may be captured in some kind of 'mission statement'). The syllabus represents the way these beliefs, values and theories are realized in terms of a step-by-step instructional programme. The curriculum is, therefore, both larger than the syllabus, and more general. Occupying an intermediate position between the two is the design of particular courses (→ **course design**), whose planning is often driven by the needs of a particular group of learners.

It is often the case that a school's curriculum is implicit, and can only be inferred from documents such as publicity material, or from the choice of coursebook, or the kinds of tests it uses. Sometimes there is a built-in contradiction, as when a school advertises itself as following a **communicative approach**, but sets examinations which are entirely grammar-based.

declarative GRAMMAR

A declarative sentence is a sentence which takes the form of a statement (eg *Robin likes olives*), as opposed to an *interrogative* one (*Does Robin like olives?* → **question**) or an **imperative** (*Try the olives*). Grammatically, the subject of a declarative sentence goes before the verb. Not all declarative sentences function as statements, though. According to context, the declarative sentence *Robin likes olives?* could function as a question. Declarative sentences can be either positive (also called affirmative) or negative (*Robin likes olives. Kim doesn't like olives.* → **negation**).

deductive learning, deduction PSYCHOLOGY

Deductive learning occurs when a rule or generalization is first presented to the learners, and then they go on to apply it in practice activities. This contrasts with an **inductive** approach, where the learners themselves generalize the rule from examples, before practising it. A deductive presentation of the past tense, for instance, might go like this:

T The past tense of regular verbs is formed by adding *-ed* to the base form of the verb, so, *walk – walked, start – started, climb – climbed*. OK, can you turn these verbs into the past? *Clean?*
S *cleaned*
T Good. *Work?* etc.

Deductive presentations are associated with approaches such as **grammar-translation** and have therefore been branded as old-fashioned. However, they can be very effective, especially in teaching rules of **form** (such as the form of the past tense) as they get straight to the point, as well as satisfying many learners' preferred **learning style**. Research that has compared the effectiveness of deductive vs. inductive learning is not conclusive. The relative merits of each approach seem to depend on the choice of grammar rule. A deductive approach works well if, for example, the rule is a rule of form, or if it is easily explained, or if there are few or no exceptions. What's more, providing examples along with the rule works better than simply providing the rule on its own. Whatever its merits, the deductive approach is the one favoured by most self-study grammar practice books.

definite article → **article**

deixis, deictic reference GRAMMAR

Deixis (pronounced /ˈdaɪksɪs/, adjective *deictic*) describes the way language 'points to' spatial, temporal, and personal features of the **context** (→ **reference**). For example, in the sentence *I have been here three weeks now*, the referents (ie, what is being referred to) of the words *I*, *here*, and *now* cannot be identified without knowing the context. The speaker's location is (generally speaking) the *deictic centre*, and deictic expressions distinguish between 'near the speaker' and 'away from the speaker'. Thus, we interpret *Come here now* as meaning 'come to where I am at this present moment of time'. A version of the sentence *I have been here three weeks now* that referred to events *away* from the deictic centre would be *She had been there three weeks then*.

In English, person deixis is a three-way system of first, second and third persons (as in *I*, *you*, *she*). But spatial deixis distinguishes between only two points: near and far, as in *here*, *there*; *this*, *that*. (This is unlike some languages, which have a three-way distinction). The same near/far distinction applies to time (temporal deixis), so that we distinguish between *now* and *then*, the latter referring to either past or future, as in *I met him then*; *OK, I'll meet you then*.

The deictic system is sensitive to changes in perspective, as when we report what people say. So *I have been here three weeks now* becomes *She said she had been there three weeks by then*. (→ **reported speech**). Deixis is also expressed by certain verbs, which have direction built into their meaning, such as *come* and *go*, and *bring* and *take*. The first of each pair means 'towards the deictic centre' and the second means 'away from it': *Guess who's coming to dinner? Take the money and run*. In English, the use of these verbs is complicated by the fact that (unlike Spanish, for example) we can project the deictic centre to the place where the person we are talking to is, as in *I'm coming over to your place. What shall I bring?* and not (usually) *I'm going over to your place. What shall I take?*

In the following extract from a play,[1] instances of deixis are highlighted:

> SLOANE *enters.*
> SLOANE. Ready? Come on[1], then.
> ED. *nods to* KATH, *waiting. She looks from one to the other. Notices the case.*
>
> KATH. Why is he[2] taking[3] his[4] case?
> ED. He[5]'s coming[6] with me[7]. He[8] can't stay here[9].
> KATH. Why not?
> ED. They[10]'ll suspect.
>
> *Pause.*
>
> KATH. When is he[11] coming back[12]?
> ED. Day after next[13].

[1] Orton, J. 1976, 'Entertaining Mr Sloane' from *The Complete Plays*, (Eyre and Methuen) p 138.

KATH. He[14] doesn't need that[15] big case. (*She exits.*)

ED. Get in the car, boy[16].

1. spatial deixis: movement away from the centre but *with* the speaker
2, 5, 8, 11 14: person deixis = Sloane
3. spatial deixis: movement away from the centre
4. person deixis = Sloane's
6. movement with speaker away from the centre
7. person deixis = speaker (Ed)
9. spatial = the centre
10. person = some other people who are not present, but who are known to the speakers
12. spatial = movement to the centre from further away
13. temporal deixis; *next* = the following day
15. spatial = referring to something not near the speaker
16. person (vocative) = Sloane

Practising deictic language is best done, initially, with things and actions in the classroom. The techniques of **Total Physical Response** are particularly good for this.

denotation → **word**; → **connotation**

derivative → **word family**

determiner GRAMMAR

Words like *the, her, many,* and *this* belong to the **word class** of determiners. These words come before nouns, and their function is to limit the meaning of the noun in some way. So, in the exchange *What have you got? ~ Apple*, the word *apple* is not limited in any way, compared to, say, *an apple, some apples, my apple, these apples, all six apples …* etc.

There are various sub-categories of determiner:

- **articles** such as *a, the*
- demonstratives: *this, that*
- possessives: *my, their*
- **quantifiers**: *some, few, no*
- numerals, including *cardinal numbers*: *one, two,* etc, and *ordinal numbers*: *first, second,* etc
- *wh*-determiners: *what, which, whose*

The choice of determiner can depend on whether the noun that follows is countable or uncountable (→ **noun**). Thus, *there wasn't <u>much</u> food* vs *there weren't <u>many</u> guests*.

There are also constraints on the order of determiners. *Central* determiners, such as the articles, demonstratives, and possessives, can be preceded by *predeterminers* like *all* and *both*, as in <u>*all the*</u> *pretty horses,* <u>*both my*</u> *sons*, but never by another central determiner: *the my son. They can also be followed by *postdeterminers*, such as numerals: <u>*her two*</u> *films,* <u>*the third*</u> *man*. In the order of elements in a **noun phrase**, determiners always come first: <u>*my other*</u> *red sports car;* <u>*all the many*</u> *different French cheeses*. Many determiners are also **pronouns**, as in <u>*all*</u> *of my children; Would you like* <u>*some*</u>*?* and *What's* <u>*that*</u>*?*

Countability and word order, as well as the wide range of meanings they express, make the learning of determiners problematic. This is especially the case for learners whose first language uses a very different way of limiting the meaning of nouns (such as Russian or Turkish). One approach, initially, may be to learn determiners as a part of fixed phrases, such as *all the* time, *the other* day, *no* problem, *any* day now, *a few too* many, etc.

developmental error → **error**

diagnostic test, diagnose → **testing**

dialect SOCIOLINGUISTICS

A dialect is a regional or social variety of a language. It has words and features of grammar that are not shared by other forms of the language, and is spoken with a different **accent**. Distinguishing a dialect from a language, or from a differently accented variety, is not always easy, and is often based on political as much as on linguistic factors. Dialects of English include Scots, African American Vernacular English, and informal Singapore English ('Singlish'). Most dialect speakers also speak a standard variety of the language (such as British or **American English**). This fact is used to justify teaching **Standard English** to learners, rather than a dialect.

dialogue METHODOLOGY

In the language classroom, a dialogue is either the text of a (usually) two-way spoken exchange, or it is the activity of having such an exchange. Dialogues have always been a popular means for presenting and practising language, one reason being that dialogue is the most common and most widespread way that language is used in real life. Dialogues have a long history. Here, for example, is an extract from one of the earliest known ELT coursebooks, called *Familiar Dialogues* (1586) and written for French-speaking refugees to Britain. Barbara, a domestic servant, is helping Peter get ready to go to school:

Barbara	Peter, where layde you your nightcap?
Peter	I left it vpon the bedde.
Barbara	Are you ready?
Peter	How should I be ready? You brought me a smock insteade of my shirt.
Barbara	I forgat myselfe: Holde, here is your shirt.
Peter	Now you are a good wenche …

Dialogues such as this one would probably have been memorized. After a period of neglect during the **grammar–translation** period, the **direct method** revived the use of dialogues as a means for practising 'oral language'. In the **audiolingual approach**, a structurally graded dialogue would usually form the starting point of each lesson, and it would be thoroughly drilled. Nowadays most coursebook dialogues are less strictly graded, and include more natural examples of language use. And the practice of memorizing or drilling dialogues has largely been replaced with such activities as: listening to recorded dialogues (or watching them on video); working out the meaning of specific language items from the context of the dialogue (→ **inductive learning**); reading dialogues aloud in pairs; writing, rehearsing and performing dialogues in class; and *dialogue building*, ie, constructing a dialogue around prompts supplied by the teacher.

dictation METHODOLOGY

Dictation is the transcribing, by students, of words, sentences or whole texts, usually read aloud by the teacher. Dictations were for a long time used simply as tests of spelling (and possibly as a form of crowd control). More recently the dictation has been rehabilitated, first as a form of integrative **testing**, and more recently as a popular activity type in its own right. As integrative tests, dictations were thought to have similar properties to **cloze tests**, in that they tested a whole range of skills. Doing a dictation involves not only recognizing individual sounds and words, but grouping these into grammatically well-formed sentences and into cohesive text. For this reason, it is best if the text is read aloud in at least sentence-length chunks. In this way the learner is not simply copying down the 'echo' of individual words, but is having to mentally process each chunk (→ **memory**). Claims for the usefulness of dictations as tests of overall **competence** may have been exaggerated, but dictations certainly test more than the processing of only surface level features of texts.

Many non-testing dictation-based activities are now common practice. These include *running dictations*, in which a text is posted on the far wall of the classroom, or even outside the classroom, and students, working in pairs, have to reconstruct it. This means that one of each pair has to run to the text, remember as much of it as possible, and ferry the information back to the other member of the pair, who writes it down. The first pair to reconstruct the complete text are the winners.

The *dictogloss* (also called both *dictocomp* and *grammar dictation*) is a form of dictation in which students hear the complete text (it should be a short one), and then reconstruct it from memory. To do this, they work individually, then in pairs, and then, if practicable, in larger groups, each time comparing their versions of the text and negotiating changes. Finally, they compare their consensus version with the original (which can be displayed using an overhead projector). Dictogloss is an effective technique both for encouraging learners to pool their language knowledge, and also for discovering features of the language that they hadn't noticed before (→ **consciousness-raising**).

dictionary VOCABULARY

Dictionaries are indispensable aids to the language learner, and they come in many forms. Bilingual dictionaries have definitions in the learner's first language, and are therefore often preferred by beginners; monolingual dictionaries use only one language throughout. Monolingual learners' dictionaries usually control the level of language used in their definitions, by using a defining vocabulary restricted to some 2000–3000 words. As well as definitions and examples (called *citations*), dictionaries usually contain information about **pronunciation**, **word class** membership, **frequency**, **style** (eg formal or informal), **collocation** and derivation (→ **word formation**). They also include grammatical information, such as whether nouns are countable or uncountable, and whether verbs are **transitive** or intransitive.

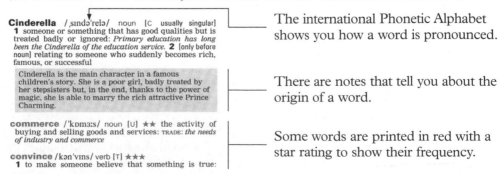

Cinderella /ˌsɪndəˈrelə/ noun [C usually singular] **1** someone or something that has good qualities but is treated badly or ignored: *Primary education has long been the Cinderella of the education service.* **2** [only before noun] relating to someone who suddenly becomes rich, famous, or successful

Cinderella is the main character in a famous children's story. She is a poor girl, badly treated by her stepsisters but, in the end, thanks to the power of magic, she is able to marry the rich attractive Prince Charming.

commerce /ˈkɒmɜːs/ noun [U] ★★ the activity of buying and selling goods and services: TRADE: *the needs of industry and commerce*

convince /kənˈvɪns/ verb [T] ★★★ **1** to make someone believe that something is true:

The international Phonetic Alphabet shows you how a word is pronounced.

There are notes that tell you about the origin of a word.

Some words are printed in red with a star rating to show their frequency.

Specialized dictionaries exist for different subject areas (such as business, medicine, or technology) as well as for different categories of language, such as **phrasal verbs**, **idioms**, **collocations** and **synonyms**. Picture dictionaries are especially useful for younger learners. The use of online and electronic dictionaries is becoming increasingly popular, and nowadays many print dictionaries also have an accompanying CD-ROM. The benefits of a CD-ROM dictionary include their data-storing capacity, allowing the inclusion of many more examples of words in their contexts. This capacity, combined with their search ability, means that CD-ROMs can be used to find and group words according to particular characteristics, eg words with a certain suffix, Australian words, or formal phrasal verbs.

Nowadays learners' dictionaries in English are based on large corpora of naturally occurring language, both spoken and written (→ **corpus**). This helps ensure that the information they provide is representative and up to date.

There are a number of ways that dictionaries can be used productively in the classroom, such as in activities that involve sorting words into different categories, for expanding knowledge of lexical sets and word families (by, for example, mapping words onto 'spidergrams' or mind maps), for checking words whose meaning has first been guessed from context, and for editing first drafts of written work.

dictogloss → **dictation**

diphthong → **vowel**

direct method METHODOLOGY

This is an umbrella term for a wide range of language teaching methods that emerged in the later part of the nineteenth century. They shared the belief that only the target language should be used in the classroom, and that therefore translation should be avoided at all costs. Instead of translation, form–meaning associations should be established using real objects, pictures, or demonstration. The teacher's role was to maintain an extended 'conversation' with the learners. One of the direct method's most successful proponents was Maximilian Berlitz, whose *First Book* (1906) has this typical question-and-answer sequence:

> I am opening the door. Am I opening the door? (You are.) Are you opening the door? (I am not.) Who is opening the door, you or I? (You are.) Carry the chair towards the door. Are you carrying the chair towards the door? Is Mr. B. carrying the chair towards the door?

The direct method was a response to the growing demand for learning languages for the purposes of international commerce and tourism. It also made a virtue out of necessity, in that it enabled teachers to teach a second language without any knowledge of their learners' mother tongue. Nevertheless, the direct method offered a refreshing alternative to the bookish **grammar–translation method** that prevailed at the time. It also produced a succession of linguists, such as Henry Sweet (the prototype of Henry Higgins in Bernard Shaw's *Pygmalion*) and Harold Palmer, who laid the foundations of what was to become **applied linguistics**. In the USA, the direct method ingested behaviourist theory and metamorphosed into **audiolingualism**. In the UK and Europe it became the fairly short-lived *situational approach*, but its core principle, the exclusive use of the target language, survives as an article of faith amongst many teachers to this day.

direct/indirect question → **question**

direct speech → **reported speech**

discourse, discourse analysis DISCOURSE

Discourse is any connected piece of speaking or writing (like this). Discourse analysis is principally the study of how such stretches of language achieve both **cohesion** and **coherence**. Whereas traditional grammar is concerned only with sentences and their components, discourse analysis seeks to identify patterns and regularities of language 'beyond the sentence'. It is closely related to, and partly overlaps with, other text-based fields of study, including **conversation analysis**, **genre** analysis, **pragmatics**, and text linguistics. Critical discourse analysis examines the relation between texts and ideology, and how readers are 'positioned' by the language choices made by writers.

For the language teacher, the main implications of discourse analysis are in the teaching of writing, especially with regard to the ways that texts are made cohesive. But discourse analysis also offers insights into areas of grammar whose functions are best understood *across* sentences, rather than *within* them. For example, the sequencing of information in a sentence is sensitive to the sentences that precede and follow it (the *co-text*). Given a sentence such as *Radium is a radioactive substance,* and given the choice between two possible ways of following up this sentence: (a) *Marie and Pierre Curie discovered it in 1902*; or (b) *It was discovered by Marie and Pierre Curie in 1902*, the second is preferred. This is because the organization of sentence (b) follows the principle of *end-weight*, by which new information is placed at the end of the sentence rather than at the beginning, which is normally reserved for given information (ie, *radium/it*). This in turn calls for the use of the **passive** (*was discovered*). In other words, the passive is not an arbitrary choice, nor a sentence-internal one, but is governed by rules of discourse.

Other grammar areas that are often affected by discourse choices include **tense**, **aspect**, and **modality**. For example, in spoken narratives, speakers typically set the scene for the narrative by using past tense forms (*I was on my way to the station … it was raining …*) but shift into the present tense for key events (*… when this bloke stops me, and says ….*). And in news reporting, an account will typically begin in the present tense, **perfect** aspect, before shifting into the past:

> A parrot up a power pole has sparked a four hour rescue operation in Auckland. The green parrot was trapped by its foot at the top of a rather wobbly old power pole in the Auckland suburb on New Lynn …[2]

discourse intonation → **intonation**

discourse marker DISCOURSE

Discourse markers (also called *pragmatic markers*) are words or expressions like *well, anyway, I mean, right, actually,* that normally come at the beginning of an utterance, and function to orient the listener to what will follow. They do this either by

[2] 'Firefighters free parrot up pole' *One Network News* website (www.tvnz.co.nz/ news/general) 17 May 1997.

indicating some kind of change of direction in the talk, or by appealing to the listener in some way. Here are some common discourse markers and their meanings:

right, now, anyway	These mark the beginning or closing of a segment of talk.
well	This is a very common way of initiating a *turn* (→ **conversation analysis**) and linking it to the preceding *turn*, often to mark the onset of a contrast, eg a difference of opinion.
oh	This is typically used either to launch an utterance, or to respond to the previous speaker's utterance, often with implications of surprise or unexpectedness.
then	This is often used to signal an inference based on what someone else has said.
y'know, I mean	These markers serve to gain attention or to maintain attention on the speaker – the first by appealing to the addressee's shared knowledge, and the second by signalling that some kind of clarification is going to follow.

Linkers, which connect what has been said to what follows, are sometimes classified as discourse markers as well. In spoken language, the most common linkers are:

and, but, or	*And* marks some kind of continuity, *but* marks a contrast, and *or* marks an option.
so, because	These signal that what follows is (respectively) the *result* or the *cause* of what has been mentioned.

In this short extract,[3] in which three people are talking about ballroom dancing, the discourse markers and linkers are highlighted:

\<Speaker 1\>	But[1] you're not doing it any more are you?
\<Speaker 2\>	No we're not. But[2] when you start dancing you, it's like getting a high on exercise and[3] when Alison started she was going three times a week which, you know[4], is a fairly big commitment, and[5] just in, you know[6] she had some relationship problems and[7] she decided okay[8] I'll see if I, take up dancing, and[9] for six months, three times a week she just, her dancing improved
\<Speaker 3\>	Well[10] she was having personal tuition lessons wasn't she?

1, 2	linker: contrastive
3, 5, 7, 9	linker: additive
4, 6	discourse marker: appealing to shared knowledge
8	discourse marker: indicating decisiveness
10	discourse marker: indicating continuation but with some qualification

discovery learning → **inductive learning**

discrete item → **syllabus**; → **test**; → **whole language learning**

discussion METHODOLOGY

Discussions and debates provide learners with opportunities to interact freely and spontaneously, to cope with unpredictability, and to voice opinions using

---

[3] OZTALK: Macquarie University/UTS Spoken Language Corpus.

language that is both complex and fluent. They are generally more structured than **conversation**, and involve arguing for or against a particular point of view. For this reason, there is always the risk that they might get out of hand, or that learners might feel unduly constrained by the target language and revert to their first language, or that certain learners will dominate while others remain silent. Some ways of minimizing these risks include:

- To start with, focus on the specific rather than the general. For example, rather than start a general discussion on the topic of drug use in sport, give learners a short news item describing a particular case.
- Allow learners time in advance of an open class discussion to formulate their point of view, to access vocabulary (using dictionaries, for example), to compare opinions (in pairs or small groups);
- Appoint a chairperson, whose job it is to allocate turns and ensure all learners participate;
- Establish some ground rules, such as:
  - Only one person can speak at a time.
  - Ask permission to speak.
  - Use people's names (not *She/You said …* but *Marta said …*), etc.
- Equip learners with a repertoire of expressions for voicing strong agreement, strong disagreement, and all the shades of opinion in between (→ **agreeing/disagreeing**; → **opinion, giving and asking for**). These could be available on posters around the room.
- Take advantage of discussions that emerge spontaneously, as a result of something that someone says, or from the coursebook, for example. The best discussions are often those that happen naturally.

Ways of organizing discussions include:

- *pyramid discussions*: Learners have to reach an agreement, in pairs, about an issue by, for example modifying a statement (*Children must not be smacked*) so they both agree on it, or by ranking a list of items (eg qualities of a good friend) in the order they think are most important. They then form groups of four, and then eight, and then sixteen, etc, each time repeating the process.
- *balloon debate*: Learners represent different jobs or famous people (alive or dead). One member of the group must be sacrificed to save the sinking balloon, so each has to argue why they should be spared.
- *formal debate*: Learners form teams and each team alternates to argue for a motion (eg *Homework should be banned*) and to rebut the arguments of the opposing team. Other learners form the audience and vote for the winning team.

display question METHODOLOGY

Display questions are questions asked by teachers in order that learners can 'display' their knowledge, such as *What's the capital of France?* They typically initiate a three-part exchange that is characteristic of classroom interaction, and is called an *IRF* (*interaction–response–follow-up*) sequence. For example:

(I)	Teacher:	*What's the capital of France?*
(R)	Student:	*Paris.*
(F)	Teacher:	*Good.*

In language classrooms, display questions are usually aimed at finding out what learners can say in the target language. Asking a sequence of display questions is called *eliciting*. In this sequence, the teacher is eliciting vocabulary:

Teacher   What does Phil Collins do?
Student 1 … singer
Student 2 … plays drums I think.
Teacher   He's a singer and he …?
Student 3 Plays drums.
Teacher   He's a singer and he plays the drums so he's a …?
Student 4 Drummer, he's a drummer.
Teacher   OK.

Display questions contrast with real questions (also called *referential questions*), which are motivated by the need to find out something that the person asking the question doesn't know. For example: *Have you ever been to France?* or *Do you like Phil Collins?* Some researchers suggest that both the quality and quantity of communication in the classroom improves when teachers ask more real questions than display questions. Others go so far as to argue that this kind of 'contingent' communication provides more **affordances** for learning than do interactions of the IRF type.

Dogme ELT METHODOLOGY

Dogme ELT is the name of a loose collective of teachers who challenge what they consider to be an over-reliance on **materials**, including published coursebooks, in current language teaching. It was triggered when, in an article, Scott Thornbury suggested that what was needed in English language teaching was a movement like DOGME 95, a group of Danish film makers who have vowed to rid cinema of a dependence on technology, and to produce films using minimal means but for maximum effect. Accordingly, Dogme ELT argues for 'a pedagogy of bare essentials, that is, a pedagogy unburdened by an excess of materials and technology, a pedagogy grounded in the local and relevant concerns of the people in the room'.[4] Critics of Dogme point out that working without materials benefits only experienced, native-speaker teachers, and typically those who are teaching small classes of adults in cultures where there may be a greater tolerance for a non-book-centred methodology. In their defence, proponents of a Dogme approach argue that they are not so much anti-materials, as pro-learner, and thus align themselves with other forms of **learner-centred instruction** and **critical pedagogy**.

drama METHODOLOGY

Drama activities, including *roleplay* and *simulation*, can provide entertaining practice opportunities, as well as offering a useful springboard into real-life language use. Situations that learners are likely to encounter when using English in the real world can be rehearsed, and a greater range of **registers** can be practised than are normally available in classroom talk.

A distinction is often made between roleplays and simulations. The former involve the adoption of another 'persona', as when students pretend to be an employer interviewing a job applicant. Information about their roles can be

[4] http://groups.yahoo.com/group/dogme/

supplied in the form of individualized role cards. In a simulation, on the other hand, students 'play' themselves in a simulated situation: they might be meeting each other after a long absence, for example. A more elaborate simulation might involve the joint planning and presentation of a business plan. Drama activities also include play-reading, recitation, improvisation, and acting out **dialogues**, sketches, or scenes from a play written by the students themselves.

Drama activities suit learners who may feel uncomfortable 'being themselves' in a second language. On the other hand, there are also learners who feel self-conscious performing in front of their peers. Just as in the real theatre, a preparation stage, including rehearsal, is generally recommended, in advance of the performance stage.

drill METHODOLOGY

A drill is repetitive oral practice of a language item, whether a sound, a word, a phrase or a sentence structure (→ **repetition**). Drills that are targeted at sentence structures are sometimes called *pattern practice drills*. Drills follow a prompt–response sequence, where the prompt usually comes from the teacher, and the students respond, either in chorus (a *choral drill*) or individually. An *imitation drill* simply involves repeating the prompt, as in:

Teacher They have been watching TV.
Student They have been watching TV.

A *substitution drill* requires the students to substitute one element of the pattern with the prompt, making any necessary adjustments:

Teacher They have been watching TV.
Student They have been watching TV.
Teacher She
Student She has been watching TV.
Teacher I
Student I have been watching TV.

etc.

A *variable substitution drill* is the same, but the prompts are not restricted to one element of the pattern:

Teacher They have been watching TV.
Student They have been watching TV.
Teacher She
Student She has been watching TV.
Teacher radio
Student She has been listening to the radio.
Teacher We
Student We have been listening to the radio.

etc.

Drills were a defining feature of the **audiolingual** method, and were designed to reinforce good language 'habits'. The invention of language laboratories allowed sustained drilling without the need for a teacher to supply the prompts. With the demise of audiolingualism, drilling fell from favour. However, many teachers – even those who subscribe to a **communicative approach** – feel the need for some form of repetition practice of the kind that drills provide. This may be for the purpose of developing **accuracy**, or as a form of **fluency** training, ie, in order to develop **automaticity**. Hence, communicative drills were developed. A communicative drill is still essentially repetitive, and focuses on a particular structure or pattern, but it has an *information gap* element built in (→ **communicative activity**). Learners can perform the drill in pairs, or as a *milling activity* (→ **classroom interaction**) and they are required to attend to what they hear as much as what they say. The milling activity popularly known as *Find someone who …* is one such activity. Students are set the task of finding other students in the class who, for example, can ride a horse, can speak French, can play the guitar, etc. They mill around, asking questions of the type *Can you …?* until they have asked all the other students their questions, and then they report their findings.

dynamic verb → **stative verb**

dynamics: group, classroom METHODOLOGY

Dynamics are the actions and interactions, both conscious and unconscious, that take place between members of a group, whether the whole class or sub-groups. Group dynamics are instrumental in forging a productive and motivating classroom environment. They are determined by such factors as: the composition of the group (including the age, sex, and relative status of the members, as well as their different attitudes, beliefs, learning styles and abilities); the patterns of relationships between members of the group, including how well they know each other, and the roles they each assume, such as group leader, spokesperson, etc; physical factors such as the size of the group and the way it is seated; and the tasks that the group are set, eg: Does the task require everyone to contribute? Does it encourage co-operation or competition? Are the goals of the task clear to the group members?

Ways that the teacher can promote a positive group (and class) dynamic include:

- ensuring all class or group members can see and hear one another, and that they know (and use) each other's names
- keeping groups from getting too big – three to six members is optimal
- setting – or negotiating – clear rules for groupwork, such as using only the target language, giving everyone a turn to speak, allowing individuals to 'pass' if they don't want to say anything too personal
- using 'ice-breaking' activities to encourage interaction, laughter, and relaxation
- ensuring that group tasks are purposeful, interactive, and collaborative
- personalizing tasks, ie, setting tasks that involve the sharing of personal experiences and opinions
- defining the roles and responsibilities within the group, and varying these regularly, eg by appointing a different spokesperson each time
- monitoring groupwork in progress, and being alert to any possible conflicts or tensions between members, and reconstituting groups, if necessary
- discussing the importance of groupwork with learners, and getting feedback on group processes

EAP (English for academic purposes) → **English for special purposes**

eclecticism METHODOLOGY

If you are eclectic you combine techniques and activities from different **methods** in your teaching. You might, for example, intersperse pattern practice **drills** with **communicative activities,** or use both **deductive** and **inductive** approaches to teaching grammar. Eclecticism is motivated by different reasons, one being a general distrust of 'one-size-fits-all' methods, such as the **direct method**, **audiolingualism**, or **task-based learning**. There is a widespread view among many teachers that methods are not sensitive enough to such variables as the context, **culture** and **learning styles** of the students. Also, some teachers reject certain practices, such as mistake **correction**, because they run counter to their own beliefs and values. Finally, many teacher training courses, especially pre-service ones, promote a 'pick-and-choose' approach to lesson design, and this is reinforced by the eclectic approach adopted by most current ELT coursebooks. However, eclecticism has been criticized on the grounds that it lacks principle, and encourages an 'anything goes' approach to teaching. Accordingly, some scholars have put the case for *principled* (or *informed*) *eclecticism*, in combination with *exploratory* (or *reflective*) *teaching* (→ **reflection**). Activities, they argue, should be selected, and lessons designed, according to a set of core principles (or *macrostrategies*) that are grounded in classroom-based research. At the same time, the teaching–learning process should be subject to ongoing self-monitoring and reflection. Importantly, the learners themselves should be involved in the evaluation process. By analogy to 'post-modernism', *principled eclecticism* subscribes to a 'post-method' philosophy.

EFL → **English as a foreign language**

EIL → **English as an international language**

elementary METHODOLOGY

'Elementary' describes the level of language proficiency after **beginner**, and before **intermediate**. It corresponds to level A2 according to the **Common European Framework**. Most coursebook series for adults now include both an elementary level and a pre-intermediate level, although it is not always clear what the difference is. It may be the case that *elementary* has replaced *false beginner* as the preferred term to describe learners who have had some exposure to English, and may even have studied English at school, but have never put it to practical use.

ELF (English as a lingua franca) → **English as an international language**

eliciting → **display questions**

elision → **connected speech**

ellipsis DISCOURSE

Ellipsis is the leaving out of elements of a sentence because they are either unnecessary or because their sense can be worked out from the immediate context. For example, the second utterance in the following exchange is *elliptical*, and its missing element (ie, *at work today*) can be recovered only by reference to the previous utterance:

> **A** *Is Rob at work today?*
> **B** *No, but Jan is.*

Ellipsis is very common in spoken language (→ **spoken grammar**). Ellipsis of **function words** is also a common feature of certain **text** types, where brevity is a priority, as in postcards (*Having a wonderful time. Wish you were here.*) or instructions: *Remove from container. Boil 2–3 minutes. Serve hot.* Learners, too, tend to omit function words, as in **Jan not at work*, or **I having wonderful time*, but this is a consequence of development processes, and is less ellipsis than *omission* (→ **error**). (Note, also, that ellipsis shouldn't be confused with *elision*, which is the omission of sounds in **connected speech**).

email → **computer-mediated communication**

emergentism, emergent grammar, emergent property → **usage-based acquisition**; → **connectionism**

English as a foreign language (EFL) SOCIOLINGUISTICS

English is a foreign language for learners in whose community English is not the usual language of communication. They may be learning English as a school subject, or for travel, business, or academic purposes. For learners who are living in an English-speaking environment and who need English in order to become integrated into this environment, the term *English as a second language* (or *ESL*) is commonly used. *TEFL* and *TESL*, respectively, stand for the *teaching* of these subjects. The general term for both fields is called, in the UK, *English language teaching* (ELT), and, in the USA, Canada, and Australia, *Teaching English to speakers of other languages* (or *TESOL*). None of these terms is unproblematic. The distinction between a foreign language and a second language is not always clear in practice. And many learners of English may already be multilingual in their home environment, so English may well be a third or even fourth language, not necessarily a second. For this reason, some scholars prefer the term *English as an additional language*. Moreover, a further distinction is now made, between EFL and ELF (or EIL), that is, *English as a lingua franca* or **English an international language**. This recognizes the fact that, for many learners, their most likely context for using English will not be with native-speakers but with other non-native speakers.

English as an international language (EIL) SOCIOLINGUISTICS

The number of people who speak English as an additional language now exceeds the number of those who speak it as their **first language**. The term EIL (or ELF: *English as a lingua franca*) recognizes this fact, and the fact that English is used as a global means of communication as much as a foreign or second language (→ **English as foreign language**). This in turn suggests that the goals and methods for the teaching of this variety of English may need to be re-defined. Accordingly, researchers are attempting to identify the characteristics of EIL (or of EILs, since it is not yet clear if EIL is a uniform entity or a host of different varieties, such as German English, Japanese English, Brazilian English, etc). The most suggestive findings, so far, have been in the area of phonology (→ **phonological core**). Corpora of learner language (→ **corpus**) are already providing clues as to what a grammar and lexis of EIL might look like. Some likely features include:

- no third person *s* in the present tense: *he go*
- all-purpose question tags, such as *isn't it?*: *You work here, isn't it?*
- reliance on certain common verbs with lots of meanings: *do, have, get, take*

(Note that these are features that already exist in some **dialects** of English.) It is unlikely, however, that most teachers – and many learners – will accept anything less than some notion of 'Standard English' as their goal, at least for the foreseeable future.

English as a second language (ESL) → **English as a foreign language**

English for academic purposes (EAP) → **English for special purposes**

English for special purposes (ESP) SOCIOLINGUISTICS

ESP contrasts with general English (sometimes facetiously called TENOR, or *Teaching English for no obvious reason*) in that the content and aims of the course are determined by the specific needs of the particular group of learners. These needs are normally identified by means of **needs analysis**. They might be occupational (as in **business English**) or academic (as in *English for academic purposes*, or EAP). It was the growing demand for ESP courses in the early 1970s that powered the development of the **communicative approach**. Scholars, teachers and course designers recognized that the practical, communicative needs of the learners, rather than abstract linguistic description, should dictate the design of language courses. Accordingly, the content of an ESP course consists of more than just topic-specific vocabulary mapped on to general English grammar. It also includes **skills** development (or the development of key **competencies**), such as the reading and writing of the kinds of **texts** associated with the field (as in *academic writing*), plus attention to the way these texts are used by the target discourse community (→ **genre**). Another area related to ESP that has emerged more recently is *intercultural communication* and the development of *intercultural competence* (→ **culture**).

ergative → **transitivity**

error SLA

An error is an instance of the learner's language that does not conform to accepted norms of usage, and which is attributed to incomplete or faulty learning. These norms by which errors are judged are usually defined in terms of adult **native speakers** of Standard English. Errors are sometimes distinguished from *mistakes*, the former being due to lack of knowledge (ie, **competence**), and the latter being due to the demands of performance. In these terms, a slip caused by lack of attention, or speaking too fast, would be a mistake. In principle, the test of a mistake is whether the learner can self-correct effortlessly. In practice, however, it is not always easy to distinguish errors from mistakes.

Errors are categorized in a number of ways: for example, in terms of the language system that is involved, eg **pronunciation**, **vocabulary** (lexical), **grammar**, or discourse; or according to the way that they depart from the norm. An error of *omission* is where an obligatory element is left out, as in **Is very hot*; an error of *addition*, on the other hand, is one such as **He made us to go*, where *to* has been added unnecessarily. A *mis-selection* error is one where the wrong item has been used, as in **Men like fairs* (for *Gentlemen prefer blondes*); a *misformation* is the wrong form of the right word, as in *★He is a good cooker*, and a *misordering* error is when sentence components are in the wrong order, as *★I like very much football*.

The following short text was produced by a Mexican learner of English in response to the question: *Do you use English in your work (or your studies)?* and the learner's errors have been categorized:

> Yes I use[1] all[2] time because I'm trying to apply to[3] some[4] position at[5] university or some[6] college and I need the idiom[7] urgently. Of course I need the[8] traduction[9] by[10] my career. I need[11] quickly[12] learn English and [13]my[14] next[15] months, I think [16]need to dedicate time to learn[17] this language.

1. omission (of *it*; grammar error)
2. omission (of *the*; grammar error, or lexical error, ie, formulaic phrase)
3. mis-selection (instead of *for*; lexical error, ie, collocation)
4. mis-selection (instead of *a*; grammar error)
5. omission (of *a*; grammar error)
6. as 4
7. mis-selection (instead of *language*; lexical)
8. addition (of *the*; grammar)
9. mis-selection (instead of *translation*; lexical)
10. mis-selection (instead of *for*; grammar)
11. omission (of *to*; grammar)
12. misordering (for *I need to learn English quickly*; grammar)
13. omission (of *in*, or *over*; grammar)
14. mis-selection (for *the*; grammar)
15. omission (of *few*; lexical error, ie, formulaic phrase)
16. omission (of *I*; grammar)
17. misformation (for *learning*; grammar)

Errors are also classified according to their possible cause. This is the particular concern of *error analysis*. Error analysis is a field of **second language acquisition** research that collects, collates and explains errors, and, in this way, offer insights into the internal processes of language acquisition. Thus, **transfer** errors are those that result from the influence of the learner's first language (such as the use of the word *idiom* in the above text; *idioma* means *language* in Spanish). On the other hand, *developmental errors* are those that occur as a natural part of the learning process. It used to be thought that all errors were transfer errors (what was then called *interference* → **contrastive analysis**). Research has shown, however, that there are certain errors that all learners appear to make, regardless of their first language, and in a predictable chronological order (→ **order of acquisition**). Many of these are due to the *overgeneralization* of a rule: for example, the application of the past tense *-ed* ending to verbs that are in fact irregular, as in *★she buyed* ....

Errors can also be evaluated in terms of their severity. A *global error* is one that affects the overall intelligibility of the message, whereas others have only a relatively insignificant and *local* effect.

Judgments as to the type, origin and gravity of an error influence teachers' decisions as to what, when and how to correct (→ **correction**). For example, an error that indicates lack of knowledge may not respond as well to correction as will a performance *mistake*. Likewise, teachers may consider a global error more deserving of correction than a local one. Failure to respond to learners' errors may arguably result in **fossilization**, that is, the state where the errors become a permanent feature of the learner's **interlanguage**.

evaluation METHODOLOGY

This generally refers to either **curriculum** evaluation or **materials** evaluation, or both. Evaluation should not be confused with **assessment**, which is a general term for **testing**. The main purpose of curriculum evaluation is to determine whether the goals and objectives of a course have been achieved, or whether the course meets externally imposed standards, such as those set by an educational authority. It is usually thought of as involving two types:

• ongoing (or *formative*) evaluation – that is, a process of getting feedback on the curriculum in action
• final (or *summative*) evaluation – that is, when the outcomes of the programme are evaluated according to the goals that were established at the outset

The evaluation may be conducted by an external authority, or by those directly involved – the 'stakeholders'. Evaluation procedures involve the use of questionnaires and interviews (of students, teachers, and administrators, for example), the observation of classes, and the holding of meetings or focus groups. Teachers, too, evaluate their classes in many informal ways. Asking learners to fill out a checklist at the end of a lesson (*What I liked about the lesson …What I learned …*) is a form of evaluation.

examination, exam METHODOLOGY

An examination is the name given to a formal test that is usually administered by some examining body. Although the terms *test* and *examination* are often used interchangeably, it is useful to distinguish between an institution's own procedures for internal assessment (ie, **testing**), which can often be informal, and external assessment procedures (ie, examinations). In the UK the main ELT examinations are administered by University of Cambridge ESOL (previously UCLES), by Trinity College, London, or by City and Guilds, London (previously Pitmans). Cambridge ESOL runs a range of examinations at different levels, for different age groups, and in different subject areas (including business English). Its suite of general English examinations are shown in the following table, alongside their equivalent levels according to the **Common European Framework** (CEF) of Reference:

CEF	Exam Targets
C2	Certificate of Proficiency in English (CPE)
C1	Certificate in Advanced English (CAE)
B2	First Certificate in English (FCE)
B1	Preliminary English Test (PET)
A2	Key English Test (KET)

The IELTS (or International English Language Testing System) examination is jointly managed by Cambridge ESOL, the British Council, and IDP: IELTS Australia, and is primarily used by learners seeking places in English-speaking universities. Trinity offers a progressive series of twelve graded levels in spoken English, as well as Integrated Skills in English examinations (ISE) which assess speaking, writing, listening and reading. Among a wide range of exams, City and Guilds offers an examination in Business Communication at three different levels.

Preparing learners for public examinations involves not just preparing them for the content of the exam, but also for the relevant skills and strategies that will be necessary to do it successfully – what is known as *exam technique*. This will, in turn, assume familiarity with the different examination **rubrics**, ie, the ways that tasks are worded and laid out. Practice doing mock exams is one obvious way of preparing for the real thing.

exercise METHODOLOGY

An exercise is an **activity** that involves the controlled manipulation of the **forms** of the language. This contrasts with more meaning-focused, and less tightly controlled, activities such as **tasks**. They are also usually written. In fact, they are often the written equivalent of **drills**. *Closed exercises* are those for which there is only one correct answer, and they are therefore popular with writers of workbooks, since they allow for self-checking, using a key. *Open exercises*, on the other hand, permit more than one possible answer. **Personalization** exercises – of the type: *Write five true sentences about yourself using 'used to'* – are a kind of open exercise.

Popular exercise types include:

- *gap-filling exercises*, where spaces in a sentence or text have to be completed (see also **cloze test**)
- *sentence transformations*, where sentences have to be reformulated according to a prompt (such as rewriting *If I had known …* so that it begins with *Had I known …*), or according to some grammar rule (such as changing active sentences into a passive ones)
- *ordering exercises*, eg putting the words of a sentence in order
- *matching exercises*, such as matching the two halves of sentences
- *insertion exercises*, such as inserting words into the correct place in a sentence or text
- *deletion exercises*, such as deleting unnecessary words from a sentence or text
- *translation exercises*
- *error-correction exercises*

experiential learning METHODOLOGY

Experiential learning is a general term for 'deep-end' approaches to learning that rate direct practical experience over the learning and application of abstract rules. In language learning terms, this might take the form of **task-based learning**, of discovery-learning, or of **content-based learning**. Experiential learning belongs to the **constructivist** school of learning theory. According to this view, knowledge is a mental 'construct' which is subject to constant re-evaluation and reconstruction, as we accommodate new information and experience. The experiential 'cycle', by which existing knowledge is tested and reshaped, consists of alternating stages of action and **reflection**. Experiential language learning shares with **mentalist** theories of learning (→ **mentalism**) a belief in the value of learners actively working things out for themselves (→ **inductive learning**). It also shares with **humanism** a commitment to whole-person learning (→ **whole language learning**), and, with **critical pedagogy**, a belief in the transformative power of direct experience rather than simply applying knowledge that has been 'handed down' by some higher authority. Classroom-based experiential learning consists simply of doing things using language, whether playing games, or performing **tasks**. No explicit teaching of language takes place in advance of these activities, although language-focused feedback may take place as a result of them. An experiential approach is particularly appropriate for the teaching of **young learners**.

explaining → **teacher talk**

extensive reading → **reading**

F

face → **politeness**

facilitation METHODOLOGY

To facilitate a process, such as language learning, is to help make it happen. Facilitation is a way of thinking about teaching that recognizes the fact that teachers do not directly *cause* learning, but that they can provide the conditions in which learning happens. The notion of the teacher as *facilitator* comes partly from **humanist** educational theory and partly from **critical pedagogy**, both of which credit the learner with **agency** in the learning process. That is, the learner should not be seen as the object of the verb *to teach*, but the subject of the verb *to learn*. The teacher facilitates the process by managing the learning situation, including the **dynamics**, in a way that is conducive to learning. The role of facilitator, therefore, involves not just knowledge of teaching techniques and subject matter knowledge (such as grammar), but interpersonal skills as well. A good example of the 'teacher-as-facilitator' is in **community language learning**, where the teacher's role is primarily that of a consultant, providing learners with the language they need to construct their own conversations.

false friend → **cognate**

FCE (First Certificate in English) → **examination**

feedback SLA

Feedback is the information, either immediate or delayed, that learners get on their performance. At least some of this feedback may have a long-term effect on their knowledge of the language (their **competence**). Traditionally, feedback takes the form of **correction**. Correction, of the sort *No, that's not right*, is called *negative feedback*: it is a clear message that the learner has produced an **error**. But feedback can also be *positive*, as in this exchange:

> **Teacher** What's the past of *I go*?
> **Student** *I went.*
> **Teacher** Right.

Feedback can be *explicit* (as in the above exchange) or it can be *implicit*. In the following exchange the teacher's response is an instance of implicit negative feedback, since the teacher does not overtly indicate that the learner has made an error:

> **Student** I go to the beach yesterday.
> **Teacher** You went to the beach, did you?

Here, the teacher responds naturally to the student's utterance, but, in so doing, *recasts* it in a more accurate form. Recasts are common in parent-child talk, and it has been suggested that they might play an important part in **first language acquisition**. Researchers into second language acquisition are in two minds, however. There is evidence that learners do not perceive recasts as feedback at all, or that they perceive them as positive, not negative. If the learners' errors elicit only positive feedback, and therefore go unnoticed and uncorrected, these errors may become fossilized, ie, resistant to change (→ **fossilization**). Other researchers, however, have argued that even explicit negative feedback, such as *No, not 'I go'. 'I went'*, has no long-term effect either. This may be because the learner's developing mental grammar is not yet 'ready' for the correction (→ **order of acquisition**). To counter this argument, supporters of negative feedback argue that, while the effect of correction might not be either immediate or predictable, constant 'nagging' serves to remind learners to pay attention to **form**. And paying attention to form is good for them in the long run.

There is also an argument that the most effective type of feedback is the feedback that learners get when their *message* is not understood or when it is misinterpreted. Thus, the learner who says *I am leaving here*, meaning *I am living here*, and gets the response *Bye, then!* may pay greater attention to avoiding this pronunciation error when it next comes up. This is a case for sometimes 'acting dumb' when learners make errors, in order to demonstrate the potential effect of such errors outside the classroom. This is also an argument for sometimes 'forcing' learners to make errors, especially of *overgeneralization* (such as using the present progressive with **stative verbs**: *I am liking it*), in order to be able to provide the necessary negative feedback. This strategy is called 'leading the learner up the garden path' (→ **grammar teaching**).

Finally, some **humanist** writers caution against negative feedback, because of the potential anxiety it could cause. Others argue against giving even positive feedback (such as praise) as this misleads learners into thinking that language learning is harder than it is. A compromise position might be to show positive feedback on the *content* of what the learner says, but negative feedback (if appropriate) on the *form*:

> **Student** I go to the beach yesterday.
> **Teacher** Lucky you. But not *I go* …
> **Student** I went …

field → **context**; → **register**

filler → **pause filler**

finite verb GRAMMAR

Verbs may be either *finite* or *non-finite*. Finite verbs show that they are related to a **subject** by having **person**, **number** and **tense**. For example, *Brad <u>works</u> for his uncle. They <u>work</u> together. Before that Brad <u>worked</u> for his father.* Non-finite verbs do not show these person, number and tense contrasts: *Before <u>working</u> for his uncle, Brad used <u>to work</u> for his father.* The **infinitive** (with or without *to*) and the present and past **participles** are non-finite. **Clauses** whose main verb is finite are called *finite clauses*: eg *Before he worked for his uncle* …. Clauses whose main

verb is non-finite are called *non-finite clauses*, eg *Before working for his uncle* ....
When there is more than one verb in a verb phrase, the finite verb comes first:
He <u>has</u> been working for his uncle for a year now.

first language (L1) SOCIOLINGUISTICS

A learner's first language, also known as their native language or their mother
tongue, is referred to as their *L1*. This contrasts with their **second language** (L2)
or their third (L3), etc. The concept of first language is relatively unproblematic
in societies that are primarily monolingual. But for children brought up in a
multilingual environment, it is not always clear-cut as to which is their first
language, or whether they might have more than one (→ **bilingualism**). A
distinction can also be made between the *home language*, ie, the language spoken
in the home, and the public language, as used at school, for example.

first language acquisition PSYCHOLOGY

How do people acquire their first language? And what bearing might this have on
second language acquisition (SLA)? These questions continue to underpin a
great deal of research and theorizing in SLA. This is what we now know about
first language (or L1, or mother tongue) acquisition:

- It takes place relatively quickly: by the time children are five years old most of
  their adult grammar will be in place. They will also have accumulated a
  vocabulary of some 5000 words, having uttered their very first words only four
  years previously.
- It is systematically staged: children move through a *pre-linguistic stage* of
  babbling and cooing, to a one-word stage, and then a two- and three-word
  stage, before acquiring grammar at around the age of two. This grammar,
  too, seems to follow a natural order. In English, the *-ing* form appears first,
  then the regular plural *-s*, followed by irregular past tense forms (eg *said*,
  caught), and then regular past tense forms (eg *played*, *watched*) (→ **order of
  acquisition**).
- It happens despite 'the poverty of the stimulus': that is, the mental grammars
  that children construct seem to be more elaborate and complex than the
  language that they are exposed to (ie, their **input**).
- It results simply from contact and interaction, and not from any formal
  teaching, nor correction, nor carrot-and-stick-type conditioning.
- Given a reasonable amount of exposure (and no brain damage), it is always
  a hundred per cent successful, irrespective of factors such as intelligence,
  personality, or the language being acquired.

These factors have led some theorists to propose the existence of an innate
language acquisition faculty (or a *language instinct*). This includes a set of
procedures, sometimes called the *language acquisition device (LAD)*, for
constructing the grammar of the language (→ **universal grammar**). According
to this view, we are 'hard-wired' to learn a first language. This raises the burning
question as to whether – or to what extent – this language faculty is available for
the acquisition of additional languages, especially into adulthood. The *critical
period hypothesis* argues that it is not: that neurological factors occurring at
puberty mean that thereafter you can't just pick up a language as you did when
you were a child. (→ **age**)

Other theorists discount the existence of a distinctive language faculty (or language *module*) in the mind. They argue instead that language acquisition can be explained as simply one manifestation of more general human cognitive capacities, such as perception, pattern-recognition, generalizing and memorizing. According to this view, language learning develops in conjunction with learning in general, and as a result of socialization processes, as the child interacts with parents, peers, and the world at large. This *interactionist* view is represented in both **cognitive learning theory** and **sociocultural learning theory**. These theories, in turn, are enlisted to explain how general learning mechanisms also account for second language acquisition (→ **language acquisition**; → **second language acquisition**; → **usage-based acquisition**).

fluency SLA

If someone is said to be fluent in a language, or to speak a language fluently, it is generally understood that they are able to speak the language idiomatically and accurately, without undue pausing, without an intrusive accent, and in a manner appropriate to the context. In fact, research into listeners' perceptions of fluency suggests that fluency is primarily the ability to produce and maintain speech in *real time*. To do this, fluent speakers are capable of:

- appropriate pausing, ie:
  - their pauses may be long but are not frequent
  - their pauses are usually filled, eg with **pause fillers** like *erm, you know, sort of*
  - their pauses occur at meaningful transition points, eg at the intersections of clauses or phrases, rather than midway in a phrase
- long runs, ie, there are many syllables and words between pauses

All of the above factors depend on the speaker having a well-developed grammar, an extensive vocabulary, and, crucially, a store of memorized *chunks* (→ **formulaic language**). Being able to draw on this store of chunks means not having to depend on grammar to construct each utterance from scratch (→ **automaticity**). This allows the speaker to devote **attention** to other aspects of the interaction, such as planning ahead. Speakers also use a number of 'tricks' or *production strategies* to convey the illusion of fluency. One such strategy is disguising pauses by filling them, or by repeating a word or phrase.

Some proponents of the **communicative approach** re-defined fluency so as to distinguish it from **accuracy**. Fluency came to mean 'communicative effectiveness', regardless of formal accuracy or speed of delivery. Activities that are communicative, such as information-gap activities, are said to be *fluency-focused*. This is the case even for activities that produce short, halting utterances. Separating accuracy and fluency, and defining the latter as *communicative* language use, is misleading, though. There are many speech events whose communicativeness depends on their accuracy. Air traffic control talk is just one. Moreover, many learners aspire to being more than merely communicative.

Classroom activities that target fluency need to prepare the learner for real-time speech production. Learning and memorizing lexical chunks, including useful conversational gambits, is one approach (→ **conversation**). **Drills** may help here, as will some types of **communicative activity** that involve repetition. Research has also shown that fluency improves the more times a **task** is repeated.

Fluency may also benefit from activities that manage to distract learners' attention away from formal accuracy so that they are not tempted to slow down. (This has been called 'parking their attention'). Some interactive and competitive language **games** have this effect. **Drama** activities, such as roleplays, recreate conditions of real-time language use, and are therefore good for developing fluency. Finally, learners can achieve greater fluency from learning a repertoire of **communication strategies**, ie, techniques for getting around potential problems caused by a lack of the relevant words or structures.

focus on form SLA

When learners focus on form, they direct conscious attention to some formal feature of the language **input**. The feature may be the fact that the past of *has* is *had*, or that *enjoy* is followed by verb forms ending in *-ing*, or that adjectives do not have plural forms in English. The learners' attention may be self-directed, or it may be directed by the teacher or by another learner. Either way, it has been argued that a focus on **form** is a necessary condition for language learning. Simply focusing on the **meaning** of the input is not enough. Focusing on form is, of course, not a new idea: most teaching methods devote a great deal of time to the forms of the language, eg when new grammar items are presented (→ **form, highlighting**). But the term *focus on form* captures the fact that this focus can, theoretically, occur at any stage in classroom instruction. Thus, **correction**, especially in the form of negative **feedback**, is a kind of focus on form. In fact, some researchers argue that the most effective form focus is that which arises incidentally, in the context of communication, as when the teacher quickly elicits a correction during a classroom discussion. This incidental approach contrasts with the more traditional and deliberate approach, where teaching is based on a **syllabus** of graded structures (or *forms*), and these are pre-taught in advance of activities designed to practise them (→ **PPP**). This traditional approach is called – by some researchers – a *focus on formS*.

form LINGUISTICS

The form of a word is the way it is written or pronounced, and is independent of its **meaning**. Thus, the meaning represented by the English word TABLE takes the form *mesa* in Spanish and *Tisch* in German. In the same way, grammatical form is the way grammatical meaning is represented in speech or writing. Thus, the *present perfect* is the name of the grammatical form that comprises the **auxiliary verb** *have* and the past **participle**: *She has left*. (The *meaning* of the present perfect is much less easy to define; → **perfect**). Much of what is involved in learning a second language is the matching of new forms to existing meanings, as (for a Spanish speaker) matching the idea of MESA to the form *table*. Or the idea SE HA IDO to the form *she has left*. The situation is complicated by the fact that there are many cases where there is no one-to-one match of form and meaning. Many forms have more than one meaning, as in the case of the English words *left* and *right*. Or the grammatical form *-s*, which can sometimes mean plurality (*the collected works of Shakespeare*), and at other times is the third person singular marker in present tense verbs (*she works*). Also, in a number of instances, the same meaning can be expressed using different forms, as in *cab* and *taxi*, or *it could rain/it might rain*. To make matters worse, a form in one language may have different meanings to a similar form in another language, as does the word *will*, which in English has future meaning, but which in German means *want* or *wants*.

Form is also often contrasted with **function**. Thus, the form called a **noun phrase**, such as *last week*, can function in different ways in a sentence: as a **subject** (*Last week was very hot*) and as an **adverbial** (*I was there last week*).

Learning the forms of a second language without learning the meanings that they express is clearly a waste of time. Similarly, focusing solely on meaning without paying attention to form is unlikely to get you far. Teaching needs to direct learners' attention to both aspects of language, so as to help forge strong form–meaning associations (→ **focus on form**).

formal test → **testing**

formal language SOCIOLINGUISTICS

Formal language is a **style** of language that is appropriate in situations where there is social distance between speakers (or writer and reader), or where the situation or topic requires a degree of seriousness. Formal language is more common in print, such as in official documents, business letters, and academic papers. But it is also used in some spoken contexts, such as giving speeches, where language is first written down and then read aloud. Formal English is characterized by the following features:

- **complex sentences**, ie, sentences with subordinate **clauses**
- frequent use of the **passive**
- use of **reported speech**
- use of past forms with present meaning, and past forms of **modal verbs**, as in *I was wondering if I could* …
- long and complex **noun phrases**
- long words, often with Greek or Latin roots, such as *inebriated* (for *drunk*)

The following is a (genuine) example of formal language. It was a broadcast announcement at an underground station in London:

'Your attention please. Passengers alighting at the next station are advised to be aware of the gap between the train and the platform'.

An informal version of the same message is: 'Please mind the gap'.
Formal language should not be confused with **politeness**. While politeness is often conveyed using formal language, it is not the case that informal language is necessarily impolite. You can be informal and polite (as in 'Mind the gap'), just as you can be formal and rude.

form, highlighting METHODOLOGY

When presenting new language items, teachers customarily choose from a variety of techniques to highlight the **form**, either spoken or written, or both. These include:

- *modelling*: the teacher repeats the item a number of times, clearly articulating its component parts, as well as demonstrating how these components are connected in natural speech (→ **connected speech**)
- *finger-coding*: the teacher uses his or her fingers to identify each element (eg each syllable or word) of the item, as well as showing which elements are stressed, joined or omitted in natural speech
- *Cuisenaire rods*: these are small blocks of wood of different lengths and

colours, originally designed for teaching numeracy, but good for demonstrating formal features of language, such as the component parts of a grammatical structure, or the syllables in words (→ **Silent Way, the**)

- *boardwork*: the teacher writes the item on the board, and, using symbols and phonemic script (→ **phoneme**), highlights features of its pronunciation, such as weak forms, contractions, and stress, for example:

		□
You	should've	phoned.
	[should have]	
/juː	ʃʊdəv	fəʊnd/

- *substitution tables*: the components of a grammar structure can be displayed in the form of a table, with items that can substitute for one another arranged in the same column

It is important that any highlighting of form takes place in close association with the **meaning** of the item, eg straight after the meaning has been established. In this way, learners are optimally primed to make the right form–meaning associations.

formulaic language LINGUISTICS

Formulaic language refers to those sequences of two or more words that operate as a single unit. This means that they are not generated word by word, but are stored in the memory, and retrieved, as if they were one-word vocabulary items. Also called *(lexical) chunks, multi-word units, ready-mades, prefabricated language* and *holophrases*, formulaic language can be classified into the following categories:

- **collocations** – such as *densely populated, rich and famous, set the table*
- **phrasal verbs** – such as *get up, log on, run out of, go on about*
- **idioms**, catchphrases and sayings – such as *part and parcel*; *make ends meet*; *down in the dumps*; *you live and learn*
- sentence frames – such as *Would you like a …? The thing is …*; *What we're going to do is …*
- social formulae – such as *See you later. Have a nice day. You're welcome.*
- **discourse markers** – such as *By the way*; *I take your point*; *To cut a long story short …*

Many formulaic sequences are invariable (or fixed); others allow for a limited degree of variation (they are semi-fixed). Typical fixed chunks include such idiomatic expressions and sayings as *out of sight, out of mind*; *hook, line, and sinker*; *over the moon*. Certain social formulae are also fairly invariable, such as *Beg your pardon? Long time no see. Have a nice day*. More common are semi-fixed chunks, ie, those that have open slots, such as the sentence frame *I remember -ing*, as in *I remember going to the circus once …*, often used to begin an anecdote.

One advantage of having a memorized store of formulaic language is that it makes for easy access in real-time speaking conditions. This saves planning time, thus aiding **fluency**. Also, because these formulae reflect accepted usage, the use of them can help make the speaker sound idiomatic. **Idiomaticity** identifies the speaker as a member of the target speech community. There are also some researchers who believe that formulaic language might provide the 'raw material' for language acquisition. That is, sequences that are first acquired as unanalysed chunks (such as *I don't know*) may be later analysed into their component parts. They are then capable of generating original phrases, such as *I don't understand*, *You don't know*, *I know* ..., etc. All these reasons suggest that there are good grounds for encouraging the learning of formulaic language. This is the central platform of the **lexical approach**.

Corpus linguistics is starting to provide information as to which of these chunks are the most frequently used. For example, in a recent study[5] of a corpus of spoken US English idioms, one researcher listed the following as some of the most frequent: *kind of, sort of, of course, in terms of, in fact, deal with, at all, as well, make sure, go through, first of all, in other words.*

fossilization SLA

A fossilized **error** is one that has become a permanent feature of a learner's **interlanguage**. In theory, such errors are resistant to correction. Some researchers doubt this, and prefer the term *stabilization* to fossilization. There are various theories as to what causes fossilization. It is a well-known phenomenon in learners who have acquired their second language in naturalistic (non-classroom) conditions. So it has been hypothesized that the lack of instruction, especially the lack of a **focus on form**, is the main cause. This is used as an argument for giving explicit attention to grammar. Another theory is that fossilization may be due to the lack of negative **feedback** on errors, a view that is used to justify **correction**. Fossilization may also be due to the fact that learners have not been 'pushed' to make their output more accurate (→ **output hypothesis**). Yet another theory argues that some learners have no social motivation to improve their interlanguage. Once they can meet their basic communicative needs, fossilization is likely to occur, because they are not sufficiently motivated to want to pass as members of the target language community (→ **acculturation**). Now that it is accepted that few if any second language learners achieve native-like proficiency, the concept of fossilization is viewed less negatively. It is being replaced by the idea of *partial competence*. In other words, for many learners it may be more realistic to aim for a 'working knowledge' of the target language. This is also consistent with the more pragmatic objectives of learning **English as an international language**.

frequency LINGUISTICS; SLA

The frequency of a word, or other language item, is the number of times the item occurs in a **text** or a **corpus**. Frequency data, derived from large corpora, provide valuable information for syllabus and materials designers. Nowadays, for example, compilers of learner **dictionaries** take frequency into account when deciding which words to include and which meanings of these words to prioritize, and the relative frequency of a word is usually indicated in some way. Word frequency is also a factor in judging the readability of texts. It has been estimated that around eighty per cent of any text consists of the two thousand most frequent words in English. (In this paragraph, for example, the figure is eighty-three per cent). The most frequent words are **function words**, such as *the, of, in, and*, etc. Corpus research also provides frequency information about

[5] Liu, D. 2003. 'The most frequently used spoken American English idioms: A corpus analysis and its implications.' In *TESOL Quarterly*, 37/4.

grammar items, but this has made less of an impact on teaching materials than has the research into word frequency. It has been shown, for instance, that simple verb forms are roughly twenty times more frequent than continuous ones (→ **aspect**). Proponents of a form of **lexical approach** argue that frequency should be a major priority when selecting items for a **syllabus**. This is because the most frequent words and structures in the language express its most frequent meanings. Frequency does not always equate with usefulness, however. Travellers know that it is often quite low frequency words, such as *toothbrush* and *bill*, that are of more immediate utility.

The frequency of an item in the input that learners are exposed to may also be a critical factor in the acquisition of that item. It has long been known that the more times a learner encounters a new word the more likely they are to learn it. (One figure quoted by researchers is that at least seven encounters over spaced intervals are necessary → **repetition**.) Now, scholars who subscribe to **usage-based acquisition** theories argue that acquisition is simply the result of exposure, over time, to language data (or 'usage'). From this data, regularities, or patterns, are abstracted using natural human processes of perception, pattern recognition, and association (→ **connectionism**). The more often a pattern occurs in the input, the greater the chance that the pattern will be observed and remembered. Indeed, the more or less fixed **order of acquisition** of grammar structures can be accounted for, at least in part, by the relative frequency of these items in naturally occurring input. The implications for teaching are that the learning of grammar and vocabulary might be speeded up by using texts that have a high frequency of occurrences of the target items. (The technique is known as *input flood* → **input**.) The 'frequency hypothesis' also justifies frequent recycling of recently taught items (→ **revision**).

function LINGUISTICS

The function of a language item is its communicative purpose. Language is more than simply **forms** and their associated meanings (ie, **usage**). It is also the communicative **uses** to which these forms and meanings are put. These two sentences, for example, share the same forms, but function quite differently:

> [in an email] *Thank you for sending me the disk.*
> [a notice in a taxi] *Thank you for not smoking.*

The function of the first is *expressing thanks*, while the second is more like a *prohibition*. Likewise, the same function can be expressed by different forms:

> [a notice in a taxi] *Thank you for not smoking.*
> [a sign in a classroom] *No smoking.*

Thus, there is no one-to-one match between form and function. Assigning a function to a text or an utterance usually requires knowledge of the **context** in which the text is used. The study of how context and function are interrelated is called **pragmatics**.

Communicative functions can be categorized very broadly and also at increasing levels of detail. The 'big' functions, or macrofunctions, describe the way language is used in very general terms. These include the use of language for *expressive* purposes (eg poetry), for *regulatory* purposes (eg for getting people to do things), for *interpersonal* purposes (eg for socializing), and for *representational* purposes (eg to inform). More useful, from the point of view of designing language syllabuses, are microfunctions. These are usually expressed as **speech acts**, such as *agreeing and disagreeing, reporting, warning, apologizing, thanking, greeting*, etc. Such categories form the basis of **functional syllabuses**, a development associated with the **communicative approach**. They often appear as one strand of a coursebook **syllabus**. Functions differ from notions (→ **notional syllabus**) in that the latter describe areas of meaning – such as *ability, duration, quantity, frequency*, etc – rather than the uses to which these meanings are put.

One way to teach functions is to adopt a 'phrasebook' approach, and teach useful ways of expressing common functions (what are called *functional exponents*), such as *Would you like …? (inviting)* and *Could you …, please?(requesting)*. More memorable, though, is to teach these expressions in the contexts of **dialogues**, so that the functional exponents are associated not only with common situations in which they are used, but with related functions (such as *accepting* and *refusing*). The term *function*, in contrast to **form**, is also used in linguistics, specifically with regard to the functions of the different elements of a **clause** (such as subject and object). (→ **systemic functional linguistics**)

functional exponent → **functional syllabus**

functional syllabus METHODOLOGY

A functional syllabus is a syllabus based around a list of language **functions**, such as *asking for information; making requests; greeting people; making, accepting and refusing invitations*. Each function is realized by one or more *functional exponents*. So, functional exponents for the function of *making requests* include *Can you …? Could you …? Would you mind …-ing?* (There is usually more than one way of expressing a function, and any one grammar structure can express a wide variety of functions). Functional syllabuses were first developed to support a **communicative approach**. In contrast to the prevailing *structural syllabuses* of the time, they were meaning-, rather than form-, based. They were often combined with language *notions* (→ **notional syllabus**) to form what was called a *functional–notional syllabus*. In practice, the distinction between functions (such as *narrating*) and notions (such as *past-ness*) became rather blurred. The purely functional syllabus was relatively short-lived. It soon became apparent that the criteria for the selection and grading of functions were rather arbitrary. Coursebook writers tended to order the functions according to the kinds of grammar structures that were typically associated with them. Moreover, functional exponents lack generalizability in the way that grammar structures are generalizable. So there was always the problem of function-based courses becoming nothing more than an elaborate list of expressions to remember, rather like a phrasebook. If functional syllabuses have survived at all, it is usually as one strand in a *multi-layered syllabus*.

function word VOCABULARY

Function words, also called *grammar words*, are those words which have a mainly grammatical function. They contrast with **content words**, which carry the main informational load. Function words are **auxiliary verbs**, **determiners**, **pronouns**, **prepositions**, **conjunctions**, and some **adverbs**, such as adverb particles (*up, down, in*) and words like *not* and *to* (in infinitive constructions). As well as being generally very short, they are also very common: of the fifty most common words in English, forty-nine are function words. They also have enormous coverage, making up a third to a half of all text. That is to say, every second or third word in a text is likely to be a function word. (The function words in the last sentence are underlined). Because English is not a heavily inflected language – that is to say, because its grammar is not realized through word endings – a great deal of grammatical meaning is conveyed by these small words.

future tense → **futurity**

futurity FUNCTION

There is no future **tense** in English, in the sense that there are no specific verb endings that express future meaning in the way that the -*ed* ending expresses past-ness. Instead there are many different ways of expressing futurity, the most common being:

- *will* + infinitive (sometimes called the future simple): *He will turn seventy next month.* This is by far the most common way of expressing the future in English, especially in writing, and expresses a neutral, predicted future. With personal subjects, especially the first person, it can also express willingness, as in offers: *I'll put the rubbish out.* In a diminishing number of English varieties, *shall* is also used: *I shall be in the office tomorrow,* but its use is mainly confined to questions: *What shall we get Robin?* (*Will* and *shall* also have a number of non-future uses, such as talking about typical behaviour (*Boys will be boys*) and obligation: *Passengers shall remain seated at all times.*)
- *going to* + infinitive: This expresses the future 'as a fulfilment of the present', either a present intention (*I'm going to resign*), or a prediction based on present evidence (*You're going to fall off*). It is more common in speech than in writing.
- present simple: This is used mainly to talk about scheduled events (*The train leaves at six*) or in subordinate clauses: *It will be late when we arrive.*
- present progressive (or continuous): This is used to talk about arrangements: *Tom's coming round for dinner tonight.*
- *will* + *be* + present participle – the 'future progressive (or continuous)': This is commonly used to talk about plans and arrangements (*I'll be seeing Jackie tomorrow*), and to talk about future events that are seen as happening as 'a matter of course': *The plane will be landing in ten minutes.*
- *will* + *have* + past participle (the 'future perfect'): This expresses 'the past in the future': *Phone me at two: I'll have had lunch by then.*

The fact that there are so many ways of expressing futurity, some of which are interchangeable in certain contexts, makes the teaching of futurity especially difficult. Another source of difficulty is the fact that the choice of form is often determined by the speaker's perception of, or attitude to, the future event being referred to. And, of course, the future is inherently vague and indefinite: it is not easy to formulate clear-cut rules. The few rules that there are are often expressed in language that is difficult (eg *spontaneous vs planned decisions*). Moreover, **register** factors (eg speech vs writing; formal vs informal) can influence the choice of form. For all these reasons, it is probably best to teach futurity in close association with typical contexts of use, and in conjunction with related **formulaic language**. Thus, *going to*, to talk about plans, is often taught in the context of holidays and travel, while *will* for predictions is often taught alongside expressions like *I [don't] think, I guess, I bet, I reckon ...* (→ **plans and intentions**; → **prediction**)

games METHODOLOGY

Games have a long history in language teaching. This is partly because many non-classroom games are language-based and therefore lend themselves to use (or adaptation) in the language classroom. Traditional word games, such as *Hangman*, guessing games, such as *Twenty Questions*, and grid-completion games of the *Bingo* type, are ever popular, as are more recent inventions such as *Pictionary*®. Also popular are adaptations of dice and board games, which involve learners correctly answering questions in order to gain points. Puzzles, including crosswords, word searches and anagrams have a long history in the language classroom. Computers have helped make puzzles both more sophisticated and more visually appealing (→ **computer-assisted language learning**). Action games, of the type *Simon says*, are popular with children, and have been elaborated by borrowing **Total Physical Response** techniques. Guessing games, especially those that involve asking questions, such as *Spot the difference* and *What's my line?*, are essentially communicative, and are therefore now standard practice within the communicative repertoire (→ **communicative activities**). Classic classroom games of the **roleplay** type include *Alibis* (where learners have to devise and defend an alibi) and *Balloon debates* (where learners, assuming the role of historical persons, have to justify their *not* being jettisoned from a sinking balloon → **discussion**). These games can be highly language-productive, an important criterion in choosing a game. But other factors, such as the effect on **motivation** of relatively light-hearted competitive activities, are also important, especially for **young learners**. In fact, any mechanical language exercise can be turned into a game, simply by dividing the class into teams and allocating points for correct answers, or by turning the task into a race.

gap-fill → **exercise**; → **cloze test**; → **computer-assisted language learning**; → **testing**

gender LINGUISTICS

In many languages, some word classes (mainly **nouns, determiners, pronouns** and **adjectives**) are marked for gender. That is, they are assigned different masculine or feminine (or sometimes neuter) forms. There is no grammatical gender in English, apart from the pronouns *he/she, him/her*, etc, plus a residual set of noun distinctions, such as *prince/princess* and *spokesman/spokeswoman*, many of which have been replaced by non-gender-specific terms such as *spokesperson*. The tradition of using masculine pronouns as the default form (as in *If a student makes an error, try to get him to self-correct it*) is now regarded as sexist. Writers are advised to avoid it, and to use some form of non-gender-specific alternative instead, even if this is either awkward (*If students make an error, try to get them to self-correct it*), or 'ungrammatical' (*If a student makes an error, try to get them to self-correct it*).

genitive → **possession**

genre LINGUISTICS

A genre is any type of spoken or written **discourse** which is used and recognized by members of a particular culture or sub-culture. As a genre becomes established, it acquires a conventionalized structure and often a characteristic vocabulary and grammar. Examples of written genres are news reports, academic papers and magazine horoscopes. Spoken genres include sports commentaries, answerphone messages and business presentations. The specialized nature of many genres can make them difficult for non-members of the 'in-group' to understand. For example, the following is an instance of a genre that botanists would recognize as being a *botanical description*: [1]

> **Corncockle**. *Agrostemma githago* L., plant grey with shaggy hairs, 30–100cm; lvs opposite, linear; sepals 5, united into a bell-shaped tube, with long spreading lobes; corolla purple, 3–5cm wide, much exceeded by the free calyx teeth; seeds poisonous! Fl.6–7. Cornfields; formerly widespread, but now rare due to efficient seed cleaning. Almost all of Europe. Protected!

The specialized vocabulary, the long **noun phrases**, the use of abbreviations and **ellipsis**, as well as the way the information is sequenced and punctuated are generic features of this type of text. They are also consistent with the text's **function**, which is 'to describe for the purposes of identification'. (Imagine how different the text would be if it were a poem about the corncockle, or the instructions on a packet of corncockle seeds). Anyone wishing to become a member of the discourse community that uses this genre (ie, botanists) will need to know how to interpret – and maybe even how to reproduce – these generic features. This will involve choices at the *macro* level, that is, the overall organization, and the *micro* level: the specific grammatical and lexical features.

There are several schools of *genre theory*, the most influential being that associated with **systemic functional linguistics**. Practitioners of *genre analysis* investigate not only the formal features of genres, but they also attempt to relate these to their social contexts and purposes. The fact that genre knowledge provides 'entry' into a culture supports the case for the teaching of specific genres, especially in ESP (→ **English for special purposes**) and English as a second language (ESL) contexts.

gerund → *-ing* **form**

graded reader → **reader**

grammar LINGUISTICS

'Grammar' can mean any one of a number of different things:

1. In popular use (such as in indignant letters to newspapers), the term 'grammar' describes what people – usually native speakers – *ought* or *ought not* to say or write. Style guides and many traditional books on grammar have formalized this advice, providing 'rules' of the type: *Don't say 'less than 10 items',* *say 'fewer than 10 items'*; *Never begin a sentence with 'and'*; *Don't say 'Hopefully, she passed the exam', say 'I hope she passed the exam'*; etc. This is called *prescriptive grammar* because it prescribes correct usage, according to the standards of some (usually privileged) group. In these terms, grammar is seen as a marker of group membership, and the word *grammar* frequently collocates with evaluative terms

---

[1] Schauer, T. 1992 *A Field Guide to the Wild Flowers of Britain and Europe* (Collins) p 62.

like *good* or *bad*, as in *It's bad grammar to say 'between you and I'*. This is *not* what is meant by grammar when the term is used with regard to teaching second or foreign languages.

2. A *descriptive grammar*, on the other hand, simply describes, in a systematic way, the rules that govern how words are combined and sequenced in order to form sentences in a given language. If a prescriptive grammar is about how people *should* speak, a descriptive one is about how people *do* speak. This description is usually based on actual data gathered from speakers of the language, eg in the form of a **corpus**. Descriptive grammars deal with **morphology** and **syntax**. Morphology is the way words are inflected for grammatical purposes, such as the verb-endings *-s* in *she works*, and *-ed* in *I worked*. Syntax describes the rules that govern the way the elements of a sentence (including **phrases** and **clauses**) are assembled and sequenced. A descriptive grammar tries to account for the fact that sequences like *★Love my is like a rose red, red*, and *★My love are like a red, red rose*, are considered ungrammatical (or *ill-formed*), whereas *My love is like a red, red rose*, is considered grammatical (or *well-formed*). Descriptive grammars tend to fall into one of two camps, depending on their theoretical bias. Most take as their starting point the **forms** of the language, independent of their meanings, and are therefore called *formal grammars*. But some are concerned with the meaning-making potential of grammar, and organize their descriptions around these meanings, as is the case with *functional grammars*. For example, the headings in a formal grammar might include *adjectives, adverbs, articles, auxiliary verbs*, etc, while the headings in a functional grammar might be *ability, advice, agency, apologizing*, etc.

3. A *pedagogical grammar* is a kind of descriptive grammar designed for teaching and learning purposes. It focuses on grammar as a subsystem of overall language proficiency, as distinct from **vocabulary**, **phonology** or **discourse** (→ **discourse analysis**). It is more selective than a linguist's grammar, and while it is not intentionally prescriptive, it will probably be based on a standard form of the language (→ **Standard English**). It will therefore exclude usages that are considered *non-standard* (such as *I ain't got none*; *Me and my sister went shopping*), even when these are used by a large number of native speakers. Most pedagogical grammars are *formal* rather than *functional*: they are organized around structural categories (such as *present simple, past continuous*, etc), rather than functional ones (such as *reporting, expressing time*, etc). A good pedagogical grammar will be sufficient for most teachers' everyday classroom needs.

4. Your *mental grammar* is the way that a language is represented in your mind: it is the internalized, and usually implicit, knowledge about the way the language works. It is part of every user's **competence**. It can be partially accessed through the use of *grammaticality judgment tests*. This is when speakers are asked if they consider sentences such as the following to be grammatical: *My love be like a red, red rose*; *The rose my love is like is a red, red one*. A *learner's* mental grammar is a system in its own right. It has its own patterns and regularities, although it may bear only a slender relation to either a native speaker's mental grammar or a descriptive grammar of the target language. This is why grammar should not be confused with **accuracy**, which is simply those points where the learner's grammar conforms to an external standard, usually that of adult native speakers. (→ **grammar teaching**)

grammaring LINGUISTICS

Grammaring is a term coined by the applied linguist Diane Larsen-Freeman in order to capture the notion of grammar being more a skill than an inert body of knowledge. Grammaring is the process by which a sequence of words is fine-tuned in order to create a more complex message than mere words can express. Consider how that last sentence would be if its grammar were 'removed': *Grammaring process sequence word fine-tune create complex message mere word express.* By adding grammar (or by grammaring) the message is made less ambiguous. This grammaring process is particularly necessary when speakers or writers cannot rely on immediate contextual clues to clarify what they mean. For example, it may be sufficient, at the end of a meal in a restaurant, to say to the waiter 'The bill, please'. But it would not be sufficient when phoning the receptionist in a hotel to ask that the bill be sent to such-and-such an address. This would require a considerable amount of complexity, and much of that complexity would take the form of grammar.

The term 'grammaring' has also been used to describe the way the learner's *mental grammar* develops, over time, from a mainly lexical mode (as in *Me Tarzan, you Jane*), to a more fully *grammaticized* one – a process that is also shared by children acquiring their first language.

grammar interpretation task → **grammar teaching**

grammar, spoken → **spoken grammar**

grammar teaching METHODOLOGY

Like the word **grammar** itself, the topic of grammar teaching is a controversial one, and teachers often take opposing views. Historically, language teaching methods have positioned themselves along a scale from 'zero grammar' to 'total grammar', according to their approach to grammar teaching. Proponents of *natural methods*, who model their approach to teaching second languages on the way that first languages are acquired, reject any explicit teaching of grammar at all. (They may, however, teach according to a grammar **syllabus**, even if no mention of grammar as such is made in the classroom). This implicit approach is common both to the **direct method** and to **audiolingualism**. Through exposure to demonstrations, situations or examples, learners are expected to pick up the rules of grammar by **inductive learning**. At the other end of the spectrum, there are approaches, such as **grammar-translation**, that adopt an explicit and **deductive learning** approach. From the outset, learners are presented with rules which they study and then practise. Occupying a midway point between zero grammar and total grammar is the approach called **consciousness-raising**. Instead of being given rules, learners are presented with language data which challenge them to re-think (and *restructure*) their existing mental grammar. This data might take the form of **input** that has been manipulated in some way. For example, pairs of sentences, such as the following, have to be matched to pictures, forcing learners to discriminate between them, and, in theory, **notice** the difference (→ **noticing**):

The Queen drove to the airport.
The Queen was driven to the airport.

(This is sometimes called a *grammar interpretation task*, or *structured input*.) In order to do the task, learners have to process not just the individual words, but also their grammatical form. That is why this approach to teaching grammar is sometimes called *processing instruction*. There are other researchers who argue that it is by means of manipulating the learner's output, eg through productive practice, that mental restructuring is best effected (→ **output hypothesis**).

The **communicative approach** accommodates different approaches to grammar teaching. Proponents of **task-based learning**, for example, argue that, if the learner is engaged in solving problems using language, then the mental grammar will develop of its own accord. However, advocates of the weaker version of the communicative approach (and the version that is most widespread) justify a role for the pre-teaching of grammar in advance of production. This view finds support in **cognitive learning theory**, which suggests that conscious attention to grammatical form (called **focus on form**) speeds up language learning, and is a necessary corrective against premature **fossilization**. There is some debate, though, as to whether this form focus should be planned or incidental. Incidental grammar teaching occurs when the teacher deals with grammar issues as and when they come up, eg in the form of **correction**, or task **feedback**. In this way (it is argued) grammar teaching follows the learners' own 'syllabus'. Such an approach attempts to address one of the dilemmas of grammar teaching: the fact that the learner's mental grammar, and the way it develops, bears only an accidental relation to a formal grammar syllabus (→ **order of acquisition**).

Nevertheless, the research into these different choices is still inconclusive. It may be the case that some items of grammar respond better to explicit teaching, while others are more easily picked up through exposure. There are also different learner types: some prefer learning and applying rules, while others are happier with a more 'deep-end' approach (→ **learning style**). Most current teaching materials hedge their bets on these issues. They offer both deductive and inductive grammar presentations, and opportunities for incidental as well as for planned learning.

grammar–translation method METHODOLOGY

Grammar–translation is a language teaching method that developed out of the way that classical languages (such as Latin and Greek) were traditionally taught. It wasn't fully formalized until the mid-nineteenth century, when it became institutionalized in schools in Germany. First known as the Prussian Method, it was only later called *grammar–translation*. The *grammar* part comes from the fact that grammar is taught deductively (→ **deductive learning**) and that grammatical **accuracy** is highly prioritized. The *translation* part owes to the fact that the grammar rules are practised (and tested) through the translation of isolated sentences, both from and into the target language. It is the contrived nature of these sentences, more than any other feature of the method, that has given it a bad name. For example, the following sentences for translation come from a 1925 edition of a grammar–translation course for Spanish speakers (*The New British Method*, by L.T. Girau):

> I don't like your hat, it is too dark. / We do not understand the meaning of this sentence. / Did you give the razor to Mr. Martin? No, I did not. / We did

not guess his name./ He does not know this word. /They do not pronounce well. /Did they kill the wolf? No, they did not. /I do not explain the lesson to you, because it is too late.

Grammar–translation was seriously challenged by the advent of the *Reform Movement* in the late nineteenth century. This was a pan-European initiative aimed at a radical reform of existing language teaching practices in schools. Translation as a means of teaching foreign languages was rejected, in favour of the **direct method**. Grammar–translation proved very resilient, however. One reason for its survival was that it was a relatively easy method to implement, especially in large classes of unruly schoolchildren. **Translation** has been making something of a come-back in recent years, and it is not impossible to imagine a rehabilitated form of grammar–translation. Inductive presentations would replace deductive ones, whole texts would replace isolated sentences, and there would be a focus not only on reading and writing but also on speaking and listening.

grammatical metaphor → **metaphor**

greeting DISCOURSE

Greetings (and farewells) are the first language functions that most learners are taught. They are frequently reinforced through natural practice at the beginning and end of every lesson. And they may be one of the few functions that some learners will get to use outside the classroom. They also provide an ideal opportunity to focus on a number of important features of language in general. For a start, greetings are good examples of purely **phatic language**. That is, they have an entirely interpersonal **function**. They also involve the use of **formulaic language**, and often consist of several successive turns (→ **conversation analysis**): they therefore have a generic structure (→ **genre**). The mode is also important: face-to-face greetings are often accompanied by **paralinguistic** features, such as hand-shaking or kissing, while telephone greetings, and written greetings – as in letters, emails or text messages – have their own conventions. Greetings are especially sensitive to differences in tenor, from the very formal to the very informal. Finally, they are an important indicator of personal and cultural **identity**, and hence are useful for sensitizing learners to issues of intercultural awareness (→ **culture**).

Grice's maxims → **co-operative principle**

group dynamics → **dynamics: group, classroom**

groupwork METHODOLOGY

Groupwork is a form of **classroom interaction** where learners work together, part or all of the time, in small groups. The best size for a group is probably from three to five learners: anything larger may mean that not all learners will contribute often or equally. Groupwork is suitable for the preparation and performance of tasks such as **discussions**, roleplays (→ **drama**) and many **games**. Groupwork works best if there is a clear outcome to the task, such as making a decision, producing a text, or performing to the rest of the class. It can be a good idea to assign roles to individual members, such as chairperson, secretary, time-keeper. It is also important that the seating arrangement permits all the members of the group to see and hear one another. Finally, the teacher needs to **monitor** groupwork to ensure that learners are *on-task*, to be available to answer questions, and to provide **feedback** (including **correction**) on task performance.

At the completion of any groupwork, it is usual for at least one member of the group to report to the class on the outcome of the task. Alternatively, groups can be re-grouped to form new groups, each consisting of members from all the original groups. One way of doing this is to assign each member of the group a number (1, 2, 3, etc), and then ask all the 'number ones' to sit together, the 'number twos' to do likewise, and so on. Each person can now report to the new group what the original group had achieved.

guided discovery → **inductive learning**

Halliday, Michael → **systemic functional linguistics**

holistic approach → **whole language learning**

homework METHODOLOGY

Homework is the out-of-class work learners do between lessons, and is an important way of reinforcing learning. Few language learners will achieve high levels of proficiency solely on account of the time they spend in classrooms. In fact, there are grounds to believe that what happens *between* lessons may be of as much importance as what happens *during* lessons. Homework traditionally involves doing written **exercises** such as those provided in a workbook, or writing more extended texts such as compositions or diaries. Reading activities – including the use of graded **readers** – are a useful means both of incidental vocabulary learning and of practice in extended reading. Listening activities, using cassettes or CDs, are also a viable, although less practised, homework activity. Learners who have access to English-language resources, such as books, films, or even native speakers, can be set **project work** to do in out-of-class time. The internet, of course, provides a virtually unlimited source of reading and listening texts, as well as reference material in the form of on-line dictionaries and encyclopedias. It also allows learners to interact with one another by, for example, posting messages on discussion lists, communicating with email pen pals, sharing blogs, and taking part in live chat (→ **computer-mediated communication**). Finally, many schools have their own libraries and **self-access** centres, providing space and resources for out-of-class, *self-directed learning*.

homonym VOCABULARY

Homonyms are words that are written and pronounced the same way, but have different meanings. *Like* is a homonym: *What would you like to eat?* vs *Who do you look like?* English is particularly rich in homonyms, which can confuse language learners but which is a rich source of jokes. For example:

> Two elephants went on holiday and sat down on the beach. It was a very hot day and they fancied having a swim in the sea. Unfortunately they couldn't: they only had one pair of trunks!

Words that are written the same way, but pronounced differently, and which have different meanings, are called *homographs* (= same writing). For example: *a long and windy road* vs *a dark and windy night*. And words that are written differently, and have different meanings, but which are pronounced the same, are called *homophones* (= same sound). *To*, *two*, and *too*, are all homophones, as are *so* and *sew*.

humanism, humanistic approaches METHODOLOGY

The term *humanistic* describes learning approaches that assert the central role of the 'whole person' in the learning process. Humanistic approaches emerged in the mid-twentieth century partly as a reaction to the 'de-humanizing' psychology of **behaviourism**, but also as a counterbalance to exclusively intellectual (or cognitive) accounts of learning, such as **mentalism**. The titles of some of the key texts on humanistic education give a flavour of its concerns: Carl Rogers' *On Becoming a Person* (1961) and *Freedom to Learn* (1969); Abraham Maslow's *Towards a Psychology of Being* (1968) and Gertrude Moscowitz's *Caring and Sharing in the Foreign Language Class* (1978). Some basic tenets of humanistic education include the following:

- Personal growth, including realizing one's full potential, is one of the primary goals of education.
- The development of human values is another.
- The learner should be engaged affectively (ie, emotionally) as well as intellectually (→ **affect**).
- Behaviours that cause anxiety or stress should be avoided.
- Learners should be actively involved in the learning process.
- Learners can – and should – take responsibility for their own learning.

Of course, there have always been teachers who have shared some or all of these values, without necessarily calling themselves humanistic. Moreover, humanistic approaches share many of the values and beliefs of other progressive educational movements, such as the **autonomy** movement, **learner-centred instruction**, **whole language learning**, and **critical pedagogy**. In language teaching terms, humanism is generally associated with a number of methods that emerged in the 1960s and 1970s, principally **the Silent Way**, **community language learning** and **suggestopaedia**. But, to most teachers, humanistic practice is probably better known in the form of certain activity types, such as ice-breakers, ie, activities designed to create good group **dynamics** by tapping into learners' feelings and experiences. More recently, certain 'new age' training approaches, such as **neuro-linguistic programming** and the theory of **multiple intelligences** have amplified the repertoire of humanistic activities. Sceptics argue that some of the claims made in the name of humanism (such as those made for *accelerated learning*) are unsupported by research evidence. Others have voiced concern that, in the wrong hands, humanistic practices might intrude on learners' personal feelings and histories. Nevertheless, in affirming the interdependency of language, learning and personal identity, humanism has had a profound and lasting effect on language teaching.

hyponym VOCABULARY

Hyponymy describes the relationship between words represented by the formula *X is a type of Y*, as in *A mango is a type of fruit*. In this case, *mango* is a hyponym of *fruit*. And so are *banana* and *kiwi fruit*. *Fruit* is known as the *superordinate* term, while *mango*, *banana* and *kiwi fruit* are *co-hyponyms*. The relationship can be represented like this:

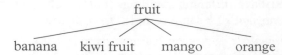

fruit

banana   kiwi fruit   mango   orange

A similar, hierarchical kind of semantic relation is the *whole–part* relation (also called *meronymy*) as in *a windscreen/steering wheel/bumper, etc is part of a car*. Hyponymy is one of a number of ways in which words can be related by meaning, others being *synonymy* (same or similar meaning) and *antonymy* (opposite meaning). These kinds of sense relationships are useful in helping learners structure their mental *lexicon* (the way vocabulary is stored in the brain). It is, in theory, easier to retrieve a word like *vehicle* if it is already connected with its hyponyms *car* and *lorry*.

hypothetical meaning FUNCTION

Hypothetical meaning contrasts with *factual meaning*, and refers to situations that are assumed to be improbable or impossible. (Sometimes the term *counterfactual* is used to describe impossibility). For example:

factual:	I think it will snow.	[future]
	I think it's snowing.	[present]
	I think it snowed.	[past]
hypothetical:	I wish it would snow.	[future]
	I wish it was snowing.	[present]
	I wish it had snowed.	[past]

Hypothetical meaning is frequently expressed by **conditional** constructions: *If you were the only boy in the world and I was the only girl ....* Other ways of expressing hypothetical meaning (apart from *wish*) include the following:

- *it's time* + past tense: *It's time you had a haircut.*
- *(not) as if* + past tense: *It's not as if she was married to him.*
- *(Just) suppose* + past tense: *Just suppose you won the lottery ...*
- *if only* + past tense: *If only it was mine. If only you had phoned ...*
- *in your place* + past form of modal verb: *In your place I would've walked out.*
- *if I were you*: *If I were you I'd leave him.*
- *I'd rather*: *I'd rather you didn't tell Norma.*
- *should*: *If you should need me/Should you need me, here's my number.*

identity PSYCHOLOGY

One of the most important functions of language is as a marker of identity. Speakers make **accent** and **dialect** choices in order to identify themselves as belonging to particular socially and geographically defined groups. Likewise, the use of jargon or slang, or insider references to local 'in-group' culture, identify the speaker as being part of (or wanting to be part of) a particular *discourse community*. Hence, the degree to which a language learner identifies with speakers of the target language is likely to affect their **motivation** and contribute significantly to their success or failure. Similarly, their 'second-language identity' may either support or threaten their first language identity, and this in turn will affect their success. To complicate matters, it is now thought that identity is not a stable, unified entity. Instead, people construct multiple identities out of attributes of their gender, ethnicity, job, family relationship, etc, and these identities are in constant flux.

Issues of identity have only recently started to attract the attention of researchers. Previously, language learners were generally thought of as having no identity apart from being simply learners or non-native speakers. Yet identity issues may explain why some learners seem to resist 'losing their accent', or will not participate in groupwork, or even drop out of the language class altogether. Issues of identity are particularly acute in **English as a second language** contexts, where speakers may no longer identify with their original language group, and may not yet be accepted into the target language community. Teachers can help reduce the chances of this occurring by acknowledging and valuing their learners' identities, eg by incorporating into the content of their classes their learners' experiences, narratives, cultures, and even their languages.

idiom VOCABULARY

An idiom is a word sequence (usually a phrase or a clause) whose meaning is not literal, ie, it cannot easily be worked out from its individual words. Thus, when somebody calls your argument *a red herring*, they do not mean that your argument is 'a fish of the genus *Clupea* that is coloured red', but that it is irrelevant and distracting. Idioms are also formulaic (→ **formulaic language**) in that they are used and understood as if they were a single unit. You do not normally say 'your argument is a herring which is red', or 'your argument is a reddish herring' or 'the red herring of your argument is ...'. It is always *a red herring*. The degree of transparency of idioms can vary on a scale from the almost literal, as in the expression *to feel like a fish out of water* (meaning to feel awkward in unfamiliar surroundings), to the semi-literal, as in *to fish something out* (meaning to retrieve something), to the totally obscure, as in the case of *a red herring* or *a different kettle of fish*.

There are a number of ways of classifying idioms, according to both their form and function. The following are some of the more common types:

- metaphorical compounds/phrases: *a hot potato*; *a king's ransom*; *the tip of the iceberg*; *a lone wolf*
- restricted collocations (ie, **collocations** that are relatively fixed): *pitch black, breakneck speed, the bitter end, fat chance*
- **phrasal verbs**: *pick up* (eg *a language*); *get on* (*with somebody*)
- frozen similes: *as old as the hills*; *as easy as pie*
- *binomials* and *trinomials*: *kith and kin, spick and span*; *hook, line and sinker*; *lock, stock and barrel*
- proverbs and catchphrases: *waste not, want not*; *get a life!*
- euphemisms: *spend a penny*; *pass away*
- 'true' idioms (ie, fixed and non-literal 'turns of phrase'): *spill the beans*; *fly off the handle*; *let the cat out of the bag*

Idioms occur in certain contexts more frequently than others, being used more often in informal spoken than in formal written language, and often with an interpersonal function. Those written texts that do use a lot of idioms tend to be 'conversational' in tone, as in magazine horoscopes: [1]

---

[1] Dena's Life Stars, in *Take a Break*, 11 November 2004, p 34.

… family members may expect you to wait on them <u>hand and foot</u>, do all the chores, and even <u>cough up</u> money as if you were the local bank. <u>You know your trouble</u>? You're too soft. <u>Put your foot down</u> now, before the situation gets <u>out of hand</u>.

… Trying something different is <u>on the cards</u>. Just be careful not to <u>blot your copybook</u> on the 7th, a day when you could get <u>too big for your boots</u>.

Many learners enjoy acquiring idioms, since they convey a sophisticated, 'insider-like' knowledge of the target language (→ **idiomaticity**). But their 'frozen' and often informal nature makes using them a risky business. In the above text, consider the effect of getting the idioms slightly wrong:

… family members may expect you to wait on them <u>hand on foot</u>, do all the chores, and even <u>cough out</u> money as if you were the local bank. You know your trouble? You're too soft. <u>Put your feet down</u> now, before the situation gets <u>out of hands</u>.

idiomaticity LINGUISTICS

The word 'idiomaticity' comes from *idiomatic* and describes the extent to which a person's language sounds native-like. A sentence may be grammatically well-formed but not idiomatic. For example, in response to the question *What's the time?* the following are all grammatically well-formed: *It's six less twenty*; *It's two-thirds past five*; *It's forty past five*; *It's ten minutes after half past five*; *It's twenty to six*. But only one (the last one) is idiomatic, ie, it is what is actually *said*. The others lack *idiomaticity*. Idiomaticity is one of the 'puzzles' of linguistics. How is it that native-speakers select only a small proportion of the sentences that are theoretically available to them? It also presents an enormous challenge to learners: how are they to know which of the many different possible ways of expressing an idea is the idiomatic one? Recognition of both the formulaic and idiomatic nature of language has been a key influence on the development of the **lexical approach**, which foregrounds idiomaticity over grammaticality.

immersion SLA

An immersion programme is one in which children, as a group, are taught some or all of their school subjects in a language that is not their mother tongue. It is aimed at fostering **bilingualism**. In the Basque country in Spain, for example, children who speak Spanish as their first language receive primary education in Basque. *Total immersion* describes the situation when all curriculum subjects are taught in the second language; immersion is *partial* when only some subjects are taught in this way. Immersion should be distinguished from *submersion*, which is what happens when individuals (rather than groups) who speak one language are placed in a situation in which their education is mediated using another. This is often the case with the children of immigrants. Immersion programmes originated in Canada in the 1960s, where English-speaking children took their school subjects in French. These programmes have been extensively studied. Results show that, in general, immersion education is not prejudicial, either to the ongoing development of the pupils' first language, or to their overall academic performance. Moreover, they achieve a near-native level of understanding of the second language, although, in production, their grammatical accuracy falls short of native speakers. The earlier and the more total the immersion, the better the results overall.

imperative GRAMMAR

The imperative in English takes the base form of the verb, ie, the form that is not inflected for **tense** or **person**, such as *enter, be, sit down*, etc. The negative imperative is formed by placing *do not (don't)* before the base form: *Do not enter, Don't be silly*, etc. A positive imperative can be emphasized using *do: Do sit down.* Imperative sentences normally have no overt subjects: *you* is implied, and may sometimes be added, either as a *tag: Sit down, won't you?* or for emphasis: *You be quiet! You take that end and I'll take this end.* Third person subjects are also possible: *Nobody move! Somebody open the door.* English does not have a first person plural imperative form but the meaning can be expressed by using *let* followed by an object pronoun: *Let's (= Let us) go out for dinner.* This is a common way of making **suggestions**.

Imperative sentences are used as *directives*, ie, to get people to do things. They are therefore common in instructions and directions (*Remove contents from tin and boil for 2–3 minutes. Take the A train, and get out at Harlem*), in requests (*Give me a hand. Wait for me*), and in making offers (*Have a chocolate. Help yourself*). However, 'bald' imperatives can be *face-threatening*, especially if used when interacting with strangers. More indirect forms of directives are normally preferred, ie, *Would you mind opening the window?* rather than *Open the window!* Thus, while imperatives are relatively easy to teach – in terms of their form – learners need clear guidance about the kinds of contexts in which they are appropriate. Giving and responding to commands and directions, through the use of techniques such as those associated with **Total Physical Response**, is a good way of practising the use of imperatives.

indefinite article → **article**

indirect speech → **reported speech**

individual learner differences PSYCHOLOGY

As most teachers know, individual learners are different, with very different learning styles, abilities, needs and drives. This is reflected in differences in the rate at which learners learn, and in their eventual levels of attainment. The study of individual differences aims to describe and explain these disparities. The key factors are often grouped into *biological factors*, such as **age** and gender; *personality factors*, such as confidence and self-esteem; *cognitive factors*, such as **aptitude**, **learning style** and **memory**; and *affective* (ie, emotional) *factors*, such as **motivation** and anxiety. (You can find more information about these factors under separate entries.) One of the outcomes of this research has been the development of **learner training** procedures, which target those factors that are susceptible to change and improvement. These include the learner's use of **learning strategies**, or techniques for improving memory. Another way of responding to the fact that learners are all different has been in the *individualization* of learning, through, for example, **one-to-one teaching**, and the use of **self-access centres**. Teachers who don't have access to such options can nevertheless still cater for individual differences by adopting an **eclectic** approach (→ **eclecticism**), in which they vary the activities and materials they use in the classroom, and by changing the focus from individual, to pair and group, to whole class work, as appropriate.

inductive learning, induction PSYCHOLOGY

Induction is the process of working out rules on the basis of examples. It is also called *discovery learning*. It contrasts with **deductive learning**, in which learners are presented with rules which they then go on to apply. Because inductive learning is thought to be the way that the rules of one's first language are internalized, it has been a core principle in such 'natural' methods as the **direct method** and **audiolingualism**. More recently, the use of inductive procedures to work out rules from data has been promoted as a means of **consciousness-raising**. It is thought that the mental effort invested by learners in working out rules for themselves pays dividends in terms of the long-term memory of these rules. In an inductive approach, learners might be given successive examples of a grammar item (or two contrasted items), and then be challenged to work out a rule for the use of the item(s). For example, to help learners work out the difference between *for* and *since*, they are given these examples:

1. I have been here <u>since six o'clock</u>.
2. Tom and Anna have been married <u>for six years.</u>
3. It hasn't rained <u>since last September.</u>
4. I've been waiting <u>for nearly an hour.</u>
5. We last met at a conference but I haven't seen her <u>since then</u>.
… etc.

At various points, learners can be asked to formulate a rule. Or they can complete further examples in order to test their grasp of the rule.

So as to speed up the process of hypothesis formation, and to steer learners away from making a wrong hypothesis, the teacher can guide the learners by asking leading questions, such as *Is 'six o'clock' a point in time, or a period of time?* (→ **concept questions**). This approach, where the teacher or the materials writer intervenes in the induction process, is called *guided discovery*. The rules themselves can be left unstated (in which case, the approach is an *implicit* one). Or, by asking learners to state the rules, they can be made *explicit*. One advantage of an inductive approach over a deductive one is that it can help develop learners' capacity for autonomous learning. Also, the rules are more likely to 'stick' if they have required mental effort. On the other hand, there is a risk that learners might formulate the wrong rule. This is one reason for asking them to state their rule. Also, inductive approaches tend to favour learners who like working out language puzzles, as opposed to those who prefer simply to be told (→ **learning style**). Many learning materials for classroom use encourage an inductive approach to grammar learning, on the assumption that teachers are present to guide the process. But those designed for self-study – such as self-study grammars – usually adopt a deductive approach.

infinitive GRAMMAR

The infinitive is the form of the verb that consists of the infinitive marker *to* and the base form of the verb, as in *to be, to work, to take*. The form without *to* is called the *bare infinitive*: it is the form that, for example, follows **modal verbs**: *You must* *be prepared. It might <u>work</u>.* Like the **participle**, the infinitive is a *non-finite* form of the verb: it is not marked for **person**, nor does it have any **tense** (→ **finite verb**). However, infinitives can be marked for **aspect** and **voice**, as this table shows:

	active	passive
	(to) take	(to) be taken
present progressive	(to) be taking	(to) be being taken⋆
perfect	(to) have taken	(to) have been taken
perfect progressive	(to) have been taking	(to) to have been being taken⋆

(The forms marked with an asterisk are very rare, but are theoretically possible: *Where's my shirt? ~ It must <u>be being washed</u>. Why did you run? ~ I might <u>have been being followed</u>*).

The main uses of the infinitive are:

- (bare infinitive) to follow modal auxiliaries: *Can you <u>drive</u>? I won't <u>be using</u> the computer this afternoon.*
- (bare infinitive) to follow verbs like *help, make, let*: *You made me <u>love</u> you. Can you help me <u>put</u> the toys away?*
- (bare infinitive) after verbs of perception: *I saw someone <u>enter</u> by the side door. I thought I heard a seal <u>bark</u>.*
- (*to*-infinitive) after many verbs, including *reporting verbs*, to form an *infinitive construction*; these can be verbs with or without an object: *She offered <u>to help</u>. I advise you <u>to re-think</u>. I hope <u>to see</u> you soon. Did you remember <u>to book</u>? She wants your boss <u>to phone</u>. Can you ask Dan <u>to take</u> over?*
- (*to*-infinitive) after some nouns: *That's a strange thing <u>to have done</u>. It's time <u>to be going</u>. This is the way <u>to do</u> it.*
- (*to*-infinitive) after some adjectives: *I'm sorry <u>to hear</u> you're leaving. He's afraid <u>to stay</u> here alone.*
- (*to*-infinitive) after *wh-words*: *We don't know where <u>to have</u> lunch. Did she remember what <u>to do</u>?*
- (*to*-infinitive) to express purpose (also called the *infinitive of purpose*): *I'm writing <u>to ask</u> about the job. We stopped <u>to have</u> lunch.*
- (*to*-infinitive) as the subject of a sentence: *<u>To err</u> is human; <u>to forgive</u> divine.*
- (*to*-infinitive) after constructions beginning *it* + linking verb + adjective: *It's easy <u>to forget</u> how hard it is. It was nice <u>to sit</u> down. It is not unusual <u>to see</u> two turtledoves together.*

A *split infinitive* is an infinitive construction in which the *to* particle and the base form are separated by an adverb, as in *to boldly go*. Some people consider this bad style, and prefer either *boldly to go* or *to go boldly*.

inflection → **word family**; → **word formation**

informal language → **formal language**

information, exchanging FUNCTION

Exchanging information is one of the key **functions** of language. Language that is used in this way is called *transactional* language. It is typically performed by the asking of **questions** (also called interrogatives) and by answering with statements (called **declaratives**), which may be either positive or negative:

Does the 73 stop here?
No. It stops on the other side of the road.

Teaching learners how to ask for and give information is a core component of most syllabuses, right from the outset. It is especially important for learners who are studying in the target language context, either as temporary visitors or long-term stayers. Common situations for introducing and practising the language of information exchange are: in bureaucratic situations such as at passport control on arrival, or when applying for a bank account, a job, a course of study, or seeking accommodation; in social contexts such as meeting someone for the first time; and for utilitarian purposes, such as making travel enquiries. Popular activities for practising this function include **dialogues** and information gap activities (→ **communicative activity**).

information gap activity → **communicative activity**

-ing **form** GRAMMAR

The -*ing* form is formed by adding the -*ing* suffix to the base form of the verb (and making any necessary spelling adjustments), as *walk* ⇨ *walking*, *smoke* ⇨ *smoking*, *stop* ⇨ *stopping*, *travel* ⇨ *traveling/travelling*. There are some -*ing* words that have no related verb, but instead are formed from nouns or adjectives, and 'verbalized' through the addition of -*ing*: eg *neighbouring*, *balding*, *enterprising*, and *appetizing*. All -*ing* forms express a sense of ongoing activity.

The -*ing* form is the term that is now generally used to describe (1) what are also called *present participles*, as in *Who is <u>smoking</u>?*, or *a <u>smoking</u> gun*, where *smoking* has properties of both verbs and adjectives (→ **participle**), and (2) what were once called *gerunds* (as in <u>*Smoking* is bad for you</u>; *No <u>smoking</u>*), where *smoking* is more noun-like. (The term *gerund* may still be found in some grammars and coursebooks.) The reason for collapsing the participle–gerund distinction is that there are many instances of -*ing* forms that do not fit comfortably into either of these two categories. It is perhaps more accurate to think of -*ing* forms as covering a spectrum of meaning from the purely noun-like to the purely verb-like. For example:[2]

NOUN   *A painting of Brown's ...*

The painting of Brown is as skilful as that of Gainsborough.

Brown's deft painting of his daughter is a delight to watch.

I dislike Brown's painting his daughter.

I dislike Brown painting his daughter.

I watched Brown painting his daughter.

The silently painting man is Brown.

VERB   *He is painting his daughter.*

---

[2] examples from Quirk, R. and Greenbaum, S. 1973 *A University Grammar of English.* (Longman)

Likewise, -*ing* forms that precede nouns can be either noun-like, as in *a swimming pool* (a pool for swimming) or verb-like, as in *a swimming dog* (a dog which is swimming). And there are words that end in -*ing* that are really adjectives, since they can be qualified with *very* or *extremely*, and with *more/less*: *a very boring talk*; *an extremely appetizing meal*; *The book was more interesting than the film*.

The -*ing* form is used in the following ways:

- as a noun, with a **determiner**: *Have you done the shopping? Your writing has improved.*
- as an **adjective**: *a flying visit; the falling snow; your loving nephew.*
- as a **conjunction**: *Providing that you don't make any noise …. Supposing it rains?*
- as a **preposition**: *Regarding your offer…. They were all there, including her father.*
- as the verb in a non-finite (participle) **clause**:
  - as the subject, object, or complement of a clause: *Seeing is believing. Eating people is wrong.*
  - after *it* + *to be* adjective constructions: *It's funny seeing yourself on TV. It was awful not knowing.*
  - after certain verbs, such as many verbs expressing likes and dislikes: *I enjoy watching tennis.* Also: *He's given up smoking. They denied doing it. Jim doesn't remember being there.*
  - after some adjectives: *That book's not worth reading. Fred was busy doing the ironing.*
  - after prepositions: *Oil is used for cooking. The talk was about teaching children.*
  - as an **adverbial** clause: *Laughing to herself, she left the room. You can see better standing.*
  - as a way of modifying the noun: *The woman sitting on her own is my Aunt Vera. A lorry carrying bananas turned over. There is someone waving at you.*
  - after verbs of perception plus an object: *I heard someone shouting. We watched the seals being fed.*
- as a **participle** in complex verb phrases: *Alice is staying with her mother. Someone was playing the violin. How long have you been waiting?*

initiate–respond–follow-up (IRF) → **display question**

input SLA

Input is the spoken or written language that learners are exposed to. You cannot learn a language without input. Less clear is whether input alone is enough, and what sort of input is best. In his *input hypothesis*, the linguist Stephen Krashen argues that input is *all* that is necessary for **language acquisition** to take place. But, he adds, the input must be comprehensible, and it must contain grammatical forms that are one step more advanced than the current state of the learner's **interlanguage**. This level is represented by the formula '$i + 1$' ($= input + 1$). According to Krashen, this 'roughly-tuned' input is enough to kick-start the learner's internal acquisition processes, so that no overt teaching – of grammar, for example – is required. One way the teacher can help, though, is to control or modify the input to ensure that it is intelligible. People do this naturally, when, for example, they talk to young children (using what is called *caretaker speech*) and when talking to learners (*foreigner speech*). In both cases, the input is often simplified, delivered at a slower pace, and more elaborated (ie, less is omitted). Researchers have suggested that these modifications may assist interlanguage development. Others, like Michael Long, argue that input is most effective when it has been made comprehensible through *negotiation of meaning*. Learners negotiate meaning when, for example, they ask questions in order to sort out a misunderstanding or a gap in their knowledge (→ **interaction**).

It does seem that, if input is to become more than simply 'noise', it needs to be attended to. According to **cognitive learning theory**, this conscious process of **noticing** features of the input results in *intake*. Intake is that part of the input that is taken into short-term memory, the first step in the process of accommodating it into the learner's developing interlanguage system. Ways of helping learners notice features of the input (so that it becomes intake) are known generally as **consciousness-raising** (CR) techniques. These include *input enhancement*. This is when a grammar feature is highlighted in some way, eg by being printed in a different font or by being underlined. Another CR technique is called *input flood*. This is when the grammar feature is repeated many times in a text. Both input enhancement and input flood suggest there is a place in the language class for texts that are artificially modified, ie, not authentic (→ **authenticity**). The input–output model of language learning has been criticized as being somewhat mechanistic, and of taking no account of contextual factors apart from linguistic ones. An alternative view of how the learner's environment influences acquisition is captured in the concept of **affordances**.

instructions, classroom METHODOLOGY

Instructions are the main way that teachers manage classroom learning (→ **classroom management**). They are usually verbal, although sometimes the instructions can be written on the board (→ **rubric**). The instructions for a classroom **activity**, such as a communicative **task** or a **game**, will normally include at least some of the following features:

- a *frame*, ie, a way of indicating that the last activity has finished and a new activity is about to begin. Typically this takes a verbal form, such as 'Right …', 'OK, now …'
- a brief *summary* of the task and its purpose, such as 'We're going to play a game to practise asking questions …'
- the *organization*, ie, whether the task is to be done in pairs, groups, or individually (→ **pairwork**; → **groupwork**)
- the *procedure*, ie, what it is that the learners actually will be doing, such as filling in a questionnaire, or rehearsing a dialogue, etc
- the *mode*, ie, whether it is a speaking or a writing task, for example
- the *outcome*, ie, what they will be required to do as a result of the task, eg report their results to the class, perform the dialogue, etc
- a *strategy* to adopt in order to facilitate the task, as when the teacher tells learners just to skim a text, initially, before reading it intensively
- the *timing*, ie, how long the learners have to complete the task (roughly)
- a *cue*, such as 'OK, you can start', so that learners know when they should begin the task

instructions, giving FUNCTION

Instructions have a *directive* function, and are typically realized using the **imperative**. Instructions often take the form of sequences of imperative sentences, connected with **linkers**, such as *first, next, then, finally*. They often involve the use of prepositions of place, as well. Text types whose function is to give instructions include: instruction manuals, recipes, street directions and the rules of games, eg board or card games. A good way of practising instructions in class is through the use of techniques borrowed from **Total Physical Response**, where learners perform physical instructions given by the teacher.

intake → **input**

intelligibility PHONOLOGY

If you are intelligible, other people can understand what you are saying. In the teaching of **pronunciation**, it is generally accepted that intelligibility should be the standard to aim for. This is partly realistic: few adult learners of a second language will achieve native-like pronunciation in that language. One of the factors that affect intelligibility is the speaker's **accent**. The accent is formed by the way the speaker pronounces individual sounds (or **phonemes**), and the way these are combined in order to produce **connected speech**. Generally speaking, the *suprasegmental* features of a speaker's accent – ie, their **rhythm**, **stress**, and **intonation** – have a greater impact on intelligibility than the *segmental* features, such as the pronunciation of individual sounds. Thus, a speaker can mispronounce individual vowel and consonant sounds, but still be largely intelligible so long as the stress is correctly placed on the appropriate syllables and words. Nowadays the notion of intelligibility has been adjusted to take into account the fact that most learners of English are more likely to be interacting, not with native, but with non-native speakers (→ **English as an international language**). What is of interest, therefore, is less the speaker's intelligibility according to native-speaker standards, but how intelligible they are to other non-native speakers. Research into this area has produced a set of features – known as the **phonological core** – that are crucial in affecting intelligibility. This core, it is argued, offers a more realistic goal for those learners who need to be intelligible in an international context. It should be remembered, however, that it is not an accent that is intelligible or unintelligible: it is the speaker. Successful communicators can make themselves intelligible despite having a strong accent. They can do this by using **communication strategies**, for example, including knowing how to recognize and **repair** communication failure.

intensifier GRAMMAR

Intensifiers are words like *very, rather, absolutely*, that modify adjectives, adverbs and verbs by heightening or lowering their intensity: *How was the film? ~ It was rather/quite /extremely/totally boring. I kind of/really/absolutely hated it.* In informal speech, some prefixes, like *super-*, and *mega-*, function as intensifiers, too: *The film was mega-boring.* Intensifiers are particularly common in spoken language, and they fulfil an *interpersonal function*, ie, they signal high involvement on the part of the speaker (→ **appraisal**).

intention, expressing → **plans and intentions**

interaction SLA

Interaction occurs when learners communicate with one another, or with their teacher, or with other speakers of the target language. All three kinds of interaction have been researched, with a view to finding out whether interaction promotes language learning, and, if so, how. Learner–learner interaction, where learners engage with each other to perform **communicative activities** such as **tasks**, is a defining feature of the **communicative approach**. Arguments for learner–learner interaction include the fact that it increases opportunities for language practice, that it promotes good group **dynamics**, and that it is a step towards learner **autonomy**. Indeed, some early proponents of the communicative approach (such as Dick Allwright) argued that small-group interaction, where learners solve tasks using language, was all that was needed to promote language acquisition. The evidence to support this view has been mixed, however. While some studies show that **pairwork** and **groupwork** produce more, and richer, language than is the case with teacher-led interaction, other researchers have been less enthusiastic. Often, it seems, learners do not push themselves in groupwork, resorting to the use of **communication strategies** or even their mother tongue. The quality of interaction seems to depend quite a lot on the nature of the task, including its structure and outcomes.

Michael Long's *interaction hypothesis* claims that tasks that promote *negotiation of meaning* are beneficial. This is because exchanges where learners jointly resolve a communication problem provide a source of *comprehensible input*. Long subscribes to Krashen's view that comprehensible input is necessary for language acquisition (→ **input**). But, unlike Krashen, Long argues for the need for interaction, primarily because it is a site for negotiating meaning. The interactional modifications that are involved in negotiating meaning are known as *discourse repair strategies* (→ **repair**). However, some researchers have found that learners are often reluctant to negotiate meaning when confronted with a communication problem. Instead, they prefer to adopt a 'wait and see' policy. Nor has it been convincingly demonstrated that such exchanges do in fact provide the 'raw material' for language acquisition.

Teacher–learner interaction has also been the subject of study. Researchers have compared teacher–learner interaction with the kind of interaction that occurs in non-classroom contexts, such as between parents and children, or between social equals. Traditionally, teacher–learner exchanges are teacher-led and consist of sequences of **display questions**. Some researchers now argue that such interactions may not provide the best language environment for learning. According to **sociocultural learning theory**, learning opportunities arise where interaction is more 'conversational'. This theory suggests that learners should be given more control over the direction of the discourse and the choice of topic, and that the teacher's role should be more facilitative (→ **facilitation**). This includes providing the interactional support (or **scaffolding**), within which the learner feels safe enough to take risks. Interactions of this type are aimed at instruction, but they also reflect many features of naturally occurring talk. Hence they have been called *instructional conversations*.

intercultural competence → **culture**

interference → **transfer**

interlanguage SLA

Interlanguage is the term used to describe the grammatical system that a learner creates in the course of learning another language. It is neither their first language system, nor the target language system, but occupies a transitional point between the two. This interlanguage is seen as an independent system in its own right, and not simply a degenerate form of the target language. It reflects the learner's evolving system of rules. Some of these rules may be influenced by the first language (through **transfer**), others by the target language, while others are attributed to innate and universal principles (→ **universal grammar**). One way that interlanguages show that they are systematic is that they follow predictable stages, no matter what the learner's first language is (→ **order of acquisition**). At a very early stage, interlanguage takes on the form that has been called the *basic learner variety*. This is characterized by very basic **syntax** and few if any grammatical word endings (*inflections*). Interlanguages are constantly evolving. When they stop doing so, they stabilize, or even fossilize, at a point some way from the target (→ **fossilization**). As it happens, very few second language learners achieve native-like proficiency. This is an argument for recognizing the legitimacy of interlanguage, and for accepting that *partial competence*, rather than full competence, is a valid objective in second language learning.

intermediate learner METHODOLOGY

Intermediate learners are those who are no longer **beginners**, but not yet **advanced**. Often divided up into pre- (or lower) intermediate, mid- and upper-immediate, this broad band corresponds with levels B1 and B2 of the **Common European Framework**. [3] The CEF descriptor for B1 is a good summary of what a learner at this level can achieve:

> Can understand the main points of clear standard input on familiar matters regularly encountered in work, school, leisure, etc. Can deal with most situations likely to arise whilst travelling in an area where the language is spoken. Can produce simple connected text on topics which are familiar or of personal interest. Can describe experiences and events, dreams, hopes and ambitions and briefly give reasons and explanations for opinions and plans.

Passing an **examination** like Cambridge First Certificate in English (FCE) is considered a form of graduation from the intermediate level into advanced. However, for many intermediate learners, this goal seems impossibly remote. The sensation of being trapped on what is called the *intermediate plateau* can be very demotivating. Likewise, many teachers are frustrated by the apparent inability of intermediate learners to achieve an acceptable level of either **fluency** or **accuracy**. One response is to concentrate on the latter, in the belief that grammatical accuracy is a prerequisite for fluency. A great deal of time, therefore, might be spent reviewing previously taught structures. A less demotivating approach might be to equip intermediate learners with the means to experience fluency (often for the first time) by concentrating on vocabulary teaching,

---

[3] *Common European Framework of Reference for Languages: Learning, Teaching, Assessment*, Council of Europe, 2001, p 24.

including the teaching of **formulaic language**. It has been calculated that learners need a critical mass of about 3000 **word families** in order to break through the intermediate ceiling. At the same time, learners can be given opportunities to use this language in real communication, and without the threat of constant correction.

internet → **computer-mediated communication**

interrogative → **question**

intonation PHONOLOGY

Intonation has been called the 'music' of speech. It is the meaningful use that speakers make of changes in their voice pitch. Intonation is a *suprasegmental* feature of pronunciation, meaning that it is a property of whole stretches of speech rather than of individual segments (such as **phonemes**). It is inseparably linked to other suprasegmental features of pronunciation such as **stress**, **rhythm**, pausing and speech rate. In combination these are called the *prosody* of speech. The basic unit of intonation is the *tone unit* (also called *tone group*), which centers on a *nucleus*. The nucleus is the most prominent syllable in the tone unit, due to the fact that it is here where there is a major pitch change. Changes in pitch direction are usually described in terms of rising and falling *tones*. Particular configurations of these tones are called *intonation contours*. Thus, the following sentence is usually spoken as two tone units, with a change in pitch direction (marked by an arrow) on each nucleus (the words in block capitals):

It's not ↑ WHAT you know | it's ↑ WHO you know.

The contour for each tone unit can be illustrated like this:

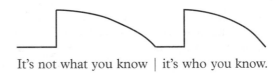

It's not what you know | it's who you know.

Many theories have been advanced as to the function of intonation, and the kinds of meanings it expresses. The main candidates are:

* *grammatical function*, such as indicating the difference between statements and questions
* *attitudinal function*, such as indicating interest, surprise, boredom, and so on – what is called high and low *involvement*
* *discoursal function*, such as contrasting new information with information that is already known, and hence shared between speakers

Current theories tend to favour the last of these, with intonation functioning primarily as a means for speakers to achieve **coherence** over stretches of talk. According to this view, intonation is a property of connected **discourse** rather than of isolated sentences or grammatical structures. It serves both to separate the stream of speech into blocks of information (the tone units), and to mark information within these units as being significant. In English, there is a strong association between high pitch and new information. So, within each tone unit, information that is being added to the discourse is made prominent through the use of a step up in pitch. Intonation also serves to signal the connections *between* tone units. Typically, a rise in pitch at the end of the tone unit (that is, after the last stressed word) implies some kind of continuation; a fall in pitch suggests completion. Likewise, an utterance that begins on a *high key* (ie, it starts high), implies a contrast in attitude with respect to the preceding utterance. Conversely, *low key* is used when the speaker is adding something that is obvious or by the way (what in written language would be enclosed in brackets). *Mid-key* implies no marked change in attitude.

Even from this brief description it should be obvious that intonation is difficult to pin down. This has implications in terms of teaching. Any attempt to 'explain' intonation is likely to fall on deaf ears – almost literally, since it is very hard for non-experts to distinguish rises from falls, and fall-rises from rise-falls. It is even harder to make sense of intonation when its features are removed from their contexts of use. Traditional 'rules', such as: 'use a rising intonation in yes/no questions, and falling intonation in *wh*-questions' are, at best, rules of thumb. Moreover, intonation, like other **paralinguistic** features of language, seems to be a system that is best acquired through exposure rather than learned through formal study.

intransitive → **transitivity**

introvert/extrovert → **learning style**

inversion GRAMMAR

Inversion happens when two grammatical elements are reversed. Inversion of the **subject** and the **auxiliary verb** is the main way of forming **questions** in English: *Kim is having lunch.* ⇨ *Is Kim having lunch? You have been there.* ⇨ *Have you been there?* Less commonly, inversion also occurs in these cases:

- after adverbial expressions of place: *Here comes the judge. Under the bridge lived a wicked troll.*
- when reporting direct speech: *'You're late,' said Terry. 'I'm sorry,' replied Robin.*
- after certain negative expressions: *Seldom have I been so angry. Never before had so many people taken to the streets.*
- as a substitute for *if*: *Had I known, I would have phoned. Were he to phone, I would soon know.*
- after *(not) only* …: *Only then did I understand. Not only was she late, but she had forgotten her book.*

(These last three uses are rather literary.)

inviting, accepting and refusing FUNCTION

The function of inviting is an interpersonal one. It can be realized in a number of ways, depending on the degree of formality, and whether the invitation is spoken or written. In speech, the invitation is usually prefaced by an opening move, such as:

Are you doing anything later on?
Are you free on Friday?
What are you doing this evening?

The invitation itself then follows. For example:

spoken or written (from informal to formal)	written only (formal)
Come round and have a bite to eat. *Do you fancy a meal?* *How would you like to come and have dinner with us?* *Would you like to come to dinner?* *Maybe you'd be interested in joining us for dinner?* *I'd like to invite you and Kim to dinner.*	*It would give us great pleasure if you and your partner would be free to dine with us on Friday night.* *Mr and Mrs Evan Jenkins request the pleasure of the company of Mr Sam Hayes on the occasion of Thanksgiving.*

Accepting requires less 'work' than refusing, since accepting presents no threat to face (→ **politeness**).

> *Thanks, I'd love to.* (= spoken)
> *Thank you for your kind invitation. We are delighted to be able to accept.* (= written, formal)

Refusing *is* threatening, so, rather than saying *no* outright, the person refusing usually notionally accepts, then apologizes, then gives an excuse:

> *Oh, thank you very much. That would be really nice, but I'm afraid I can't. I've arranged to …*

The language of inviting is usually taught early on, since it is very useful. Although it can require the use of **modal verbs** and **conditional** constructions, teaching these as grammar items can be avoided by teaching the expressions as social formulae (→ **formulaic language**).

irregular verb → **verb**

---

jigsaw techniques → **communicative activity**

juncture → **connected speech**

KET (Key English Test) → **examination**

key → **intonation**

keyword DISCOURSE

A keyword is a word in a text that occurs significantly frequently in that text. In other words, it appears in the text much more often than might be predicted on the basis of its **frequency** in a large **corpus** of texts. As an example, the word *text(s)* has occurred five times in this present paragraph (in the space of around 50 words). This is out of all proportion to its relative frequency in the British

National Corpus, for example, where it is recorded as being the 1007th most frequent word. *Text*, then, is a keyword in this text. This means, among other things, that the text is probably *about* text: keywords are a good indication as to a text's topic. Keywords are also the words that learners will most need in order to get the gist of a text, so they are good candidates for pre-teaching. Some software programs that are used for searching corpora come with a keyword program, which will quickly identify the keywords in a text.

keyword technique → **memorization**

kinesthetic learner → **learning style**

Krashen, Stephen → **input**; → **language acquisition**

L

L1 → **first language**

L2 → **second language**

language acquisition SLA

The terms *acquisition* and *learning* are used interchangeably by some writers. Others follow Stephen Krashen's distinction: *acquisition* means the non-conscious and 'natural' process of internalizing the rules of a language, as in first language acquisition. This is what is popularly called 'picking up a language'. On the other hand, *learning* involves conscious, usually classroom, study, including attending to rules of grammar. Krashen argues that **first language acquisition** and **second language acquisition** (SLA) are essentially the same process. More controversially, he goes on to claim that second (or third, fourth, etc) languages can *only* be acquired. According to Krashen, learning plays no part in the process. The only value of learning rules is that you can use these to check (or **monitor** (→ **monitoring**)) your output and make last minute corrections. Krashen claims that learners simply need exposure to comprehensible **input**, in conditions of low anxiety, and they will construct a mental grammar of the language 'naturally' by a process called *creative construction*. The claim that acquisition and learning are separate, independent processes, that do not influence one another, is called the *no-interface position*. Most researchers reject it. But the distinction between natural, non-instructed learning ('acquisition') and instructed learning is a necessary one. There are many second language users (and not only children) who have achieved impressive levels of skill without any formal instruction. How they have done this is of enormous interest to researchers and teachers alike.

language acquisition device (LAD) → **first language acquisition**; → **mentalism**; **universal grammar**

language analysis LINGUISTICS

Language analysis is the study of the systems of a language, such as **grammar** and **phonology**, for the purposes of teaching the language. Courses to prepare teachers of EFL (**English as a foreign language**), for example, usually include a language analysis component. Typical topic areas are **tense**, **modality**, **vocabulary**, **discourse analysis**, **phonemes**, **stress** and **intonation**. Typical tasks include identifying and explaining features of grammar in samples of language, analysing learners' errors, and identifying the linguistic content of EFL materials.

language awareness LINGUISTICS

Language awareness is a teacher's or learner's explicit knowledge about language, often gained through **language analysis**. It includes not only knowledge of the systems of the subject language, such as its **grammar** and **phonology**, but also knowledge of its social and cultural role. Language awareness of English, for example, includes knowing how its standard and non-standard forms differ, and how different **registers** of English are used in different contexts. Language awareness for teachers can also extend to knowledge about the language (or languages) of their learners. Language awareness helps inform the design and choice of materials, syllabuses, classroom teaching methods, and tests. It is also a professional responsibility of language teachers: the minimum expectation of most learners is that their teacher will know something about the language that they are being taught, rather than simply being able to speak it.

language instinct → **first language acquisition**

language laboratory → **drill**

language play LINGUISTICS

Language is often regarded as simply a vehicle for communicating information. This rather utilitarian view ignores a universal tendency to play with language simply for the fun of it. Puns, riddles, jokes, 'nonce words' (ie, one-off word inventions), expressions of endearment, the words of many pop songs (such as *Awopbopaloobop alopbamboom!*), all exhibit the creative use of language for purposes that are not simply informative. It has been argued (eg by Guy Cook) that the repetitive, playful manipulation of sounds, words and sentences, in the form of tickling rhymes, nursery rhymes, and playground chants, plays an important role in the development of child language. Consider this example:

> *Diddle diddle dumpling my son John*
> *Went to bed with his trousers on*
> *One shoe off, and the other shoe on,*
> *Diddle diddle dumpling my son John*

The fact that the rhyme makes no real sense as a story has not bothered generations of children. This suggests that it fulfils a different kind of purpose, one that is less concerned with language *meanings*, rather than with language *forms*. Writers, like Cook, argue that this playful use of language, and especially the creative manipulation of forms, may also serve a useful function in *second* language learning. They believe that the communicative emphasis on teaching purely functional language (such as asking for information, making requests, etc), on using only **authentic** language data (→ **authenticity**), and on learning through the performance of language **tasks**, has meant that the playful element in learning has been neglected. Ways of restoring a playful element might include focusing on the more creative use of language, the inclusion of more literary texts, and the greater use of **repetition**, **memorization**, and recitation as aids to learning. In other words, less work, more play, makes Jack a good learner.

learner autonomy → **autonomy**; → **learner training**

learner-centred instruction, learner-centredness METHODOLOGY

Learner-centred instruction aims to give learners more say in areas that are traditionally considered the domain of the teacher or of the institution. Learner-centred instruction is true to the spirit of progressive education, including the movement towards providing learners with greater **autonomy**. For example, a learner-centred **curriculum** would involve learners in negotiating decisions relating to the choice of syllabus content, of materials, of activity-types, and of assessment procedures. Learner-centredness also describes ways of organizing **classroom interaction** so that the focus is directed away from the teacher, and on to the learners, who perform tasks in pairs or small groups. This contrasts with traditional, teacher-centred, classroom interaction. Some writers believe that the dichotomy between learner-centred (= good) and teacher-centred (= bad) is a false one. It might be more useful to talk about *learning-centred instruction*, ie, instruction which prioritizes sound learning principles. In a learning-centred approach there would be room for both learner-centred *and* teacher-centred interactions.

learner training METHODOLOGY

The aim of learner training is to help learners make the most of the learning opportunities that are available to them. In the long term, it is directed at achieving **autonomy** in language learning. Learner training techniques originated in research into the kinds of **learning strategies** used by successful language learners. Typical learner training procedures include: having learners complete questionnaires designed to help them identify their own **learning style**; showing learners how to get the most out of available resources, such as dictionaries and grammar books; training them in effective reading and listening strategies; and experimenting with techniques to aid **memorization**. Learner training can be programmed as a separate component of a course, or, more usually, it is integrated into lesson content. Most coursebooks, for example, now include sections devoted to raising learners' awareness about effective learning strategies.

learning strategy PSYCHOLOGY

Learning strategies are techniques or behaviours that learners consciously apply in order to enhance their learning. For example, while reading, learners may look up and record new words for later review. They may even do this in a way that helps memorization, eg by writing a translation or a synonym alongside. But simply looking the words up without recording them is less a learning strategy than a reading strategy. It becomes a learning strategy when the intention is long-term learning rather than solely immediate understanding. Interest in identifying learning strategies grew out of research into how successful learners learn (the *good language learner studies*). Some of the characteristics of good learners include:

- actively seeking out real-life opportunities to use the L2
- not being afraid of appearing foolish in using the L2
- paying attention to the formal properties of the L2 (such as tense endings)
- monitoring their own performance in the L2 and trying to learn from their errors
- making intelligent guesses, eg about unfamiliar words

Learning strategies are often grouped according to whether they are *cognitive strategies*, *metacognitive strategies* or *social/affective strategies*. Cognitive strategies are those that are linked to the way learners process data and perform specific tasks in the target language. For example, when learners repeat, under their breath, what they have just heard, they are using an effective cognitive strategy called *sub-vocalization*. Metacognitive strategies are those that are used to regulate and manage learning in general, such as this example, reported by one learner: 'I sit in front of the class so I can see the teacher's face clearly'.[1] Reflecting on the learning process is also a metacognitive strategy: this may take the form of keeping a language-learning journal (→ **reflection**). Social strategies are those that learners use in order to interact with other learners or native speakers, such as asking for repetition or clarification. Affective strategies are those that they use to give themselves encouragement and to deal with anxiety (→ **affect**). Observed learning strategies form the basis for many of the recommendations made in **learner training** activities. But this raises the question as to how generalizable such strategies are: what may work for one learner may not be effective for another. A less prescriptive approach might be to offer learners a 'menu' of learner strategies and invite them to experiment until they find the ones that best suit them.

learning style PSYCHOLOGY

Your learning style is your preferred way of learning. This style may be influenced by biographical factors (such as how you were taught as a child) or by innately endowed factors (such as whether you have a 'good ear' for different sounds). Types of learning style are often presented in the form of polarities (some of which may overlap), such as

- analytic versus global (or holistic) thinkers, ie, learners who tend to focus on the details, versus learners who tend to see 'the big picture'
- rule-users versus data-gatherers, ie, learners who learn and apply rules, versus those who prefer exposure to lots of examples
- reflective versus impulsive learners
- group-oriented versus solitary learners
- extrovert versus introverted learners
- verbal versus visual learners
- passive versus active learners

Attempts have been made to group these polarities and relate them to brain lateralization. So, a bias towards left-brain processing correlates with analytic, rule-forming and verbal learners, while a bias towards right-brain processing correlates with their opposite. A less binary view of learning style is that proposed by the psychologist Howard Gardner. He identified at least seven distinct intelligences that all individuals possess but to different degrees. These include the *logical/mathematical*, the *verbal/linguistic*, and the *visual/spatial* (→ **multiple intelligences**). Similarly, proponents of **neuro-linguistic programming** distinguish between different sensory orientations, including the *visual*, *aural* and *kinesthetic* (ie, related to movement, touch). So far, though, there is no convincing evidence that any of these dispositions correlates with specific learning behaviours. Nor has it been shown that a preference in one area predicts success

[1] Ellis, R. 1994 *The Study of Second Language Acquisition* (OUP) p 538.

in language learning. In fact, it is very difficult to separate learning style from other potentially influential factors, such as personality, intelligence, and previous learning experience. Nor is it clear to what extent learning style can be manipulated, eg through **learner training**. The best that can be said is that, if the learner's preferred learning style is out of synch with the type of instruction on offer, then success is much less likely than if the two are well matched. This supports the case for an **eclectic** approach (→ **eclecticism**), on the one hand, and the individualization of learning, on the other.

lesson design METHODOLOGY

'Lesson design' refers to the way that individual lessons are structured. Like the rules of a game, the structure provides a secure framework within which a certain amount of spontaneity and improvisation can be accommodated. Experienced teachers, when they plan a lesson, usually choose from a 'menu' of lesson models the particular shape of lesson that suits their needs and style.

Some popular lesson shapes are:

- **PPP** (presentation–practice–production) in which a pre-selected grammar item is first presented, then practised in a controlled way, and then practised by means of a freer, productive activity such as a roleplay.
- TTT (**test–teach–test**, or task–teach–task) in which learners first perform a task, eg improvising a dialogue around a theme; the teacher uses this in order to identify the learners' specific language needs; they are then taught whatever it is they need in order to re-do the task more effectively (→ **task-based learning**).
- 'model–muddle–meddle': the teacher models a task, eg telling an anecdote; the learners attempt to do the same in pairs or small groups, while the teacher monitors, intervening where necessary in order to help the learners perform the task effectively; finally, individuals perform the task to the whole group.
- text-based lesson: learners listen to, or read, a text; the teacher asks **comprehension questions**; selected features of the text then become the focus of some kind of language analysis; these features are practised in isolation; learners then write their own texts, incorporating the targeted features.

Other writers on classroom methodology have proposed general principles for designing lessons, rather than specific models. For example, Jim Scrivener argues that effective language lessons will always include stages that focus on *authentic language use* (A), *restricted language use* (R), and *clarification* (C), but in no strict order. (Scrivener has since revised the ARC principle, substituting these components: *input–learning–use*). In a similar attempt to avoid prescriptivism, B. Kumaravadivelu has proposed a number of *macrostrategies* for language teaching, such as 'facilitate negotiated interaction', and 'contextualize linguistic input'. Some other useful design principles include the following:

- start with some kind of warm-up activity (or ice-breaker)
- find out what the learners already know (eg by 'brainstorming' vocabulary related to a topic)
- maximize on the learners' attention when they are at their peak – usually in the first ten to twenty minutes of a lesson, or just after any break: these are

good times to introduce new material
- sequence the activities in a way that is logical, and ensure that this logic is obvious to the learners
- ensure maximum learner participation in the progress of the lesson, and include activities that require learners to interact
- vary the focus, eg from open class work to pairwork, and back again; or from their books to the blackboard; or from reading to listening, etc
- vary the pace and intensity of the lesson, without losing the flow
- allow time near the end for a recap of the lesson, to field questions, or to set homework, etc.

lesson plan METHODOLOGY

A lesson plan is a document that maps out the teacher's intentions for the lesson. It reflects the teacher's planning decisions as well as the teacher's understanding of the principles of **lesson design**. Many schools and training courses require teachers and teachers-in-training to produce lesson plans, usually for periodic assessment purposes, and in conjunction with a class observation. The layout of the lesson plan is normally prescribed by the relevant institution, but typically it will include the following features:
- *aims*: these may be worded in purely linguistic terms (eg *to teach the present perfect progressive*) or in terms of some skill or sub-skill (eg *to practise reading for gist*), or both
- *timetable fit*: how the lesson fits into an overall scheme of work
- *assumptions*: eg what the teacher assumes the learners may already know that is relevant to the achievement of the lesson aims, eg *familiarity with present perfect simple, and with present progressive*
- *anticipated problems*: ie, problems that are specific to the lesson aim, such as difficulties in understanding a concept or in manipulating a form; the plan should also mention some possible strategies to deal with these problems
- *materials*: ie, the materials and/or aids that the teacher plans to use
- *class profile*: a description of the class, including the class composition, the students' level, their needs, and any other relevant information that may affect the achievement of the lesson aims
- *developmental aims*: the teacher's personal aims, in terms of what he or she hopes to learn from teaching the lesson
- *procedure*: a stage-by-stage outline of how the teacher anticipates the lesson will progress. It may include such details as:
  - the aim of each stage
  - a brief description of the activity
  - the time that the activity is predicted to take
  - the interactional focus, eg pairs, groups, teacher–class

Despite the apparent inflexibility of planning a lesson in such detail, most observers allow for the fact that no lesson is entirely predictable. They will not expect the teacher to follow the plan slavishly. In reality, most lessons are a dynamic mix of the planned and the unplanned, and it is often during the unplanned moments that the most rewarding learning opportunities occur. Nevertheless, it is generally felt that the exercise of planning lessons in detail is a useful training practice, and a reliable indicator of the quality of a teacher's expertise.

lexeme → **lexical item**

lexical approach METHODOLOGY

A lexical approach to language teaching is one that has chosen vocabulary (ie, **lexis**) as the main focus for syllabus design and classroom teaching. This contrasts with traditional approaches, which usually focus on grammar. This lexical bias emerged out of developments in **corpus** linguistics, especially research into **collocation** and word **frequency**. Corpus research has shown that a great deal of language in use is highly predictable. Words are 'primed' to co-occur with other words (→ **priming**). That is, the choice of words that go with any given word is often tightly constrained, not just by grammar, but by habits of association. These associations are what we call **collocations** and **formulaic language**, or, more loosely, *chunks*. (In fact, some linguists regard grammar as just another kind of collocation). These chunks account for the **idiomaticity** of language. The fact that a good deal of language is formulaic is also an aid to **fluency**. These findings prompted Michael Lewis to propose an approach to teaching called the Lexical Approach. Lewis argues that 'language consists of grammaticalized lexis, not lexicalized grammar'. In other words, he challenges the traditional view that speaking a language means slotting words into previously learned grammatical structures. Instead, we draw on a huge bank of memorized words, phrases and collocations. In fact, Lewis is very sceptical as to the value of studying traditional grammar rules at all.

In a parallel development, Jane and Dave Willis worked on the assumption that the most frequent words in any language express its most frequent meanings. A syllabus of high frequency words, therefore, would be a syllabus of high frequency meanings. Corpus data not only show which words are the most frequent, but also the kinds of words and structures that commonly co-occur with these high-frequency words. For example, the word *way* is one of the most frequent words in English, and it is commonly found in these patterns:

> way + of + -ing: *There's no way of knowing. That's one way of putting it.*
> the + way + noun + verb: *That's the way I like it; the way we were*
> the + way + adverbial: *all the way home; on the way to the forum; no way back*

A syllabus based on these high-frequency words and patterns is arguably more useful to learners than a list of grammar structures. This is because it is based on actual usage, rather than on linguistic theory.

Michael Lewis's Lexical Approach and the lexical syllabus of Dave and Jane Willis share a number of features. Both acknowledge the important meaning-making function of vocabulary, and both question the traditional distinction between vocabulary and grammar. In their view, words are really 'small grammar' and grammar is 'big words'. Where these writers differ is in their classroom approach. Dave and Jane Willis favour **task-based learning** for their meaning-based syllabus. Lewis argues for a more analytic, text-based approach, in which texts are examined for the kinds of chunks that are embedded in them.

lexical density → **content word**

lexical item VOCABULARY

The term 'lexical item' (or, more technically, *lexeme*) is used in order to get round the fuzziness of the word *word*. For instance, are *go, going, goes* and *went* all different words, or simply different forms of the same word? Likewise, is *get up* one word or two? And *of course*, *in case*, and *for example* – are these single words or pairs of words? 'Lexical item' means 'any item that functions as a single meaning unit, regardless of its different derived forms, or of the number of words that make it up'. So, *go*, *get up* and *for example* are all lexical items (lexemes). So, too, are **idioms** like *spill the beans* and *hell for leather*. And *go*, *went*, *been* and *gone* are all forms of the same lexeme (*go*). As a rule of thumb, dictionary entries are organized into lexemes, rather than individual words.

lexical set VOCABULARY

Lexical sets are sets of words that share a meaning relationship, eg because they relate to a particular topic or situation. Thus, the words *drive*, *steering wheel*, *starter*, *windscreen*, *change gear*, *hand-brake* and *reverse* all belong to the lexical set 'car'. Likewise, *menu*, *starter*, *napkin*, *wine glass*, *tip* and *bill* are associated with a restaurant situation. (Note that many words – like *starter* – can belong to more than one lexical set). Lexical sets can be assembled using a **corpus**. By looking at the words that co-occur with a key word (such as *car*), and then by looking at the words that co-occur with *those* words, a network of commonly associated words can be constructed. Most **vocabulary teaching** is organized around lexical sets (*furniture*, *jobs*, *sport*, etc), on the principle that it is easier both to teach and to learn words that are closely associated. Such a view fits in with what we know about the way words are stored in memory. That is, they are stored in interconnecting networks according to their meaning associations. Sometimes, however, a close association can cause 'interference', so that a learner might say *Bring me the tip* instead of *Bring me the bill*. This has led some researchers to suggest that it might in fact be better to learn vocabulary items which have *not* been grouped into lexical sets, but which, instead, have been selected more randomly. Such a view, however, seems to run counter to common sense.

lexical verb GRAMMAR

Verbs are either lexical or auxiliary. A lexical verb is distinguished from an **auxiliary** verb in that it is a **content word**, not a **function word**. That is to say, it has a dictionary meaning, rather than serving a grammatical function. Thus, all the verbs in the following sentence are lexical: *I came, I saw, I conquered*, whereas none of the verbs in this sentence are: *I would if I could but I can't*. There is an intermediate class of verbs, called *de-lexicalized verbs*, which form the verb element in a large number of multi-word expressions, and which have little or no dictionary meaning on their own. Examples are *take*, *get*, *make* and *go*, as in *take your time*, *get lost*, *make an appointment*, and *go shopping*.

lexis LINGUISTICS

Lexis is a technical term for the **vocabulary** of a language, as opposed to its **grammar**. From lexis are derived a number of other terms relating to vocabulary, including the adjective *lexical*, as in the **lexical approach**. A *lexicon* is a collection of words, and is often used to talk about the way vocabulary is stored in the mind, as in *the mental lexicon*. *Lexicography* is the study of words for the purpose of compiling dictionaries (→ **lexical item**).

liaison → **connected speech**

lingua franca → **English as an international language**

linguistic imperialism SOCIOLINGUISTICS

Linguistic imperialism refers to the often destructive effect that majority languages have on minority languages and cultures. It has been estimated, for example, that of the present 6000 or so languages spoken in the world, only ten per cent will still be around in a hundred years' time. The problem is especially acute where the dominant language is associated with economic, political, or military power, as is currently the case with English. Rather than accepting the view that English has become a neutral *lingua franca*, some scholars, such as Robert Phillipson and Alistair Pennycook, argue that the teaching of English not only threatens local languages, but does so in ways that perpetuate colonial attitudes and practices. One example of this that they identify is the assumption that native-speaker teachers are better than non-native-speaker ones. (This has been termed *native-speakerism*). Another is the notion that the English classroom should be monolingual and that the use of the learners' L1 should be discouraged. A third is the way that teaching methods and materials that originated in western contexts (the 'centre') are exported to contexts where they may not be appropriate (the 'periphery').

It is not necessarily the case that learners in the so-called periphery have accepted the spread of English uncritically, however. Researchers have begun to document ways that learners resist and subvert the dominance of English. Meanwhile, the notion of linguistic imperialism is a useful corrective to the triumphalism that is often associated with the global spread of English.

linguistics LINGUISTICS

Linguistics is the study of human language in general. This includes not only the structure of language (eg **grammar**, **phonetics**, **semantics**), but also the purposes for which language is used (eg **pragmatics**). Prior to the twentieth century the main focus of linguistics (then called *philology*) was the comparative study of languages (always written and often dead). Early in the twentieth century, the Swiss philologist, Ferdinand de Saussure, shifted the focus on to the principles governing the structure of living languages. Saussure's primary concern was *semiotics*, or the study of signs. His ideas were taken up by what came to be called the Prague School (founded in 1926), which in turn led to the development of **functional** approaches to language description (→ **function**). Meanwhile, anthropologists studying Native American languages, such as Franz Boas and Edward Sapir, initiated field studies that laid the foundations of linguistic research. This early descriptive work, coupled with **behaviourist** psychology, developed into the school of linguistics known as 'structuralism'. Structural linguistics was concerned with describing linguistic structures, with little or no reference to their meaning or use. Language learning was seen as the acquisition of these structures through habit formation (→ **audiolingualism**).

A radical departure from this tradition occurred in the late 1950s, when Noam Chomsky refuted the prevailing view of 'language as behaviour'. Instead, Chomsky sought to look 'inside the mind' for the in-built mental structures that underpin the way language develops and is used (→ **mentalism**). He hypothesized the existence of an innate capacity for language acquisition, based on principles common to all languages, called **universal grammar**.

Nevertheless, Chomskyan linguistics, like structural linguistics, is interested more in linguistic forms than in how these forms are realized in use. It was left to linguists working in the functional tradition, including Michael Halliday, to account for the way linguistic forms are related to their contexts of use (→ **systemic functional linguistics**).

The study of language has combined with other disciplines to give rise to many specialized fields, including *psycholinguistics* (the study of the relationship between language and the mind), *historical linguistics* (the study of language change), **sociolinguistics** (the study of the relationship between language and society), **corpus** linguistics (the use of data bases of authentic language for linguistic description), *critical linguistics* (the study of the relationship between language and ideology) and **applied linguistics**. It is in this last area that the study of second language teaching is located. It would be misleading, though, to think of language teaching as being solely a branch (of a branch) of linguistics. It is as much concerned with psychology, education and sociology as it is with language description.

linker DISCOURSE

Linkers (also called *conjuncts*) join what has already been said (or written) to what follows. They do so by showing the sense relationship between the two linked elements. The main kinds of sense relations that linkers express are:

- additive: *and, what's more, moreover, firstly, secondly ...*
- summative: *all in all, in sum ...*
- appositive: *that is to say, ie, namely, in other words ...*
- contrastive (also called adversative): *but, instead, on the other hand ...*
- concessive: *however, still, all the same ...*
- resultative (also called causal): *so, as a result, therefore, in consequence ...*
- temporal: *then, next, meanwhile, eventually ...*

Linkers are one means by which **cohesion** is achieved in texts. Linkers can join parts of sentences (phrases and clauses), sentences, and whole paragraphs. In spoken language, many **discourse markers**, such as *so, yes but, I mean*, have a linking function, and there is considerable overlap between these terms.

Discursive texts often have a high frequency of linkers, but less formal kinds of text achieve cohesion by other means. There is a tendency in ELT materials to over-emphasize linkers at the expense of other cohesive devices. The most commonly used linkers in casual conversation are *and*, *so*, *but* and *then*, and these often do quite well for written texts as well.

linking verb GRAMMAR

Linking verbs (also called *copular verbs*) are the small set of verbs, including the verb *to be*, that take an obligatory **complement**. The complement is either a noun phrase (*This is my tailor*) or an adjective phrase (*My tailor is rich*). The complement either expresses a current attribute (*My tailor seems rich*) or a resulting one (*My tailor became rich*). The most common linking verbs are:

(current attribute): *be, appear, feel, look, seem, smell* (+ adjective only), *sound, taste* (+ adjective only)

(resulting attribute): *become, get* (+ adjective only), *go* (+ adjective only), *grow* (+ adjective only), *turn* (+ adjective only)

Some linking verbs can also be followed by **adverbials**, usually of place, as in *My tailor is in prison*.

listening METHODOLOGY

Listening is the skill of understanding spoken language. It is also the name given to classroom activities that are designed to develop this skill – what are also called *listening comprehension* activities – as in 'today we're going to do a listening'. Listening is one of the four language **skills**, and, along with **reading**, was once thought of as being a 'passive' skill. In fact, although receptive, listening is anything but passive. It is a goal-oriented activity, involving not only processing of the incoming speech signals (called *bottom-up processing*) but also the use of prior knowledge, contextual clues, and expectations (*top-down processing*) in order to create meaning (→ **comprehension**). Among the sub-skills of listening are:

• perceiving and discriminating individual sounds
• segmenting the stream of speech into recognizable units such as words and phrases
• using **stress** and **intonation** cues to distinguish given information from new information
• attending to **discourse markers** and using these to predict changes in the direction of the talk
• guessing the meaning of unfamiliar words
• using clues in the text (such as vocabulary) and context clues to predict what is coming
• making inferences about what is not stated
• selecting key information relevant to the purpose for listening
• integrating incoming information into the mental 'picture' (or **schema**) of the speech event so far

Also, since listening is normally interactive, listeners need to be capable of

- recognizing when speakers have finished their turns, or when it is appropriate to interrupt
- providing ongoing signals of understanding, interest, etc. (*backchannelling*)
- asking for clarification, asking someone to repeat what they have just said, and repairing misunderstandings (→ **repair**)

These sub-skills exist across languages, so, in theory, learners should be able to transfer them from their first language into their second. In fact, there are a number of reasons why this does not always happen. One is that speakers of different languages process speech signals differently, depending on the phonetic characteristics of the language they are used to. This means that speakers of some languages will find it harder than others to match the spoken word to the way that the word is represented in their mind. They simply do not recognize the word. Another problem is lack of sufficient L2 knowledge, such as vocabulary or grammar. A third problem is that learners may lack the means (and the confidence) to negotiate breakdowns in understanding. Finally, many learners simply lack exposure to spoken language, and therefore have not had sufficient opportunities to experience listening. These problems can be compounded in classrooms because:

- Listening to audio recordings deprives the learners of useful visual information, and allows the learners no opportunity to interact and repair misunderstandings.
- Classroom acoustics are seldom ideal.
- If learners do not know what they are listening for (in the absence, for example, of some pre-set listening task) they may try to process as much information as possible, rather than being selective in their listening. This can lead to listening overload, which in turn can cause inhibiting anxiety.
- Listening texts that have been specially written for classroom use are often simplified. But if this simplification means eliminating a lot of redundant language, such as speaker repetitions, pause fillers and vague language (→ **conversation**), the density of information that results may make it harder – not easier – to process.

For this reason, the use of audio recordings to develop listening skills needs to be balanced against the advantages of using other media, such as video, and face-to-face interaction with the teacher or another speaker.

Nevertheless, the use of audio recordings is an established part of classroom practice, so it is important to know how to use them to best advantage. The following approach is one that is often recommended:

- Provide some minimum contextual information, eg who is talking to whom about what, and why. This helps to compensate for lack of visual information, and allows learners to activate the relevant mental **schema**, which in turn helps top-down processing, including the sub-skill of prediction.
- Pre-teach key vocabulary: this helps with bottom-up processing, although too much help may mean that learners don't get sufficient practice in guessing from context.

- Set some 'while-listening' questions. Initially, these should focus on the overall *gist* of the text. For example: true/false questions, selecting, ordering or matching pictures, ticking items on a list, following a map (→ **comprehension questions**).
- Play a small section of the recording first, to give learners an opportunity to familiarize themselves with the different voices, and to trigger accurate expectations as to what they will hear.
- Play the recording right through, and then allow learners to consult on the answers to the pre-set task. Check these answers. If necessary, re-play the recording until satisfied that learners have 'got the gist'.
- Set a more demanding task, requiring more intensive listening, such as listening for detail, or inferring speakers' attitudes, intentions, etc. If the recording is a long one, it may pay to stage the intensive listening in sections. Again, allow learners to consult in pairs, before checking the task in open class.
- On the basis of the learners' success with these tasks, identify problem sections of the recording and return to these, playing and re-playing them, and perhaps eliciting a word-by-word transcription and writing this on the board.
- Distribute copies of the transcript of the recording (if available) and re-play the recording while learners read the transcript. This allows the learners to clear up any remaining problems, and also to match what they hear to what they see.

The above approach can be adapted to suit different kinds of recorded texts and different classroom needs. For higher level learners, for example, it may be counter-productive to make listening *too* easy. The approach can also be adapted to the use of video, and even to *live listenings*, such as listening to the teacher or a guest.

literacy SOCIOLINGUISTICS

Literacy is the ability to read and write in a language, usually one's own. However, increasingly learners of a second language, especially those living in an English as a second language (ESL) context (→ **English as a foreign language**), require native-like literacy skills in order to function effectively in the target culture. In other words, they need to achieve *functional literacy*. Literacy training is a major component of *workplace language training*, where it may be taught as a set of skills, or **competencies**. Alternatively, the learners' needs may be defined in terms of the different social practices that they will have to participate in. These, in turn, will be realized as specific written **genres**. Either way, simply 'doing reading and writing' in class is unlikely to meet the special needs of such learners.

literature DISCOURSE

Literature refers to texts that have a mainly expressive function and which are highly valued in a particular culture. Texts are described as *literary* if they have achieved the status of literature or aspire to be literature. Literary texts do not feature much in ELT materials. This is mainly because they are considered difficult, in terms of both their language and the interpretative work involved in reading them. However, attitudes towards the classroom use of literature are changing. For a start, the whole concept of literature has been re-assessed. It is now recognized that many qualities that were once considered purely literary, such as the playful and figurative use of language, are shared by other genres, such as advertising. Moreover, the notion of a literary canon of exclusively British (or American) 'classics' has been challenged. Many writers from what was once the English-speaking 'periphery', including writers writing in dialect, are now considered mainstream. This means that literary texts need not be treated with any more reverence than other authentic texts used in the classroom. As an example of how 'easy' literary texts can be, here is a poem by the contemporary poet Christopher Logue,[2] which, incidentally, plays on the fact that *literature* has two senses:

> Last night in London Airport
> I saw a wooden bin
> labeled UNWANTED LITERATURE
> IS TO BE PLACED HEREIN.
> So I wrote a poem
> and popped it in.

The way that a poem like this one could be used in the classroom is not necessarily any different from the way other written texts can be used (→ **reading**). However, because literary texts often achieve their effects through what is *not* said, as much as through what is said, it is important to set tasks that encourage learners to 'read between the lines' and 'to fill in the gaps' themselves. This may mean asking them to identify (a) the point of view of the writer; (b) the person addressed (if anyone); and (c) the mood of the text (humorous, ironic, reflective, etc). Identifying and discussing any instances of language use that are expressive, figurative, playful, ambiguous, or otherwise unusual, is also important. In the above poem, this might mean drawing attention to the double meaning of *literature*, and the poet's use of the informal phrasal verb *pop in*. And, since literature usually aims to provoke some emotional response in the reader (eg pleasure, empathy, wonder), the sequence of post-reading tasks should include a task where learners are asked to say how the text affected them.

Longer literary texts, such as novels, can be read out of class. It's a good idea, though, to put class time aside for learners to report on their reading, compare opinions, and seek help if needed. Asking learners to summarize the story so far, and to predict what happens next, are useful ways of checking understanding, comparing interpretations, and motivating reading. It can also help if the texts that are chosen have an accompanying audio recording, or a film which is based on them, as these can help ease the difficulty of the language or lack of familiarity with the cultural context.

[2] 'London Airport' from *Selected Poems* by Christopher Logue © Christopher Logue 1996. (Faber and Faber) Re-printed in *Poems on the Underground* (ed. Benson et al.) 1991, 2001. (Cassell) p 69.

materials METHODOLOGY

Materials in the language classroom include anything that is used to support the learning process. This includes coursebooks, workbooks, **visual aids**, charts, board games, Cuisenaire rods, audio and video materials, as well as the software that is run by computers, data projectors and interactive whiteboards. Nowadays, it is generally the case that learners will have access to a coursebook for classroom use as well as some form of homework book (workbook). The coursebook itself will consist of texts, both spoken and written, with accompanying tasks, grammar and vocabulary presentations and exercises, speaking and writing tasks, and usually some form of grammar reference section at the back. The coursebook is usually supplemented with recorded material, and, increasingly, a photocopiable resource pack as well as a CD-ROM of extra exercises, and access to a web page. Coursebooks for children come with even more components, including charts, games, and even puppets.

The arguments in favour of materials are: they relieve the teacher of having to do copious preparation; they are a stimulus to language production; they provide immersion-like language exposure; they allow learners to continue studying outside class time; they provide variety and entertainment, thereby engaging and motivating the learners. The variety also caters for different individual **learning styles**. On the downside, an over-reliance on materials can create a materials-centred classroom, at the expense of a person-centred one (→ **Dogme ELT**). It is important, therefore, to select and use materials judiciously, taking into account the learners' needs and interests, so that the materials are a help rather than a hindrance.

meaning LINGUISTICS

Language consists of **forms** that express certain meanings. The study of meaning is called **semantics**. A basic principle in semantics is that the forms of a language are simply *signs* – they are arbitrary and bear no resemblance to the things that are *signified* by them. Thus the word *table* does not look or feel or sound like a table. Any other word, like *Tisch*, or *mesa*, or *tarabeza* (which all translate as *table* in their respective languages), would do as well. Learning a second language, then, is first and foremost a job of matching a whole new set of (arbitrary) forms to existing meanings. The teacher's job is to help in the matching process. In fact, establishing meaning is probably one of the most important functions of a language teacher.

Language teaching methods have evolved different approaches to dealing with meaning. Some, like the **direct method**, relied on visual aids, mime, and gesture, to convey the meanings of words and grammatical structures. Others, like **grammar–translation**, used translation. Either way, meaning is often elusive. The direct method approach, ie, pointing to a real table and saying the word *table*, works well with words like *table*. But it works less well for an expression like *under the table*, as in *The deal was done under the table*. Here, the meaning is not literal but *figurative*, or *metaphorical*. Nor does a direct method approach deal well with the fact that 'table' is *polysemous*, ie, that it has several meanings, one of which is a way of displaying information in rows and lines on a page.

Translation is equally problematic. It is easy enough to translate the literal meaning of words, ie, their *denotations*. But it is less easy to capture a word's associations, often cultural, ie, its **connotations**. For example, the English word *chuffed* translates as *contento* in Spanish, but this does not distinguish it from other words that are translated by *contento*, such as *happy*, *content* and *pleased*.

It is not always easy to say what something means, eg by giving a definition. (Dr Johnson famously defined *network* as 'anything reticulated or decussated, at equal distances, with interstices between the intersections'.) For teaching purposes, it is often easier to say what something is *like* (using a **synonym**), what it is a *kind of* (using a **hyponym**), or what it is *not* (using an **antonym**).

memorization METHODOLOGY

If you memorize a word or expression, you intentionally commit it to **memory**. Memorization has been out of favour in language teaching, as it has been associated with *rote learning*. Rote learning (or *learning by heart*) is the endless, often mindless, repetition of a rule, text, word list or grammatical pattern (eg *write, wrote, written; drive, drove, driven*, etc). Nevertheless, memorization doesn't have to be mindless, nor meaningless. In fact, the memorization of meaningful words, phrases, and even sentences is now considered to be an essential ingredient of language learning. Researchers have calculated that, to achieve the status of an independent user, learners need to be familiar with 3000 or more vocabulary items. Moreover, it is now generally accepted that a speaker's **fluency** depends on their having a bank of memorized chunks which they can draw on (→ **lexical approach**). Some researchers have estimated that this bank comprises literally hundreds of thousands of items. Learners will acquire some of the words and chunks they need simply as a by-product of exposure to language through listening and reading – what is called *incidental learning*. But for most adult language learners, incidental learning will satisfy only a very small proportion of their needs. This is because the likelihood of any but the most frequent words re-occurring is too small to make a lasting impression. The bulk of the lexicon must be learned *intentionally*. That is, most words must be deliberately committed to long-term memory. How can this be done?

Essentially, there are three key processes involved in transferring material from working memory to long-term memory. These are:

- *elaboration*: Processing new information more elaborately improves its chances of being remembered. This means attending to, and making conscious decisions about a new word at the level of form (both written and spoken), and of meaning. For example: Which other words (L1 or L2) does the word sound like? How many syllables has it got? Where's the stress? Which other words are derived from it? What part of speech is it? Which other words are associated with this word? Which words collocate with it? What images does it evoke? (These are questions that learners can address individually or working in pairs or small groups.)
- *rehearsal*: This is mental recycling of material for the purposes of memorization. Typically it takes the form of silently saying the word to yourself. This is the process usually associated with rote learning. But rehearsal is insufficient for long term retention, unless it is accompanied by retrieval.
- *retrieval*: The more times a word is retrieved from long-term memory, the easier it will be to access in future. The best way of doing this is by means of regular self-testing over intervals of increasing duration (called *distributed*

practice). The teacher can help by regularly recycling previously studied material (→ **revision**).

Few learners come to language learning fully aware of the importance or the procedures of memorization, and this is where **learner training** can play a really useful role. Techniques to aid memorization include the following:

- *mnemonics*: These are 'tricks' to help retrieve items or rules that are stored in memory and that are not yet automatically retrievable. The spelling rule '*i* before *e* except after *c*' is a mnemonic. A well-known mnemonic technique is the *keyword technique*. This involves devising a mental image that connects the pronunciation of the L2 word with the meaning of an L1 word. So, if a Spanish-speaking student was learning the English word *carpet*, they might associate it with the Spanish word *carpeta*, meaning a folder, and visualize a folder made of carpet material.
- *word cards*: These are sets of small cards, on one side of which the learner writes an L2 word, and on the other its L1 translation. Learners test themselves regularly, alternating the direction of recall (L2 ⇨ L1, then L1 ⇨ L2) and periodically changing the order of the cards. As words are learned they can be discarded and new ones added to the pack.

memory PSYCHOLOGY

There is no learning without memory, and language learning in particular, with the enormous load of vocabulary that it requires, is largely a memory task. It demands the ability to store and retrieve enormous amounts of memorized information. This information includes both the phonological forms of words (and of multi-word *chunks*), and the associations between the forms of words and their meanings. Unsurprisingly, therefore, having a good memory is considered to be a key factor in a learner's **aptitude** for language learning.

Current models of memory distinguish between:

- *sensory memory*: This is an echo or visual impression that lasts only seconds.
- *working memory*: This holds and processes information in the short term. The information may come from an external source or may have been 'downloaded' from long-term memory (see below). The capacity of working memory is limited, and only so much information can be processed at any one time. This is why it is important to develop processes that are automatic (→ **automaticity**). These make fewer demands on working memory than do controlled processes. Most cognitive tasks, such as reasoning, learning and understanding, depend on working memory.
- *long-term memory*: This is the part of the memory system that stores information more permanently. Unlike working memory it has enormous capacity and durability. Information can be transferred from working memory to long-term memory, sometimes after a period of silent mental repetition (called *rehearsal*) which strengthens the memory trace. But it may decay if it is not frequently retrieved: the more often it is retrieved, the easier it is to access.

For language learning purposes, what is important is, firstly, moving material from working memory into long-term memory, and, secondly, being able to access and retrieve this material in real-time conditions. The first process is helped by the use of **memorization** techniques, as well as by frequent encounters with the new material (→ **frequency**; → **repetition**). The second process, ie, access and retrieval, is entirely dependent on **practice**, and the principle *use it or lose it*.

mentalism, mentalist theory PSYCHOLOGY

Mentalism is the theory that language is an innate property of mind. It is primarily associated with the work of Noam Chomsky, and represents a reaction to a purely **behaviourist** view of language acquisition, and a return to the rationalist philosophy of Descartes ('I think, therefore I am'). The mentalist view assumes the existence of a built-in **universal grammar**, and presupposes an inborn *language acquisition device*. In this sense, mentalist models differ from those other **cognitive learning theories** that attribute language acquisition to non-language-specific processes of cognition.

metalanguage LINGUISTICS

Metalanguage is the language that is used to talk about language, and is better known as *terminology*. (This dictionary is, essentially, a dictionary of metalanguage). There is some debate as to the value, for learners, of knowing metalanguage, especially grammar terms such as *adjective, adverbial, auxiliary*, etc. This is part of a larger debate as to the role of explicit knowledge in language learning. In the past, methods such as the **direct method** and **audiolingualism** rejected any role for explicit knowledge, and, by association, metalanguage. Since the advent of **cognitive learning theory** there has been a greater tolerance for talking *about* language in the classroom. However, no studies have convincingly shown that knowledge of metalanguage results in more successful language learning. For language teachers, though, it would be virtually impossible to talk about their subject without the use of metalanguage (or what outsiders would call *jargon*).

metaphor LINGUISTICS

A metaphor is a *figure of speech* where one thing is stated in terms of another. For example, in the sentence *The teacher blew her top*, the teacher's anger is described as if it were literally a volcanic explosion. While metaphor tends to be associated with literary language (as in *The moon was a ghostly galleon, tossed upon cloudy seas*), a great deal of day-to-day language use is also metaphoric. In fact, some scholars have suggested that the fundamental roots of language are figurative rather than literal, and that metaphors structure the way we think about, and perceive, the world. Metaphors of this type are called *cognitive metaphors*. Thus, when we say *I look forward to hearing from you*, or *Picasso was ahead of his time*, we are (unwittingly) construing time as if the future was physically in front of us. Likewise, directional terms can express improvement (*Things are looking up*), or its opposite (*Why are you so down?*). Knowing the way that spatial language is used metaphorically may help learners make sense of **phrasal verbs**, and the way **prepositions** are used in time expressions, such as *in January, at 10 o'clock, on the 4th of July*, etc. A lot of **formulaic language** is also metaphoric in origin, as in these 'weather' **collocations**: *a stormy relationship, a sunny disposition, thunderous applause, an icy smile*.

Grammatical metaphor is the term used to describe the way in which concepts that are normally expressed in one grammatical form (such as verbs) are expressed in another (such as nouns). For example, in the sentence *Using fossil fuels is destroying the ozone layer*, the words *using* and *destroying* are verbs expressing processes. In more **formal language**, such as in academic or technical writing, these verbal processes are often turned into 'things' through the use of nouns: *The use of fossil fuels is causing the destruction of the ozone layer*. Because *use* and *destruction* are not really things, but processes, this operation (also called *nominalization*) is considered metaphorical.

Often, metaphorical language thinly masks a particular ideology or mindset. So, if someone talks about *a flood of immigrants*, it is reasonable to infer that they think the situation is disastrous. And, in our own field, terms like *input*, *output*, and *feedback*, are used unquestioningly, implying that language learning is a form of information processing. So ingrained do these metaphors become that it becomes hard to think 'out of the box' (another metaphor). Major theoretical advances often come about because someone 'discovers' a new metaphor. The metaphor of **scaffolding**, for example, which is central to **sociocultural learning theory**, challenges the input–output metaphor of information processing theory.

method METHODOLOGY

A method is a system for the teaching of a language that is based either on a particular theory of language or on a particular theory of learning, or (usually) on both. These theories will underpin choices of **syllabus** type, **materials**, and classroom **activities**. For example, **audiolingualism** is a method that drew on a structuralist description of language (→ **linguistics**) and **behaviourist** views of learning. Accordingly, syllabuses for audiolingual courses were organized around a graded list of structures, and the main classroom activity was the drilling of the structures so as to instil correct language habits. Other well-known methods are **grammar–translation**, the **direct method**, and the **communicative approach**.

Method should not be confused with *coursebook*: a coursebook is simply the material support for a method. In fact, some methods, such as **the Silent Way**, do not have coursebooks at all. Nor should *method* be confused with *methodology*, which is a general word to describe classroom practices, such as **classroom management**, irrespective of the particular method that a teacher is using. Some theorists distinguish between method and *approach*, as in the **communicative approach** or the **lexical approach**. 'Approach' denotes a more general theoretical orientation, while a method is just one way that the approach is realized in practice. Nowadays, the term *approach* is used almost exclusively, *method* having fallen from favour. This is due to a strong reaction, in the late twentieth century, away from the 'method concept', on the grounds that methods are too prescriptive and too insensitive to local contextual factors. It is now recognized that language learning is a more complex process than any single method can hope to address. Hence, there has been an attitude shift in favour of **eclecticism** and of customizing teaching approaches to suit the particular and local needs of the learners – sometimes called a *post-method pedagogy*. In practice, however, most teachers tend to teach using the method in which they were originally trained, supplemented by activities gleaned from coursebooks.

methodology → **method**

minimal pair PHONOLOGY

A minimal pair is a pair of words which differ in meaning when only one sound (one **phoneme**) is changed. *Pair* and *bear* are minimal pairs, since their difference in meaning depends on the different pronunciation of their first sound: /p/ versus /b/. However, *pair* and *pear* are not minimal pairs, since, although they differ in meaning, they are pronounced the same. Minimal pairs are widely used in pronunciation teaching to help learners discriminate between sound contrasts, for the purposes of both recognition and production. So, for example:

- The teacher first presents a contrast, by pronouncing a set of minimal pairs: *pair, bear; bin, pin; bark, park;* etc. (It helps if the words are illustrated, using visual aids, so that they do not become divorced from their meaning).
- The students then hear a sequence of words, such as *pair, pin, bark, bin, park, bear,* and have to assign them to one category or another: /p/ or /b/, or to identify which picture is being referred to.
- And/or they have to listen to pairs of words and say if they are the same or different: *pair, pair; bin, pin; park, park; bear, pear;* etc.
- Or they listen to the words in sentence-length contexts, and decide which sound they have heard. For example:

  There were some bears under the tree/There were some pears under the tree.
  Our dog likes a good bark/Our dog likes a good park.

- Finally, prompted by the visual aids, or reading aloud words from a list or sentences, the students attempt to produce the contrast.

mistake → **error**

mixed ability METHODOLOGY

Classes where there is a marked difference among the learners in terms of **aptitude**, **learning style** or **motivation**, are generally described as being mixed ability classes. Mixed ability classes should be distinguished from classes of *mixed levels*, where students with different levels of proficiency are grouped together. Of course, a mixed ability class is likely to become a mixed level class, over time. All classes are mixed ability classes to some extent. Mixed ability classes become a problem when the diversity threatens the general **dynamics** of the classroom. This may be the case in large and potentially unruly classes. The problem is also compounded in situations where learners' progress is frequently assessed, and where all learners are expected to achieve similar results. Mixed ability classes can be viewed either as a **classroom management** issue, or as a **syllabus** and **materials** issue. As a management issue, one approach is to increase the amount of **groupwork**. Learners are grouped according to their abilities and set different task objectives. Or stronger students are paired with weaker ones, so that the former can teach the latter. As a syllabus and materials issue, the problem of mixed ability is more acute in classes following a *narrow-band curriculum* versus those following a *broad-band curriculum*. A narrow-band curriculum is one where each stage of the syllabus is highly specified, usually in terms of discrete items of grammar, and where mastery of one stage is a prerequisite for the next. Learning is viewed as segmented, incremental and sequential. A broad-band curriculum, on the other hand, is one where the objectives are more broadly defined, eg in terms of general **competencies**, such as *to be able to talk about one's free-time activities*. Such an objective allows each learner to contribute to the best of their ability. It also allows for the teaching and learning of a variety of language areas concurrently. Learning is viewed as holistic, emergent, and concurrent. It is argued that a broad-band curriculum is not only better suited to cope with diversity, but is able to exploit diversity and turn it into a resource rather than a problem.

mnemonics → **memorization**

modality GRAMMAR

Modality refers to the lexical and grammatical ways used by speakers to express their attitude to what they are saying. For example:

1. *Charles is married.* (no modality)
2. *Maybe Charles is married.* (lexical modality: adverb)
3. *I wonder if Charles is married.* (lexical modality: verb)
4. *I wish Charles was married.* (lexical modality: verb)
5. *Charles might be married.* (grammatical modality: modal verb)
6. *Charles ought to be married.* (grammatical modality: modal verb)

The attitudes expressed by modality divide into two groups, sometimes called *extrinsic* and *intrinsic* modality, respectively. Extrinsic modality refers to the speaker's assessment of the *likelihood* of the situation, as in sentences 2, 3 and 5, above. Intrinsic modality refers to the speaker's attitude to the *necessity* or *desirability* of the situation, as in sentences 4 and 6 above. By means of extrinsic modality we can talk about the world 'out there'. By means of intrinsic modality we can act on the world. Intrinsic modality allows us to express a range of *interpersonal* meanings, such as obligation, volition (willingness) and ability.

Modality is expressed grammatically through the use of **modal verbs** (*modal auxiliaries*). All modal verbs can express both extrinsic and intrinsic modality. Modality can also be expressed lexically, such as through the use of these verbs and adverbs:

[extrinsic modality]: *wonder, guess, think; perhaps, maybe, possibly*
[intrinsic modality]: *wish, promise, suggest, allow; hopefully, ideally, luckily, unfortunately*, etc

In the following text,[1] instances of modality are identified:

How to help your postie deliver your mail early and safely

Your mail box should[1] be clearly in view. Maybe[2] you and your neighbour can[3] arrange it so your mail boxes sit next to each other on your adjoining boundary. This could[4] save the postie a stop and you'll[5] get your mail earlier.

Posties shouldn't[6] have to[7] bend over backwards to deliver your mail. Make sure[8] your mail box is not too low, or too high.

Australia Post recommends[9] you protect your mail by fitting a lock to your mail box.

You could[10] consider[11] adding something like a newspaper holder. This would[12] be sufficient to hold enough advertising material for even the largest Christmas sale. You may[13] even like to label your mail box with a 'Mail Only' inscription.

[1] brochure distributed by *Australia Post* (PM 35) July 1990.

Of course,[14] your box can[15] be made larger if you receive a large amount of mail.

1. *should*: modal verb (intrinsic)
2. *maybe*: adverb (extrinsic)
3. *can*: modal verb (intrinsic)
4. *could*: modal verb (extrinsic)
5. *will*: modal verb (extrinsic)
6. *should*: modal verb (intrinsic)
7. *have to*: semi-modal verb (intrinsic)
8. *make sure*: verbal idiom (intrinsic)
9. *recommends*: verb (intrinsic)
10. *could*: modal verb (extrinsic)
11. *consider*: verb (extrinsic)
12. *would*: modal verb (extrinsic)
13. *may*: modal verb (extrinsic)
14. *of course*: adverbial (extrinsic)
15. *can*: modal verb (extrinsic)

modal verb GRAMMAR

The most common way of expressing **modality** in English is through the use of modal verbs. Modal verbs are a class of **auxiliary verb**. There are nine 'pure' modals: *can, could, may, might, will, would, shall, should* and *must*. They are pure in the sense that they fulfil the formal requirements of auxiliary verbs: eg they form their negatives with not (*You mustn't write*) and they form questions by inversion with their subject (*Can I go?*). Modal verbs do not have infinitive forms, participles, or third person *-s*. They are always placed first in the verb phrase: *It <u>may</u> have been raining.*

Each modal verb can express two kinds of meaning: 1. likelihood, possibility (called *extrinsic* meaning) and 2. a range of meanings to do with the speaker's attitudes, wishes, etc. (*intrinsic* meaning) (→ **modality**). For example, the sentence *Camilla may become Queen* can mean both *Camilla is likely to become Queen*, and *Camilla is allowed to become Queen*. The main meanings expressed by the modal verbs are:

can	theoretical possibility ability permission	*Grammar can be fun.* *Can you speak French?* *Can we take photographs?*
could	possibility ability	*It could be fun.* *We could see the top.*
may	possibility permission	*It may rain.* *You may go in now.*
might	possibility permission	*It might be Gary.* *Might I use the phone?*
will	prediction/predictability volition	*It will be a nice day.* *Boys will be boys.* *I'll give you a hand.*
would	predictability volition	*He would say that.* *Would you lend me the car?*

shall	prediction volition	*We shall overcome.* *Shall we dance?*
should	possibility obligation	*It should be a nice day tomorrow.* *You should try harder.*
must	logical necessity obligation	*You must be exhausted.* *I must phone Dad.*

In addition to the 'pure' modals, there are a number of other single-word and multi-word verbs that combine with other verbs to express modal meaning, and are known as *semi-modals* or *marginal modals*. The main ones – and the meanings they most commonly express – are:

ought to	obligation	*You ought to phone her.*
need (to)	necessity	*I need to see the supervisor.*
have(got) to	logical necessity obligation	*You've got to be joking.* *I have to feed the baby.*
be able to	ability	*Will he be able to walk?*
be going to	prediction volition	*It's going to be crowded.* *I'm going to complain.*
used to	habitual past	*It used to be cheap here.*

Because of the wide range of meanings – especially interpersonal – that they convey, modals allow speakers to express a variety of **functions**, such as asking **permission**, making **requests**, giving **advice**, and making **offers**. They also express a variety of *notions*, such as **obligation**, **necessity**, **ability**, **futurity**, and **possibility** (→ **notional syllabus**). Not surprisingly, language syllabuses include modals almost from the outset, especially the most frequent and the most versatile, such as *can, could, would, will, have to* and *going to*. However, modals present a number of problems for learners, such as:

- Problems of form: The pure modals are not inflected (*he cans), nor followed by *to* + infinitive (*he can to play), nor can they combine with other auxiliaries (*they don't can); the semi-modals, however, do all these things: *he has to play, he doesn't have to play*. Some modals are *defective*, that is, they have no past or future forms, so that, for example, the past of *I must work* is *I had to work*.

- Problems of meaning: In many cases the meanings of the different modals are similar or overlap (*It will rain. It's going to rain*), but in many cases they are not (*I'll phone you. I'm going to phone you*). It is sometimes the case that affirmative forms are similar in meaning, but negative forms are not, as in *You must dress up/You have to dress up* versus *You mustn't dress up/You don't have to dress up*.

- Problems of use: Because modals express interpersonal meanings, they are sensitive to context factors. Some modals are avoided where they may risk causing a threat to face (→ **politeness**). For example, *I think you ought to do X* or *I would do X* are less face-threatening than *You must do X*. Some modals, such as *shall*, are rarely or never used in some varieties of English.

modifier GRAMMAR

The modifier in a **noun phrase** adds further information to (or *modifies*) the main word of the noun phrase (the *head*). The modifier can go before the head, and after any **determiners**, in which case it is called a *premodifier*. Or it can go after the head, in which case it is called a *postmodifier*. For example:

	determiner	premodification	head	postmodification
1	*the*	*white*	*peacock*	
2		*animal*	*farm*	
3		*Portnoy's*	*complaint*	
4	*the*	*electric, kool-aid acid*	*test*	
5	*a*		*room*	*with a view*
6			*lord*	*of the flies*
7	*a*		*streetcar*	*named desire*
8	*the*		*spy*	*who loved me*

The premodifier is typically an **adjective** or adjective phrase (as in 1 in the table above); or a **noun**, in which case it is called a *noun modifier* (as in 2); or a **possessive** form (*genitive*) as in 3; or any combination of these (as in 4). The postmodifier is typically a *prepositional phrase* (as in 5), an *of*-construction (as in 6), a non-finite **clause** (as in 7) or a **relative clause** (as in 8).

Modification of the noun phrase is an important way of building complex noun phrases in English. These in turn are a generic feature of certain text-types, especially journalism and technical or academic writing. For example (the noun phrases are underlined):

Police investigations that preceded the collapse of the trials of two royal butlers were fundamentally sound, an external review published last week concluded.

Previous studies of content-based second language (L2) programs have shown that students learning their L2 through immersion develop high levels of comprehension skills as well as considerable fluency and confidence in L2 production.[2]

monitor → **classroom management**

monitoring (output) SLA

Speakers monitor their output when they attend to what they are saying as they say it. This often involves repairing their output (either by self-correcting or clarifying → **repair**), using expressions like *I mean* and *or rather*. Stephen Krashen's *monitor hypothesis* claims that learners use knowledge that they have

[2] Lyster, R. 2004 'Differential effects of prompts and recasts in form-focused instruction.' In *Studies in Second Language Acquisition*, 26/3: 400.

learned in order to edit utterances that are generated by knowledge that they have acquired (→ **language acquisition**). He goes on to claim, more controversially, that this monitoring function is the *only* use of learned knowledge. He distinguishes between *monitor-over-users*, ie, learners who monitor their accuracy to such an extent that they sacrifice fluency, and *monitor-under-users*, who do the opposite.

morpheme LINGUISTICS

A morpheme is the smallest meaningful unit in a language. The word *meaningful*, for example, consists of three morphemes: *mean*, *ing*, and *ful*. None of these can be broken down further to form meaningful grammatical units, and all of them can be used as the building blocks for other words, such as *mean**s***, *speak**ing***, and *beauti**ful***. Note that, while *mean* can stand on its own (it is a *free morpheme*), *ing* and *ful* cannot. They are *bound morphemes*, and must combine with free morphemes to form complete words. Bound morphemes are mainly **affixes**. The description of the way morphemes combine is called **morphology**.

morpheme studies → **order of acquisition**

morphology GRAMMAR

Morphology is the area of grammar that is concerned with the formation of words. It contrasts with **syntax**, which is concerned with the structure of sentences, including the order of words within them. The basic unit of morphology is the **morpheme**. Morphology is divided into two branches: (1) *inflectional morphology*, which describes the way that words, such as verbs, are *inflected* in order to convey different grammatical meanings, as in *she work**s***, *she work**ed***, *she is work**ing***, where *-s*, *-ed*, and *-ing* are different inflectional **affixes**; and (2) *derivational morphology*, which describes the way lexical words are formed, by, for example, *affixation* and *compounding* (→ **word formation**). Thus, the words *inflection* and *inflectional* are derived from *inflect*.

motivation PSYCHOLOGY

Motivation is what drives learners to achieve a goal, and is a key factor determining success or failure in language learning. The learner's goal may be a short-term one, such as successfully performing a classroom task, or a long-term one, such as achieving native-like proficiency in the language. With regard to long-term goals, a distinction is often made between *instrumental motivation* and *integrative motivation*. Instrumental motivation is when the learner has a functional objective, such as passing an exam or getting a job. Integrative motivation, on the other hand, is when the learner wants to be identified with the target language community. Intersecting with these two motivational *orientations* are two different *sources* of motivation: *intrinsic* (eg the pleasure of doing a task for its own sake) and *extrinsic* (eg the 'carrot and stick' approach). Another motivational source that has been identified is success: experience of succeeding can result in increased motivation (called *resultative motivation*), which raises the question as to whether motivation is as much a result as a cause of learning.

Various theories of motivation have been proposed. Most of these identify a variety of factors that, in combination, contribute to overall motivation, such as:

- *attitudes*, eg to the target language and to speakers of the language
- *goals*, both long-term and short-term, and the learners' *orientation* to these goals
- how much *value* the learner attaches to achieving the goals, especially as weighed against *expectancy of success*; expectancy of success may come from the learner's assessment of their own abilities, and how they account for previous successes or failures
- *self-esteem*, and the need to achieve and maintain it
- *intrinsic interest, pleasure, relevance* or *challenge* of the task
- *group dynamic*: is it competitive, collaborative, or individualistic?
- *teacher's attitudes*, eg what expectations does the teacher project about the learners' likelihood of success?

As the last point suggests, teachers can play a key role in motivating learners, not just in terms of choosing activities that are intrinsically motivating, but in the attitudes they project. Two researchers on motivation offer the following advice for teachers:[3]

> Ten commandments for Motivating Language Learners
>
> 1. Set a personal example with your own behaviour
> 2. Create a pleasant, relaxed atmosphere in the classroom.
> 3. Present the tasks properly.
> 4. Develop a good relationship with the learners.
> 5. Increase the learner's linguistic self-confidence.
> 6. Make the language classes interesting.
> 7. Promote learner autonomy.
> 8. Personalise the learning process.
> 9. Increase the learners' goal-orientedness.
> 10. Familiarise learners with the target language culture.

multiple-choice questions → **testing**; **comprehension questions**; **computer-assisted language learning**

multiple intelligences PSYCHOLOGY

Intelligence is usually thought of as being a single, inborn capacity. But the theory of multiple intelligences (MI), as first proposed by Howard Gardner, views intelligence as being multi-dimensional. Proponents of this view have identified at least seven different kinds of intelligence that individuals possess in different strengths and combinations. These are:

- verbal/linguistic
- logical/mathematical
- visual/spatial
- bodily/kinesthetic
- musical/rhythmic
- interpersonal, ie, the ability to understand other people's feelings and wishes
- intrapersonal, ie, the ability to understand oneself

The last two share characteristics of what has also been called *emotional intelligence*.

[3] from Dörnyei, Z. and Csizér, K. 1999 'Ten commandments for motivating language learners: results of an empirical study': *Language Teaching Research*.

Advocates of MI argue that learning (including language learning) is optimized when these different intelligences are engaged. One way of doing this is to vary the kinds of classroom activity so that no single intelligence is being targeted at the expense of others. A lesson might include, for example, a warm-up action game (*bodily/kinesthetic*), a story-telling activity (*verbal/linguistic*), a problem-solving task (*logical/mathematical*), and a song (*musical/rhythmic*). In this way, the inherent diversity of the classroom can be catered for. Since the theory of multiple intelligences is consistent with the concept of **individual learner differences**, other approaches to dealing with diversity, such as **learner training**, might also apply. However, it is not clear to what extent these different intelligences are susceptible to training and development. Like **neuro-linguistic programming**, with which it has a lot in common, MI belongs to those **humanistic approaches** that have a distinctly 'new age' flavour.

multi-word verb → **phrasal verb**

narrating FUNCTION

Narrating, or telling stories, whether real or fictional, is a universal function of language. Narratives may be spoken or written. They embrace a number of sub-genres, such as *anecdotes*, *jokes*, *fables*, *urban legends*, *news reporting* and re-telling the *plots* of films and soap operas. Anecdotes are a common feature of casual conversation, where they often serve an *interpersonal* function. Through telling and responding to personal stories, speakers can express shared experiences and values. Essentially, a narrative is the recounting of a series of past events. The structure of spoken narratives has been analysed into the following components:

- an *abstract* – which tells you what the story is going to be about
- an *orientation* – which establishes the setting, time, and characters
- a *complicating event*
- a *resolution* – which tells how the complication was resolved
- a *coda* – which signals the end of the story and connects it back to the ongoing talk

Running through this structure are frequent *evaluative* comments, which express the speaker's attitude to the events, and help position the listeners so that they can respond appropriately. Written narratives share a number of these features, but the sequence may vary, according to the **genre**. For example, newspaper narratives typically begin with the complication or the resolution and then back-track to fill in the details. In this example, the orientation, complicating event, and resolution are concentrated into one sentence:

> **Man bites dog**
> A MAN who was attacked by an Alsatian dog in a park in Denepropetrovsk, Ukraine, killed the animal by biting its throat. The dog's owner said the man had been drinking and her pet disliked the smell of alcohol.[1]

As in the above example, narrating typically involves the use of the past **tense**, on its own (*was attacked*, *killed*), or marked for continuous or perfect **aspect**, or both (*had been drinking*). However, some narrative forms, such as jokes, are often told in the present tense:

[1] *Weekly Telegraph*, Issue 137, 23 February 1994.

> This penguin goes into a bar and he says to the barman 'Have you seen my brother?', and the barman says, 'What does he look like?'

Narratives also include the following features:

- time **adverbials**: *once upon a time, the other day, last summer, when I was at school*, etc
- **linkers**: *and then, all of a sudden, however, eventually*, etc
- **appraisal** language, ie, language that expresses the storyteller's attitude to the story: *unfortunately, it was awful, amazing, totally and utterly exhausted*, etc

The ability to tell a story in a second language, whether a simple joke or the account of a weekend outing, is extremely satisfying. It can also be very important, as when reporting an accident, for example, or filing an insurance claim. It is a good idea, therefore, to introduce learners to narrating language, and to provide opportunities to practise it, at an early stage in their learning. This in turn assumes that learners are able to use past tense forms, so the sooner these are taught, the better. Many teachers customarily start their lessons with some chat about recent activities: this is a good opportunity to support (through **scaffolding**) the learners' emerging story-telling skills. Other narrative-telling techniques are the use of *picture stories* (a sequence of pictures that tell a story); *chain stories* (where each learner writes the continuation to an introductory sentence, such as *It was a dark and stormy night* ...; they then pass their sheet of paper to the learner sitting on their right, and each student continues the story in their own way, and so on, until each sheet of paper has returned to its owner); and *mini-sagas*, where learners have to write a story that is exactly fifty words long.

native speaker SLA

A native speaker (NS) of a language is a person who has acquired the language as their first language in childhood. Native speakers are considered to know this language intuitively, and to use it accurately, fluently, and appropriately. The educated native speaker's command of the language has long been considered the standard by which the language should be taught to *non-native speakers* (NNSs). Hence, dictionaries, grammars and teaching materials are based on the intuitions of native speakers, or, more recently, on databases, or *corpora* (→ **corpus**) of native-speaker language. And in many teaching contexts, NS teachers are preferred to NNS teachers, irrespective of their training or experience. Many of these assumptions are contentious, however. For a start, many people develop a native-like command of more than one language (→ **bilingualism**). It is often difficult to say which is their native language, or which language group they principally identify with. Furthermore, the terms *native* and *non-native* have in-group and out-group, or centre and periphery, associations. For these reasons, some scholars have argued for different classifications, such as *expert user* and *L2 user*. An expert user is a proficient speaker of the language, regardless of whether it is their first language or not. And the term *L2 user* avoids the negative associations of *non-native speaker*. At the same time, many learners do not necessarily aspire to a native-like command of the target language, especially those who are learning **English as an international language**. This has called into question the value of native-speaker models. Finally, the privileged status of native-speaker teachers has been challenged on many counts, one of which is the fact that, unlike non-native speakers, they have never had to learn the target language in a classroom situation, and so are not as well-positioned to teach it.

natural approach METHODOLOGY

The term 'natural approach' (or *natural method*) was first used in the nineteenth century to describe teaching methods, such as the **direct method**, that attempted to mirror the processes of learning a first language. Translation and grammar explanations were rejected, learners were exposed to sequences of actions, and the spoken form was taught before the written form. The term was resurrected by Tracy Terrell in the 1970s to describe a similar kind of approach. Learners were initially exposed to meaningful language, not forced to speak until they felt ready to, and not corrected or given explicit grammar instruction. The method was characterized by a lot of teacher talk, made intelligible through the use of visual aids and actions. The method was endorsed by Stephen Krashen, whose *input hypothesis* (→ **input**) gave it theoretical validity. It also shared many principles in common with **Total Physical Response**. These included the importance of comprehensible input, and of promoting positive **affect** in the learning process. The natural approach seems to have become absorbed into what are generally known as **humanistic** teaching practices and **whole language learning**.

natural order hypothesis → **order of acquisition**

naturalistic language acquisition SLA

Naturalistic language acquisition refers to language acquisition that takes place in naturalistic (ie, non-classroom) settings. It contrasts with *instructed language acquisition* (or *learning*). Many educators have attempted to replicate the conditions for naturalistic language acquisition in classroom contexts (→ **natural approach**; → **immersion**), believing that it is intrinsically better. After all, everyone knows someone who has just 'picked up' a foreign language while living or working abroad. However, while some learners achieve impressive levels of proficiency this way, the evidence suggests that, on balance, classroom instruction is more effective in the long run. Of course, for many learners, it is the only option.

necessity, expressing FUNCTION

The verb *need* is the most common way of saying that something is necessary, as in:

I need a new keyboard. (= *need* + noun phrase)
That plant needs watering. (= *need* + -*ing*)
You need to lie down. (= *need* + *to*-infinitive)

Constructions that include words like *necessary* and *essential* are more formal ways of expressing necessity: *It's not necessary to book in advance.*
There are at least two other senses in which we can talk about necessity. For example:

1. *I must get going: it's late.*
2. *You must be Robin's brother: you look exactly like him.*

The first of these conveys **obligation**, the second expresses *logical necessity*. Note that, in the negative, these concepts are expressed quite differently:

    3. *I don't have to go yet: it's not late.* (= no necessity or obligation)
    4. *You can't be Robin's brother: you look totally different.* (= logical impossibility)

Ways of expressing the first kind of necessity include the **modal verbs** *must, have (got) to, need to, ought to.* (For other ways of expressing obligation, see **obligation**.) Ways of expressing logical necessity include: *must* and *have (got) to*, as well as adverbs like *(not) necessarily, certainly, inevitably* and adjective constructions such as *bound to, certain to, sure to: It's bound to rain on Saturday: it always does.*

For other ways of expressing logical necessity, see **possibility**.

Contexts in which the language of necessity is likely to occur include: bureaucracy (eg the requirements for getting a driving licence), talking about the qualifications for a job, and making excuses.

needs analysis METHODOLOGY

Needs analysis is the process of specifying the learners' language needs in advance of designing a course for them (→ **course design**), especially an ESP (**English for special purposes**) course. Data are usually collected by means of questionnaires or interviews. Observations of the kinds of situations in which the learners will be using English are also helpful. So is an analysis of the kinds of texts and interactions that the learners will be dealing with. Subjective information, such as the learners' attitudes, expectations and preferred **learning style**, can also feed into the overall analysis. The analysis can then be used to inform both the content of the course, including the syllabus and choice of materials, and also the methodology. Finally, the needs analysis can be used in the design of **assessment** and **evaluation** procedures.

negation GRAMMAR

There are a variety of ways, both grammatical and lexical, of contradicting the meaning of a sentence, or of part of it. These include:

- NOT-negation: *We <u>can't</u> go on meeting like this. <u>Don't</u> do anything I <u>wouldn't</u> do! It's <u>not</u> cricket!* To make a clause negative, the particle *not* is placed after the first **auxiliary**, or after the verb *to be*; in the absence of an auxiliary the operator *do* has to be introduced. In spoken and informal language, *not* is usually contracted.
- negative **determiner** *no*: *<u>No</u> way, José! Thanks, but <u>no</u> thanks!*
- *not* + time or quantity expression: *<u>Not</u> tonight, Josephine! <u>Not</u> a lot of people know that!*
- negative **pronouns**: *<u>Nobody</u>'s perfect. It's <u>none</u> of your business!*
- other negative words: *<u>Never</u> say die! It's <u>neither</u> one thing <u>nor</u> the other.*
- negative **affixes**: *<u>Un</u>accustomed as I am … As use<u>less</u> as a chocolate kettle …*

The order in which learners acquire negation has been studied by researchers of second language acquisition. Typically, and irrespective of the learner's first language, this follows the sequence:

    1. *no* + verb: *She no eat meat.*
    2. *not* + verb: *She not eat meat.*

3. *don't* + verb: *She don't eat meat.*
4. operator + *not* + verb: *She doesn't eat meat.*

Sequences like this are evidence of there being a fixed **order of acquisition**. They also demonstrate how complex negation is in English, and why learners take so long to master it.

negative → **negation**

negative feedback → **feedback**

negotiation of meaning → **interaction**

neuro-linguistic programming (NLP) PSYCHOLOGY

NLP is a theory about the way the mind processes experience and language. It has generated a great deal of literature, much it of the 'self-help' variety. Because it is concerned with the brain (*neuro-*), language (*linguistic*), and learning (*programming*), its principles and techniques have been applied to second language teaching. NLP shares with the theory of **multiple intelligences** the view that the mind is predisposed to process experience in different ways (or *modalities*): through sight, smell, hearing, movement, touch and taste. According to NLP, individuals differ in the extent to which one or more of these modalities dominates. As well as being predisposed to a particular modality, learners have preferred thinking styles, or *metaprograms*. Some learners, for example, favour rules while others favour examples. It follows that communication (and hence both counselling and teaching) can benefit if it is adjusted to match the individual's particular sensory predisposition and thinking style. Learners themselves can realize their potential for 'excellence' by re-configuring their mental 'maps' so that they match the way they are being taught.

Although under-investigated, and rather narrowly focused on sensory experience, NLP finds some support in the research on **learning styles**. Many of its practical recommendations – such as for ways of establishing rapport – are already well established in the literature on **affect**, and on **humanistic approaches**.

non-finite verb → **finite verb**

non-native speaker → **native speaker**

noticing SLA

If you notice a feature of the language that you are exposed to, it attracts your attention and you make a mental note of it. For example, a learner might notice (without necessarily understanding) the sign *Mind the gap*, repeated several times on a railway station platform. That same day, the learner hears the teacher say *would you mind* in the context of making a request in class. A day or two later, the same learner hears someone else say *I don't mind*. Each successive 'noticing' both primes the learner to notice new occurrences of *mind*, and at the same time contributes to a growing understanding of the use and meaning of *mind*. Proponents of **cognitive learning theory** believe that noticing is a prerequisite for learning: without it input would remain as mere 'noise'. The *noticing hypothesis*, then, claims that noticing is a necessary condition for acquisition, although not the only one. Some kind of mental processing of what has been noticed is also necessary before the **input** becomes *intake*, ie before it is moved into long-term **memory**.

Teachers obviously play an important role in helping learners to notice features of the language. They do this when they repeat words or structures, write them on the board, or even drill them (→ **form, highlighting**). One way of increasing the chance of learners' noticing an item is to include it lots of times in a text, a technique called *input flood* (→ **frequency**). For example, learners read a text with the word *mind* included several times. They then categorize these examples according to their meaning. A set of **concordance** lines for a particular word can be used in the same way.

There is another type of noticing, called *noticing the gap*. This is when learners are made aware of a gap in their language knowledge. This might happen when they do a **dictation**, for example. When they compare their version with the correct version, they may notice certain differences, such as the lack of past tense endings, that represent a gap in their **interlanguage**. It has been argued that noticing the gap can trigger the **restructuring** of interlanguage. That is, 'minding the gap' leads learners to 'fill the gap'.

notion → **notional syllabus**

notional syllabus METHODOLOGY

A notional syllabus is a syllabus that is organized according to general areas of meaning that are used in most grammars. Thus, meanings like *location, frequency, duration, possibility* and *past-ness* are all universal concepts, and are each associated with particular grammatical forms. So, *frequency* is associated with adverbs of frequency (*often, usually, never,* etc) as well as with certain **modality** forms, such as *used to, tend to* and *would* (*We would always spend our summers at the beach*). These general meaning categories are called *notions*.

Traditionally, syllabuses consist of an ordered list of language structures, such as the present simple, the first conditional, etc. These are then taught in association with their common meanings and uses. A major development in syllabus design occurred in the mid-1970s when a number of theorists suggested that this form-to-meaning organization could be reversed. That is, instead of listing the forms and then teaching their meanings, they started with the meanings and then listed their associated forms. Accordingly, syllabuses were devised where the organizing feature was notional: *habits, cause and effect, probability, quantity,* etc. Very early on, these notional categories were combined with language **functions** – such as *requesting, suggesting, apologizing,* etc – to form what became known as *functional–notional syllabuses*. These syllabuses formed the backbone of the **communicative approach**. There has been some resistance, however, to meaning-based syllabuses, perhaps because structure-based syllabuses seemed easier to teach and to test. The functional–notional syllabus now survives as just one strand of what are known as *multi-layered syllabuses* (→ **functional syllabus**).

noun GRAMMAR

Nouns are by far the largest **word class** in English, with new ones being coined on a daily basis. (The following appeared in *The Guardian* newspaper in 2003: *nerd-fest, frumpsville, accentism, Jill-of-all-trades*). They comprise that class of words that refer to people (and other creatures), places, things and abstract entities. In grammatical terms, nouns act as the head of **noun phrases**. Nouns can occur as the **subject** or **object** of a verb, after a **preposition** (_out of_ control; _under_ the boardwalk) or after a **determiner** (_some_ girls; _no_ expectations; _one more_ try), and can be modified by **adjectives** (_brown_ sugar; _wild_ horses; _little red rooster_). Most nouns have singular and plural forms, and many can take 's to indicate possession (_yesterday's_ papers; _mother's_ little helper). Many nouns are formed from the addition of an affix to a verb, adjective or other noun: _satisfaction_, _happiness_, _undercover_.

Nouns can be subdivided into _proper nouns_ and _common nouns_. Proper nouns are names of specific people, places, and so on: _Carol_, _Route 66_. Common nouns can be further divided into _countable_ and _uncountable_ nouns, the former having both singular and plural forms (_neighbours_, _horses_), the latter only singular (_money_, _sugar_). Both countable and uncountable nouns can be further classified in terms of whether they are _concrete_ or _abstract_. Concrete nouns refer to things that can be observed and measured (_horses_, _money_), while abstract nouns refer to unobservable ideas or qualities (_satisfaction_, _luxury_).

Nouns are the first words most learners learn, and are often taught in the form of **lexical sets**, such as _food and drink_, _furniture_, _parts of the body_, _jobs_, etc. Decisions as to which nouns to teach will need to take into account _usefulness_ (words like _board_, _video_ and _homework_ will be immediately useful in the classroom); _teachability_ (concrete nouns are more easily taught than abstract ones); and _frequency_. The ten most frequent nouns in both spoken and written English are: _time_, _people_, _way_, _man_, _years_, _work_, _world_, _thing_, _children_ and _life_.

noun modifier → **modifier**

noun phrase GRAMMAR

A noun phrase (NP) is one of the five types of **phrase** in English, and typically forms the **subject**, **object** or **complement** of a **clause**.

> _The whole town's talking_. = (subject)
> _She wore a yellow ribbon_. (= object)
> _I was a fugitive from a chain gang_. (= complement)

Noun phrases consist of an obligatory _head_ – that is the main word in the phrase – and optional elements that go before or after the head. The head is either a noun or a pronoun. The elements that go before it include **determiners**, **adjectives** and other **nouns**. Those going after include prepositional phrases and **relative clauses** (→ **modifier**):

pre-modification	head	post-modification
	Gigi	
my beautiful	_laundrette_	
duck	_soup_	
Rosemary's	_baby_	
	father	_of the bride_
the	_bridge_	_on the River Kwai_
the	_spy_	_who came in from the cold_
those magnificent	_men_	_in their flying machines_

The following quotation consists of a series of complex noun phrases. These are underlined, and the head of each noun phrase (where there is more than one word) is in bold:

Down here it was still the **England** I had known in my childhood: the railway **cuttings** smothered in wild flowers, the deep **meadows** where the great shining horses browse and meditate, the slow-moving **streams** bordered by willows, … and then the huge peaceful **wilderness** of outer London, the **barges** on the miry river, the familiar **streets**, … the **men** in bowler hats, the **pigeons** in Trafalgar Square, the red **buses**, the blue **policemen** – all sleeping the deep, deep **sleep** of England, from which I sometimes fear that we shall never wake till we are jerked out of it by the **roar** of bombs.[2]

Note that many of the noun phrases have other noun phrases nested in them: [*the England* [*I*] *had known in* [*my childhood*]]. On the other hand, some noun phrases consist of a single word: *it, we, all.*

The structure of noun phrases differs from language to language, and learners often have problems accommodating to a different system, as these NP errors by learners of English indicate:

It was a film very interesting.
He is a mechanic of cars.
All people can not be rich.
He live in a house that he built it.

nucleus → **intonation**

number GRAMMAR

Number refers to the grammatical distinction between singular and plural. In English countable **nouns** can be either singular or plural: *one blind mouse; three blind mice.* Some **pronouns** and **determiners** are also marked for number: *see how it runs; see how they run; she cut off its tail; she cut off their tails.* The third person in the present simple is the only verb form that makes a distinction between singular and plural in all verbs: *see how it runs; see how they run.* Otherwise, only the verb *to be* is marked for number (*I am; the mice are*). In this respect, English is less complicated than languages such as German, where adjectives, articles, and all verb forms are marked for number.

Some singular nouns can be used with either singular or plural verbs and pronouns:

The committee meets on Wednesday, doesn't it?
The committee meet on Wednesday, don't they?

Plural pronouns are often used to refer to the singular impersonal pronouns *anybody, somebody*:

If anybody wants a ticket, they'd better hurry.

[2] Orwell, G. 1938, 1962 *Homage to Catalonia.* (Harmondsworth: Penguin) p 221.

object GRAMMAR

The object of a **sentence** or **clause** refers to the person or thing that is affected by the action of the verb:

Can I phone a friend?
Let them eat cake!
Take the money and run.

The object is usually a **noun phrase**, as in the above examples, or a **pronoun**:

Can you hear me, mother?
Play it again, Sam.

Some **clauses** can also be objects:

I didn't know you cared. (Compare: *I didn't know that*).
I'll have what she's having. (Compare: *I'll have that*).

Only *transitive* verbs can take objects (→ **transitivity**). Some verbs take two objects: a *direct object* and an *indirect* one:

Give the man a cigar.
I never promised you a rose garden.

Here *a cigar* and *a rose garden* are the direct objects of their verbs, and *the man* and *you* are the indirect objects. The sentences can be rephrased with *to*:

Give a cigar to the man.
I never promised a rose garden to you.

An *object question* is a question about the object of the verb:

What are you doing after the show? (= you are doing *something*)

This compares with a *subject question*, which is a question about the **subject** of the verb:

What's new, pussycat? (= *something* is new)

obligation FUNCTION

Obligation is expressed using **modal verbs**, principally *must, have to* and *have got to.*

I must phone Zoe.
Children under 12 must be accompanied by an adult.
Do you have to leave so soon?
We've got to get that window repaired.

Must generally suggests that the obligation comes from the speaker. *Have to* suggests the obligation is imposed from 'outside', eg from some authority who is not the speaker.

I must phone Zoe. (*It's her birthday so it's my duty*).
I have to phone Zoe. (*Her mother asked me to*).

For this reason, *you have to* (= it's the rule) is generally less threatening than *you must* (= I say so). Hence Queen Elizabeth I's indignation at being told that she must go to bed: 'Must! Is *must* a word to be addressed to princes?'

The negative of *must* (*mustn't*) means 'obligation not to' ie 'prohibition', whereas *don't have to* means 'no obligation to':

You <u>mustn't</u> eat that (… *because it's bad for you*).
You <u>don't have to</u> eat that (… *if you don't want to*).

Must has no derived past form or future forms. Instead *had to* is usually used:

I <u>had to</u> phone Zoe yesterday
If her mother doesn't phone Zoe, I'<u>ll have to</u>.

In British English *have got to* usually refers to a single, non-habitual instance of obligation:

I'<u>ve got to</u> work this Saturday.

For habitual obligations, *have to* is more usual:

I <u>have to</u> work on Saturdays.

Other ways of expressing obligation include:

- *should* and *ought to*: *Applicants <u>should</u> enclose a stamped addressed envelope. We <u>ought to</u> leave a tip.* (*Ought to* implies a moral obligation).
- *need to*: *The government <u>needs to</u> get its priorities sorted out.*
- *had better*: *We'<u>d better</u> hurry or we'll miss that train.*
- *(not) supposed to/not allowed to*: *You're <u>supposed to</u> be a member.*
- *be obliged to/be under an obligation to* (formal): *I'm <u>obliged to</u> ask you for a reference.*

(→ **necessity**)

Useful contexts for teaching obligation include: rules and regulations, eg the rules of a club, or the steps involved in getting a visa; the rules of games, including team sports, card games and computer games; and classroom and school rules.

offering, making an offer FUNCTION

The function of offering is made either with **questions** or **imperatives**. Question forms typically involve the use of **modal verbs**:

Would you like *Can I get you* *How about* *What about*	*something to drink?*

The customary response is either *Yes, please* or *No, thanks*. Refusals usually include an explanation: *No thanks. I've just had one.*

Offers expressed as commands are usually less formal:

Have a drink.
Let me pay.

The following sequence from a TV comedy demonstrates an informal sequence of offers:[1]

Barbara Oooh, Emma, would you like a drink?
Emma Erm, well, I'm driving – so just an orange please.
Barbara Oh, I don't think I've got any orange. Would you like some Vimto?
Emma Er, I'm all right thanks.
Barbara Help yourself to the buffet. Can I get you a ham sandwich?

[1] *The Royle Family: The Complete scripts.* 2002. (Granada Media) pp. 322–3.

Emma   Oh, no thank you, I'm a vegetarian.
Barbara Ooh, can I do you a Dairylea instead?
Emma   No, honestly, I'm fine thank you.

one-to-one teaching METHODOLOGY

One-to-one teaching is individualized instruction, in contrast to the teaching of small or large groups. One-to-one teaching usually occurs face to face, and at times, over the phone. Increasingly, and with the advent of **computer-mediated communication**, one-to-one teaching is being conducted at a distance by means of the internet, email, and video conferencing. The one-to-one situation is a familiar one for many ESP teachers, particularly those teaching English for business or professional purposes (→ **English for special purposes**). There are obvious advantages for the student: students have the undivided attention of the teacher, they have optimal opportunities for participation, and the classes can be tailored to their particular needs, pace and **learning style**. Teachers, too, do not have to deal with the kinds of diversity frequently encountered in groups, such as mixed levels, **mixed ability**, diverse interests, and different learning styles. Moreover, the teacher can allow the learner some choice in the content and direction of the lesson, thereby reducing the amount of preparation necessary. On the down side, one-to-one classes can be intensive, tiring experiences for both teacher and learner. And, if there is a lack of rapport, it is less easy to disguise than in a large group. More importantly, the possibilities for communication are limited to just the one channel: the teacher and the learner. **Groupwork** is obviously out of the question, as are milling activities. This rules out a number of **communicative activities** – such as surveys, discussions, and many games – that are associated with a **communicative approach**. Moreover, it is sometimes difficult to base lessons on coursebook material, which is usually designed for classroom groups.

Nevertheless, one-to-one teaching need not be a hard slog. There are a number of techniques that can maximize its effectiveness. These include:

- doing a detailed analysis of the learner's needs (→ **needs analysis**)
- keeping a written record, in note form, of the progress of the lesson, eg recording errors and noting down vocabulary that comes up, for use in subsequent lessons, or as the basis for writing up a record of the lesson for the student
- varying the interactional focus by setting up role plays or information gap activities in which the teacher takes part, and then reversing roles
- encouraging the student to become the 'teacher' – ie explaining to the teacher some aspect of their job or field of study; this can be prepared in advance
- reformulating the student's output, eg asking the learner to talk about a topic, and then recasting the learner's language in a more acceptable form; the learner can then have another attempt at the task, and the cycle can continue
- recording the learner, and then going back over the recording, commenting on it, improving it, even transcribing parts of it
- encouraging the learner to bring to the class texts that are relevant to their specific needs, eg business letters, emails, catalogues, and using these as the content of the lesson

- if possible, changing the focus by leaving the class and going somewhere else together, eg a library, café, or shopping centre
- using time between lessons to stay in contact using email, eg for sending homework assignments, or for discussing something such as a news item found on the internet

opinion, giving and asking for FUNCTION

The language of asking for, giving and comparing opinions is useful not only in 'real life', but in the classroom context too, especially where learners are encouraged to take part in discussions and debates. It is therefore helpful to have some common expressions of opinion displayed in the classroom, along with other useful classroom language.

To ask for and state opinions, judgments, beliefs, etc, the following verbs are common: *think, believe, find, suppose, feel, assume, imagine*:

> *What did you think of the movie? ~ I found it a bit dull.*
> *Who do you think will win? ~ I imagine Nadal will.*

Other common expressions for framing an opinion include: *in my opinion, if you ask me, it seems to me (that), to my mind, quite frankly* and *to tell (you) the truth.* Comment clauses, beginning with *it*, are also used to introduce an opinion: *It seems to me that …. It worries me that ….*

Opinions are often *hedged* so as to make them less assertive, eg by the use of expressions that reduce the force of an adjective: *I found it a bit dull. It was rather long.* Verbs like *seem* and *appear* are also used to reduce the assertiveness of an opinion: *I don't know but she seemed a bit distracted.*

To make opinions more emphatic, intensifying expressions are used: *He was definitely off side, without a doubt. I thought it was absolutely brilliant.*
More formal, particularly written ways of stating or reporting opinions can involve the use of the **passive** with verbs of cognition:

> *The house is believed to have been unoccupied at the time.*
> *It is thought that the fire started in the basement.*

To practise the language of opinion, the following topics are usually productive: films, books, music, etc; sports and sportspeople; local, national and international politics, particularly topical issues; and moral issues, such as cloning or animal rights. (→ **discussion**)

opposite → **antonym**

oral test → **testing**

order of acquisition SLA

The order of acquisition is the order in which grammar items are thought to be acquired. It is also called the *natural order* and the *order of development*. Research into the order of acquisition was first carried out on **first language acquisition**, by means of what are called *morpheme studies*. These are tests that attempt to elicit the correct use in context of specific **morphemes**, such as the *-ing* ending, or the definite article *the*. Researchers found what seemed to be a fixed order of acquisition in early first language development. In the 1970s, the same methods were used to investigate **second language acquisition** (SLA). These studies seemed to confirm that there is indeed a natural order for at least some morphemes. This order is the same, irrespective of the learners' first language, their age, or the order in which they are taught these items. The order of acquisition can be represented like this, where items in the higher boxes are acquired sooner than items in the lower boxes.

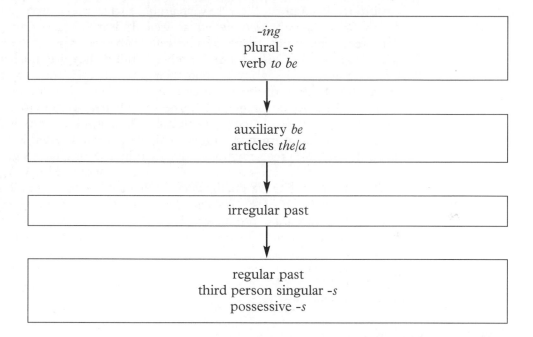

These findings prompted Stephen Krashen to formulate his *natural order hypothesis*. This states that the rules of language are acquired in a predictable order, regardless of the order in which they are taught. The suggestion that learners are 'programmed' to acquire grammar in a fixed order clearly has major implications. For Krashen there was only one implication: don't teach grammar – it is a waste of time. Other theorists have been more cautious. Some suggest that grammar teaching is not a waste of time, but that we shouldn't expect it to emerge in the order we teach it. According to this view, teaching can't change the *route* of acquisition, but it can speed up the *rate* of acquisition.

Other researchers have cast doubt on the reliability of the morpheme studies. Still others have investigated the acquisition of different features of language, such as syntax. For example, there seems to be a fixed order for acquiring negative structures (→ **negation**), question forms, and relative clauses.

However, no one has come up with a convincing explanation of the natural order. Some believe that it confirms the view that we are genetically 'programmed' for language (→ **universal grammar**). Others have suggested that the order of acquisition of grammar items reflects the relative **frequency** of the items in naturally-occurring input. Still others claim that certain forms are acquired sooner because they stand out more: the invariable and relatively audible *-ing* ending is more obvious than the variable, and sometimes hard-to-hear, *-ed* ending.

output hypothesis SLA

Output is the language that learners produce, either spoken or written. The output hypothesis is the theory that output, especially spoken output, is a necessary condition for language acquisition. This contradicts the view first proposed by Krashen in his *input hypothesis*. Krashen claimed that all that is necessary to ensure second language acquisition is *comprehensible input* (→ **input**). In contrast, Merrill Swain argues that learners also need to be pushed to produce *comprehensible output* as well. If learners are simply exposed to comprehensible input, they may understand the message but overlook the way the message is formulated. On the other hand, if they are 'pushed' to produce language at a level slightly beyond their present level, they are forced to pay attention to features of the grammar that they might otherwise not notice. Being pushed to produce language puts learners in a better position to notice the 'gaps' in their language knowledge (→ **noticing**). The output hypothesis developed out of the experience of **immersion** teaching in Canada, where it was observed that students who were receiving their education in a second language (French) had achieved native-like levels of understanding, but not of production. This led some researchers, including Swain, to conclude that simply understanding their classes was not enough. This also confirms the feeling shared by many teachers that an insistence on accurate production is good for learners. Pushing the learners means saying to them: *OK, that was good. Now say it again, but faster and more accurately.*

overgeneralization → **error**

overhead projector → **aids**

pairwork METHODOLOGY

Pairwork is a form of **classroom interaction** in which learners work in pairs to achieve a task. Pairwork can take the form of *open pairs*, where one student interacts across the class with another student while the rest of the class listen. Or it can take the form of *closed pairs*, where all the students are simultaneously interacting with their immediate neighbour. Setting up a **dialogue** activity, for example, may first start as a teacher–student interaction, followed by an open pairs stage. Once students are sufficiently familiar with the task, they can then go into closed pairs. Apart from dialogues, pairwork is good for practising any question-and-answer activity, such as an information gap task (→ **communicative activity**).

Other ways of organizing pairwork include: (1) *mingling* or *milling*: the students stand up and move about, interacting with other students in turn in order to ask and answer the questions of a prepared survey, for example. (2) *dyadic circles*: half the class sit in a circle in the centre of the room, facing outward, while the other half sit opposite them. In pairs they perform the task (such as interviewing each other about their free time activities). Then the students in the outer circle move around one place, and the task is repeated. (3) *parallel lines*: students sit or stand in two lines, facing one another, and at the end of the task the students in one line move up one place, the head of the line moving to the end of the line, so that each student has a new partner. (4) *Poster carousel*: Learners, working individually, first prepare a poster on a pre-selected theme. Half the students then stand by their posters, while the others circulate, moving from poster to poster, asking questions about each one, with a view to getting as clear as possible an idea of its content. Once all the presenters have been 'interviewed', the roles are reversed, and those who have been asking the questions then stand by their own posters and become the interviewees.

paradigm LINGUISTICS

A paradigm is a way of displaying the different forms of a word in the form of a list or table. For example:

singular		plural	
present	past	present	past
I *am*	I *was*	we *are*	we *were*
you *are*	you *were*	you *are*	you *were*
he/she/it *is*	he/she/it *was*	they *are*	they *were*

The words *am*, *are*, *is*, etc are said to have a *paradigmatic relation* with one another. This means that they fill the same 'slot' in a sentence, and only one of them may be present at any time in a given slot. Vertical slots contrast with horizontal 'chains'. Chains are elements in sequence, such as *I + am*, or *I + was*. The relationship between elements in a chain is called a *syntagmatic relationship*. Thus, the elements in the sentence *This little pig went to market* have the same syntagmatic relationship to one another as do the elements in *This little pig stayed at home*. On the other hand, the words *went and stayed* share the same paradigmatic relationship, as do the words *market* and *home*. All language choices consist, ultimately, of making chains and filling slots. For teaching purposes, these choices are typically displayed in the form of **substitution tables**.

paragraph DISCOURSE

A paragraph (like this one) is a way of organizing written texts into a sequence of topic-related sentences. The division of a text into paragraphs is an indication of its *macro-structure*. That is, the paragraphs represent the different stages of the text, such as introduction, problem, solution, conclusion. By dividing the text into meaningful units, paragraphing contributes to the overall **coherence** of a text. Typically, a paragraph begins with a *topic sentence*, and then the topic is developed in different ways, such as by elaboration or exemplification. A transitional sentence may then pave the way to the conclusion.

paralinguistics LINGUISTICS

Paralinguistics is the study of non-linguistic means of vocal communication. This includes the use of different kinds of *voice quality*, such as speaking in a 'breathy' voice or a 'gravelly' voice, as well as the use of loudness, **intonation** and tempo to convey particular emotions and attitudes. The term is also used to describe *non-vocal* features of communication, such as the use of gesture, facial expression, and eye contact. This is what is popularly known as 'body language'. (The technical term is *kinesics*.) For example, in face-to-face conversation, speakers will use a sharp intake of breath and a raising of the shoulders to signal the wish to take a turn (→ **conversation analysis**). At the same time, the speaker-to-be typically glances away from the current speaker: it's not customary to start talking when looking directly at your interlocutor. During a speaking turn, little head-nods from listeners tend to encourage speakers to speak faster, but if someone stands with their arms crossed, most speakers slow down. As speakers approach the end of their turn, there is a tendency to let the shoulders fall, and to redirect their gaze back at their interlocutors, as if to say 'I'm done'.

A related area is *proxemics*. This is the study of how speakers use and interpret variations in interpersonal distance, posture, and touch, during face-to-face communication.

parameter SLA

According to Chomsky's theory of **universal grammar (UG)**, the grammar that we are pre-programmed (or 'hard-wired') with consists of two components: principles and parameters. For example, all languages have **verb phrases** and **noun phrases**; that is a principle. But different languages construct phrases differently. The limited choice of variants is controlled by parameters. These are 'switched' to one setting or another when the child is exposed to language data. Thus, English phrases are switched to a *head-first* order. This means that verbs come before their complements, and prepositions come before nouns: *The picture is hanging on the wall*. In Japanese, on the other hand, phrases are switched to *head-last*, so that verbs come after their complements and nouns have *postpositions* (instead of prepositions): *e wa kabe ni kakatte imasu* ('picture – the wall on – is hanging'). The choice between head-first and head-last is governed by a parameter. So, principles are universal, but parameter settings are language-specific. According to the theory, learning a second language involves discovering its particular parameter settings. The question as to whether – and how – these parameters can be re-adjusted for a second language is hotly debated.

parsing GRAMMAR

Parsing is the process of analysing sentences into their component parts. It was once a staple activity in traditional grammar teaching. Here, for example, is one way of parsing the sentence: *Yankee Doodle stuck a feather in his cap*.

Yankee Doodle	*stuck*	*a feather*	*in his cap*
SUBJECT	VERB	OBJECT	ADVERBIAL
noun phrase	verb phrase	noun phrase	prepositional phrase

Parsing is also the term used to describe the largely unconscious mental processes by which a reader or listener works out the grammatical structure of sentences or utterances. To do this the 'parser' employs a number of processing strategies, such as assuming that the first noun phrase in a sentence (*Yankee Doodle*) is the subject. In English, the 'default' structure of a sentence is subject–verb–object (SVO) unless there is evidence to the contrary. Machine translation also depends on the capacity of computer programs to parse input, and this is a major research focus in computational linguistics.

Sensitizing learners to the way that sentences are structured in English can help them with both understanding and production. This is especially the case with learners in whose first language the structure of sentences is quite different. Asking learners to identify the main verb, its subject, and any other **clause** elements, may help them to 'unpack' the meaning of **complex sentences**, such as *The tourist who the guide claimed that the hotel manager had insulted wants to go home.*

participle GRAMMAR

Participles are words like *going* and *gone*. They are *non-finite* forms of the verb (→ **finite verb**). That is, they don't show contrasts of **tense**, **number** or **person**, and they can't occur alone as the main verb of a sentence. There are two types of participle: the *present participle* eg *working*, *writing*, and the *past participle* eg *worked*, *written*. Present participles are always formed by adding *-ing* to the verb stem. Regular past participles are formed by adding *-ed* to the verb stem, and so have the same form as the *past simple*. There are several different types of *irregular* past participle. These can be classified according to whether the form of the past participle is the same as the past simple (type 1), or the same as both the infinitive and the past simple (type 2), or whether all three forms are different (type 3). Further divisions are made according to whether they take a suffix such as *-en*, or whether there is an internal vowel change:

Type	infinitive	past simple	past participle
1a ('t' group)	*spend* *learn* *feel*	*spent* *learnt* *felt*	*spent* *learnt* *felt*
1b ('ght' group)	*teach* *buy*	*taught* *bought*	*taught* *bought*
1c ('d' group)	*say* *sell*	*said* *sold*	*said* *sold*
1d (vowel-change only group)	*hang* *win*	*hung* *won*	*hung* *won*
2	*hit* *put* *set*	*hit* *put* *set*	*hit* *put* *set*
3a ('-(e)n' group)	*break* *know* *eat*	*broke* *knew* *ate*	*broken* *known* *eaten*
3b (vowel-change only group)	*drink* *swim* *begin*	*drank* *swam* *began*	*drunk* *swum* *begun*

There are a number of common past participles that fit none of these categories, such as *come (come, came, come)*, *gone (go, went, gone)*, and *run (run, ran, run)*.

Very generally, the present participle expresses the course of a process, and the past participle describes its result or effects, as in the auctioneer's call: *Going, going, gone!* The terms *present* and *past* participle are misleading since the former is not restricted to present time reference (*it was raining*), nor is the latter restricted to past reference: (*it is written*). Hence, the terms *-ing participle* (or **-ing form**) and *-ed participle* (or *-en participle*) are sometimes used.

Participles are used:

- in conjunction with **auxiliary verbs** to form **verb phrases**: *As I was going to St. Ives …. I've been to London to look at the Queen.*
- after certain verbs: *Tom went howling down the street. Jill came tumbling after.*
- to post-modify nouns (→ **modifier**), in the form of a reduced **relative clause**: *Simple Simon met a pieman going to the fair. There was an old woman tossed up in a basket …*
- like adjectives: *I went out to the roaring sea, and saw a tossing boat.*
- on their own, as the verb in a non-finite participle **clause**: *The maid was in the garden, hanging out the clothes. In spring I look gay, dressed in handsome array.*

particle → **phrasal verb**

part of speech → **word class**

passive GRAMMAR

The passive contrasts with the *active* and together they make up the system called *voice*. Voice is the way the relationship between the **subject** and the **object** of the verb can be changed without changing the basic meaning of the sentence. For example, compare these newspaper headlines:

1. Man bites dog.
2. Dog is bitten by man.

The subject in the first (active) sentence is *Man*, while the subject in the second (passive) one is *Dog*. Yet the *agent* of the verb, ie, the person performing the action, is *man* in both cases. The *patient*, ie, the person or thing affected by the action, is *dog* in both cases.

There are many reasons for putting the patient into the subject position (ie, for using the passive). One reason is in order to distribute information according to what is not known (or *given*) and what is known (or *new*), Very generally, there is a tendency to place *given* information at the beginning of the sentence and *new* information at the end. So, in the following two versions of a news story, the second version is easier to process, because its second sentence follows the order of *given* to *new*:

1. *A dog got a big fright yesterday. A man bit it.*
2. *A dog got a big fright yesterday. It was bitten by a man.*

A passive construction followed by a *by*-phrase, identifying the agent, is called the *long passive*: *This pyramid was built by the Aztecs.* The *short passive* (ie, the passive without a *by*-phrase) is used because the agent is not known (*My bike's been stolen*), or is obvious (*A man has been arrested*), or because the speaker doesn't wish to identify the agent (*Your application has been turned down*). The short passive is often used in a formal, written style, eg in public notices:

Passengers are reminded that baggage should not be left unattended.
Baggage found unattended will be removed and may be destroyed.

In fact, the passive is much more common in written language than in spoken, making up around twenty-five per cent of all finite verbs in academic writing, but occurring only rarely in casual conversation.

The passive is formed by combining the **auxiliary verb** *be* with the past **participle**. Note that only *transitive* verbs (ie, verbs that take an object → **transitivity**) can take the passive voice. Passive verbs can be marked for **tense**, **aspect** and **modality** in the same way as active verbs:

	simple	progressive aspect	perfect aspect
present tense	*it is written*	*it is being written*	*it has been written*
past tense	*it was written*	*it was being written*	*it had been written*
future (modal *will*)	*it will be written*	*it will be being written***	*it will have been written*

* Forms with *be being* and *been being* are rare.

Passive meaning is also conveyed in non-finite verb structures, through the use of the past **participle**: *Baggage should not be left <u>unattended</u>.* Passive constructions can also be formed with the verb *get* in the role of an auxiliary: *My best friend is getting married. I got given the wrong book.*

The passive is often taught in the context of manufacturing processes (*Tea is grown mainly in the Indian sub-continent and China. It is usually picked by hand and then dried …*), and to talk about discoveries, inventions and historical events: *Pluto was discovered in 1930. The first atomic bomb was dropped on Hiroshima.* The passive is also quite common in biographical information: *Rutherford was born in … He was awarded … He was knighted …* The present perfect and the passive combine to talk about recent changes: *The old railway station has been turned into a shopping centre. The bridge has been widened …*

past perfect → **perfect**

past progressive → **progressive**

past simple GRAMMAR

The past simple is the name given to the past **tense**: *Something <u>happened</u>. The train <u>left</u>.* It is 'simple' because, like the **present simple**, it is not marked for **aspect**. This distinguishes it from other past forms, like the past **progressive** (*Something <u>was happening</u>. The train <u>was leaving</u>*), and the past **perfect** (*Something <u>had happened</u>. The train <u>had left</u>*).

The past simple in regular verbs is formed by adding -*ed* to the verb stem: *happened, liked, carried.* This is the same form as the past **participle**. The pronunciation of the -*ed* ending varies. After the sounds /t/ and /d/ it is pronounced /ɪd/: *started, ended.* After all other voiced consonants (→ **voiced sound**), and after vowel sounds, it is pronounced /d/: *sobbed, climbed, stayed.* After unvoiced consonants it is pronounced /t/: *shopped, watched, missed.*

Irregular verbs fall into several groups, according to whether they take the same form as their infinitive and past participle forms, or a different one (see the table under **participle**). Many of the most common verbs, such as *be, go, do, make, put* and *give*, are irregular. The **modal verbs** (apart from *must*) have forms that, in certain contexts, such as **reported speech**, are equivalent to past forms: *can* ⇨ *could, will* ⇨ *would, shall* ⇨ *should, may* ⇨ *might.*

Except for the verb *to be*, the question form and negative of the past simple are formed by using the operator *did*: *How did it happen? Did the train leave? It didn't happen. The train didn't leave.*

The past simple is used to express these meanings:

- states, events, and habits in the past, and unconnected with the present: *We were lost. It rained. Tomás always paid.*
- present situations reported in the past: *I told him I was married …* (→ **reported speech**)
- present or future hypothetical situations: *I wish I had the time. If no one came to work tomorrow …* (→ **hypothetical meaning**)
- politeness in the present: *Did you want to see me? Do you think I could …*

Because it is used to talk about events disconnected from the present, or to hypothesize, or to indicate social distance, the past simple has sometimes been called the *remote form*. Some theorists (such as Michael Lewis) argue that this term is more accurate, since it captures the basic meaning of the past simple, from which all other meanings flow.

The past simple is one of the most common verb forms in English, not only in fiction and news reporting, but also in conversation. One reason for its frequency in conversation is that it is used to tell stories, and stories are very common in casual talk (→ **narrating**). The frequency of the past simple suggests that it should be taught as soon as possible. The main difficulties it presents learners are its question and negative forms, and the somewhat mystifying forms of its irregular verbs. Contexts for presenting and practising the past simple include: talking about recent activities, holidays, etc; personal biography and curriculum vitae; the biographies of famous people; history; personal anecdotes, jokes, urban legends, and folk tales.

pause filler DISCOURSE

In order to maintain **fluency**, speakers need to avoid frequent, long or silent pauses. One way of doing this is to use pause fillers, also called simply *fillers* or *hesitators*. The most common are *er* and *erm* (usually written as *uh* and *um* in American English). A number of common **discourse markers**, such as *well*, *actually*, *you know* and *I mean* also double as pause fillers. Some vague expressions like *sort of*, as well as the hedging device *like*, are also commonly used, as in *It's like sort of erm you know tropical*. Another way of filling pauses is to repeat a word or phrase a number of times, as in *It's, it's, it's tropical*. It's arguable whether learners need to be taught pause fillers, but not to use any may contribute to an impression of lack of fluency.

perfect GRAMMAR

The perfect is one of the two verb **aspects** in English, the other being the **progressive**. It combines with tense to form the *present perfect*, *past perfect* and *future perfect* structures. It also combines with the progressive to form the present, past, and future *perfect progressive*. The perfect is formed by combining the **auxiliary verb** *have* with the past **participle**: *The Eagle has landed.*

The basic meaning of the perfect is 'before – and connected to – a point in time'. In the case of the present perfect, the point in time is the present, ie, *speech time* (the time at which an utterance is spoken, or a sentence written). Thus, *I've lived in Italy* means 'at some time in the period that extends back from the time of speaking I lived in Italy'. The time itself is *indefinite*. Contrast this with *I lived in Italy in the late 90s*. Here the time is definite and disconnected from the moment of speaking. With the past perfect, the point of time is in the past and is defined by the context. Thus, *They gave me the job because I'd lived in Italy* situates the 'living in Italy' in a period of time prior to being given the job. Compare this with *They gave me the job because I lived in Italy*.

There are at least two reasons for choosing to view an event in this retrospective way. One is that, although finished, it is still relevant, as in *The Eagle has landed* (= it is still there); *I've lived in Italy* (= that's why I speak Italian). The other reason for viewing the situation as being connected to speech time is to indicate that it is unfinished, eg *I've lived in Italy all my life*. This is why the perfect often combines with expressions of *duration*, such as *how long ...?, ... for ages, ... since I was a child*, etc.

The combination of **progressive** and perfect aspects unites their two basic meanings, that of the event being in progress, and of the event being viewed retrospectively: *How long has this been going on? I hadn't been waiting long before the bus arrived*.

The present perfect is baffling for many learners – even those, like French or German speakers, who have a similar structure in their L1. This is because notions such as relevance, connectedness, and unfinishedness are subjective and difficult to pin down. Rather than try and teach rules, therefore, it may be easier to relate the perfect with the kinds of time expressions it co-occurs with (such as *yet, just, already*), and to relate it to the typical contexts it is used in. In the case of the present perfect, typical contexts are: talking about work and travel experiences, talking about things that have changed, and announcing news.

performance → **competence**

permission FUNCTION

The most common way of asking permission is to use the **modal verbs** *can, could* and *may*, in that order of formality:

> <u>Can</u> *I bring a friend?*
> <u>Could</u> *we have a look around?*
> <u>May</u> *I use the phone?*

The verb *let* and the semi-modal construction *be allowed* are also frequent, as are questions with *mind*:

> *Would you <u>let</u> me leave my bags here?*
> *Are we <u>allowed</u> to start writing?*
> *Do you <u>mind</u> if I start?*

Less formal expressions include: *Is it OK if ...? Is it all right if ...?*

In more formal, written, contexts, the word *permission* can be used: *I am writing to ask <u>permission</u> to take photographs in the library ....*

To give permission, the following expressions are used: *Of course. Go ahead. No problem. That's fine by me.* To give permission to questions with *mind*, a negative construction is often used:

> *Would you mind if I opened the window? ~ Not at all.*

To refuse permission, the refusal is usually softened with an apology:

> *Would you let me leave my bags here? ~ I'm sorry, but it's not allowed.*

Contexts for practising the language of permission include any situation where rules are strictly enforced, such as when dealing with officialdom or in situations where security is a priority, eg on planes. The classroom also offers an ideal context for authentic practice, especially for young learners.

person GRAMMAR

Person is the way some pronouns and verbs refer to either the speaker (*first person*), the addressee (*second person*), or others (*third person*). In English, personal **pronouns** (*I, me; you; he, him*, etc), possessive forms (*my, mine, your, yours*, etc), and reflexive pronouns (*myself, yourself, herself*, etc) are all marked for person. *You* usually refers to the addressee, but it can refer to people in general: *You learn something every day!* Likewise, *we* is sometimes used to refer to the addressee: *How are we today?*

But, apart from the verb *to be*, the only verb form that is inflected for person is the third person in the present simple, which is marked with an *-s*: *Power corrupts. Time flies. Grammar rules.* The third person singular *-s* is one of the great mysteries of English grammar for learners of English, not least because it is the same suffix that is used to indicate plurality. All other verbs are uninflected for person, except for the auxiliary *be*, where person is indicated: *I am not joking. Are you kidding? He's pulling your leg.*

personalization METHODOLGY

When you personalize language you use it to talk about your knowledge, experience and feelings. Personalization of the type *Now write five true sentences about yourself using 'used to'* is often motivated by the need to provide further practice of pre-taught grammar structures. But it is also good preparation for the kinds of situations of genuine language use that learners might encounter outside the classroom. These advantages are lost, though, if the teacher's response is to treat the exercise as *only* an exercise, and correct the learners' errors without responding to the content. The influence of **humanistic approaches** has given a fresh impetus to personalization, both in terms of providing a more coherent rationale and suggesting a broader range of activity types. For a start (it is argued), personalization creates better classroom **dynamics**. This is because groups are more likely to form and bond if the individuals in them know more about one another. And the mental and emotional effort that is involved in finding personal associations with a language item is likely to make that item more memorable. This quality is called cognitive and affective *depth* (→ **affect**; → **memory**). Finally, lessons are likely to be more interesting, and hence more motivating, if at least some of the content concerns the people in the room, rather than the characters in coursebooks. On these grounds, some writers have suggested that personalization should not be considered simply as an 'add-on', but should be the principle on which most, if not all, classroom content should be based. One teaching approach that is committed to this view is **community language learning**. In this approach, all the content of the lesson comes from the learners themselves. Personalization is not without risks, though. Teachers need to be sensitive to learner resistance: learners should have the right to 'pass' on questions that they consider too intrusive. And teachers should be authentic in the way that they respond to learners' personalizations. This means that they should respond to *what* their learners are saying, not just how they say it.

personal pronoun → **pronoun**

phatic language DISCOURSE

Phatic language is language whose purpose is to smooth the conduct of social relations. Unlike *transactional* language, which serves in the exchange of goods, services and ideas, phatic language has an *interpersonal* **function**. Phatic communication is typically formulaic (→ **formulaic language**), as in the case of **greetings**, and is a characteristic of what is called *small talk*. Despite the implication that small talk is trivial, phatic communication plays a very important role in the formation and maintenance of social groupings. It may even have been the origin of language itself. Most learners recognize the need for a handful of useful expressions for handling small talk situations, and these can be easily practised at the beginnings and endings of lessons.

phoneme PHONOLOGY

A phoneme is one of the distinctive sounds of a particular language. That is to say, it is not *any* sound, but it is a sound that, to speakers of the language, cannot be replaced with another sound without causing a change in meaning. Thus, the sounds /p/ and /b/ are both phonemes in English, since there is a meaning difference between the two words *pin* and *bin*, or between *cap* and *cab*. (These minimally different pairs of words are known as **minimal pairs**). In some languages such as Arabic, however, /p/ and /b/ are not differentiated: replacing one with the other does not make a difference of meaning. Hence, they are not phonemes in Arabic. On the other hand, Arabic has phonemic distinctions that an English-speaker would not recognize as such. The set of phonemes of a particular language is its *phonemic system*, and the study of it is called **phonology**. This contrasts with **phonetics**, which is the study of speech sounds in general, irrespective of their meaning-making role.

The fact that a language has a phonemic system does not, of course, mean that all speakers of that language pronounce the phonemes in exactly the same way. The way a US speaker of English says *cab*, for example, is quite different from the way a South African might pronounce the same word: they realize these sound combinations differently. But both speakers would still make a distinction between their own pronunciations of *cab* and *cap*. Or *cab*, *cob* and *cub*, for that matter. Differences in **accent** are mapped on to the same phonemic system (apart from some minor differences → **American English**).

Phoneme sounds are also pronounced differently even by an individual speaker, according to the different phonetic environments in which the sound is uttered. Thus the sound that is normally spelt *sh*, and which is represented by the phonemic symbol /ʃ/, is produced differently at the beginning of the word *shoe* than it is at the beginning of the word *she*. In *shoe* the lips are rounded whereas in *she* they are spread. However, saying *she* with the rounded lips of *shoe*, or vice versa, does not alter a listener's perception of the difference in meaning between the two words. These different ways of realizing the same phoneme are called *allophones*.

Since there is rarely a one-to-one match between a language's written alphabet and its sound system, the phonemes of a language are represented by symbols. These symbols, called *phonemic script*, are written within slashes: /p/, /b/. British English, in its **Received Pronunciation** form (RP), has forty-four phonemes, distributed between twenty-four **consonants** and twenty **vowels**. The following list of English phonemes comes from the *Macmillan English Dictionary for Advanced Learners*:

Consonants

p	press	ʒ	measure
b	bag	h	hot
t	time	x	loch
d	card	tʃ	chair
k	can	dʒ	jam
g	dog	m	more
f	staff	n	snow
v	vote	ŋ	sing
θ	thin	w	water
ð	that	r	ring
s	sit	l	small
z	zebra	j	you
ʃ	shine		

Vowels and diphthongs

ɪ	bit	ɔː	caught
e	bed	uː	boot
æ	bad	ɜː	bird
ɒ	hot	eɪ	bay
ʌ	cut	aɪ	buy
ʊ	book	ɔɪ	boy
ə	about	əʊ	go
i	pretty	aʊ	now
u	annual	ʊə	poor
iː	bee	eə	hair
ɑː	father	ɪə	hear

For teaching purposes, the phonemes are often displayed in the form of a *phonemic chart*.

Underhill, A. 2005 *Sound Foundations* (Macmillan)

The phonemic chart might imply that learners need to be *taught* the phonemic system of English. After all, the English system is sure to be different in several ways from the phonemic system of their own language. However, the issue is less clear-cut than simply 'replacing' one phonemic system with another. It ignores the fact that there will be areas where the two systems may coincide. It also ignores the difference between *reception* (discriminating between the sounds as a listener) and *production* (producing the different sounds as a speaker), which may require quite different classroom approaches. Finally, there is the question of priorities, especially where **intelligibility** is concerned: some sounds may play a greater role in a speaker's intelligibility than others. For example, it has been found that the ability to produce the English phonemes /θ/ and /ð/ (as in the initial sounds in the words *thin* and *that*) does not contribute a great deal to a speaker's intelligibility, especially when interacting with other non-native speakers of English (→ **phonological core**). These, and other issues, determine the approach that teachers take to **pronunciation teaching**.

phonetics PHONOLOGY

Phonetics is the science of speech sounds, including the ways that these sounds are produced, transmitted, and received. Phoneticians are interested in *all* speech sounds, not just the sounds of a particular language (the study of which is called **phonology**). Nor are they interested in the differences in meaning that some sounds (called **phonemes**) make. Again, this belongs to phonology. In phonetics, sounds are described and classified according to the way they are physically articulated (→ **articulator**). The International Phonetic Alphabet (IPA) is a way of representing all attested sounds. Because there are many more sounds than there are phonemes in English, the IPA is a much bigger alphabet than the phonemic alphabet. To make a phonetic transcription of spoken language, the phonetic symbols are written between square brackets: eg [t], [ʔ]. (The second of these represents the *glottal stop*, as in some pronunciations of *bottle*. Note that pronouncing *bottle* with or without a glottal stop makes no difference to the meaning. So, in English at least, the glottal stop is *phonetic*, not *phonemic*.) Generally speaking, language teaching is less concerned with *phonetics* than with *phonology*. But an understanding of the way sounds are produced, interpreted and described can help inform the teaching of the latter.

phonics METHODOLOGY

Phonics is an approach to the teaching of first language reading that is based on the principle of identifying sound–letter relationships, and using this knowledge to 'sound out' unfamiliar words when reading. Phonics has been criticized because it encourages an exclusively 'bottom-up' approach to reading, ignoring the value of recognizing whole word shapes, or using context clues to decode new words. Phonics contrasts with more holistic, 'top-down' approaches to teaching literacy, such as those advocated in **whole language learning**. Typical top-down activities include being read to while following the words on the page, or reading aloud with the assistance of an adult or a slightly more proficient classmate. Nowadays, literacy training often involves a combination of approaches, where the sounding out of words is only one of several effective reading strategies. In second language teaching, the phonics debate is less of an issue since most adult second language learners are already literate. Where it may still be relevant is in the teaching of **young learners**.

phonological core PHONOLOGY

The phonological core is the name given to those features of pronunciation that are considered essential in order to be understood when speaking **English as an international language (EIL)**. These are the features that have been shown to be crucial in ensuring **intelligibility** between non-native speakers of English.

Proponents of the phonological core challenge the traditional view that the best model for teaching English pronunciation should be a **native speaker** one, and **Received Pronunciation** (RP) in particular. RP is used in native speaker–native speaker communication, but it is considered both unrealistic and inappropriate as a standard for English in its role as a global lingua franca. Instead, learners can be safe in the knowledge that they can speak English with their own accents, so long as they are attentive to the following features (as proposed by Jennifer Jenkins):

1. most **consonant** sounds (but not the *th* sounds in either *thing* or *that*)
2. **consonant clusters** at the beginnings of words, but not necessarily at the ends
3. **vowel** length distinctions, ie, the difference between long and short vowels
4. nuclear **stress** (ie, the correct placement of stress in an utterance)

This is obviously a much more simplified syllabus for pronunciation, particularly with regard to vowel sounds, than one that is based on replacing learners' **accents** with RP.

phonology PHONOLOGY

Phonology is the study of the sound system of a particular language, and how this system is used by its speakers to express meaning. Phonology is distinct from **phonetics**, which is concerned with describing the sounds of speech in general, regardless of their role in conveying meaning. Phonology, on the other hand, describes the abstract system that allows the speakers of a language to distinguish meaning from mere verbal noise.

The basic unit of study in phonology is the **phoneme**, of which there are forty-four in standard British English. Phonemes are divided into **vowels** and **consonants**, and the former into *monophthongs* and *diphthongs*. It is customary to transcribe speech using *phonemic symbols*. This is the way that the pronunciation of a word is represented in most dictionaries. But phonemes do not exist in isolation, and even words with the same sequences of phonemes can have different meanings, according to which syllable is emphasized. Compare a *black bird* with a *blackbird*, for example, or an *arch bishop* with an *archbishop*. Hence, phonology is also concerned with not just the smallest units of speech (the *segmental* features), but with the larger elements as well, such as **stress**, **rhythm** and **intonation** (the *suprasegmental* features). These latter elements, especially when considered along with tempo, loudness and voice quality, are sometimes referred to as the prosodic features, or *prosody*, of speech.

The importance attached to phonology in the teaching of second languages has fluctuated over the years. At one time it was thought that the mastery of the sounds of the language was absolutely essential, even before the teaching of other systems, such as grammar and vocabulary, had started. Nowadays, it is generally thought that, for most learners, native-like mastery is neither a realistic nor even a desirable goal, and that **intelligibility** should be the standard by which a learner's pronunciation is judged. (→ **accent**; → **phonological core**; → **pronunciation teaching**)

phrasal verb GRAMMAR

A phrasal verb is a combination of a verb and one or two *particles*. The particle is either an adverb or a preposition, or both, as in (respectively): *look up* (*a word in the dictionary*), *look after* (*the children*), *look up to* (*someone you respect*). Sometimes the term *phrasal verb* is reserved for verb + adverb combinations (like *look up*), while verb + preposition combinations (like *look after*) are called *prepositional verbs*, and verb + adverb + preposition combinations (like *look up to*) are called *phrasal-prepositional verbs*. They are also all called *multi-word verbs*.

Phrasal verbs are different from verbs that happen to be followed by a preposition, as in *I looked at the painting*. Sometimes the difference is not always clear, as some words can be both a preposition and an adverb, depending on their function in the sentence. For example:

1. *Ivan looked up the chimney.*
2. *Ivan looked after the children.*
3. *Ivan looked up the word.*
4. *Ivan looked up.*

In sentence (1) *up the chimney* is a *prepositional phrase* (→ **preposition**), and *up* is the preposition that forms an inseparable part of it. *Up the chimney* is a single syntactic unit, and forms a sentence **adverbial**, answering the question *where?* It could be moved to another position in the sentence, as in *Up the chimney Ivan looked*. (Or, more plausibly, *Up the hill Ivan ran*). We could also insert an adverb between *looked* and *up*: *Ivan looked carefully up the chimney*. But we cannot say *⋆Ivan looked the chimney up*. Finally, in the question *What did Ivan look up?* (answer: *The chimney*), the stress is on *look*. For all these reasons, the combination of *look* and *up* is not a phrasal verb, but simply a verb followed by a preposition.

In sentence (2) *after* behaves like a preposition in that it has a noun complement (*the children*) from which it cannot be separated: *⋆Ivan looked the children after*. But nor can we say *⋆After the children Ivan looked* or *⋆Ivan looked carefully after the children*. Nor can we ask *Where did Ivan look?* and answer *⋆After the children*. All this suggests that *look* and *after* form a tighter combination than *look* and *up* do in sentence (1). Therefore, *look after* qualifies as a phrasal verb (or prepositional verb, in some grammars).

In sentence (3) *up* functions as an adverb. It does not meet any of the preposition 'tests' above. We cannot say *⋆Ivan looked carefully up the word*. Nor *⋆Up the word Ivan looked*. But we can say *Ivan looked the word up*. In this sentence, the verb is *looked up*, and *the word* is its object, answering the question *What?* And, in the question *What did Ivan look up?* (answer: *The word*) the stress is on *up*. For all these reasons, *up* is an adverb, and forms the particle of the phrasal verb *look up*.

Finally, in sentence (4) *up* is clearly not part of a prepositional phrase: it is closely tied to the verb. It is also an adverb, and *look up*, in this case, is a phrasal verb too. But, unlike *look up* in sentence (3) which is transitive, *look up* in sentence (4) is intransitive – it takes no object (→ **transitivity**).

What about meaning? In sentence 1, *look* and *up* comprise two separate units of meaning. But, in sentence 2, *look after* is a single unit of meaning, meaning something like *take care of*. Likewise, *look up* in sentence 3 is a single unit of meaning and one, moreover, that is not entirely literal (Ivan didn't literally look *up*). The meaning of many phrasal verbs is idiomatic in this way: their meaning is not simply a combination of the meanings of their component parts: *They don't get on. The plane took off. Do you give up?* But there are many verb + adverb combinations that are not idiomatic, such as sentence (4): *Ivan looked up*, so idiomaticity is not as reliable a test of a phrasal verb as syntax is.

Taking into account all of the above, phrasal verbs are customarily divided into four types:

Type	Syntax	Examples
1 (prepositional verbs)	verb + preposition particle + object	*Can you <u>deal with</u> it?* *I <u>ran into</u> Jacob yesterday.* *I'm <u>looking for</u> my keys.*
2 (intransitive phrasal verbs)	verb + adverb particle	*A storm <u>blew up</u>.* *It pays to <u>shop around.</u>* *How do the two of them <u>get by</u>?*
3. (transitive phrasal verbs)	verb + adverb particle + object verb + object + adverb particle	*Can you <u>write down</u> your address?* *I'll <u>pick</u> you <u>up</u> at eight.* *We'll have to <u>put</u> the wedding <u>off</u>.*
4. (phrasal-prepositional verbs)	verb + adverb particle + preposition + object	*We've <u>run out of</u> gas.* *You should <u>cut down on</u> fats.*

Note that in Type 1 phrasal verbs, the particle cannot come after the object (it is *inseparable*), whereas in Type 3, the particle can be separated by the object (and must be separated by the object if the object is a pronoun), hence it is *separable*.

Due to the complexity of their grammar, phrasal verbs present enormous problems to learners. The fact that so many are idiomatic does not help either. And, on top of that, many are restricted in terms of style, tending to be informal or even slang (such as *faff about, nod off, chill out*). Not surprisingly, many learners avoid using them altogether. Traditional approaches to the teaching of phrasal verbs tend to focus on the syntax rules, ie, whether they are transitive or intransitive, and, if the former, whether they are separable or not. These rules are often quite mystifying for most learners (and many teachers!). Phrasal verbs are also often grouped according to their lexical verb: *get up, get back, get off, get over*, etc, and exercises are designed to test the learner's knowledge of the difference. This may seem systematic but it can easily lead to confusion, since the verbs are so similar in form. An alternative is to focus on the meanings of the particles. A focus on particles aims to sensitize learners to the shared meanings of a group such as *carry on, drive on, hang on, go on* and *come on*.

It may be the case, however, that phrasal verbs are best learned on an item-by-item basis, and preferably in short contexts that demonstrate their syntactic behaviour. The teacher can increase the probability of learners coming across phrasal verbs by providing texts that are likely to have a high frequency of phrasal verbs in them. Some books on phrasal verbs present theme-related sets of verbs in specially written texts. Thus, a text about relationships may include such phrasal verbs as *go out with, get on with, fall out, split up, make up, get back together*, etc. A looser and more natural relationship may be more effective, such as the way words occur in authentic texts. In this example, a restaurant review, the phrasal verbs are underlined:

Rocket is one of those places that you just keep <u>coming back</u> to. Its secluded location – <u>tucked away</u> in a charming cobble-stoned lane in Mayfair – ensures you feel a world away from central London. And don't be <u>put off</u> by the expensive-looking décor: Rocket's menu is sensitive to the needs of budget diners and the portions are huge. We <u>started off</u> with a generous serving of parmesan and garlic pizza bread (£2.50), then I ordered a goat's cheese, courgette and sundried tomato pizza (£7) while my friend <u>went for</u> the spicy couscous-crusted chicken, <u>served up</u> with french beans and squash (£8). We <u>washed</u> it all <u>down</u> with a bottle of Chilean merlot (De Gras 1999, £12) and the whole bill <u>came to</u> less than £15 each. Provided you're dressed to <u>blend in</u> with posh city folk, then give Rocket a try. [1]

To exploit such a text – and assuming basic comprehension of the text has first been checked – learners could search for and underline the phrasal verbs. They could then check their understanding of them by searching for a synonym in the dictionary. They could then classify the verbs (according to the chart above). Finally, they could write their own text (about a restaurant of their choice, for example), trying to include as many of the phrasal verbs as possible.

phrase GRAMMAR

Phrases occupy the level on the grammatical hierarchy between individual words and **clauses**. They are a unit of one or more words that form a single element of clause structure. There are five types of phrase, each one associated with one of five word classes: **noun**, **verb**, **adjective**, **adverb** and **preposition**. For example, each of the elements in the following sentences can be grouped according to one of the five different phrase types:

adverb phrase (AdvP)	noun phrase (NP)	verb phrase (VP)	adjective phrase (AdjP)	prepositional phrase (PP)
Quite often	*my older brother*	*would get*	*totally lost*	*in the woods.*
Unsurprisingly	*Alice*	*feels*	*lonely*	*at the weekends.*
As soon as we arrived	*the wind that had been blowing all morning*	*turned*	*cold as ice.*	
Very slowly	*the aircraft carrier*	*began to sink*		*beneath the waves.*

Note that some of the examples of phrases consist of a single word (eg, *Alice*, *lonely*). But they have the potential to be expanded into multi-word units: *poor old Alice, extremely lonely*).

The structure of adverb phrases, noun phrases and adjective phrases is similar in that each consists of a *head* (the main word in the phrase) which can be modified both before and after (→ **modifier**):

pre-modification	head	post-modification
quite	*often*	
my older	*brother*	
	lonely	
the	*wind*	*that had been blowing all morning*
as	*soon*	*as we arrived*
	cold	*as ice*

[1] *TNT Magazine*, 23 September, 2001.

Prepositional phrases consist of a preposition and a noun phrase complement: *in the woods*; *at the weekends*. Verb phrases consist of a main verb and any **auxiliary verbs**. Some verb phrases consist of two main verbs *in phase*. This means that the two verbs are closely linked, and the first verb needs the second verb to complete its meaning: *began to sink, wanted to leave, kept barking*, etc.

Phrase structure differs from language to language, so it is not necessarily the case that learners will know how phrases are internally sequenced in English. This is particularly the case with the **noun phrase**, arguably the most complex and certainly the most common. Activities involving **parsing**, ie, analysing phrases into their components, may help some learners.

pitch → **intonation**

placement test → **testing**

planning → **lesson plan**

plans and intentions FUNCTION

Plans and intentions are frequently expressed by the semi-modal construction *going to* and the **modal verb** *will*:

I'm going to wash that man right out of my life.
I'll build a stairway to Paradise.

The difference in meaning is subtle, and quite often the two forms are interchangeable. Some grammar books suggest that *going to* is used to talk about plans and intentions that have already been made, and which are therefore notionally connected to the present. By contrast, *will* is used, at the *moment of deciding*, to talk about events in the future. In other words, *will* is used to make plans; *going to* is used to report them. **Discourse analysis** has shown that *going to* is often use to *frame* a future situation, after which *will* is preferred. This is quite common in restaurant contexts:

What are you going to have?
I think I'll start with a salad and then I'll have the fish.

It's also the case that *going to* is more common in spoken language and *will* more common in written, suggesting a difference in **style**.

The use of *going to* and *will* to talk about plans and intentions parallels their use to make **predictions**:

It's going to work out fine.
You'll never walk alone.

That is, *going to* is notionally connected to the present, while *will* is not.

To emphasize the determination of an intention, *will* can be stressed: *I WILL go to the ball!* In British English *shall* is also used with *I* and *we*, and sounds slightly formal.

Other ways of expressing plans and intentions include:

- the present **progressive**, especially to talk about arrangements: *I'm coming home next week. Who are you staying with in Brussels?*
- using the verbs *plan, intend, mean, aim, decide*: *They are planning to retire soon. Did you mean to do it? The USA aims to have a man on Mars by the year 2020. I've decided to paint the kitchen.*

- (more formally) using nouns like *aim, plan, intention*: *My aim is to become a champion snooker player. It is our intention to lower taxes.*

Situations for talking about plans and intentions include: travel and holidays, business plans, political programmes, or simply the immediate leisure plans for the evening or the weekend.

play → **language play**

plural → **number**

plurilingualism → **bilingualism; Common European Framework**; → **critical pedagogy; translation**

politeness DISCOURSE

Politeness can mean showing respect to differences in social rank. Use of honorifics, such as *sir, madam,* or titles and surnames (*Dr Dolittle, Lady Bracknell*) are ways of showing such respect. In this sense, politeness is more like courtesy or good manners But, politeness also means showing respect for other people's *face*. Face is defined in two ways: it is the desire to be appreciated (called *positive face*), and it is the desire not be imposed upon (called *negative face*). For example, I want you to appreciate that I cooked dinner. But I don't want you to ask me to do the dishes.

Social behaviour which expresses positive attitudes to other people is called *positive politeness*. Positive politeness can take the form of thanking: *Thanks for the meal,* or paying compliments: *That's a nice shirt!* or showing agreement: *That's exactly what I thought!* or using terms of address that increase the hearer's sense of importance, such as *Certainly, officer,* or (in less formal situations) using terms of familiarity that imply a close friendship, even if there isn't one, such as *mate* or *sweetheart*.

On the other hand, social behaviour which avoids imposing on others is called *negative politeness*. There are many ways that negative politeness is achieved in language. Saying *please* is the best known. Another common way is to acknowledge that you are imposing and even to apologize for it:

> *I hate to ask this, but could you take you shoes off?*
> *I'm really sorry, but you're not supposed to smoke in here.*

Another way is to use language that minimizes the potential threat to face, by using diminutives (ways of making something sound small), or by using indirect language, including **modal verbs**, the past tense and **conditionals**:

> *If I could just have a tiny moment of your time.*
> *I think you might have broken it.*
> *I was wondering if you did deliveries?*

Finally, the use of some kind of lead-in (or pre-sequence) is common in requests and invitations. Requests and invitations are *face threatening acts (FTAs)* since they expose both the speaker and the addressee to the risk of a refusal. Hence, they are often prefaced by a question which gives the addressee a let-out:

> *Are you using your car tonight? ~ Yes, I am, actually. Why? ~ Oh, nothing.*
> *Are you free on Friday? ~ No, I'm all booked up, I'm afraid. ~ Oh, well, never mind.*

The concepts of positive and negative politeness are universal, and there is no culture that can be said to be more or less polite than another. Different cultures, though, have different ways of avoiding, minimizing and negotiating potential threats to face. This usually involves the use of language that is often quite complex, and not necessarily directly transferable from one language to another. So, in order not to appear impolite, learners need to learn at least two things: they need to learn the particular behaviours associated with potential FTAs in the target language culture, and they need to learn the way that these behaviours are expressed through language. A learner of English preparing to visit the USA, for example, might need to know that it is customary there to respond to a compliment by downplaying it, but without denying it, as in:

What a great scarf! ~ Oh, do you like it? It's just an old thing I have.

This behaviour might differ in other cultures. Indeed, in some cultures, such as Egypt, it is customary to respond to a compliment by offering the item to the person who made the compliment. All this makes the teaching of politeness quite face-threatening in itself, as it may involve teaching behaviours that fit uncomfortably with the learners' own **culture**. This sometimes takes the form of teaching learners a list of *dos and don'ts*. More useful might be to teach learners particular all-purpose language devices that can be used in a range of situations, such as formulaic expressions (*Would you like …? Do you mind if …?*), minimizing language (*a bit, just*), and modal verbs. A good way of practising politeness language and strategies is through *roleplays* (→ **drama**).

polysemy VOCABULARY

Polysemy means 'many meanings' and refers to the case where one word has more than one related meaning. Thus, the word *chip* can mean (1) a piece of deep-fried potato, (2) a small piece of wood, and (3) an electronic component. Because the words have a common, or core, meaning (ie, small piece of some solid material), they are said to be *polysemes*. This distinguishes them from **homonyms**, such as *bat*, whose different meanings (*to bat one's eyelashes, a vampire bat, a cricket bat*) do not overlap in any way. There are some cases, however, where it is not always easy to differentiate a polyseme from a homonym. These meanings of the adjective *fair*, for example, are only very distantly related: *this fair city of ours; one fair day; let's be fair; her long fair hair*. From a practical point of view, the *polysemous* nature of many English words complicates the task of learning vocabulary: how many meanings of a word do you need to know in order to be able to say you know the word? It also means that there is not much sense in talking about the most frequent words in English without reference to their different meanings.

portfolio TESTING

A portfolio is a collection of original work that is put together by a student for the purposes of **assessment**. It may include examples of classwork, such as written compositions, or of homework, such as projects, or even audio or video recordings. It may also include some form of self-assessment or **reflection**. The *European Language Portfolio (ELP)* is designed to encourage learners to assess their own progress according to criteria described in the **Common European Framework**. It also includes a 'language biography' in which learners record their learning experiences, including contacts with other languages and cultures.

positive → **declarative**

possession FUNCTION

The concept of possession is expressed mainly by possessive **determiners** (sometimes called *possessive adjectives*) and by possessive **pronouns**. These are:

possessive determiners		possessive pronouns	
singular	plural	singular	plural
my	*our*	*mine*	*ours*
your	*your*	*yours*	*yours*
his, her, its	*their*	*his, hers, its*	*theirs*

For example: *My Fair Lady*; *Forever mine*; *Our man in Havana*

Nouns are marked for possession by the addition of the possessive *'s* (sometimes called the *Saxon genitive*): *Sophie's choice*; *Nobody's child*; *The teddy bears' picnic*. This is used mainly with short noun phrases that refer to humans and animals, plus some time words: *A long day's journey into the night*. Otherwise, an *of* construction is used: *A taste of honey*; *The thief of Bagdad*.

Verbs that express possession include *have, have got, belong* and *own*:

To have and have not; *You've got mail*; *Paris belongs to us*.

Possession is easily demonstrated and practised in the classroom using objects that students possess or clothes that they are wearing. Describing families also involves possessive *'s*: *My brother's girlfriend* …, etc.

possibility FUNCTION

To talk about possibility is to talk about degrees of likelihood of past, present and future events and situations. (Other, partly overlapping, senses of possibility, such as **ability**, **permission**, logical **necessity**, and **prediction**, are dealt with separately). Degrees of possibility range from certainty, through probability, to impossibility. The chief ways of expressing these notions are by means of:

- **modal verbs**: *It may rain. She could have forgotten. They might not be home.*
- **adverbials**: *Perhaps it will rain. Maybe she forgot. They're probably not home.*
- **adjectives**: *It's likely to rain. It's possible she forgot. They're unlikely to be home.*
- **nouns**: *There's a chance of rain. One possibility is that she forgot. There's not much likelihood of their being home.*

A distinction is also made between *factual possibility* and *theoretical possibility*:

The beach may be crowded. (= it's possible that the beach is crowded).
The beach can be crowded. (= it's possible for the beach to be crowded).

There is no shortage of contexts for teaching the language of possibility. For past possibility, any situation where it is not clear what happened or what caused the situation – such as a crime or a mystery – can be productive. Speculating on the whereabouts and activities of people not immediately present practises present possibility. Talking about the outcomes of future sports events or political developments practises the language of future possibility.

post-method pedagogy → **eclecticism**; → **method**

postmodification → **modifier**

PPP METHODOLOGY

PPP stands for *presentation–practice–production*. It describes the three-stage model of **lesson design** that has prevailed in ELT methodology for the past half-century. It also underpins the sequencing of most published ELT materials. A pre-selected grammar item is first presented to the learners, eg by means of a text or through demonstration using **direct method** techniques. Its rules of form and use are either explained or elicited from the learners (→ **presentation**). The item is then practised in isolation, and with an emphasis on **accuracy** (→ **practice**). Teacher control is gradually relinquished, and activities, such as roleplays, are set up to encourage free production of the grammar item in context, and with an emphasis on **fluency**. The cycle (which may take place in one single lesson, or be spread over several lessons) is then repeated with a new grammar item.

When **audiolingualism** dominated, lesson design was limited to just PP: presentation and practice. The practice itself consisted mainly of controlled pattern practice **drills**. The production stage was added when the need for more fluency practice was recognized. The need for production was reinforced by the advent of the **communicative approach**, where fluency was prioritized. In fact, an alternative 'deep end' model of lesson design was proposed by some scholars, where lessons *started* with the production stage. This evolved into what is now known as **task-based learning**. Nevertheless, the PPP model has proved extremely resilient, despite the many criticisms that have been levelled at it.

One complaint is that the first two Ps receive undue emphasis at the expense of production, which, coming last, may be sacrificed. More seriously, the basic principle of the PPP approach – that language learning can follow a **syllabus** of pre-selected grammar items – was challenged by second language acquisition research in the 1970s. This research suggested that there is a natural **order of acquisition** of language structures, independent of the order they are taught in. Even if the *natural order hypothesis* remains unproven, most experienced teachers acknowledge that there is a mismatch between what teachers teach and what learners learn. Hence, the PPP model is felt by many to represent an idealized, linear, and somewhat mechanical model of learning. Moreover, its emphasis on presentation, rather than discovery, and on production, rather than on comprehension, has also been questioned. Alternative models promote **consciousness-raising** techniques and **experiential learning**.

Nevertheless, there are also theoretical grounds to support a PPP approach. These come mainly from **cognitive learning theory**. According to this theory, learning a complex skill involves successive stages of (1) *cognition* (where a description of the procedure is learned), (2) *association* (where a method for performing the skill is worked out), and (3) an *autonomous* stage (where the skill becomes more rapid and automatic). It is not difficult to see that the three-step cognitive model maps neatly on to the PPP one. The question remains, though, as to whether language learning involves the same kind of learning processes as, say, learning to drive, or playing the guitar.

Apart from these theoretical debates, PPP offers teachers – especially inexperienced ones – a useful template for lesson planning. It is less risky than a deep-end approach, and it is one which probably matches most learners' expectations of how teaching should be sequenced.

practice METHODOLOGY

If you practise a skill, you experience doing it a number of times in order to gain control of it. The idea that 'practice makes perfect' is fundamental to **cognitive learning theory**. It is through practice that the skill becomes automatic (→ **automaticity**). **Sociocultural learning theory** finds room for practice too. Performing a skill with the assistance of someone who is good at it can help in the **appropriation** of the skill. At issue, then, is not so much whether practice is beneficial, but what form it should take, when, and how much of it is necessary. In addressing these questions, it is customary to distinguish between different kinds of practice, such as *controlled practice* vs *free practice*, *mechanical practice* vs *meaningful/communicative practice*, and *receptive practice* vs *productive practice*.

Controlled practice is associated with the second P of the **PPP** instructional model. Practice can be controlled in at least two senses: *language control* and *interactional control*. In the first, the language that is being practised is restricted to what has just been presented (hence it is also called *restricted practice*). For example, if the first **conditional** has been presented, learners practise this, and only this, structure, and in a repetitive way, eg through a sequence of **drills**. Practice is also said to be controlled if the learners' participation is overtly managed and monitored by the teacher, such as in open-class work, as opposed to closed **pairwork** or **groupwork**. One reason for this degree of control is that it maintains a focus on accuracy, and pre-empts or corrects errors. *Free practice*, on the other hand, allows learners a measure of creativity, and the opportunity to integrate the new item into their existing language 'pool'. It is also less controlled in terms of the interactions, with pairwork and groupwork being favoured. Typical free practice activities might be **games**, **discussions** or **drama**-based activities.

Mechanical practice is a form of controlled practice, where the focus is less on the meaning of an item than on manipulating its component parts. Mechanical practice can be either oral or written: many traditional **exercises** are mechanical in this sense, such as when learners transform sentences from active into passive, or from direct speech into reported speech. The arguments in favour of controlled and mechanical practice have lost their force since the decline of **behaviourism** and its belief that learning is simply habit-formation.

Meaningful practice requires learners to display some understanding of what the item that they are practising actually means. One way of doing this is through **personalization**. *Communicative practice* involves the learners interacting in order to complete some kind of task, such as in an *information gap* activity (→ **communicative activity**). Proponents of a communicative approach argue that it is only this kind of practice that is truly effective. This is because learners are not simply practising language, but are practising the behaviours associated with the language, and this is a pre-condition for long-term behavioural change.

Finally, some practice activities are purely *receptive*. They involve the learners in identifying, selecting, or discriminating between language items, but not actually producing them. Many **consciousness-raising** activities are receptive, on the grounds that learners first need to understand a new structure before they can properly internalize it. Receptive practice is also associated with comprehension-based approaches to teaching (→ **input**). *Productive practice*, on the other hand, requires learners to produce the targeted items (either orally or in writing), and is associated with output-based models of learning (→ **output hypothesis**).

There is fairly general agreement nowadays that the most effective practice activity combines at least some of the following features:

- It is meaningful, which may mean that is personalized.
- It is communicative, thus it will require learners to interact.
- It involves a degree of repetition – not of the mindless type associated with imitation drills, but of the type associated with many games (→ **language play**).
- It is language-rich, ie, learners have to interpret or produce a lot of language.
- Learners can be creative and take risks, but support is at hand if they need it.
- Learners are pushed, at least some of the time, to the limits of their competence
- Learners get **feedback**.

pragmatics LINGUISTICS

Pragmatics is the study of how language is used and interpreted by its users in real-world situations. For example, it attempts to explain how the following exchanges might make sense to the people who are engaged in them:

1. **A** *How do you like the soup?*
   B *It's nice and hot.*
   A *What's wrong with it?*
2. **A** *Are you the fish?*
   B *No, I'm the meat balls.*

A's second remark in the first exchange is explained by the **co-operative principle**. She infers that B's response to her first question is less than entirely informative, and therefore that he must mean something else, ie, he *doesn't* like it. Exchange 2 is explained by reference to the context (a restaurant) and the speakers' roles (waiter and customer). Of course B is not literally *the meat balls*, and nor does she intend A to think as much. In both instances, contextual factors rule out a literal interpretation of these two sentences: *It's nice and hot. I'm the meat balls*. Instead, they are interpreted pragmatically.

The fact that *semantic meaning* (ie, the literal meaning of an utterance) and *pragmatic meaning* (or intended meaning) may not correspond is central to the study of pragmatics. For example, a sentence like *Thank you for not smoking* might appear to be an expression of thanks, but in its context of use (eg as a sign in a taxi) it functions as a request or even a prohibition.

Pragmatic competence is the knowledge that language users have that enables them to take contextual factors into account when using and interpreting language. Even in native speakers this ability takes time to develop, as the following exchange demonstrates:

George (a six-year-old, answering the phone): Hello?
Caller Hello, George. Is your dad there?
George Yes.
[longish pause]
Caller Well, can I speak to him?

George's literal interpretation of the caller's question nearly resulted in *pragmatic failure*. In fact, most adult learners of a second language are able to transfer their L1 pragmatic competence to their L2 without too much trouble: we are used to having to 'read between the lines'. However, differences in cultural conventions may lead to misunderstandings. In some cultures, for example, it is customary to decline an offer several times before accepting. But if the first refusal is taken literally, and the offer is not renewed, ill-feeling might result – a case of what is called *sociopragmatic* failure.

The main effect that pragmatics has had on language teaching, apart from confirming the importance of contextualizing language, is to show how a speaker's intentions can be expressed in a variety of ways, not all of them to be taken literally. This has implications on the teaching of **politeness**, for example. It's less threatening to say *It's a bit warm in here, isn't it?* than *Do you think you could open the window?*

predicting → **reading**

prediction FUNCTION

Prediction is a broad notional area that overlaps with both **futurity** and **possibility**. We make predictions about the future, but we can also talk about predictable situations in the present and in the past. For example:

> *I will be home at seven tomorrow.* (future prediction)
> *On work days I will normally be home by seven.* (present predictability)
> *When I was working I would normally be home by seven.* (past predictabilty)

The most common ways of expressing prediction and predictability are through the use of **modal verbs**. For future predictions, *will* and *going to* are common. The use of *will* is more factual, whereas *going to* implies that the prediction is linked to the present in some way, eg that there is present evidence:

> *It will be a nice day tomorrow* (so the weather report says).
> *It's going to be a nice today tomorrow* (because I can see the stars now).

Should can be used to make predictions, especially about desirable outcomes:

> *It should be a nice day tomorrow.*

For present predictability, both *will* and *must* are common:

> *There's someone at the door. ~ That will be the postman./That must be the postman.*

Will implies a strong likelihood (→ **possibility**), while *must* implies logical necessity (→ **necessity**).

Conditional sentences often express future prediction or present predictability:

> *If you break a mirror, you will have seven years' bad luck.*
> *If you heat plastic, it will melt.*

Habitual, hence predictable, behaviour in the past can be expressed by *would*:

> *We would often spend all day at the beach.*

As well as these modal verbs, there are other ways of expressing prediction and predictability, including:

• verbs such as *predict, forecast, expect,* especially in the passive: *It is predicted that house prices will continue to fall. Rain is forecast for this weekend.*

- sentence adverbs, such as *hopefully, predictably, unexpectedly: Predictably, Graham was late.*

Contexts for presenting and practising the language of future prediction include: horoscopes and superstitions; the weather; sporting events; elections; economic trends; the environment; and personal biography.

Here, for example, is a text about weather which includes a variety of exponents of prediction:[2]

2005 looks like being a busy hurricane year

One of the USA's most noted long-range hurricane forecasters predicts an active season for the Atlantic-Caribbean this year.

William Gray, Colorado State University professor, believes 13 tropical storms will form this year. Of these, seven are predicted to become hurricanes, of which three will become major storms with winds over 110mph.

On a more positive note Gray also added that coastal residents should not expect a disastrous season like the last one when four hurricanes tore through Florida.

preference FUNCTION

Stating a preference means saying which of two or more alternatives you like better. This can be expressed in a variety of ways:

Questions	Answers
Which do you <u>prefer</u> – the green one or the blue one?	*I <u>prefer</u> the blue one (to the green one).*
Who do you <u>like best</u> in your drama class?	*I like Jan <u>best</u> (of all).*
What <u>would you rather</u> have – a herbal tea or normal tea?	*I'd <u>rather</u> have coffee, if you've got it.* *I'd <u>rather not</u> have tea. I'd <u>prefer</u> coffee.*

Contexts for practising the language of preference include: talking about tastes in music, art, clothes, etc; shopping; making offers and issuing invitations. Conducting class surveys about preferences ensures repeated practice of questions like: *Who's your favourite …? Which do you like best: X or Y?* Learners can then report their results: *Most of the class prefer ….*

prefix → **affix**

premodification → **modifier**

preposition GRAMMAR

Prepositions are a class of words (→ **word class**) which show a relationship between two parts of a sentence, such as how they are related in space or time: *Mr Smith goes <u>to</u> Washington. Born <u>on</u> the fourth of July.* Prepositions are highly

[2] http://www.bbc.co.uk/weather/features/understanding/hurricane_predictions2005.shtml, 11 June, 2005.

frequent: *of, in, for, on, with, by* and *at*, are all in the top 20 words in English. Many prepositions also double as **adverbs**: *on the beach* (= preposition); *and the ship sails on* (= adverb) and many form the *particles* of **phrasal verbs**.

Prepositions typically precede **noun phrases**. The combination of preposition and noun phrase is called a *prepositional phrase*. For example: *On the waterfront; In the heat of the night; After midnight; About Schmidt*. Prepositional phrases typically function as the **adverbial** element in clause structure, providing circumstantial information of time or place: *Meet me in St Louis. Guess who's coming to dinner. They live by night. One flew over the cuckoo's nest*. Prepositional phrases also postmodify nouns: *The bridge on the River Kwai. A room with a view. Men in black*.

Some prepositions consist of more than one word: *Out of Africa; Back to the future*.

Most prepositions have a range of meanings, both literal and metaphorical. They can be classified into several broad categories, but note that many prepositions belong to more than one category:

- *at*-type: eg *at, around, before, by, near*, which identify a relationship to a fixed point in space or time: *at Tiffany's; after dark; round midnight*.
- *on*-type: eg *on, off, along, behind, over, under* which identify a relationship to a line or surface in place or time: *on Golden Pond; never on Sunday; over the rainbow*.
- *in*-type: eg *in, during, inside*, which identify a relationship with an area or volume in space or time: *in the bedroom; during World War 2; inside San Quentin*.
- *towards*-type: eg *towards, to, (away) from, into, out of, since, until*, which identify a relationship of motion to or from a point in space or time: *back to the future; from here to eternity; out of Africa; a river runs through it*.

A number of other meanings are also expressed by prepositions, including *means*: *burnt by the sun*; and *accompaniment*: *travels with my aunt; rebel without a cause*.

Apart from these general meanings, prepositions express a vast range of metaphorical meanings: *in love; on the way; out of order; under investigation; beyond doubt; against all odds*, etc. Many nouns, verbs and adjectives take *dependent prepositions*: *the trouble with Harry; you can count on me; looking for Shorty; who's afraid of Virginia Woolf?*

Prepositions are usually first taught in terms of their most literal spatial meanings (*next to, in front of, between*, etc) with reference to people and objects in the classroom, or on a street plan, or in a group photo, for example. Prepositions of time are best presented in association with common time expressions such as clock times, days of the week, months, etc. For the more metaphorical uses of prepositions, these are probably best learnt as fixed expressions (→ **formulaic language**).

prescriptive grammar LINGUISTICS

A prescriptive grammar is a manual that states rules for how language *should* be used, rather than how it *is* used (which is the domain of a descriptive grammar). Many traditional grammars were of this type, and most manuals of correct *usage* and 'style guides' still are. Here are some examples of the kind of advice you might find in these:

- Never end a sentence with a preposition.
- *None* is always singular, hence *None of the students have failed* is incorrect.
- *Than* is a conjunction, not a preposition, hence *I am older than he* is correct, while *I am older than him* is not.
- *Who* is a subject pronoun, and *whom* is an object pronoun, so *Who were you talking to?* is incorrect.

For many people this *is* grammar. But for most linguists and language teachers, *prescriptivism* is considered at best a curiosity and at worst reactionary. Nevertheless, because coursebooks aspire to teach some kind of **Standard English** they tend to edit out usage that is considered non-standard although very common, such as *Me and my brother did it* (for *My brother and I ...*), *If I would've known ...* (for *If I had known ...*) and *There were less people than I expected* (for *There were fewer people ...*), a practice which could be considered a form of prescriptivism by default.

presentation METHODOLOGY

The presentation stage of a lesson is the stage when a new language item – typically a grammar structure – is introduced to the learners. Presentation is the first stage in the **PPP** model of lesson design, where it is followed by **practice** activities at decreasing degrees of control, and finally a freer production stage. Grammar presentations can be either **deductive** or **inductive**. The former begins with a statement of the rule and is followed by examples. The latter begins with examples from which learners work out the rule. In a deductive presentation the rule is always made explicit, but in an inductive presentation the rule may be left unstated, on the assumption that learners will internalize it unconsciously. This was the approach adopted in the **direct method** and **audiolingualism**, but current practice favours making rules explicit, since unconscious processes are considered unreliable.

Presentations are aimed at matching a language **form** (such as the modal verb *must*) with a **meaning** (eg obligation). It is important, therefore, that the examples that are used are meaningful to the learners. To this end the examples in a presentation can be illustrated using visual aids, or demonstrated using mime and gesture. Or they can be contextualized in a text, or in a situation. A *situational presentation* is one in which a situation is established, eg using board drawings, which generates a number of examples of the target structure. It is also important that the examples are representative of the particular form that is being presented. There should be enough examples to ensure that the learners can detect the key features of the rule or pattern that is being taught.

Presentations should normally include some check on the learners' understanding of the presentation. This can be done by asking for an explicit statement of the rule, by eliciting further examples, by asking learners to personalize the new item (→ **personalization**), by asking **concept questions**, and by asking for translations of the example sentences into the learners' L1.

The value of grammar presentation has been questioned by some scholars, and research on the long-term effectiveness of presenting pre-selected grammar items is not encouraging. Language learners seem to learn not what they are taught but what they immediately need, or what they are developmentally ready for, or what they get feedback on when they are communicating. This suggests that, if presentation is to be included in lessons, it should be kept short and simple, to allow maximum time for communicative practice.

Items of vocabulary, or features of pronunciation or of connected discourse are also candidates for presentation. In the case of vocabulary, the means of presentation can vary from visual **aids** to mime, to situations, depending on the choice of words. Pronunciation features are typically presented using tapes, the teacher's own voice, and a *phonemic chart* (→ **phoneme**). Features of discourse are best presented using texts.

presentation–practice–production → **PPP**

present perfect → **perfect**

present simple GRAMMAR

The present simple is the name of the present **tense**. It is 'simple' because it is not marked for **aspect**, either **progressive** or **perfect**. It is formed from the base form of the verb, ie, the **infinitive** form without *to*: *You only live once. Some like it hot.* The third person singular takes an *-s* ending (the 'third person *-s*'): *Destry rides again; Mr Deeds goes to town.* Question and negative forms use the operator *do/does*: *Where does it hurt? Alice doesn't live here anymore.*

The present simple is used to express a wide variety of meanings. For example (in order of frequency):

- states and habits in a 'time-less' present: *They live in New York. Marc never cooks.*
- actions happening at the moment of speaking: *Federer sends the ball to the back of the court, Nadal returns it …*
- future scheduled events: *The bus leaves at noon tomorrow …*
- future events in adverbial clauses of time or condition: *When the plane leaves … If it rains…*
- 'historic present': *This guy walks into a bar … As Shakespeare says… My daughter tells me that you …*

The present simple is the most frequent verb form in English. It is at least twenty times more common than the present progressive, for example. However, many of the occurrences of the present simple are with a small set of verbs. In conversation, for example, over half of all present simple forms are made up of the verbs *know, think, mean, see* and *get*. The present simple occurs in a wide range of contexts, including both casual conversation and academic writing.

Its frequency, range, and usefulness, and the fact that its most common uses pose few conceptual problems, mean that it is taught very early in most syllabuses. Indeed it is often the first verb structure that beginners meet. The main difficulties relate to its form, particularly the third person *-s*, and the formation of questions and negatives. Typical contexts for teaching the present simple include: daily routines, jobs, likes and dislikes, and scientific, geographic, cultural, etc, facts. It is often taught in conjunction with adverbs of frequency (*always, never, sometimes*). It is also the structure from which many useful classroom expressions are formed, such as *I don't understand. What does X mean? How do you spell it? I don't know.* This suggests that one way of 'feeding in' the present simple is to teach these expressions as unanalysed 'chunks' (→ **formulaic language**).

present tense → **present simple**

pre-teaching vocabulary → **vocabulary teaching**

primary METHODOLOGY

Primary schooling usually begins when children are aged between five and seven, and continues until secondary schooling starts at around the age of 12. Primary school is usually preceded by a pre-primary stage, known either as pre-school or kindergarten. Increasingly, English as an additional language is being introduced at primary and even pre-primary stage in schools in many countries (→ **age**). Typically, English will be taught either as one of many subjects by the class teacher. Or it will be taught by a specialist teacher, who teaches only English but usually teaches several classes. Sometimes **immersion** teaching is introduced at primary level. This is when some or all the subjects on the curriculum are taught in English (→ **content-based learning**). Primary school children differ from secondary school children in that they have yet to acquire the ability to deal with abstract concepts (such as singular and plural, or past and future) and decontextualized language, hence their need for a clear context accompanied by visual and other support. They learn best through activities which engage them in doing things and using language in ways that are purposeful and which they can relate to, such as playing games, singing songs, and listening to stories. They are generally not self-conscious about making mistakes. They have short attention spans, and therefore need lots of variety, but also tolerate repetition, so long as it is purposeful. However, in the later primary years, children are better able to work more independently, to set their own learning goals, to review their own progress, and to begin to understand **metalanguage** and language rules.
→ **young learners, teaching**

priming LINGUISTICS

Priming describes the process by which, through repeated encounters, a word gathers particular associations. These associations may be with other words, as is the case with **collocations**. For example, the word *encounter* is primed to occur with adjectives like *chance, first* and *close*: *a chance encounter with an applied linguist*. Or words may be primed to occur in association with particular meanings (called *semantic associations*). Thus, the verb *to encounter* is often associated with problems and difficulties, as in *Krashen's theory encountered widespread rejection*. Or words may be primed to occur in particular grammatical patterns and not in others (this is sometimes called *colligation*). For example, the noun *encounter* is twice as likely to occur in indefinite contexts (*an encounter, encounters*) than in definite ones (*this encounter, her encounter*). And when it occurs in definite contexts it almost never occurs with the definite article *the*. This contrasts with the word *meeting*, a word of similar meaning to *encounter*, which occurs twice as often in definite contexts as it does in indefinite ones, and mostly with the article *the* (*The meeting went on and on*). The primings of *meeting* and *encounter* are almost mirror images of each other, which is frequently the case with synonyms. They tend to divide up their shared semantic territory.

Recent research into how the brain works (neurobiology) helps explain how priming happens. The brain extracts recurring patterns from the input it receives. These patterns are strengthened through repeated encounters, and 'chunked' into larger units before being stored in long-term memory (→ **usage-based acquisition**).

The theory of *lexical priming*, first elaborated by Michael Hoey, suggests that learning a language is essentially learning the primings of its words. This includes its grammar, which itself is the accumulated effect of the primings of **function words**, like *is*, *do*, *by* and *that*. This theory, in turn, supports a **lexical approach** to teaching. According to this approach, learners need massive exposure to input, and guidance in extracting patterns from it.

probability → **possibility**

process writing → **writing**

processing instruction → **grammar teaching**

production → **PPP**

productive skills → **skills**

proficiency SLA

A language user's proficiency is the degree of skill with which they can use the language. A proficient user is one who is considered to have a native-like, or near native-like, ability in the language. This is broadly defined in the **Common European Framework** as being equivalent to C2 level. In CEF terms a proficient user:[3]

> Can understand with ease virtually everything heard or read. Can summarise information from different spoken and written sources, reconstructing arguments and accounts in a coherent presentation. Can express him/herself spontaneously, very fluently and precisely, differentiating finer shades of meaning even in more complex situations.

A *proficiency test* is one that aims to measure a user's overall skill, independent of whatever course of study they have done. (This differs from an **achievement test** which is a test of a learner's success in a particular course). Proficiency testing used to focus on the learners' **competence**, ie, what they *know*, rather than their performance (ie, what they can do with this knowledge), and with an emphasis on literacy skills rather than oral ones. These tendencies have been corrected in most public proficiency exams nowadays. The **examination** called *Cambridge Proficiency in English* (*CPE*), or 'Proficiency' for short, is considered by many to be the summit of ELT achievement. It consists of five papers, one for each of the four **skills** plus a *Use of English* paper, in which candidates are:

> expected to demonstrate [their] knowledge and control of the language system by completing various tasks at word, sentence and text level. These include gap-filling and word formation exercises, comprehension questions and a summary writing task.

As an example of how this exam deals with performance, in the *Speaking* paper candidates are assessed on their ability:

> to interact in conversational English in a range of contexts. The paper contains three parts, which take the form of an interview section, a collaborative task and individual long turns with follow-up discussion.[4]

---

[3] *Common European Framework of Reference for Languages: Learning, Teaching, Assessment.* Council of Europe, 2001, p 24.

[4] Cambridge ESOL website: http://www.cambridgeesol.org/exams/cpe.htm

progressive GRAMMAR

The progressive (also called *continuous*) is one of the two verb **aspects** in English. (The other is the **perfect**). The progressive combines with **tense** to form the structures *present progressive, past progressive* and *future progressive*. It also combines with the perfect to form the present, past and future *perfect progressive*. The progressive is formed from the **auxiliary verb** *be* and the *-ing* **form** (also called the present **participle**): *Bells are ringing. I'll be seeing you.*

The progressive is not a tense, so it doesn't tell us *when* an action happened so much as what the action *was like*. The basic meaning of the progressive is that the event or situation is viewed as being 'in progress' (in the present or the past, depending on the tense). According to the context, and to the type of verb, this can have secondary implications. These are that the situation is not finished, and/or that it is temporary. Compare, for example, these sentence pairs:

	[no aspect]	progressive aspect
present	(1) *She plays tennis.*	(2) *She is playing tennis.*
past	(3) *She played tennis.*	(4) *She was playing tennis.*

Sentence 1 combines easily with such expressions as *on Mondays, every day, for a living*, etc, while sentence 2 is more likely with *at the moment* (= in progress now), *whenever I phone her* (= in progress at that time), *nowadays* (= in progress around now, ie, temporarily), *always* (= in progress all the time, ie, unceasingly). *She is playing tennis tomorrow* has the meaning 'arrangement in progress' (→ **futurity**). Sentence 3 combines with *yesterday, when she was younger, once*, etc. Sentence 4 combines with *yesterday* too, but also with *when it started raining*, implying that the playing was in progress at that moment, and was possibly interrupted. With certain verbs, the use of progressive aspect implies repetitiveness: compare *She tapped on the window* and *She was tapping on the window*.

Because of the inherent meaning of 'in progress', the progressive is not normally possible with verbs that describe only states (**stative verbs**), such as *be, like, want, see, think*, etc, unless a dynamic meaning is intended: *You're being stupid. I'm seeing Paul tomorrow. She was thinking of retiring.*

Progressive verb forms are more common in conversation than they are in writing. Even so, they are much less frequent than simple verb forms (→ **present simple**; → **past simple**). The past progressive (*We were driving home*) is more common than the present progressive (*We are driving home*).

The general meaning of the progressive (*in progress*) is not a difficult concept for most learners to grasp. But because progressive forms are taught as if they were independent tenses (as in the *present* progressive, the *past* progressive), learners tend to associate its meaning with the time of the event, rather than with the nature of the event. As a consequence, they may find it difficult to distinguish between the following:

While she did the ironing, he did the dishes.
While she was doing the ironing, he was doing the dishes.
While she did the ironing, he was doing the dishes.
While she was doing the ironing, he did the dishes.

As with perfect aspect, it is probably more useful to teach the progressive in association with its common **adverb** collocations, and in its common contexts of use. The adverbs that most commonly go with progressive forms are *still, now, also, already, just,* and *always*: *It's still raining. I was just telling Jo about it. I'm always learning.* One common use of the progressive is to describe activities that form the background, or frame, for an event, as in *We were driving home. I turned on the radio, and that's when I first heard that ....* The present progressive is often used to talk about changes and trends: *Children are getting fatter... House prices are going up.* In the classroom, the present progressive is easily demonstrated using actions (*I'm opening the door. Vaclav is writing ...*), which is one reason why it was popular with teachers who were trained in the **direct method**. This usage of the present progressive has been criticized as lacking authenticity, but of course, with the advent of mobile phones, it is now very common: *I'm just getting off the bus.*

progress test → **testing**

project work METHODOLOGY

Project work is the preparation and presentation of a project, either by an individual or (more usually) a group. A typical project might be producing a magazine or website out of individually written articles. Or it might be the scripting, rehearsal and performance – and even filming – of a short play or puppet show. Another project could involve the writing-up and presenting of the results of a survey that has been conducted with, for example, the users of the local airport. The rationale for project work is essentially the same as that for **task-based learning**. The difference between classroom tasks and projects is that the preparation of projects usually extends over more than one lesson. It may also involve doing some research outside the classroom. The final product can be presented in spoken form and illustrated with visual aids, as a poster, in magazine or book form, as a film or website, or any other combination of graphic and visual media. The teacher should monitor project work at all its stages: planning, development and presentation, in order to ensure that learners are all 'on-task', and to discourage mere copying from other sources. The teacher can also 'push' learners to stretch their linguistic resources. One way of doing this is to insist that the learners present preliminary drafts in advance of the final product (→ **writing**). Another is to establish evaluation criteria which include not only an assessment of the content and presentation of the project, but also an assessment of the learners' use of English.

pronoun GRAMMAR

Pronouns are the relatively small **word class** of (relatively small) words that can be used to substitute for a **noun** or a **noun phrase**. They are classified into the following types:

- personal pronouns, eg *I, me, she, her, they.*
- possessive pronouns, eg *mine, hers, yours.*
- demonstrative pronouns: *this, that, these, those.*
- interrogative pronouns, eg *who? what?*
- relative pronouns, as in *the house that Jack built; an old woman who lived in a shoe ...*
- indefinite pronouns, eg *something, anybody, no one.*

- reflexive pronouns: eg *myself, itself, themselves*.
- reciprocal pronouns: *each other, one another*.
- **quantifiers**: *all, some, none, one*, etc, as in *The cheese is nice; would you like <u>some</u>?* and *Would you like a coffee? ~ I've just had <u>one</u>.* Note that most quantifiers can also function as **determiners**, as in *Would you like <u>some</u> cheese?*

In the following passage, in which the protagonist (referred to only as *he*) has responded to a flat-share advertisement, the pronouns have been identified:[5]

> He[1] telephones, makes an appointment.
>
> The man who[2] shows him[3] the flat is a few years older than he.[4] He[5] is bearded, wears a blue Nehru jacket with gold buttons down the front. His name is Miklos, and he[6] is from Hungary. The flat itself[7] is clean and airy; the room that will be his[8] is larger than the room he[9] rents at present, more modern too. 'I[10]'ll take it,[11]' he[12] tells Miklos without hesitation. 'Shall I[13] give you[14] a deposit?'
>
> But it[15] is not as simple as that.[16] 'Leave your name and number and I[17]'ll put you[18] on the list,' says Miklos.
>
> For three days he[19] waits. On the fourth day he[20] telephones. Miklos is not in, says the girl who[21] answers. The room? Oh, the room is gone, it[22] went days ago.
>
> … He[23] can only think that Miklos was looking for someone[24] who[25] would bring more to the economy of the household than just a quarter of the rent, someone[26] who[27] would offer gaiety or style or romance as well …

- personal pronouns: 1, 3–6, 9–15, 17–20, 22, 23
- relative pronouns: 2, 21, 25, 27
- reflexive pronoun: 7
- possessive pronoun: 8
- demonstrative pronoun: 16
- indefinite pronouns: 24, 26

Note that (1) *he*[4] is a literary usage, and that *him* would be more common in spoken language; (2) *his* in *his name* is a *possessive determiner* (also called a possessive adjective), and not a pronoun (→ **possession**); and (3) the use of *it*[15] and *that*[16] refer not to any single entities but to aspects of the whole situation. Pronouns used in this way contribute to the overall **cohesion** of texts.

As can be seen, pronouns cover a range of uses, and many are also inflected for **number** (*himself, themselves*), **gender** (*he, she*), **person** (*I, you, he*), and case (*he, him*). They can therefore be problematic for learners, but their high frequency and utility mean that they have to be introduced at an early stage. Talking about family or about famous people are contexts that are commonly used for contextualizing pronoun use at early stages of learning.

pronunciation teaching PHONOLOGY

Pronunciation is the general term for that part of language classes and courses that deals with aspects of the **phonology** of English. This includes the individual sounds (**phonemes**) of English, sounds in **connected speech**, word and

---

[5] Coatzee J.M. 2003 *Youth* (Vintage Books) pp 95–6.

sentence **stress**, **rhythm** and **intonation**. These components are customarily divided into two groups: the *segmental* features of pronunciation, ie, the individual sounds and the way they combine, and the *suprasegmental* features, ie, stress, rhythm and intonation. **Paralinguistic** features of speech production such as voice quality, tempo and loudness, are also classed as suprasegmental.

Effective pronunciation teaching needs to consider what goals, course design and methodology are most appropriate for the learners in question. The goal of acquiring a native-like **accent** is generally thought to be unachievable for most learners (and perhaps even undesirable). Instead, the goal of **intelligibility** is nowadays considered more realistic, if less easily measurable. It is often claimed that suprasegmental features play a greater role in intelligibility than do segmental ones. Unfortunately, however, some of these suprasegmental features, such as intonation, are considered by many teachers to be unteachable. Moreover, learners intending to interact with native speakers may need to set different goals from those learners whose purpose is to learn **English as an international language (EIL)**. For this latter group, the so-called **phonological core** is a checklist of those pronunciation features considered critical for intelligibility in EIL.

In terms of the design of course content, a basic choice is whether the pronunciation focus is *integrated* or *segregated*. In an integrated approach, pronunciation is dealt with as part of the teaching of grammar and vocabulary, or of speaking and listening. In a segregated approach it is treated in isolation. A classical segregated exercise is the **minimal pairs** task, in which learners are taught to discriminate and produce two contrasted phonemes (as in *hit* and *heat*). There are doubts as to whether this item-by-item approach to pronunciation reflects the way that the features of pronunciation are interconnected. Nor does it reflect the way that they jointly emerge over time ('as a photo emerges in the darkroom'[6]). A related issue is whether pronunciation teaching should be *pre-emptive* or *reactive*. That is to say, should pronunciation teaching be planned around a syllabus of pre-selected items, or should the focus on pronunciation emerge *out of* practice activities, in the form, for example, of **correction**? There is evidence that the latter approach is more effective than the former.

In 1964 the writer (and former language teacher) Anthony Burgess wrote, 'Nothing is more important than to acquire a set of foreign phonemes that shall be entirely acceptable to your hosts'. However, there is generally less emphasis given to pronunciation teaching nowadays. Indeed, some teachers are sceptical as to the value of teaching pronunciation at all. This view is reinforced by research that suggests that the best predictors of intelligible pronunciation are 'having a good ear' and prolonged residence in an English-speaking country. On the other hand, faulty pronunciation is one of the most common causes of misunderstandings. This is an argument for demanding higher standards than the learners can realistically achieve, in the hope that they will meet you 'halfway'.

proper noun → **noun**

prosody → **phonology**; → **intonation**

[6] Adrian Underhill

punctuation DISCOURSE

Punctuation is the system of marking written text with commas, full-stops, quotation marks, etc, in order to make its structure clear. The principle punctuation marks in English are listed below:

- *capital letter*: used to mark the beginning of a sentence, proper nouns, days of the week, months, nationality adjectives, and the first person pronoun *I*
- [.] *full-stop*: marks the end of a sentence
- [,] *comma*: divides sentences into separate units of meaning
- [?] *question mark*: indicates a question
- [!] *exclamation mark*: indicates surprise, anger, loudness, etc
- ['] *apostrophe*: used mainly to indicate a **contraction**, and also, with *s*, to mark the **possessive** form of nouns
- [;] *semicolon*: separates two sentences that are closely linked in meaning.
- [:] *colon*: shows that what follows is an example, or a list, or some kind of continuation
- [–] *dash*: shows incompletion, or is used like the colon
- [-] *hyphen*: joins parts of words
- [( )] *brackets*: enclose subordinate information
- [' '] *speech marks* or *quotation marks*: enclose direct speech, or other quoted material, or material that the writer wishes to separate from the rest of the text
- *indentation*: used to mark the beginning of a new **paragraph**

'One evening as I was lying flat on the deck of my steamboat, I heard voices approaching-and there were the nephew and the uncle strolling along the bank. I laid my head on my arm again, and had nearly lost myself in a doze, when somebody said in my ear, as it were: 'I am as harmless as a little child, but I don't like to be dictated to. Am I the manager-or am I not? I was ordered to send him there. It's incredible!' ... I became aware that the two were standing on the shore alongside the forepart of the steamboat, just below my head. I did not move; it did not occur to me to move: I was sleepy.[7]

Punctuation conventions vary from language to language, so some of these features will need to be pointed out to learners. Once learners have grasped the basic conventions of sentence division, the most important punctuation device in terms of conveying coherence to a text is probably the comma. Giving learners sentences with no commas, or with an excess of commas, and asking them to punctuate them correctly is a fairly conventional activity, but no less effective for all that.

quantifier GRAMMAR

Quantifiers are words or phrases which specify quantity or amount. They either precede nouns (as **determiners**) or stand on their own (as **pronouns**): *All of me*; *Every breath you take*; *A piece of my heart*; *The two of us*. (Some grammars reserve the term *quantifier* for only those combinations with *of* (*a few of, most of, lots of, both of*, etc), while single words, like *few, most, both* are labelled *determiners*.)

[7] Joseph Conrad 1899, Heart of Darkness (Penguin Classics)

The choice of quantifier is often determined by whether the **noun** that follows is countable or uncountable, and, if countable, whether it is singular or plural:

countable		uncountable
singular	plural	
each child *every child*	*(not) many children* *(a) few children* *fewer children* *a number of children*	*(not) much information* *(a) little information* *less information* *an amount of information*

Quantifiers can be categorized as being

- inclusive: eg *all (of), both (of), each (of), every, the whole*
- an indefinite quantity: eg *some (of), several (of), any (of)*
- a large quantity: eg *most (of), much (of), lots of, a lot of, loads of, plenty of*
- a small quantity: eg *a few (of), a little (of), a bit of, a couple of*
- a comparative quantity: eg *more (of), less (of), fewer (of)*
- negative quantities: eg *no, neither (of), none (of)*
- numbers: eg *one (of), two (of), hundreds of*
- partitives: *a piece of, a group of, a litre of, a bottle of*, etc.

Note that some quantifiers are used mainly in negative constructions or in questions:

> *There isn't <u>any</u> information. I haven't got <u>much</u> time.*
> *Have you got <u>any</u> children? How <u>much</u> time have you got?*

Their variety and subtlety (compare, for example, *A few of the children were there. Few of the children were there. A few children were there* and *Few children were there*) mean that quantifiers are difficult to learn, and most learners acquire only a small subset of them. Like the **noun phrase**, of which they form a part, quantifiers are generally under-represented in many coursebook syllabuses. They are typically introduced in the context of food and drink. Many are associated with fixed expressions, and this may be a good way of introducing them. For example: *most of the time, all the way, a little advice, in a couple of days*. They can also be put to good use in reporting the results of class surveys: *Most of the class think … Some students said … One of the girls disagreed*, etc.

question GRAMMAR

There is a basic distinction in all languages between *asking* and *telling*. Questions (*interrogative* forms) are the main way of performing the asking function, and they contrast with statements (**declarative** forms) which do the telling. Questions are classified according to the following types:

- *yes–no* questions: *Are you being served? Do you come here often?*
- *wh*-questions: *What are you doing after the show? How's your father?*

- alternative questions: *Shall we go to your place or mine? Did she fall or was she pushed?*
- tag questions (or **question tags**): *It's nice here, isn't it? You're not from round here, are you?*
- declarative questions (ie, questions that take the form of statements): *You are sure you're okay? That's ALL?!*
- rhetorical questions (ie, statements that have the form of questions, but do not expect a response): *Who would have thought it? What do I care?*
- indirect (embedded) questions and reported questions: *Do you know what time it is? Ask him if he speaks English.*

The basic operation in forming questions in English is the **inversion** of the subject and the (first) auxiliary of the verb. In the absence of an auxiliary the *operator do/does/did* is used. The following rubric shows how questions are formed. 1–4 are *wh*-questions; 5–8 are *yes-no* questions; 9 and 10 are tag questions:

	W (wh-word)	A auxiliary verb/ verb *to be* (+ *n't*)	S subject/ complement	V main verb	O/A object/ adverbial
1	*What*	*is*	*your name?*		
2	*Where*	*are*	*they*	*going?*	
3	*How much*	*does*	*the room*	*cost?*	
4	*Why*	*didn't*	*you*	*have*	*breakfast?*
5		*Is*	*it*	*raining?*	
6		*Couldn't*	*the others*	*have waited?*	
7		*Have*	*you*	*seen*	*Tim?*
8		*Did*	*the bus*	*arrive*	*on time?*
9		*Is*	*he?*		
10		*Aren't*	*we?*		

In indirect questions and reported questions there is no inversion (→ **reported speech**); the word order of statements is retained:

Direct question (inversion)	Indirect question (no inversion)
'Are you sure?'	*I asked her if <u>she was sure</u>.*
'Where's the bathroom?'	*He wants to know where <u>the bathroom is</u>.*
'Can you drive?'	*I'm asking you whether <u>you can drive</u>.*
'Do you know Shorty?'	*I'm being asked if <u>I know Shorty</u>.*

Questions are obviously essential to even the most basic communication, and are taught right from day one of a language course. However, there are a number of problems associated with them. Principally, these are the use of inversion and the need for the *dummy operator, do*. Initially, it's probably easier for learners to learn questions as unanalysed *chunks*, in the form of useful classroom language: *What does X mean? How do you spell Y? How do you say Z in English?* etc. A number of classroom activities generate a high volume of questions, such as surveys and questionnaires, guessing **games**, and interviews and dialogues. Learner-centred classrooms generally provide learners with more opportunities to ask questions than do traditional, teacher-centred classrooms.

question tag GRAMMAR

A question tag (or tag question) is a kind of *yes/no* **question** that is added to a statement: *It won't hurt, will it? They shoot horses, don't they?* The tag consists of two words: a subject **pronoun** and an **auxiliary verb** (or a form of the verb *to be*). The subject pronoun matches the subject of the statement *It won't hurt, will it?* And the auxiliary matches the auxiliary in the statement, except that if the statement is positive, the tag is usually negative, and vice versa. If there is no auxiliary in the statement the operator *do* is used in the tag.

> *You've been to Hong Kong, haven't you?*
> *It's not raining, is it?*
> *Chris and Robin live together, don't they?*
> *I couldn't use the phone, could I?*

The function of question tags is to invite the addressee to respond to the statement. This may be because the speaker is uncertain, in which case a rising **intonation** is used. Or it may be because the speaker expects the addressee to agree, in which case a falling intonation is used:

> *You're from New Zealand, aren't you?* (= I don't know, tell me if I'm right)

> *You're from New Zealand, aren't you?* (= I know this, but I want you to confirm it)

There are occasional exceptions to the positive–negative, negative–positive rule, as when checking the accuracy of a guess: *This is your seat, is it?* or to show surprise: *You speak Swahili, do you?* There are also some exceptions to subject–subject agreement in the statement and the tag: *Stand up, will you? Let's go, shall we? Everyone knows that, don't they?*

Question tags almost only occur in spoken language (or in direct speech in written texts). Although they are common, there is a case to be made for not teaching them except to the most advanced learners. For a start, they are notoriously difficult for learners to formulate accurately. A number of operations have to be performed simultaneously, and an appropriate intonation contour has to be chosen. All-purpose alternatives, such as *... no? ... right? ... am I right?* are also available: *You're from New Zealand, right?*

reader METHODOLOGY

Readers (also *graded readers*) are books that have been specially prepared for language learners. They provide supplementary **reading** material, mainly for out-of-class use, and for the purpose of reading for pleasure. The language of each reader is usually graded by level. This means that the range and complexity of its language, particularly its vocabulary and grammar, is controlled in order to ensure readability. The following extract from a reader targeted at elementary learners shows how this can be achieved without any undue sacrifice of literary effect:[1]

> The soldiers say that I am safe now. I want to believe them. But what's going to happen when they go away and I'm alone again?
>
> I ask Chris and he tells me that the soldiers are going to take me with them.
>
> 'You can't stay here all alone,' says Chris.
>
> I don't know where I'm going, but Chris tells me it's a long way away from the village. He says that I'm going to a place where there are lots of children like me. He says that there has been fighting in other places. And there are lots of children without families. But I have a family. They're here. The soldiers don't understand that. Chris doesn't understand. Only the ghosts understand.

Many readers are adaptations of existing books, such as English language classics. But, increasingly, readers are purpose written. They cover a range of genres, both fiction and non-fiction. Readers may include a glossary, **comprehension questions**, and often come accompanied by an audio recording. Readers can be used in the classroom, too. However, it is probably best to allow the bulk of the reading to be done out of class, and to use classroom time to check general understanding, to deal with specific problems, to focus on key passages, and to discuss the learners' response to the text.

reading METHODOLOGY

Reading is a receptive **skill**. But the fact that it is receptive does not mean that it is passive: reading is an active, even interactive, process. Readers bring their own questions to the text, which are based on their background knowledge, and they use these to interrogate the text, modifying their questions and coming up with new ones according to the answers they get. In order to do this, they draw on a range of knowledge bases. They need to be able to decode the letters, words and grammatical structures of the individual sentences – what is called *bottom-up processing*. But they also enlist *top-down processes*, such as drawing on **discourse** and schematic knowledge, as well as on immediate contextual information. Discourse knowledge is knowing how different text-types – such as news reports, recipes or academic papers – are organized. Schematic knowledge is the reader's existing knowledge of the topic (→ **schema**). Reading involves an interaction between these different 'levels' of knowledge, where knowledge at one 'level' can compensate for lack of knowledge at another (→ **comprehension**).

Readers also bring their own *purposes* to texts, and these in turn determine the way they go about reading a text. The two main purposes for reading are for

[1] Moses, A. 2000 *Jojo's Story*, (CUP) pp 14–15.

information (such as when consulting a directory), and for *pleasure* (such as when reading a novel), although these purposes may overlap. Different ways of reading include:

- *skimming* (*skim-reading*, *reading for gist*): rapidly reading a text in order to get the *gist*, or the main ideas or sense of a text. For example, a reader might skim a film review in order to see if the reviewer liked the film or not.
- *scanning*: reading a text in search of specific information, and ignoring everything else, such as when consulting a bus timetable for a particular time and destination.
- *detailed reading*: reading a text in order to extract the maximum detail from it, such as when following the instructions for installing a household appliance.
- *reading aloud*: such as when reading a prepared speech or lecture, or reading a story aloud, or an extract from the newspaper.

A reader's purpose usually matches the writer's intentions for the text. Readers seldom read telephone books from cover to cover, for example. Nor do they normally skim through a novel looking for names beginning with *Vron* .... In classrooms, however, texts are frequently used for purposes other than those for which they were originally intended. They are often used not so much as vehicles of information or of pleasure, but as 'linguistic objects', that is, as contexts for the study of features of the language. A distinction needs to be made, therefore, between two types of classroom reading: reading as *skills development*, and reading as *language study*. There is no reason why the same text cannot be used for both purposes.

Another distinction that is often made is between *intensive reading* and *extensive reading*. The former applies to the way short texts are subject to close and detailed classroom study. Extensive reading, on the other hand, means the more leisurely reading of longer texts, primarily for pleasure, or in order to accumulate vocabulary, or simply to develop sound habits of reading. This is typically done outside class, using graded **readers**, authentic texts, or literary texts (→ **literature**).

A third important distinction is between testing reading and teaching reading. Traditional reading tasks usually involve reading a text and then answering **comprehension questions** about it. This is the testing approach. A teaching approach, on the other hand, aims to help learners to become more effective readers by training them in the *sub-skills* of reading, and by teaching them *reading strategies*. Some of the sub-skills of reading are:

- understanding words and identifying their grammatical function
- recognizing grammar features, such as word endings, and 'unpacking' (or **parsing**) the syntax of sentences
- identifying the topic of the text, and recognizing topic changes
- identifying text-type, text purpose, and text organization, and identifying and understanding **discourse markers** and other cohesive devices (→ **cohesion**)
- distinguishing key information from less important information
- identifying and understanding the gist
- inferring the writer's attitude
- following the development of an argument
- following the sequence of a narrative
- paraphrasing the text

Activities designed to develop these sub-skills include: underlining topic-related words; contrasting different text-types; comparing different examples of the same text type and identifying *generic* features (→ **genre**); circling and categorizing discourse markers; identifying what the pronouns refer to (→ **reference**); predicting the direction the text will take at each discourse marker; choosing the best summary of a text; putting a set of pictures in order; extracting key information on to a grid, writing a summary of the text, etc.

Strategy training involves training learners in ways of overcoming problems when they are reading. Some useful strategies include:

* using contextual and extra-linguistic information (such as pictures, layout, headlines) to make predictions regarding what the text is about
* brainstorming background (or schematic) knowledge in advance of reading
* skimming a text in advance of a more detailed reading
* keeping the purpose of the text in mind
* guessing the meaning of words from context
* **dictionary** use

There is some argument, however, as to the value of a 'skills and strategies' approach to teaching reading. Most adult learners of English come to English texts with already well-developed reading skills in their own language. They already know how to skim, scan, use context clues, enlist background knowledge, and so on. Theoretically, at least, these skills are transferable. What makes reading difficult is not so much lack of reading skills as lack of *language knowledge*. That is, learners lack sufficient vocabulary and grammar to unpack sentences, and they cannot easily identify the ways that sentences are connected. This can result in 'tunnel vision', with readers becoming distracted by unfamiliar words, at the expense of working out meaning from context. On the other hand, it can also result in an over-reliance on guesswork, and on superficial 'text attack' strategies such as skimming. This suggests that texts needs to be chosen that do not over-stretch learners' ability to read them fluently. At the same time, texts should not be so easy that learners can process them simply by skimming. It also means that tasks need to be chosen that both match the original purpose of the text, and that encourage learners to transfer their first language reading skills. Such tasks are likely to be those that motivate learners to *want* to read the text. This might mean activating interest in the topic of the text, through, for example, a pre-reading quiz. At the same time, classroom reading texts should be exploited, not just for their potential in developing reading skills, but as sources of language input. This will involve, at some point, detailed study of the text's formal features, such as its linking devices, its collocations or its grammar.

realia → **aids**

real question → **display question**

recast → **feedback**; → **task-based learning**

Received Pronunciation (RP) PHONOLOGY

RP is the type of pronunciation of British English that is considered the regionally neutral *standard* (→ **Standard English**). It therefore provides the model most widely used in the teaching of British English. Associated with the south-east of England, RP gained prestige status as the **accent** of the court (it was called the Kings's – or the Queen's – English), and thence of government, higher education, and broadcasting (it is still called *BBC English*). RP is universally understood. However, in its pure form it is only spoken by a diminishing minority of the British population. Most educated people now speak a modified RP, incorporating regional features, such as those of *Estuary English*, an accent that emerged in and around London in the 1990s. The argument for using RP as a model for teaching has been challenged in recent years, especially since the growth of **English as an international language**. RP is considered irrelevant, or elitist, or out of date. Nevertheless, in the absence of a credible alternative, RP endures, and most UK-published ELT coursebooks and dictionaries still use RP as their standard.

receptive skills → **skills**; → **listening**; → **reading**

recycling → **lesson plan**

reference DISCOURSE

Reference is the relation between language forms and things in the real world (their *referents*). Some language is highly referential, in the sense that we can identify the particular person or thing that is referred to, as in *That towel* belongs to *me*, or *The White House* is in *Washington*. But, more often, words do not refer to specific things, but to concepts. Thus, in *I need a new towel*, the referent of the word *towel* is not a specific towel that I can see and feel. Rather, it is a *generic* towel – the concept of a towel. My addressees understand me, not because there is a towel present in the context, but because they share the concept of what a towel is. Learning a second language is largely the matching of new forms to existing concepts (→ **meaning**). But of course the process can be facilitated by using real things (*realia*) or pictures of them (**aids**) to represent the concepts we are teaching.

Reference also has a narrower sense, and describes the relation between language forms and their referents in **discourse**. Thus, in the exchange:

A *Where's my towel?*
B *I hung it on the line.*

the pronoun *it* refers back to *my towel*. This kind of reference is called *anaphoric reference*, meaning 'back' reference. In the sentence: *That's what I like, a nice dry towel*, the pronoun *that* refers forward in the discourse, and is an instance of *cataphoric reference* ('forward' reference). Finally, the use of the definite article *the*, in *I hung it on the line*, is a kind of reference, too. But it is not a reference that has a referent in the discourse. The referent is in the shared world of speaker and addressee. (Compare it to *I hung it on a line*, which has no such shared referent). Direct reference to the non-linguistic context is called *exophoric reference*. **Deicitic** terms, like *this*, *that*, *here*, *there*, typically have exophoric reference.

Reference, using **pronouns** (such as *it*, *he*, *they*) and **determiners** (such as *this* …, *that* … *the* …), contributes to the overall **cohesion** of spoken and written text. In the following extract from a play[2] the different kinds of reference are identified:

AMJAD The[1] tea has gone cold. Let's have some more[2]. (He shouts.) Amina[3] – wake up now!
BANOO You[4] never let me[5] speak, Amjad.[6]

[2] Kureishi, H. 1992 'Borderline' in *Outskirts and other plays*, (Faber and Faber) p 126.

> **AMJAD** Always.
> **BANOO** I[7] want to speak.
> **SUSAN** (*Gently*) And I'd like to hear.
> **BANOO** This[8] is my position, Susan. I get up. I clean the[9] house. I cook for my[10] husband. Then I work. I sew. He[11] says, 'Don't think. Don't think about anything.' But I am thinking all the time. I am a woman. But I am not afraid. They[12] do their[13] things to us,[14] but I will fight them.[15]

1. exophoric reference (immediate context), definite article
2. anaphoric reference (*the tea*), pronoun
3. and 6. exophoric reference (person deixis), proper noun
4, 5 and 7. exophoric reference (person deixis), personal pronoun
8. cataphoric reference (forward in discourse), demonstrative pronoun
9. exophoric reference (shared knowledge), definite article
10. exophoric reference (person deixis), possessive determiner
11. anaphoric reference (*my husband*), personal pronoun
12, 13 and 15. exophoric reference (= *men*, shared knowledge), pronouns and determiner
14. exophoric reference (= *women*, shared knowledge), pronoun

referential question → **display question**; → **teacher talk**

reflection, reflective teaching PROFESSIONAL DEVELOPMENT

When you reflect on your teaching, you think back on it, in order to understand it better, and to take steps to improve it. Reflection is seen as a key stage in an **experiential learning** cycle that also includes *planning*, *action* and *learning*. Reflection involves more than simply remembering. It means being able to think critically about experience, to identify problems, and to 're-frame' these problems, ie, to consider them in a new light, in order to identify possible solutions, and to formulate these as a plan of action. It is claimed that self-directed reflection of this type is a characteristic of professional expertise. One way of encouraging reflection is through the keeping of a teaching journal. Here, for example, is part of an entry from the journal of a teacher on a pre-service training course:

> This lesson was rather controlled and towards the end I'd wished I had something that I could've 'set them free' on. Each group (elem., interm. etc) seem to require and thus develop different skills. In light of this, I'm beginning to realise, and adjust my lesson plans to, the necessity of clarity and demonstration … In general, the beginners are great to develop and practise being utterly economical and definite. In some ways I think that listening to the students is most crucial (for beg. levels) here: not just because they're prone to make more mistakes, but also because their knowledge of how to form sentences, etc, is less and they're thus really eager to hear a correct modelling.

The idea of teachers as *reflective practitioners* is sometimes contrasted with other models of teacher development, such as the 'theory-to-practice' model, or the 'apprenticeship' model. In the 'theory-to-practice' model, trainee teachers are taught some theory, and then they are judged on how well they can apply it. In the apprenticeship model, trainee teachers work alongside – and model their teaching on – experienced teachers. Reflection is also a component of the **action research** cycle.

reflexive pronoun → **pronoun**

reflexive verb → **verb**

register LINGUISTICS

Register is the way that language use varies according to variations in the context. It is a term that is used particularly by proponents of **systemic functional linguistics**. They argue that there is a systematic correlation between the forms of language and features of the social context. In other words, the choice of linguistic form is not arbitrary but is governed by a configuration of cultural and contextual factors. Key factors are the *field* of discourse, (what is being talked or written about), the *tenor* (the relationship between the participants), and the *mode* of the discourse (whether, for example, the language is written or spoken). Together these features constitute the *register variables* of a situation. Texts whose contexts of situation are the same are said to belong to the same *register*. Thus, three holiday postcards written by three different people each to a close friend will have in common the same field, tenor and mode settings. Hence they can be said to share the same register. And, because they share the same register, they will have meanings in common, which will, in turn, be realized by similar grammatical and lexical features. The formula *Having a wonderful time, wish you were here*, for example, is so indicative of 'postcard register' that it has become a cliché. On the other hand, a travel feature in a women's magazine, while sharing the same field as the postcards (ie, leisure travel), differs in both tenor and mode. It therefore belongs to a different register. This difference, in turn, will determine differences at the level of grammar and vocabulary. The concept of register is a useful way of explaining and predicting the relationship between features of context and features of text. It is of particular relevance in the teaching of **genres**, as when teaching business or academic **discourse**.

regular verb → **verb**

relative clause GRAMMAR

A relative clause is a **clause** which modifies a **noun** or **noun phrase**. This means that it comes after a noun, and forms part of the larger noun phrase thus created (→ **modifier**). The relative clause provides additional information about the noun:

1. *This is the house <u>that Jack built</u>.*
2. *I know an old woman <u>who swallowed a fly</u>.*

In (1) *the house that Jack built* is one noun phrase. The relative clause *defines* which house we are talking about. Relative clauses are introduced by relative **pronouns** (*that, who, which*, etc). When the relative pronoun refers to the **object** of the relative clause, it can be omitted: *This is the house Jack built*. (= *This is the house. Jack built it*). Omission is not possible if the relative pronoun is the **subject** of the relative clause: **I know an old woman swallowed a fly*.

Examples (1) and (2) above are *defining relative clauses*, because they define the noun phrase that they modify. But some relative clauses, called *non-defining relative clauses*, simply add extra, non-essential, information, as in:

(3) *An old woman, <u>who lived in the house that Jack built</u>, swallowed a fly.*

A relative pronoun is obligatory in non-defining relative clauses. In writing, they are separated from the rest of the sentence by commas.

relative pronoun → **pronoun**

repair DISCOURSE

If you repair an utterance, you correct or modify what you have just said, so as to make it more accurate or more intelligible. Repair can be self-initiated or other-initiated. In the classroom, the 'other' is typically the teacher, although it may be another learner. In non-classroom contexts repair may be triggered by communication breakdowns with other speakers. In this extract,[3] between a learner and a native speaker, the speakers use three different kinds of move to try to repair a communication problem:

1. NNS: Official of ... pu public
2. NS: Ah you work for the government
3. NNS: Uhm pref-? ... No? (= *comprehension check*)
4. NS: I don't understand. No. Pre?
5. NNS: /prifek/ /prif ker/ Japan has many /prifkers/
6. NS: Factory. Factory? (= *confirmation check*)
7. NNS: No.
8. NS: What is it? Can you tell me? What is that? (= *clarification request*)
9. NNS: Uhm city

In turn 3, the speaker checks that the listener is understanding. In turn 6, the listener checks that she has understood correctly. In turn 8, the listener asks for clarification. According to the *interaction hypothesis*, this sort of repair work provides 'raw material' for language acquisition (→ **interaction**; → **conversation analysis**).

repetition METHODOLOGY

Repetition underlies many language learning activities, and it has always been considered a sound learning strategy. In 1940, Harold Palmer, an influential writer on methodology, wrote:[4]

There are three stages of learning:

1. *Receiving* knowledge.
2. *Fixing* it in the memory by repetition.
3. *Using* the knowledge by real practice.

Subsequently, **audiolingualism** helped make repetition 'scientific' and developed a sophisticated repertoire of **drills**. The common characteristic of all drills was repetition. Post-behaviourist approaches continued to promote repetition, believing, like Palmer, that it helped fix language in the memory. In fact, researchers into memory have found that rote repetition is a relatively inefficient way of learning. Unless the learner makes some deliberate attempt to organize the material being learned, no amount of repetition will guarantee that it is moved into long-term memory. Organizing language material, such as a new word, may mean making a personal association with it, or using it in context, or

---

[3] Long, 1981, cited in Larsen-Freeman D. and Long, M. 1991 *An Introduction to Second Language Acquisition Research*. (Longman), pp 146–7.
[4] Palmer, H. 1940, 1970 *The Teaching of Oral English*, (Longman) p 11.

attaching a mental image to it. Either way, it is the way that the item is processed that is critical, not the number of times it is repeated (→ **memory**).

However, this does not mean that repetition plays no part in learning. *Receptive* repetition (rather than productive repetition, as in drilling) is now believed to play an important role in vocabulary acquisition. The more encounters a learner has with a word, the more likely it is that the word will be retained. Each time learners meet a word, they need to retrieve its meaning from long-term memory. Each retrieval strengthens the path linking the form of the word with its meaning. Ideally, the first encounters should be close together, but the spacing should then gradually increase, a process called *spaced retrieval*.

More recently, **usage-based acquisition** theories claim that the bulk of language learning, grammar as well as vocabulary, is simply an effect of the frequency of encounters with individual items. These encounters strengthen associations between co-occurring elements of the language, allowing patterns to be perceived, extracted, and stored in long-term memory (→ **priming**). This theory finds some support in connectionist research (→ **connectionism**), and suggests that learners need massive exposure to input, plus some guidance in **noticing** the repetitive features of this input.

Finally, *task repetition* has been found to yield positive results in terms of the **accuracy**, **fluency** and **complexity** of learners' output. Asking learners to perform a task in pairs, and then to perform it again in different pairs, is an economical and efficient way of incorporating repetition into classroom practice (→ **task-based learning**).

reported speech GRAMMAR

When you report speech, you report what someone said without repeating the exact words. Reported speech (also called *indirect speech*) converts *direct speech* into a subordinate clause (→ **subordination**) that follows a *reporting verb*, such as *say, tell, state, ask, warn, explain*, etc:

> *You asked me once <u>what was in Room 101.</u>*
> *I told you <u>that you knew the answer already</u>.*

By contrast, direct speech quotes the actual words spoken, and, when written, encloses these in quotation marks:

> *<u>'What is Room 101?'</u> He answered drily: <u>'You know what is in Room 101,</u>*
> *<u>Winston. Everyone knows what is in Room 101.'</u>*

Reporting usually involves a shift away from the time and place of speaking to the time and place of reporting. (Technically, this is a shift in the *deictic centre* → **deixis**). This typically causes a number of 'distancing effects'. For example, if the reporting verb is in the past tense, it is usual to use *backshift* in the reported clause. That is, present tense verbs are 'shifted back' to the past tense, and past tense verbs are 'shifted back' to the past perfect:

> *'What <u>is</u> in Room 101'* ⇨ *You asked me once what <u>was</u> in Room 101.*

Also, pronouns change **person**: *<u>I</u> work* ⇨ *<u>she</u> worked*. Time and place adverbials are shifted from a 'here-and-now' focus to a 'there-and-then' one:

> *'What happens to <u>you here</u> is for ever,' O'Brien told Winston.* ⇨ *O'Brien told Winston that what happened to <u>him there</u> was for ever.*

However, these changes are not necessary if the time and place of speaking is the same as the time and place of reporting:

You just told me that what <u>happens</u> to <u>me here is</u> forever!

Statements are usually reported with *that*-clauses (also called *reporting clauses*: the *that* is often omitted). *Wh*-questions are reported with *wh*- clauses and yes/no questions are reported with clauses beginning with *if/whether*:

I told you (that) you knew the answer already.
You asked me once what was in Room 101.
O'Brien asked Winston if/whether he loved Big Brother.

Note that in *indirect questions*, the subject and verb are not inverted as they are in direct questions (→ **question**):

'Where <u>is Room 101</u>?' ⇨ *I asked him where <u>Room 101 was</u>.*

Thoughts, beliefs, decisions, etc can also be reported using the same kinds of construction:

The past, he reflected, had not merely been altered, it had been actually destroyed.
… He did not believe he had ever heard of Ingsoc before 1960.

Commands, instructions, warnings, requests and advice are usually reported using *infinitive clauses*:

She asked me to stay.
She told me to sit anywhere.

But the choice of reporting structure depends on the **verb pattern** associated with the particular reporting verb: *★She suggested me to stay.*

Reported speech is common in news reporting and in some types of formal official text, such as the minutes of meetings and police statements. It is relatively uncommon in informal speech. Instead, direct speech is favoured, and, especially in young people's talk, reporting expressions include not only *say* but *is like*, and *go*:

So, she's like, are you staying? And I'm like, are YOU? And she goes, no, I have to work …

Useful practice contexts for the classroom include: reporting phone messages, reporting gossip and rumour, complaining (*You said the room would be quiet, but …*), and interpreting, ie, explaining in English what someone has just said in their mother tongue.

reporting verb → **reported speech**

requesting FUNCTION

Requesting belongs to the general class of **speech acts** that are about getting people to do things, such as commanding, persuading, and asking favours. Because it places a potential imposition on the addressee, it is considered a *face-threatening act* (→ **politeness**). Therefore requests are usually softened with some kind of *hedging* and *indirectness*. Most requests involve the use of **modal verbs**. Typical request forms in spoken English, arranged in increasing degrees of indirectness, are:

Put the kettle on, will you?
Would/Can/Could you put the kettle on?
Would you mind putting the kettle on?
I wonder if you'd mind putting the kettle on?
I don't suppose you'd mind putting the kettle on, would you?

Extra shades of politeness can be built in by using words like *possibly* and *please*. In formal written language, conditional forms are common:

> *We would be grateful if you could confirm your attendance.*

Ways of agreeing to a spoken request include: *Of course. Right away. No problem.* With requests whose main verb is *mind*, a negative reply means agreement:

> *Do you mind putting the kettle on? ~ Not at all.*

Refusing a request is more complicated, since it usually involves apologizing and making an excuse:

> *I'm sorry, I'm in a rush.*
> *I can't, I'm afraid. I'm expecting a phone call.*

Classroom activities for practising requests include roleplays involving flatmates, work colleagues, or people – such as tourists – requesting help from strangers. The classroom, too, is an ideal context for making requests, and some frequently occurring ones can be displayed on the classroom wall: *Can you repeat that, please? Could you write that on the board?* etc.

resource → **materials**

restructuring SLA

If a system restructures, it responds to new information by re-organizing itself so as to accommodate the new information. This restructuring allows the system to function more efficiently. Restructuring is the term used in **cognitive learning theory** to describe what seems to happen to the learner's developing **interlanguage** system, as it adapts to new input. For example, learners may first learn words, such as *stayed*, *worked*, and *happened*, along with *went* and *bought*, as individual items. At some point, a rule for regular past tense formation (add *-ed*) is extracted from some of these items and applied to *all* verbs in past contexts. The system has now restructured, and this speeds up processing. But it may result in what is called *backsliding*, which is what happens when the learner over-applies the rule (or *overgeneralizes* it). For example, the *-ed* ending is added to even the irregular verbs (which, until now, the learner had been producing correctly), so that they come out as *goed* and *buyed*. A further restructuring is then required in order to discriminate between regular and irregular verbs.

There are different theories as to what triggers restructuring: whether, for example, it is exposure to *negative evidence* (→ **feedback**), or whether it is the accumulation of a critical mass of instances of a form that causes a kind of mental 'landslide'. Failure to restructure is one way of defining **fossilization**.

revision TESTING

Revision is the process of reviewing previously studied material, especially in advance of a test. In fact, one of the arguments in favour of **testing** is that it encourages revision, since the regular recycling of material makes it easier to recall (→ **memory**). However, if the revision consists of little more than rote memorization of facts it is unlikely to serve much long-term usefulness, either for learning or for testing purposes (→ **repetition**). The most effective forms of revision involve revisiting previously studied material and processing it in a novel way. For example, if the material under review is the *present perfect*, the following revision techniques are likely to be more effective than simply memorizing examples from the coursebook:

- writing original sentences using the present perfect
- searching for examples of the present perfect on the internet, followed by
- translation of the examples into the learner's L1 and back into English again

Research into memory suggests that, for optimal recall, material should be revised as soon as possible after first meeting it, and then at successively longer intervals of time. Many learners are unaware of the benefits of regular review and recycling, and a useful objective of **learner training** is to introduce them to some basic tips and strategies.

rheme → **theme**

rhythm PHONOLOGY

The rhythm of speech is the way that some words are emphasized so as to give the effect of regular beats. In the following sentence this regularity is achieved by stressing some syllables, and by lengthening or shortening intervening syllables:

If I'd KNOWN | you were COMing| I'd have BAKED | a CAKE

In slow, deliberate speech, or in reciting verse, this regularity is more obvious. It is achieved by giving equal length to each *foot* (ie, the words between each bar), so that |*you were coming*| and |*a cake*| occupy the same length of time, even though the first consists of four syllables and the second of only two. 'Squeezing' the syllables up like this is called *accommodation*. In normal fluid speech, the rhythm is less regular, but it is still there. (The alternative, ie, stressing all syllables equally, would result in speech that sounded machine-produced). Rhythm interacts with sentence **stress** and **intonation** to help speakers organize speech into meaningful units. Since the words or syllables that are given prominence by rhythm also tend to be the ones that carry the burden of the meaning, rhythm helps listeners process the message more easily.

Different languages have different kinds of rhythm. A distinction has been made between what are called *stress-timed* languages and *syllable-timed* languages. In the former, the stressed syllables tend to recur at regular intervals, and the intervening syllables are accommodated (as in the example above). In syllable-timed languages, the syllables are given equal length. English is classified as stress-timed; French and Spanish as syllable-timed. More recently, sophisticated measuring techniques have found that these distinctions are at best tendencies.

A popular technique for practising rhythm is through the use of *jazz chants*, a form of syncopated choral speaking. Simply getting learners to produce sentences of increasing length while retaining the same basic beat is a useful way of practising the skill of 'squeezing up' the syllables.

roleplay → **drama**

rote learning → **memorization**

routine METHODOLOGY

Teaching consists of routines, that is, regular procedures that impart a sense of structure, rhythm and flow to the class. Some routines are management-oriented, such as checking attendance or re-organizing seating into groups (→ **classroom management**). Others are teaching-oriented, such as checking homework, drilling, brainstorming vocabulary, or playing a game like 'twenty questions'. Research suggests that expert teachers regularly use a relatively small number – say, a dozen – routines in their classes, but that these are performed fluidly and purposefully. Learning to teach is largely a case of acquiring a repertoire of useful, automated routines that can be adapted to different classes, levels, and circumstances. At some point, of course, teachers need to re-evaluate or update their routines, which is one of the purposes of programmes of **teacher development**.

rubric METHODOLOGY

The rubric for a test or an exercise is the set of instructions (usually written) that tells the students what they have to do. For a task, the rubric may be more elaborated, specifying the purpose of the task, the steps it involves, and the kinds of interactions that are involved. It may also provide a format, or template, for displaying the outcome of the task (→ **instructions, classroom**). For example, the rubric might ask the learners to read a text, and then to use information from the text to fill in a grid.

S

scaffolding SLA

Scaffolding is the temporary support that surrounds a building under construction. The term is used metaphorically to describe the temporary *interactional* support that is given to learners while their language system is 'under construction'. It is this support – from teachers, parents, or 'better others' – that enables them to perform a task at a level beyond their present competence. The term derives from **sociocultural learning theory**, which views learning as being jointly constructed. Scaffolding is an integral part of this model. In **first language acquisition** it has been observed that children, even at an early age, are able to participate in conversations because of the verbal scaffolding provided by their caregivers. Here, for example, a two-year-old child responds to the fact that the central heating boiler had just ignited:[1]

Mark	Oh popped on
Mother	Pardon?
Mark	It popped on
Mother	It popped on?
Mark	Yeh
Mother	What did?
Mark	Er – fire on
Mother	The fire?
Mark	Yeah … Pop the … fire popped it fire
Mother	Oh yes. The fire popped on didn't it?

By asking questions, and by repeating, reformulating and extending the child's utterances, the mother draws the child out. As the child's ability to handle the skills of conversation increases, the adult's support and control will gradually be withdrawn.

Scaffolding not only provides a conversational framework, but it is believed to shape language acquisition itself. In the example above, the child is prompted to modify his original utterance (*popped on*) to *it popped on* and then *the fire popped*,

[1] Wells, G. 1981 *Learning through interaction* (CUP).

bringing it step-by-step closer to the target *the fire popped on*. This incremental accumulation of grammar over several assisted *turns* is called *vertical scaffolding*.

Similar processes are believed to occur in second language learning. The scaffolding is provided by teachers and also by peers. Experienced teachers know how to draw learners out and to engage them in conversation. At the same time, they know when it is appropriate to withhold such support.

scanning → **reading**

schema PSYCHOLOGY

A schema (plural *schemata*) is the way that knowledge about a topic or a concept is represented and organized in the mind. Schemata help us make sense of experience, and hence they are crucial in comprehension. For example, the sentence *At check-in they told me my flight had boarded* will not make much sense to anyone who does not have an 'air travel schema'. The air-travel schema not only includes the various places in an airport (eg check-in), but links these into a typical sequence (or *script*). Familiarity with the script allows us to fill in the details in a narrative, and to make predictions as to what might happen next. For example: … *so I was put on the waiting list for the next one*. A schema constitutes part of what is called the *top-down knowledge* of a text. If students do not have the schema, or if the schema is represented differently in their own culture, or if they simply fail to access it, they will have to rely on *bottom-up processing* alone, ie, working out the meaning from the vocabulary and grammar (→ **comprehension**). Thus, teachers can help learners understand a text by priming them to activate the appropriate schema. One way of doing this is to use contextual information, such as titles, headlines, pictures, as clues as to what the text is about. Another is to ask them to brainstorm what they already know about a topic. (This has the advantage of generating relevant vocabulary as well.)

Schema is also used to refer to the temporary mental 'picture' that a reader (or listener) constructs when processing a text. The schema for a narrative text, for example, would be the sequence of main events in the story. Teachers can help learners construct an accurate schema by asking questions that focus on the significant events (→ **comprehension questions**). Or they can set a task – such as putting pictures in order – that allows learners to share and compare the schema that they have each arrived at.

schwa → **vowel**

second language (L2) SLA

Second language refers to *any* language that has been learned subsequent to the acquisition of the **first language (L1)**. Since many learners have more than one 'second' language, the term *additional language* is sometimes preferred. *Second language* also contrasts with *foreign language,* especially in the terms ESL and EFL (→ **English as a foreign language**), where the former refers to the learning of English by learners who are living in an English-speaking environment and who need English in order to become integrated into that environment. *Second language* is also used to refer to a language that, while playing a major role in a particular region, is not an official language. English is a second language in many countries, such as Nigeria, Singapore, and, increasingly, Japan and the countries of the European Union.

second language acquisition (SLA) SLA

SLA is the study of how second (or additional) languages are acquired. It is a relatively new field of study, emerging in the wake of the failure of **behaviourism** to offer a satisfactory explanation of either first or second language acquisition. Among the major research questions in SLA are the following:

- To what extent are the processes of SLA the same as those of first language acquisition (FLA)?
- Why is SLA seldom, if ever, as successful as FLA?
- Why do some learners learn better and/or faster than others?
- Why do learners make errors?
- How does the first language (L1) affect the learning of the second (L2)?
- Does instruction help – and, if so, how and why?

In attempting to answer these questions, researchers draw on the findings of other 'feeder' disciplines, such as **linguistics**, psychology, neurology and sociology. Since it is still impossible to get 'inside' the brain of a learner, researchers use as data the *output* ($\rightarrow$ **output hypothesis**) that learners produce (including their errors), the **input** that they are exposed to, the various physical and psychological factors that might be implicated, such as **age**, **aptitude**, **motivation** and **learning style**, and the various contextual factors, such as whether the learning is instructed or naturalistic.

Since the demise of behaviourism, a great many new theories have emerged to account for SLA. They fall into three broad groups: **universal grammar (UG)**, **cognitive learning theory** and **sociocultural learning theory**. The lack of any one comprehensive and conclusive theory is a source of frustration to some commentators. Others accept that language acquisition is such a multidimensional phenomenon that no single theory will ever capture its complexity. One criticism of SLA research is that it is generally conducted apart from the realities of the classroom. Hence, its research questions may not be the ones that teachers want answered, or its methods and results may not be generalizable to real learning situations. This may account for the scepticism, even indifference, that many teachers feel for SLA theory. Ironically, the SLA theory that has attracted the most interest among teachers is Stephen Krashen's (now generally discredited) claim that teaching does *not* benefit acquisition ($\rightarrow$ **input**).

self-access centre METHODOLOGY

A self-access centre is that part of a language teaching institution that is allocated to self-directed study. It is usually equipped with books, computers, video monitors, and audio equipment. There may also be a bank of worksheets to guide learners in their study. Self-access centres are usually offered as an adjunct to classroom learning, although they may also be used for independent study. Self-access centres were popular at the height of the learner **autonomy** movement, but they are expensive to run and maintain, and many have become re-absorbed into the institution's library or turned into internet rooms.

self-assessment $\rightarrow$ **assessment**

semantics LINGUISTICS

Semantics is the study of **meaning**, including the way words relate to the things that they refer to in the real world ($\rightarrow$ **reference**). Of relevance to language teaching is the meaning relationships between words – what are called *semantic relations* (or *sense relations*) – such as similarity (→ **synonym**) and oppositeness (→ **antonym**). Semantic meaning is often contrasted with pragmatic meaning, the former being the literal meaning of a sentence, such as *Bob's your uncle*, and the latter being its use in context to create a certain effect (→ **pragmatics**).

sentence GRAMMAR

A sentence is the largest purely grammatical unit in a language. Everything 'beyond the sentence' is only weakly linked in grammatical terms (→ **discourse analysis**). And anything smaller than a sentence, such as a **clause**, a **phrase** or a **word**, is capable of combining to form larger units. Identifying written sentences is relatively easy, since they start with a capital letter and end with a full-stop. They also contain, at the very least, a **subject** and a **finite verb**. However, even these basic rules are flouted in some text types. For example:

> (1) Fog everywhere. Fog up the river, where it flows among green aits and meadows; fog down the river, where it rolls defiled among the tiers of shipping and the waterside pollutions of a great (and dirty) city. Fog on the Essex marshes, fog on the Kentish heights. Fog creeping into the cabooses of collier-brigs; fog lying out on the yards and hovering in the rigging of great ships; fog drooping on the gunwales of barges and small boats.[2]

Spoken sentences are even more difficult to identify. In this transcription of part of a conversation, the transcriber has broken one speaker's turn into two sentences, but the division seems fairly arbitrary:

> (2) When we were out for the walk and we walked up to the cemetery when we were walking back and and um there was a beautiful sunset and Craig, I had Jodie's camera and um Craig said you know oh why don't you take a photo of you know the old man and his dog you know. And I said I can't take a photo of him with those track suit pants on.[3]

The difficulty of breaking up speech into sentences has prompted linguists to use the term *utterance* instead. An utterance is defined variously as one speaker's *turn*, or a stretch of speech between pauses, or one that falls under a single intonation contour, or one that fulfils a single **function** – such as requesting, agreeing, etc. However, none of these definitions is entirely satisfactory in terms of segmenting extract 2 above, for example. Nevertheless, *utterance* is now generally accepted as preferable to *sentence* when talking about spoken language (→ **spoken grammar**).

Language teaching has traditionally focused on the teaching of sentences, not utterances. Coursebooks are based on descriptions of written language rather than of spoken language, and learners are taught to produce fully-formed sentences, often of a rather unlikely nature: *John was bought some books by Mary*. An utterance like (2) above would be considered a poor model for learners. If it was produced by a learner, it might be 'corrected', ie, reformulated into a 'sentence'. This privileging of sentences over utterances reflects the way that, until recently, *competence* was privileged over *performance* (→ **competence**).

sentence stress → **stress**

---

[2] Charles Dickens 1852, *Bleak House* (Wordsworth Editions Ltd)
[3] OZTALK: Macquarie University/UTS Spoken Language Corpus.

silent period SLA

The silent period refers to the fact that children learning their first language go through a lengthy period simply listening before they venture their first words. The same phenomenon has been observed in L2 learners. Some researchers have argued that this silent period is a necessary stage in language acquisition. It provides an opportunity to comprehend **input**, a prerequisite for the development of the learner's internal grammar. Accordingly, methods based on this principle – such as the **natural approach** and **Total Physical Response** – respect what they call the learner's 'right to be silent' and they do not force learners to speak until they themselves wish to. There is some evidence that learners use this period to engage in *private speech*, a kind of silent or sub-vocalized rehearsal phase.

Silent Way, the METHODOLOGY

The Silent Way is the name of a method that was developed by Caleb Gattegno in the 1960s. It is normally grouped among the **humanistic approaches** to language learning. Gattegno believed that language learning is a personal, even mystical process, one that is self-initiated and self-directed: 'Only the learner can do the learning'. Hence the teacher's role is that of a technician or facilitator. It is the teacher's deliberately unobtrusive presence and minimal interventions that give the method its name. Learning is largely mediated through the use of two aids: the *Fidel charts*, which are colour-coded charts representing the sounds of the language, and *Cuisenaire rods*, small coloured blocks of wood of varying lengths. By tapping out sounds on the charts to form words, and by manipulating these words using the rods, basic sentence patterns are created and reflected upon. Gattegno believed it is imperative that the learner should get a 'feel' for the language, and 'surrender to its melody'. He argued that this melody is largely contained in its grammar, and in its **function words** in particular. Therefore the Silent Way concentrates on these items initially, and deliberately keeps the vocabulary load low.

Few serious attempts have been made to evaluate the Silent Way. And its requirement that classes be small, teachers specially trained, and the learners willing to take responsibility for their own learning, means that it has only ever had fringe status. Nevertheless, it has contributed to more mainstream teaching in a number of ways, including the widespread use of Cuisenaire rods and the *phonemic chart*.

simple → **present simple**; → **past simple**

singular → **number**

skills METHODOLOGY

A language skill is a way in which language is used. Language skills contrast with language *systems*. The systems include the **grammar**, **vocabulary** and **phonology** of the language, whereas the skills are customarily divided into the two *productive skills*: **speaking** and **writing**, and the two *receptive skills*: **listening** and **reading**. This division into four skills has been a fundamental one in terms of course design and lesson planning. For example, the language systems aim of a lesson might be 'to present the past simple'. The skills aim might be 'to practise reading for gist'.

It was once argued that 'nothing should be spoken until it has first been heard, nothing should be written until it has first been read, and nothing should be read or written until it has first been heard and spoken'. That is to say, reception should precede production, and oral skills should precede literacy skills. This strict sequencing was based both on the priority given to spoken language in the post **grammar–translation** age, and also to avoid interference from the written form. Also, productive skills are generally considered to be more difficult to master than receptive skills. However, the separation into discrete skills overlooks the fact that most communication is interactive, involving both *reception* and *production*, and often in equal measure. Practising *productive skills* apart from *receptive skills*, and vice versa, presents a distorted view of how language is really used.

Nevertheless, this tendency to compartmentalize the skills has persisted. It is very obvious in the design of many **examinations**, which often have a separate section for each of the four skills. It has also given rise to the identification and listing of *sub-skills*, such as *skimming* and *scanning*, *gist listening*, *selective listening* and *inferencing*. It is argued that these sub-skills need to be taught and practised in isolation. A more holistic approach to skills development argues that listening is best learned by listening, and speaking by speaking, etc. (→ **whole language learning**).

skimming → **reading**

socialization SLA

Socialization is the process by which we become members of a particular social group. The social group may be the one we are born into, or the one that we aspire to belong to. Becoming socialized means adopting – or adapting to – the values and customs of the target group. This process inevitably involves language, and there is a growing school of thought that views second language learning not as a process of *acquisition* but one of *socialization*. Language is viewed less as a system to be learned than as a tool that opens the door to group membership. The dominant metaphor is an *apprenticeship* one, in which the learner is gradually inducted into the target culture, including its language. This, in turn, may involve constructing a new **identity** in relation to the host community. Viewing second language acquisition (SLA) as second language socialization (SLS) makes more sense in the context of learning English as a second language, than in the EFL (→ **English as a foreign language**) or EIL (→ **English as an international language**) contexts. On the other hand, classrooms, too, are 'small cultures' and teachers have always been aware of the need to socialize learners into the group's norms and practices. By foregrounding social and identity factors, socialization represents what has been described as the 'social turn' in SLA.

sociocultural learning theory PSYCHOLOGY

Sociocultural theory (SCT) comes from the pioneering work of Lev Vygotsky, a child psychologist working in the 1930s in what was then the USSR. Vygotsky saw learning as being a social process: through social interaction the learner is assisted from dependency towards autonomy. Unlike **mentalism**, in which development is viewed as both innately predetermined and internal to the learner, sociocultural theory situates the learning process firmly in its social context. According to this view, all learning – including the learning of a first and a second language – is *mediated* through social and cultural activity. To become an independent skill-user, a learner first needs to experience external mediation by a 'better other', whether parent, peer or teacher. This mediation typically takes the form of *assisted performance*, whereby the 'better other' interacts with the learner to provide a supportive framework (or *scaffold* → **scaffolding**). Through this shared activity, new knowledge is jointly constructed, until the learner is in a position to *appropriate* it, at which stage the scaffolding can gradually be dismantled (→ **appropriation**). The learner is now able to function independently, having graduated from a state of *other-regulation* to a state of *self-regulation*. A good example of this is the way an older child will teach a younger one the rules of a game, by both talking and walking it through, until the younger one has got the hang of it. Even then, the younger one may need to think the steps through out loud (as *private speech*) before the procedure of the game has become internalized in the form of *inner speech* or *thought*. The best state for this kind of learning is in what is known as the *zone of proximal development (ZPD)*. This is the 'window of opportunity' where the learner is not yet able to solve a problem independently, but can do so with the assistance of others.

Learning, according to this view, is fundamentally a social phenomenon, requiring both activity and interactivity. In classroom terms, it takes place in cycles of assisted performance, in which learning is collaborative, co-constructed, and scaffolded. For example, learners may set about solving a problem in small groups, during which the teacher intervenes when necessary to provide suggestions or even to model the targeted behaviour. In fact, assisted performance looks very much like **task-based learning**, despite its very different theoretical roots.

sociolinguistics SOCIOLINGUISTICS

Sociolinguistics studies the way language and society are interrelated, and in particular the way different social contexts influence language use. A speaker's choice of **accent**, for example, is likely to vary according to whom they are addressing, why, and where. It has been shown that contextual factors account for some of the variability in learners' language as well. But the major contribution of sociolinguistics to language teaching was the impetus it gave to the development of the **communicative approach**. Sociolinguistic descriptions of how language is used in different communities prompted scholars to re-think the goals of second language teaching and to describe these in *functional* rather than *structural* terms (→ **functional syllabus**). Other areas that come under the umbrella of sociolinguistics include **bilingualism**, language and gender, language and power, and language planning.

songs METHODOLOGY

Using songs in the language classroom has a long history, and for good reason. They are an entertaining and often memorable way of contextualizing language. Learners will tolerate repeated re-playings of a song, which is not the case with most classroom listening texts. Songs also have inbuilt **repetition**, such as when the lines of a chorus are repeated, which adds to their potential as sources for incidental learning. Many songs display instances of high frequency idiomatic language, including the use of **formulaic language**. And they are also imbued with significant cultural information.

On the downside, the lyrics of authentic songs are ungraded and often colloquial (sometimes even ungrammatical by conventional standards). The playful, creative use of language that is more typically associated with literature can make some songs difficult to interpret (although this can be considered an advantage, especially for more advanced learners). Recorded songs are also difficult to hear, especially in the poor acoustic conditions of most classrooms. For these reasons, specially written songs for language learning purposes are available. These are typically designed to display a particular grammar structure. Nevertheless, the popularity of 'EFL songs' for adults has waned (although purpose written songs still commonly accompany courses for young learners). Most learners prefer the challenge of listening to authentic songs, for all their difficulties. The motivation to listen is increased further if the songs are those that the learners themselves have chosen.

Songs can be played purely for the pleasure of listening to them, and for any incidental learning that might result. A more focused approach involves either eliciting the words of the song on to the board, or asking learners to complete a gapped transcript of the lyrics while listening. Tasks associated with **listening** to the gist of more conventional texts can also be used with songs. For example: learners identify the emotion that the song expresses, eg longing, regret, anger, wonder; or they identify the scenario that the song describes, eg boy meets girl, girl leaves boy; girl meets boy, discovers boy is being unfaithful, etc.

When using a song, it is appropriate, at some point, to ask the learners to talk about their personal response to the song. Asking learners to sing along to a song is also an option, but only where learners are willing.

speaking METHODOLOGY

Speaking is generally thought to be the most important of the four **skills**. The ability to speak a second language is often equated with proficiency in the language, as in *She speaks excellent French*. Indeed, one frustration commonly voiced by learners is that they have spent years studying English, but still can't speak it. One of the main difficulties, of course, is that speaking usually takes place spontaneously and in real time, which means that planning and production overlap. If too much **attention** is paid to planning, production suffers, and the effect is a loss of **fluency**. On the other hand, if the speaker's attention is directed solely on production, it is likely that **accuracy** will suffer, which could prejudice **intelligibility**. In order to free up attention, therefore, the speaker needs to have achieved a degree of **automaticity** in both planning and production. One way of doing this is to use memorized routines, such as **formulaic language**. Another is to use *production strategies*, such as the use of **pause fillers**, in order to 'buy' planning time. The situation is complicated by the fact that most speaking is interactive. Speakers are jointly having to manage the flow of talk. The management of interaction involves *turn-taking skills*, such as knowing how and when to take, keep, and relinquish speaker turns, and also knowing how to repair misunderstandings (→ **conversation analysis**).

For language learners these processing demands are magnified through lack of basic knowledge of grammar and vocabulary. For the purposes of most day-to-day talk, however, the grammar that is required is not as complex nor need be as accurate as the grammar that is required for writing (→ **spoken grammar**). Nor do speakers need an enormous vocabulary, especially if they have developed some **communication strategies** for getting round gaps in their knowledge. A core vocabulary of 1000–1500 high-frequency words and expressions will provide most learners with a solid basis for speaking.

Activating this knowledge, though, requires **practice**. This in turn suggests that the more speaking practice opportunities that learners are given, and the sooner, the easier speaking will become. Speaking practice means more than simply answering the teacher's questions, or repeating sentences, as in grammar practice activities. It means interacting with other speakers, sustaining long turns of talk, speaking spontaneously, and speaking about topics of the learners' choice.

Approaches to teaching speaking vary. Traditionally, speaking was considered to be a by-product of teaching grammar and vocabulary, reinforced with work on **pronunciation**. This view has been replaced by approaches that treat speaking as a skill in its own right. One such approach is to break down the speaking skill into a number of discrete sub-skills, such as *opening and closing conversations, turn-taking, repairing, paraphrasing, interrupting*, etc. Another approach is to focus on the different *purposes* of speaking and their associated **genres**, such as *narrating, obtaining service, giving a presentation, making small talk*, etc. This approach is particularly well suited to learners who have a specific purpose for learning English (→ **English for specific purposes**). A third is to adopt a topic-based approach, where learners are encouraged to speak freely on a range of topics, at least some of which they have chosen themselves. This is the format used in many conversation classes (→ **conversation**). Typical activity types for the teaching of speaking include: **dialogues**, **drama** activities (including *roleplays* and *simulations*), many **games**, **discussions** and debates, as well as informal classroom chat.

speech act, speech event DISCOURSE

A speech act is 'doing something' with words. Thus, when someone says *I promise to be true* the utterance *is* the promise. Likewise, *I sincerely apologize* is an apology. Most speech acts are not as direct as that, and their purpose (or *illocutionary force*) has to be inferred. For example, in certain conditions, the statement *It's freezing in here* may have the force of a *request* (→ **requesting**) – an indirect way of saying *Can you shut the window?* The conditions that determine the appropriacy and interpretation of a speech act are the concern of **pragmatics**.

Speech acts are classified as being of one of five types:

- representatives: these describe states or events in the world, eg *There is a house in New Orleans*; *I shot the sheriff*; *Baby, it's cold outside*.
- directives: these are aimed at getting people to do things, eg *Wake up, little Susie*; *Please release me*; *Let's take a walk around the block*.
- commissives: these commit the speaker to a course of action, eg *We'll meet again*; *I'll never say 'never' again*; *Will you still love me tomorrow?*
- expressives: these express feelings and attitudes, eg *Thanks for the memory*; *Congratulations! I'm in the mood for love*.
- declaratives: by uttering these, the speaker changes the situation, eg *I surrender*; *With this ring I do thee wed*; *You can have him*.

Speech act theory originated in philosophy, and is associated with the names J L Austin and John Searle. While not directly concerned with language teaching, speech act theory has informed *functional* descriptions of language. These in turn gave rise to **functional syllabuses**. Many of the functional labels in these syllabuses originated as ways of describing speech acts.

One problem with both speech act and functional labels is that they reduce communication to individual utterances. In fact many of the things that people 'do with words', such as requesting or inviting, take place over several utterances, as in this example (from a television sit-com):[4]

> **Barbara** Oh Antony, you're not going to the precinct, are ya?
> **Antony** 'Spect so. Yeah.
> **Barbara** Oh. Will you go into Boots's and get me some Sudocrem ...?
> **Antony** (*annoyed*) Ohhhhhh, why?

Barbara's first question is a *pre-request*, which allows the addressee to opt out of the request before it has actually been asked (→ **politeness**). For exchanges like this that have a specific outcome, and that follow a conventional pattern, the term *speech event* is used. Factors that determine the choice of language in a speech event are its *setting*, the *participants* and their *role relationship*, the *message* and the *channel* (eg speaking or writing). The concept of speech event is probably more useful for teaching purposes than that of the individual speech act. Speech events are typically small **dialogues**, and teaching and practising dialogues are staple classroom activities.

spelling METHODOLOGY

Knowing how to spell a word is part of knowing a word. Accurate spelling is also one of the sub-skills of **writing**. Moreover, knowing how to pronounce a word on the basis of its written form is also a useful **speaking** skill. Both spelling-for-writing and spelling-for-speaking involve recognizing *sound-spelling relationships*. However, the spelling and pronunciation of words is commonly taught in an item-by-item fashion, rather than systematically. One reason for this is the perception that there are 'no rules' to English spelling. It is true that there are a number of irregular spellings in English (the *-ough* family is one of the most often quoted examples). However, English spelling is not as irregular as is often made out. Over seventy per cent of English words have a predictable spelling, and only about three per cent are so irregular that they have to be learned as individual items. Many of these happen to be very common words like *one, two, would, are, was,* and *were*. These are met so frequently that their spellings are constantly reinforced, so that they are seldom problematic.

A systematic approach to spelling might involve teaching the different ways that individual sounds, particularly vowels, are spelt. It also helps to give some guidance as to the relative probability and likely environment for the different spellings. Thus, the sound /eɪ/, as in *pay* or *state*, is most often spelt *a ... e* as in *ape* or *plane* (eighty per cent of instances), by *ai* as in *Spain, fail* (nine per cent) and by *ay* as in *stay, delay* (six per cent).

There are also some basic spelling rules which have few exceptions and are relatively easy to teach and practise. For example:

- a silent *-e* at the end of a word 'makes the preceding vowel say its name': *pace, pipe, code, cute*
- words ending in a silent *-e* drop the *e* before a suffix beginning with a vowel: *hoping, joked, writer*.

[4] *The Royle Family: The Complete Scripts.* 2002 (Granada Media), p 394.

- after *s, x, z, sh, ch*, add *-es*, not *-s*: *buses, boxes, buzzes, bushes.*
- when a suffix is added, final consonant + *-y* is changed to consonant *-i* (or *-ie* if the suffix is *-s*): *happier, easily, carries,*
- in one-syllable words of the CVC (consonant-vowel-consonant) pattern, the final consonant is doubled before a suffix that begins with a vowel: *stopping, hottest, winner, begged.*
- '*i* before *e*, except after *c*': *field, believe; ceiling, receive.*

spoken grammar GRAMMAR

The grammar of spoken English shares the same basic structure as that of written English, but because of its 'on-line' production, there are some significant differences. The main difference lies in the fact that speech is built up clause by clause, and phrase by phrase, rather than sentence by sentence, as is the case with writing (→ **sentence**). This explains why *utterance* boundaries are less clearly defined in spoken language, and why *co-ordination* is preferred to **subordination** (the use of subordinate clauses). Spoken language typically consists of frequent sequences of short clauses joined by *and, but, then, because*:

> You know that Donna who works with me. She only does half days, afternoons and her mam usually picks up the kids. But the thing is her mam's going into hospital, means she won't be able to pick the kids up. So Donna wanted to swop to mornings. So she has to ask Pauline and she said 'Can I swop to mornings' and she told her about her mam and the hospital but Pauline was having none of it. She's got herself in a right pickle. So what's she going to do?[5]

This looser construction means that, in utterances, content can be added before or after the main body of the message in ways that sentence grammar does not allow. These before and after 'slots' are called, respectively, *heads* and *tails*:[6]

head	body	tail(s)
1. *Timpson's,*	*do you know where that is,*	*Twiggy?*
2. *Cheryl.*	*thirteen-and-a-half stone*	*she is.*
3. *Tell you what*	*she's a lucky girl*	*that Emma.*
	4. *He's a cracking show host,*	*Winton, you know.*
	5. *He's lookin' a lot better though*	*PJ, in't he.*
	6. *I'm glad we don't pay our licence fee,*	*that's all I can say.*
	7. *I think it was about last March. Or April.*	*Something like that.*

With regard to the *head* slot, (1) and (2) show the *fronting* of the topic of the utterance, while (3) is an example of an *utterance launcher* – a way of beginning a speaker turn.

[5] *The Royle Family: The Complete Scripts.* 2002 (Granada Media) pp 59–60.
[6] *The Royle Family: The Complete Scripts.* 2002 (Granada Media) pp 232, 502, 257, 234, 504, 311, 477.

The tail slot is particularly versatile, accommodating *vocatives* (ie, the use of the addressee's name as in (1); *retrospective comments*, as in 2, 4 (*you know*) and 6; *end-placing* in evaluative statements (as in 3, 4 and 5); **question tags** (5); and expressions of **vague language** (7). Notice that more than one element can go into the tail slot.

Also, unlike sentences, utterances can consist of isolated fragments. And the here-and-now context in which they are produced means that parts of utterances, such as subject pronouns, can be left out. (This is called **ellipsis**.):

Dad So life treating you all right, is it?
Joe Can't complain. (PAUSE) Nice bit of cake.
Dave Did you hear the thunder last night?
Joe No.
Dave Slept through it then?
Joe Must have done.[7]

Other characteristic features of spoken grammar include:

- a preference for direct speech rather than **reported speech**, as in:

  So Donna wanted to swap to mornings. So she had to ask Pauline and she said, 'Can I swop to mornings'

- the use of **vague language**, as in:

  I think it was about last March. Or April. Something like that.

Other differences between written and spoken grammar have to do with the distribution of particular items. For example, personal pronouns and determiners (such as *I*, *you*, *my*, *our* ...) are more frequent in spoken language than they are in written; adjectives are less common in speech than in writing; modal verbs, especially *will*, *would* and *can*, are more common in spoken language than in written; the past perfect, present perfect continuous, and passive forms are rare in spoken language.

The question as to whether learners should be *taught* these features, or simply be exposed to material that includes them, is debatable. Many of the characteristics of spoken language, such as tails, are associated with informal, even regional, varieties of English. Their use may sound strange coming from learners. What the evidence does suggest is that a looser kind of syntax and more relaxed standards of accuracy are tolerated in spoken language. To insist, therefore, that learners should speak as if they were writing may be counterproductive.

stage → **lesson plan**

Standard English SOCIOLINGUISTICS

Standard English (SE) is the variety of English that is usually used in writing, taught in schools, and used as the model for teaching non-native speakers. Because it is the variety normally spoken by educated people, it has a privileged status over other varieties. The linguistic features of SE are codified in its grammar and its vocabulary, including its **spelling**. Its pronunciation may vary, however. Standard English is not necessarily spoken with the accent that is also considered a standard, ie, **Received Pronunciation**.

---

[7] *The Royle Family: The Complete Scripts.* 2002 (Granada Media) p 85.

Each major English-speaking country has its own variety of SE: there is Standard American English (→ **American English**), Standard Australian English, and so on. The issue of whether to use SE as the model in teaching is more hotly debated in first language education than in second. However, with the increasingly widespread need for **English as an international language (EIL)** there are arguments both for and against using SE as the norm. The arguments in favour hinge on its already wide distribution and the fact that, even if not all English speakers speak it, they can understand it. Furthermore, there is no viable alternative. The arguments *against* using SE as the model for EIL are that it is too closely associated with **native speakers**. English is now 'owned' as much by its non-native speakers as its native ones. Proponents of this view argue that a new variety (or new varieties) of international English should be allowed to emerge with which these speakers can identify.

stative verb GRAMMAR

Verbs can also be classified according to whether they are *stative* or *dynamic*. Stative verbs refer to:

- states: *I am curious. It's a wonderful life.*
- inactive emotional, cognitive, or perceptual processes: *Gentlemen prefer blondes. I want to live! I know what you did last summer.*

Dynamic verbs, on the other hand, refer to actions and events: *Guess who's coming to dinner? The postman always rings twice. I shot Jesse James.* Stative verbs cannot normally be used in the continuous: **Gentlemen are preferring blondes.* However, many verbs – such as *smell, look, see, think* – have both a stative and a dynamic use: *You look nice. What are you looking at?* It is perhaps more accurate, therefore, to talk about stative and dynamic *uses*, rather than stative and dynamic verbs.

storytelling → **narrating**

stress PHONOLOGY

Stress is the effect of emphasizing certain syllables by increasing their loudness, length or pitch. A *stressed* syllable is one that is made prominent in this way, and it contrasts with the syllables that are *unstressed*. Some descriptions refer to degrees of stress, ie, *primary* and *secondary*, but for practical purposes these distinctions are unimportant. *Word stress* refers to prominence at the word level, while *sentence stress* refers to the patterns of stressed and unstressed syllables over a whole sentence.

There are few reliable rules as to which syllable is stressed in a word. But there is a tendency in two-syllable words to place the stress on the first syllable. In *polysyllabic* words, the tendency is to stress the third-to-last syllable (the *antepenultimate*), as in *communicate, economy, photographer*. However, this pattern can be overridden by certain *suffixes*, such as *-tion*, and *-ic* which attract the stress to the penultimate syllable: *communication, economic, photographic*. There are also a number of words that are spelt the same but that are stressed differently according to whether they are being used as a verb or a noun: eg *present, conduct, import*.

Words normally retain their normal stress patterns in a sentence, but one syllable of at least one word will be given particular prominence. This is usually because that word signals what is new information in the sentence, or because it marks a contrast:

> A *Where're the keys?*
> B *They're on the table.*
> A *The coffee table or the kitchen table?*
> B *The kitchen table.*

Because of the lack of useful rules, word stress tends to be dealt with on an item-by-item basis, until learners start working out stress on the basis of intuition. Nevertheless, highlighting the correct stress when teaching new words can be a useful aid to memory. There is some evidence that words are stored and recalled according to their 'shape'. Sentence stress is related to meaning, so it is easier to explain. But this depends on utterances being presented in their contexts. In the absence of context, there is no way you can decide which word is stressed in a sentence like: *My older sister doesn't live with my football coach.*

stress-timed language → **rhythm**

strong form → **weak form**

structure LINGUISTICS

A structure is a pattern that a language has for generating specific instances. Thus, the pattern *determiner + adjective + noun* generates such combinations as *my left foot, the quiet man, an American tragedy*, etc. The pattern *noun phrase + be-auxiliary + -ing* generates *the whole town's talking, the Russians are coming*, etc. The term *structure* is now used loosely to mean any grammar item that appears on a syllabus, and in particular the different combinations of **tense** and **aspect**, such as the *present progressive*, the *past simple*, the *present perfect*, etc. Structural syllabuses, in which structures are sequenced in terms of their formal complexity, underpin form-based methods such as **audiolingualism**. Since then, attempts have been made to introduce syllabuses based on criteria other than purely structural ones, such as **meaning**. Thus, the **communicative approach** tried to replace structures with **functions**. But, despite the virtually universal acceptance of communicative methodology, structural syllabuses have persisted. This is mainly because structures are easier than functions to grade. **Form**, rather than meaning, is still the main organizing principle on which coursebooks are based to this day.

style LINGUISTICS

Style is a (usually deliberate) choice of a particular way of saying or writing something. There is often more than one way of conveying the same message. The choice is determined by (1) specific contextual factors, such as the degree of formality that is required, or (2) a particular effect that the person wants to achieve. In both cases, the choice is a stylistic one. With regard to the first kind of choice, the following example (heard on an aeroplane) shows a marked shift in style:

> We are on a taxiway, so it is essential that you remain seated with your seatbelts securely fastened … Excuse me, could you sit down please? … Sit down!

The style changes from **formal** to informal, as the situation becomes more urgent. Other terms that are used to identify different context-dependent styles include *frozen, casual* and *intimate*.

An example of language being used to create a particular effect is this Valentine's day message:

To Wee Pig from Big Pig. Grunt Grunt!

Here the writer has chosen a style associated with children's literature. The study of style, in this second sense, is called **stylistics**.

Style choices affect both grammar and vocabulary. Words that are used only in certain styles are often identified as such in dictionaries. Styles include *literary*, *old-fashioned*, *humorous* and *medical*. Thus *bonkers* HUMOROUS; *lunatic* OLD-FASHIONED; *bipolar* MEDICAL. Styles that are related to particular fields, such as medicine or journalism, are also called **registers**.

stylistics LINGUISTICS

Stylistics is the study of **style**, or the way language is used to create particular effects, especially those associated with the expressive and literary uses of language. Stylistics differs from literary criticism in that, rather than simply *interpreting* different styles, it aims to *explain* them. It does so by employing the concepts and analytical techniques of linguistics and applying these to literary texts. For example, these are the opening two sentences of a novel by Monica Ali:[8]

> Nazneen waved at the tattoo lady. The tattoo lady was always there when Nazneen looked out across the dead grass and broken paving stones to the block opposite.

From a stylistic point of view, the fact that Nazneen is both named and the **subject** of activity verbs (*waved*, *looked out*) contrasts with the fact that *the tattoo lady* is unnamed and either in **object** position, or the subject of a *stative verb* (*was*). This clearly establishes Nazneen as the agent, hence the likely protagonist of the story. Furthermore, the use of the definite **article** *the* in *the tattoo lady*, *the dead grass*, *the block*, indicates that these items are known. Since they are not known to the reader, but to Nazneen, the reader is compelled (or 'positioned') to adopt Nazneen's point of view.

Stylistics is not just concerned with literary texts. It has broadened its focus to encompass non-literary genres, such as those associated with advertising and journalism. In this sense, stylistics has a lot in common with **genre** analysis. It has been argued that sensitizing learners to the ways that particular language choices can create intended or unintended effects, and the way that these effects can position readers, makes them more critical readers of texts, as well as potentially better writers.

subject GRAMMAR

The subject of a **sentence** or **clause** is the agent that causes the event expressed by the **verb**: *The postman always rings twice. Fear eats the soul.* Or the subject is in the state expressed by the verb: *Rosencrantz and Guildenstern are dead. I was a teenage werewolf.* In **passive** sentences the subject is the thing or person affected by the action: *How the West was won.*

In statements, the subject normally precedes the verb, and the verb agrees with the subject (→ **concord**): *Mr Smith goes to Washington.* The subject is usually realized by a full **noun phrase** or a **pronoun**: *The empire fights back. Gentlemen*

---

[8] Ali, M. *Brick Lane*, 2003 (Black Swan) p 17.

prefer blondes. Some like it hot. It's a wonderful life. Clauses can also take the subject role: *Who dares wins.*

Unlike some languages, subject pronouns are obligatory in English statements and questions: it's not possible to say, for example, ⋆*Is a wonderful life.*

subjunctive GRAMMAR

The subjunctive is a verb form which exists in many languages to express a range of meanings such as uncertainty, wishes and desires. It contrasts with the *indicative* which is the form of the verb used to describe real states, and the **imperative**, which is used to give commands. In English, no subjunctive form exists. Instead, the base form of the verb (ie, the infinitive without *to*) is used (mainly in **American English**) in some constructions that express suggestions or demands (the *mandatory subjunctive*):

> *I suggest he see a specialist.*
> *The opposition demands that the government act now.*

(In British English it is more usual to insert *should*, as in *… that the government should act now*). The subjunctive also survives (1) as *were* in past **conditional** constructions (*If I were you, I'd leave him*) and (2) in some formulaic expressions: *So be it. Come what may. As it were. If need be.*

subordination GRAMMAR

Subordination is one way of linking **clauses** so that one clause is embedded in another. The embedded clause is said to be subordinate to (or dependent on) the other clause:

> *When two Englishmen meet, their first talk is of the weather.* (Samuel Johnson)

> *An Englishman, even if he is alone, forms an orderly queue of one.* (George Mikes)

The subordinate clauses that are underlined in the above sentences cannot stand on their own grammatically, whereas the other clauses can. Each of these other clauses forms the *main clause* of its respective sentence: *their first talk is of the weather; An Englishman forms an orderly queue of one.*

The **conjunctions** *when* and *even if* are *subordinating conjunctions*. Other subordinating conjunctions are *although, because, while, after, unless,* etc.

There are three kinds of subordinate clause:

- *adverbial clauses* (as the above two examples): these are clauses that act like an **adverbial** in a sentence, in that they provide extra information about time, manner, reason, conditions, etc.
- **relative clauses**: These are attached to a noun phrase, which they modify by providing extra information: *There is some corner of a foreign field that is forever England.*
- reported clauses: clauses that report statements, questions, thoughts, and which typically begin with *that* or *if* or a *wh-* word (→ **reported speech**): *An Englishman believes that his home is his castle. The British dream is that the Queen drops in for tea.* (These are also called *complement clauses*, because they *complete* the meaning of the verb; or a type of *nominal* or *noun clause*, because

they typically fill the **noun phrase** slot in the sentence: *An Englishman believes this*.)

A sentence which consists of a main clause and one or more subordinate clauses is called a **complex sentence**.

sub-skill → **skill**

substitution DISCOURSE

Substitution is the replacing of a **noun phrase** or a whole **clause** by a single word. This is done in order to avoid repetition, or to make a text more cohesive (→ **cohesion**). For example, in the following line from *The Importance of Being Earnest* by Oscar Wilde, Algernon says:

> I don't really know what a gorgon is like, but I am quite sure that Lady Bracknell is <u>one</u>.

the word *one* substitutes for *a gorgon*.
And in this exchange:

> **Lady Bracknell** What are your politics?
> **Jack** Well, I am afraid I really have <u>none</u>.

the single word *none* substitutes for *no politics*.

The words *do/does*, *so* and *not* can substitute for whole clauses:

> **Algernon** I would rather like to see Cecily.
> **Jack** I will take very good care you never <u>do</u>.

Here *do* substitutes for *see Cecily*. Here are some more examples from the same source:

> All women become like their mothers. That is their tragedy. No man <u>does</u>. That's his.

> **Cecily** Then have we got to part?
> **Algernon** I am afraid <u>so</u>.

> **Algernon** I am afraid, Aunt Augusta, I shall have to give up the pleasure of dining with you tonight after all.
> **Lady Bracknell** I hope <u>not</u>, Algernon.

Do can combine with *so* to mean 'perform the action just mentioned' and with *the same* to mean 'perform the same action':

> I broke off my engagement with Ernest. I feel it is better to <u>do so</u>.

> So I am going to get rid of Ernest. And I strongly advise you to <u>do the same</u>.

substitution table METHODOLOGY

A substitution table is a way of displaying the way the different elements of a **structure** relate to one another, both on a horizontal axis, and on a vertical one. Horizontally, the table displays the order of elements. Vertically, it displays the items that may be substituted for one another. The technical terms for these horizontal and vertical relations are *syntagmatic* and *paradigmatic*, respectively (→ **paradigm**).

Here, for example, is a substitution table for the present perfect:[9]

I've	[never]	seen been to eaten worked in touched met	a kangaroo a crocodile a comet Australia a pineapple London a foreign country shark-fin soup a ghost the President a unicorn	[once.] [more than once.] [many times.]

Substitution tables were a popular aid to learning in audiolingualism, since they displayed the structural patterns of the language. They also provided material for *substitution drills* (→ **drills**). Since then they have fallen out of favour. Nevertheless, there are few clearer ways of displaying a structure's parts, and, with a little ingenuity, they can also provide a model for creativity and **personalization**.

suffix → **affix**

suggesting, making suggestions FUNCTION

If you make a suggestion, you attempt to influence the behaviour of people. It is less forceful than a command, although it may be a way of disguising a command. Explicit suggestions use the verb *suggest*: *I suggest you ask next door.* Or they involve the use of **modal verbs**: *You could try the shop on the corner. You might want to phone first.* Questions with *what about* and *how about* are common: *What about looking in the Yellow Pages?* Also: *Why don't you phone Information?* For suggestions that involve the speaker, *let's* is common: *Let's ask that policeman. Let's not.*

Asking for suggestions can, again, involve using the verb *suggest*, or the use of modal verbs: *What do you suggest? What shall we do? What do you think I should do?*

Reporting suggestions can involve the use of the **subjunctive**: *I suggested she ask next door*, although in British English *should* is more common: *I suggested she should ask next door.*

Situations and topics that involve making suggestions and which are therefore good for practising this language include: health, travel, the home (eg decorating), work-related problems, study and career choices, relationship issues (such as those dealt with in the problem pages of magazines), or, closer to home, giving tips to language learners.

[9] Thornbury, S. 1994. *Highlight Pre-Intermediate Student's Book.* (Heinemann).

218

suggestopaedia METHODOLOGY

Suggestopaedia is a method that applies principles of suggestion (or *suggestology*) to teaching. Its originator, Georgi Lozanov, believes that, in the right conditions, the human mind is highly suggestible and capable of prodigious feats of learning (called *superlearning* or *accelerated learning*). In order to tap into this potential, the learner needs to be in the right emotional state. Any negative feelings associated with learning need to be eliminated – by a process of what is called *de-suggestion*. To this end, classes are conducted to a background of soothing classical music, learners adopt fictitious names and personae, and the teacher is in conspicuous control – all of which helps make learners maximally suggestible. The teacher reads dialogues aloud, along with their translations, while the learners simply listen and follow the texts, on the assumption that learning is taking place subliminally. The emphasis on positive **affect** situates suggestopaedia firmly in the **humanistic** camp of teaching methods. Its faith in the power of effortless, unconscious learning anticipated approaches such as **neuro-linguistic programming**.

superlative → **adjective**

syllable PHONOLOGY

A syllable is a unit of pronunciation that is typically larger than a sound but smaller than a word. Syllables consist of **vowel** sounds (V) or combinations of vowels and **consonants** (C). In English, the different possibilities include V, as in *I*; CV, as in *go*; CVC, as in *got*, as well as combinations that start or finish with **consonant clusters**: CCCV (*stray*), VCC (*eats*), etc. Some consonants – notably /n/ and /l/ – can form syllables on their own, as in the last syllables of *button* and *little*, and are called *syllabic consonants*.

Apart from some words, like *medicine, library, Wednesday*, whose syllabification can vary from speaker to speaker, it is relatively easy to perceive and count syllables. It is less easy to say where one syllable ends and another begins. This is an issue that affects the *hyphenation* of written words. Most English words consist of one or two syllables – the more frequent the word, the fewer syllables it is likely to have. For words of more than one syllable, one of the syllables is given greater prominence, or **stress**. In order to identify and assign stress, it is important, therefore, that learners understand what a syllable is. Asking them to count and identify the syllables in their own name is a good place to start.

syllable-timed language → **rhythm**

syllabus METHODOLOGY

A syllabus is an item-by-item description of the teaching content of a course. On the basis of the syllabus, a timetable, or *scheme of work*, can be drawn up. This in turn can generate individual lessons. Finally, the syllabus content helps specify what should be tested (→ **testing**). A distinction is sometimes made between the **curriculum**, which is a general statement of educational beliefs and objectives, and the syllabus, which is one way that the curriculum is operationalized.

Syllabus design involves at least two sets of decisions: *selecting* and *grading*. Syllabus items are chosen and sequenced on the basis of criteria such as *usefulness* and *difficulty*. The usefulness of an item is best assessed in relation to the learners' needs (→ **needs analysis**) but other factors, such as an item's **frequency** may influence the choice. The difficulty of an item may be a function of its **form** (the present perfect progressive is formally complex, for example) or of its **meaning** (the meanings of modal verbs can be difficult to tease apart). On the other hand, an item may be difficult to explain, demonstrate, or translate: a factor called *teachability*. The present progressive is easier to demonstrate than the present simple, for example. Finally, *tradition* plays a part in syllabus design: items may be included simply because teachers and learners have come to expect them. For example, despite its relative infrequency, **reported speech** is included in many syllabuses, probably for no other reason than tradition.

The organizing principle for a language syllabus can be either in terms of forms, or of meanings. A typical example of the former is the *structural syllabus*, a sequence of grammatical structures organized in terms of their formal complexity (→ **structure**). Most current coursebooks are still organized along structural lines, consisting for the most part of *discrete items* of grammar, such as *past simple, adverbs of frequency, first conditional, -ing forms*, etc. A meaning-based (or *semantic*) syllabus, on the other hand, might be organized around a list of language **functions**, such as requesting, narrating, giving advice, etc (→ **functional syllabus**). Alternatively, a syllabus might be organized around a series of topics such as *weather, family, food and drink*. Such a syllabus is called a *topic-based*, or *thematic*, syllabus. This kind of organization is frequently used for teaching vocabulary. A *situational syllabus* is one based on the kinds of situation the learner is likely to encounter: *at the bank, renting a flat, visiting the doctor, etc.* In a *task-based syllabus*, on the other hand, instruction is programmed around a series of **tasks**, such as *planning an excursion, designing a logo, performing a scenario*, etc (→ **task-based learning**). Finally, *text-based syllabuses* are based around the text and discourse needs of the learners. They are associated with **genre**-driven approaches to teaching.

Attempts have been made to combine and interweave these different 'strands' into what are called *multi-layered syllabuses*. However, on closer examination these usually turn out to consist of a core syllabus (typically structural) on to which have been grafted elements from other syllabus types, such as a functional, topic-based, or task-based descriptors.

The above discussion might suggest that all teaching is pre-planned around a syllabus. But the degree of detail in a syllabus, or the extent to which teachers are expected to follow one, can vary enormously. The use of a syllabus is generally favoured by institutions, especially where there is standardized testing of students. However, no one syllabus will represent an accurate description of all the learners' diverse needs. Advocates of **learner-centred instruction** argue that a pre-specified syllabus runs counter to their philosophy. They have proposed a number of alternatives, including *negotiated syllabuses* (also called *process syllabuses*), where the content and direction of the program is jointly – and continuously – negotiated between the learners and the teacher.

synonym VOCABULARY

A synonym is a word that has the same meaning as, or a very similar meaning to, another one. *Prison* and *jail* are synonyms, as are *let down* and *disappoint*, and *mad* and *crazy*. This relation of similarity is called *synonymy*, and contrasts with other sense relations, such as oppositeness (or *antonymy* → **antonym**) and group membership (*hyponymy* → **hyponym**). Total synonyms, ie, words that are interchangeable in all contexts, probably don't exist. For example, words may have a similar meaning but differ in **style**, such as *mad* and *bonkers*, or in their geographical distribution (cf. BrE *petrol* with AmE *gas*), or in their **connotations**, eg *slim* vs *skinny*, or in the words that they commonly co-occur with (→ **collocation**). For example, *fair* and *blonde* are synonyms: both collocate with *hair* to mean *light-coloured*. But *blonde* collocates only with *hair*, while *fair* collocates with *complexion*, *weather*, and many other words as well. For these reasons, it is perhaps more useful to talk about *near synonyms*. A useful resource for finding synonyms is a *thesaurus*.

syntax GRAMMAR

Syntax describes the rules for sequencing words so as to show their relationships of meaning within sentences. For example, in English the rules of syntax permit the placing of two **nouns** together, so that one modifies the other: *fruit juice, bus stop, table tennis*. In other languages, like French, the rules of syntax do not allow this, so, not **fruit jus* but *jus de fruit, arrêt d'autobus, tennis de table*, etc. Likewise, the basic order of **clause** elements in English is subject–verb–object (SVO), as in *The table tennis players drank fruit juice*. In some other languages, such as Japanese, the preference is for an SOV order.

Syntax contrasts with **morphology**, which is the study of the structure of words, such as the way different endings or word forms can change the **tense** of a verb: *play, played; drink, drank*. Together, syntax and morphology make up what is conventionally known as **grammar**.

Syntax was traditionally taught by the process of **parsing** sentences. Parsing involves dividing up sentences into their constituent parts, and identifying each part. More engaging ways of teaching syntax include: ordering cards, on which are printed words and phrases, so as to make meaningful sentences; expanding very simple sentences so as to make them longer and more complex; or the opposite: reducing complex sentences to their most simple form by eliminating words or phrases, one at a time; or contrasting sentences, such as:

> *The singer that my father likes sang a song.*
> *The singer sang a song that my father likes.*
> *The singer that likes my father sang a song.*

or 'disambiguating' ambiguous sentences, such as:

> *I try to avoid boring students.*
> *Brad showed Tom a photo of himself.*

systemic functional linguistics LINGUISTICS

Systemic functional linguistics (SFL) is a model for linguistic analysis developed by Michael Halliday. It is *systemic* because it describes language as a network of *systems*, a system being 'a small fixed set of choices'. It also describes the conditions for choosing among each set of choices. For example, in the verb system in English the speaker has a choice between using a **finite** or a non-finite verb; the non-finite choice, in turn, allows a choice between **infinitives** and

participles. These systemic choices can be displayed like this:

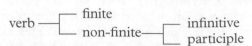

At every level (or *rank*) in the system the speaker is offered such options, and the task of grammar is to specify the total grid of options available: this represents the 'meaning potential' of the language. According to the SFL model, language is viewed not as a set of rules that generate structures, but rather as an enormous systems network for 'making meaning'.

SFL is *functional* because it incorporates a functional dimension into its description (→ **function**). SFL identifies language as having three main (or *mega-*) functions:

- an *experiential function* (also called an *ideational function*): ie, language expresses the way we experience the world
- an *interpersonal function*: ie, language is used to act upon the world and to interact with other people
- a *textual function*: ie, language can be used to make connections between a text and its context, or to make connections within the text.

These three functions are realized at every level of analysis. Thus, a **clause** acts as a *representation* (its experiential function), as an *exchange* (its interpersonal function), and as a *message* (its textual function), concurrently. Thus, the clause *Man bites dog* represents a state of affairs, functions in order to inform (eg a newspaper reader by a reporter), and takes the message form of a headline.

As representation, clauses describe some kind of *process*, and verbs are classified according to the kinds of processes they express: whether they are *mental, verbal* or *material,* for example. Mental processes are expressed by verbs like *think, believe* and *decide,* and verbal processes are expressed by verbs such as *say* and *ask*. A material process is one in which some action occurs, as in *Man bites dog.* And, rather than describe this headline as being composed of a *subject,* a *verb* and an *object,* a functional description construes it as *actor, material process* and *affected.* Notice that in the passive these functions do not change: *Dog* [= *affected*] *bitten* [= *material process*] *by man* [= *actor*].

Underlying this model of language is the claim that the grammatical system is determined by the social functions for which language is used: 'Language is as it is because of what it has to do.' SFL has been influential in educational contexts, such as in teaching immigrant populations in Australia, where language is viewed as the key to in-group membership (→ **genre**). The complexity of its description, however, can be off-putting. What's more, from a teaching point of view, there is the danger inherent in all complex descriptions, that more time is spent explaining the system than actually putting it to practical use.

---

tag question → **question**

task METHODOLOGY

A task is a classroom activity whose focus is on communicating meaning. The objective of a task may be to reach some consensus on an issue, to solve a problem, to draft a plan, to design something, or to persuade someone to do something. In contrast, practising a pre-selected item of language (such as the present perfect) for its own sake would not be a valid task objective (→ **activity**; → **exercise**). In the performance of the task, learners are expected to make use of their own language resources. In theory, tasks may be receptive or productive, and may be done individually or in pairs or small groups. However, in practice, most activities that are labelled 'tasks' in coursebooks involve production (either speaking or writing, or both) and require learners to interact with one another.

Tasks are the organizing principle in **task-based learning**. In order to devise a syllabus of tasks it is necessary both to classify tasks, and to identify the factors that make one task more difficult than another. Different criteria for classifying tasks have been suggested. For example, tasks can be *open-ended* or *closed*. An open-ended task is one in which learners know there is no predetermined solution. It might be planning an excursion, or debating a topical issue. A closed task, on the other hand, requires learners to discover the solution to a problem, such as identifying the differences in a *spot-the-difference* task (→ **communicative activity**). Tasks can also be classified according to the kinds of operations they involve, such as *ranking, selecting, sorting, comparing, surveying* and *problem-solving*.

Factors which influence the degree of difficulty of the task, and hence which affect the grading of tasks, include:

- *linguistic factors*: How complex is the language that learners will need to draw on, in order to do the task? How much help, either before, or during the task, will they get with their language needs?
- *cognitive factors*: Does the task require the processing of complex data? Is the task type familiar to learners?
- *performance factors*: Do the learners have to interact in real time in order to do the task? Do they have time to rehearse? Do they have to 'go public'?

The term *task* is now widely accepted as a useful way of labelling certain types of classroom activity, including many which have a thinly disguised grammar agenda. But the concept of task is not without its critics. Some writers feel that the associations of task with 'work' undervalues the more playful – and possibly less authentic or communicative – types of classroom activity, such as games, songs and drama (→ **language play**).

task-based learning METHODOLOGY

Task-based learning (TBL) – also called *task-based language teaching* and *task-based instruction* – is an approach that makes the **task** the basic unit for planning and teaching. This contrasts with approaches that are centred around grammar, for example. The rationale underlying TBL originated in the **communicative approach**, particularly in what is known as its 'strong' version. Proponents of this view argue that 'you learn a language *by using it*'. (This contrasts with the 'weak' version: 'you learn a language *in order to use it*'). One of the first experiments with TBL took place in the 1970s, in southern India, and is known as the *Bangalore Project*. Its architect, N.S. Prabhu, designed and taught a syllabus of tasks. Classroom instruction involved the demonstration (by the teacher) and the performance (by the learners) of these tasks. Prabhu strongly rejected any focus on (grammatical) form, either before, during, or after the task, on the grounds that it might distract the learners from a focus on meaning. Since then, most proponents of TBL have adopted a more relaxed attitude to incorporating a **focus on form**. The question remains, however, as to when and in what form this form focus should take. Purists argue that it should emerge *out of* the task, and be dealt with after the task. One way of doing this might be to ask learners to perform a task and then let them hear a recording of native speakers performing the same task. The learners then repeat the task, incorporating any features they choose to appropriate from the recording. Apart from anything else, there are positive gains in simply repeating tasks (→ **repetition**).

Others argue that the **feedback** that learners get while *on task* is more effective than *post-task*. One way of supplying a feedback on form without overt correction is through the use of *recasts*. A recast is when the teacher reformulates what learners have said in a more target-like way. For example:

Learner I am not agree.
Teacher Oh, you don't agree. Why not?

Still others have accepted that a *pre-task* focus on form – ie, pre-teaching grammar items that might be needed during the task – is justifiable as a way of 'priming' learners. It is difficult to see how this is not simply a version of **PPP**, however.

TBL shares many of the principles and practices of **whole language learning**. But it has been influential more at the theoretical and research level than in terms of actual classroom practice. One reason for this is that a focus on tasks requires a totally different **course design**, not to mention the implications for **testing**. Also, for many teachers, a task-based approach represents a management challenge. How do you set up and monitor tasks in large classes of unmotivated adolescents, for example? And how do you deal appropriately with language problems that emerge spontaneously from the task performance? A grammar-based syllabus and a PPP approach offer greater security to teachers with these concerns. Nevertheless, the value of incorporating communicative tasks into classroom teaching is generally accepted, even if the overall theoretical framework of TBL is not. Also, the notion of *task* as including the use of **computer-mediated communication** has expanded the possibilities of TBL (→ **webquest**).

teacher development PROFESSIONAL

Teacher development (TD) refers to the ongoing professional growth of teachers, particularly that which takes place after their initial training. TD may take the form of *in-service training* of a more formal kind, such as attendance on short or long courses, or at professional conferences. But it is more typically associated with informal, collegial and classroom-based programmes that incorporate cycles of classroom practice and **reflection**. These might include such activities as:

- a mentoring system, where more experienced teachers work alongside novice teachers, including taking part in team teaching
- classroom observation, by peers, mentors or supervisors, plus feedback
- keeping a teaching journal
- **action research**
- locally-based workshops and seminars
- guided reading, and discussion

TD is often contrasted with *teacher training* (TT), the latter having more technical goals, such as the acquisition of basic classroom skills and subject knowledge. TD, on the other hand, has a more 'whole person' orientation, aimed at developing the teacher's capacity for self-directed growth and professional well-being. Both TD and TT come within the larger orbit of *teacher education*.

teacher talk METHODOLOGY

Teacher talk is the term used to describe the variety of language used by teachers when addressing learners. In this sense, teacher talk shares qualities with the way speakers often adapt their language when talking to non-native speakers (*foreigner talk*) and the way that parents talk to children (*caretaker talk*). More generally, teacher talk refers to the way that teachers *interact* with their learners. Researching these interactions is of special relevance to language teaching, since the teacher provides a source of **input** as well as of **feedback**. Both are considered necessary conditions for language acquisition. Moreover, strong claims have been made for the formative role of **interaction** in language acquisition, especially interaction with a 'better other' ($\rightarrow$ **sociocultural learning theory**). These claims contradict the received wisdom that *teacher talking time* (TTT) should be kept to a minimum, in favour of maximizing *student talking time* (STT). Such advice is well-intentioned, in that it is aimed at discouraging 'lecturing', but it underestimates the value of the teacher as both a source of input, and as an interactional partner.

Teacher talk has a number of different functions, which include

- *managing*, eg giving instructions, nominating turns
- *explaining*, eg giving definitions of words, presenting grammar
- *checking understanding*
- *modelling*, ie, providing a clear model of new language items
- *giving feedback*, including correcting
- *eliciting*, ie, asking questions in order for learners to display what they know (called **display questions**)
- *providing input*, as when dictating a text, or telling a story for listening comprehension purposes
- *interpersonal talk*, such as when chatting with learners at the beginning of the lesson, or commenting on topics that might arise incidentally during the course of the lesson.

Traditionally, teacher talk has been more concerned with those functions at the top end of the above list. However, there is growing evidence to support a role for the teacher as a source of input and interpersonal talk. Also, some researchers have challenged the value of display questions (such as *How many fingers have you got?*), as opposed to *real questions* (such as *How many cousins have you got?*). It has been argued that the latter type promote greater *depth of processing* than the former. Another issue that has been investigated is whether, and to what extent, teachers grade their talk in order to make it more comprehensible, and what benefits this might have. Researchers have indeed found modifications in teacher talk, such as in pace, pause length, and complexity. But few teachers are actually ungrammatical. Of more significance, perhaps, are the *interactional* modifications that teachers engage in, when, for example, they recognize problems of understanding in their learners. Effective teachers pre-empt or negotiate such problems by frequently checking understanding, repeating themselves, rephrasing and backtracking. This suggests that being intelligible as a teacher is less a question of grading language than of being sensitive to, and knowing how to resolve, misunderstandings.

tenor → **context**; → **register**

tense GRAMMAR

'Tense' refers to the way that verbs are inflected (ie, have different forms) to express a relation with time. For example, *happen* vs *happened*; *run* vs *ran*; *can* vs *could*. The relation between tense and time is not an exact match. A present tense verb form may in fact refer to the future or the past, as in *The bus leaves at noon tomorrow. Yesterday morning, I'm lying in bed when the phone rings* …. And a past tense verb form may refer to the future or the present, as in *If we went to Mallorca next summer … Could I try it on?* Nevertheless, there is a loose relation between time and tense. In the absence of context, you are likely to interpret *it happens* as having present reference, and the sentence *it happened* as having past reference. It is important to remember, though, that grammatical *tense* and notional *time* are not the same thing.

Because tense describes the way that verbs are *inflected*, there are only two tenses in English: the *present* and the *past*. There is no future inflection in English; instead **futurity** is expressed in a variety of ways, including the use of **modal verbs**: *It'll happen. It's going to happen.*

Modal verbs can also be marked for tense, although this usually indicates a difference in certainty rather than in time: *It may rain. It might rain. I'll pay. I'd pay.* Only in reported speech is the tense-time connection obvious: *Dad says I can go. Dad said I could go.*

Tense combines with **aspect** to create the variety of verb structures in English that are commonly, if mistakenly, known as its different *tenses*. These are:

	[no aspect: simple]	perfect	progressive	perfect + progressive
present	*they work*	*they have worked*	*they are working*	*they have been working*
past	*they worked*	*they had worked*	*they were working*	*they had been working*

Since 'tenses' are strongly associated with **grammar** in general (due, in part, to the residual effect of the teaching of Latin and Greek), a focus on them has traditionally dominated **course design** – and still does. The so-called tenses are taught as independent *discrete items*. An alternative might be to teach tense and aspect as an interconnected closed system. Such an approach would, in theory, be a lot simpler. Rather than teaching eight (or more) 'different' structures, it would involve teaching the forms and basic meanings of two tenses (*present* and *past*) and two aspects (*progressive* and *perfect*). Since these forms and meanings remain stable whatever their combination, it would then be a matter of learners experiencing the various combinations in context. It is context, after all, that helps distinguish between these different uses of *they are working*:

1. *Where are the twins?* ~ <u>*They are working*</u>.
2. *The cleaners like to listen to music when* <u>*they are working*</u>.
3. *My parents can't come to the wedding next Saturday.* <u>*They are working*</u>.

testing TESTING

Testing is a form of **assessment**. It can happen at any stage of the teaching/learning process. At entry, learners are often given *placement tests* in order to ascertain their level. They may also be given some kind of *diagnostic test* in order to identify their particular needs (as in **needs analysis**). In order to monitor the learning process, learners may then be given periodic tests during their course (*progress tests*), and at the end of the course (*achievement tests*). (These are also called *formative* and *summative* tests, respectively.) One reason for setting progress tests is to encourage **revision**: the threat of a test is a powerful incentive to review previously studied material. Tests can be administered at various degrees of formality, from the very informal gap-fill exercise given to test the learners' recall of the previous lesson, to the highly formal public **examinations** of the type administered by examination boards such as Cambridge ESOL, Trinity and TOEFL. Tests can be marked according to an agreed standard, as is the case in public examinations. Candidates have to achieve the standard in order to pass: this is called *criterion-referenced testing*. Tests where there is no criterion for passing, but where a candidate's results are interpreted in relation to the results of other candidates, is called *norm-referenced*.

The criteria by which the worth of a test is judged include its *validity*, its *reliability* and its *practicability*. A test is *valid* if it measures accurately what it is intended to measure. For example, a *multiple-choice* grammar test consisting of items such as this:

How long [*are you living/do you live/have you lived*] here now?

is a valid test if the tester is interested only in the learners' ability to match grammatical forms to their contexts. But it is not a valid test of communicative ability nor of overall **proficiency**. Yet, due to their practicability, such tests are commonly used as *placement tests*. Because communicative ability is a combination of various skills and types of knowledge, it is arguably more valid to test it by means of an *integrative test*, ie, one which integrates various components of the skill, rather than by means of a *discrete-point test*, ie, one that tests the individual components in isolation. An integrative test of communicative ability might be an interview, for example, or participation in a group problem-solving task. The test also needs to be acceptable to the learner, ie, it needs to have *face validity*. Learners are likely to under-perform if the test doesn't meet their expectations of what a test should be like.

A test is *reliable* if it gives consistent results: if two learners of obviously different levels get roughly the same score on a test, or if the same learner gets a different score on two different occasions, the test lacks reliability. Reliability is often an effect of the test design: if it is easy to guess the answers to test questions it is unlikely to be reliable, since anyone who does the test has a good chance of scoring highly. Poorly designed tests of reading or listening comprehension are often of this type: the answers can be guessed using common sense, rather than through the application of any particular comprehension skills. Reliability is also at risk the more *subjective* the scoring is. A test of oral skills based on an interview, where the interviewer scores the candidate on a scale from 0–5 is unlikely to be very *objective*, especially if there is only one examiner, or if there are no scoring criteria, or if there has been no training of examiners, or no standardization of their scoring criteria.

Criteria of validity and reliability may at times be sacrificed in the interest of *practicability*. Such a sacrifice may be justifiable for informal progress testing, where the stakes are not high, or for the purposes of encouraging revision. The popularity of *multiple choice* and *gap-fill* tests lies in their practicability. A version of the gap-fill that was very popular for a while was the **cloze test**. *Computer-based testing* is becoming increasingly popular because of its practicability, in terms both of administering tests, and of scoring them.

Tests also have to be judged on the way they affect the classroom teaching that leads up to them: this is called their *washback* (also *backwash*). A test may be practicable but have little positive washback. Afer all, the only way to prepare for a cloze test is by doing lots of cloze tests. By contrast, if the test involves an interview or a roleplay, these are activities that can be easily and usefully incorporated into classroom teaching.

Finally, the *impact* of a test is its overall effect on the educational and social context. Some public examinations, such as the IELTS or TOEFL tests, are used as entry tests to tertiary education, and this *gatekeeping* function can have a significant impact on educational policy and the allocation of resources. Even at a local level, a change in an institution's achievement test can have a knock-on effect on the choice of coursebook, syllabus, and even on classroom teaching.

test–teach–test METHODOLOGY

A test-teach-test (TTT) approach to **lesson design** is one in which decisions about what to teach are based on the way learners perform particular **tasks**. Also called a *deep-end strategy*, TTT grew out of the **communicative approach**. In a TTT lesson, rather than teaching a pre-selected syllabus item, the teacher first sets up a **communicative activity** such as a role play. The purpose of this is essentially diagnostic. It serves as a means of identifying the learners' language needs, and, specifically, the language that they would need in order to perform the task more effectively. The teacher then teaches this language, and the original task (or a similar task) is then repeated. In this way, teaching is directed at the learners' immediate needs and current developmental stage, rather than at some theoretical notion of their competence. TTT was a precursor to **task-based learning** (TBL), and like TBL, has attracted mainly those teachers who are confident in their ability to respond to the immediate needs of their learners.

text DISCOURSE

A text is a continuous piece of spoken or written language. It normally consists of a number of linked sentences, and has a distinctive internal structure and an identifiable communicative function. On the basis of their structure and function, texts are classified into *text types* or **genres**. The text that you are reading now belongs to the text type 'encyclopedia entry'. It shares with other texts of that type a structure that goes from the general to the specific, or from definition to examples. There is often cross reference to other entries. Here, for example, is an entry in a children's encyclopedia:

SQUIRREL

Squirrels are small furry animals with bushy tails. They belong to the rodent family. Most squirrels live in trees. The red squirrel lives in Europe and Asia. The North American grey squirrel has spread to other countries.

Some squirrels live in holes in the ground. Gophers, prairie dogs and chipmunks are ground squirrels which live in America.

See also RODENT.[1]

Notice that the general-to-specific organization (or *text structure*) is clearly indicated in the progression from *squirrels* to *most squirrels* to *the red squirrel*.

While texts are not as rule-bound as sentences, there is the expectation that they will be coherent. There is therefore some kind of logic that determines which sentences can go in which order (→ **coherence**). Moreover, there are a number of ways that the sentences are seen to be connected (→ **cohesion**). In the *Squirrel* text, cohesion is achieved through the repetition of the word *squirrel(s)*, through the use of pronoun **reference** (*Squirrels … They …*) and through the use of the same **tense** (present) throughout. All these features contribute to the overall unity of the text, an effect that is sometimes called its *texture*.

Texture also influences the structure of individual sentences. Thus, in the *Squirrel* text, the following sentence could not replace the third sentence in the text, even though it is grammatically well-formed and contains exactly the same information:

In Europe and Asia lives the red squirrel.

Thus, the surrounding text (the *co-text*) influences not just the meaning but the form of the sentences within it (→ **theme**).

The interdependence of sentence and text is a strong argument for teaching grammar through texts. Indeed, the use of some grammar items, such as **pronouns** and **articles** cannot be fully explained without reference to the language 'beyond the sentence' (→ **discourse analysis**). Moreover, since language in use is always realized as text, rather than as decontextualized sentences, it is perhaps more useful to teach language *through* texts, rather than apart from them.

Text analysis shares many of the same concerns and methods as do both discourse analysis and genre analysis, and it is often difficult (and perhaps unnecessary) to distinguish between them.

textual function → **systemic functional linguistics**

theme DISCOURSE

In linguistics the term *theme* is used in describing the way messages are constructed. The theme is the 'point of departure' of the message. It is the first major constituent of a clause or sentence. It typically expresses *known* (or *given*) information, often information that is 'carried over' from a previous sentence. Thus, in the text in the previous entry (→ **text**), the theme of the first sentence is *squirrels* (carried over from the title), and again in the second sentence (*they*). The rest of the sentence is called the *rheme*, and constitutes the *new* information.

[1] Jack, A. 1983 *Pocket Encyclopedia* (Kingfisher Books) p 203.

theme	rheme
Squirrels	*are small furry animals with bushy tails.*
They	*belong to the rodent family.*

The tendency to place new information at the end of the sentence is called the *end-weight* (or *end-focus*) *principle*. This explains why the first and third sentences, with their message content reversed, would (in their context) sound strange:

Small furry animals with bushy tails are squirrels.

In Europe and Asia lives the red squirrel.

Learners often produce sentences like this in their writing. Drawing their attention to the end-weight principle might be one way of redressing this kind of error.

third person → **person**

timetable METHODOLOGY

A teaching timetable (also called a *scheme of work*) is the plan for a sequence of lessons that takes place over a fixed period of time, such as a week, month, term or school year. The timetable translates the information contained in the **syllabus** into a series of **lesson plans**. Timetabling takes into account the amount and distribution of time available, such as whether the course is an intensive or a part-time one, and how best to allocate this time. Decisions also need to be made with regard to the sequencing, weighting, balancing and recycling of syllabus items, as well as to the choice and use of the **materials**, such as coursebooks, that are available. Usually, teachers are responsible for designing their own timetables, but sometimes these are imposed by their institution.

tone unit, tone group → **intonation**

top-down processing → **comprehension**

topic DISCOURSE

In a *topic–comment* analysis of a sentence, the topic of a sentence is what the sentence is about. The *comment* refers to what is being said about the topic. Topic and comment often correspond to what, in grammatical terms, are called **subject** and *predicate*. In terms of message structure, they also correspond to what are called **theme** and *rheme*.

Love	*means never having to say you're sorry.*
topic	comment
theme	rheme
subject	predicate

However, the topic is not always the subject. If, for example, a new topic is being introduced, it needs to go into the 'new information' part of the sentence, ie, the *rheme* position. In order to do this, the 'dummy' subject *there* (called *existential there*) is enlisted:

There	's a fly in my soup
[zero]	topic
theme	rheme
subject	predicate

In a similar fashion, impersonal *it* is used to fill an empty subject slot: *It takes two to tango. It was a dark and stormy night.*

Topicalization is the process of moving an element to the front of a sentence so that it functions as the topic: *Nice place you got here. For this relief, much thanks.* (This is also called *fronting*). *Clefting* is another way of adding emphasis to the topic element (→ **cleft sentence**): *I am big! It's the pictures that got small. What we've got here is a failure to communicate.*

A topic–comment sentence structure is characteristic of an early stage of first language development (*car go*; *dolly sleep*), and of pidgin languages (*Mr Kurtz – he dead*). It also characterizes learners' **interlanguage**: *somebody door* (for *there's somebody at the door*); *my home four bicycles* (for *we have four bicycles at home*).

Topic is also a term used in **discourse analysis** and **conversation analysis** to refer to 'what people are talking about' over a stretch of conversation. 'Speaking to topic' is one way that speakers achieve **coherence** in talk, and *changing topic* usually needs to be overtly signalled, as in *By the way … That reminds me ….*

The concept of *topic* has also been used with reference to teaching. A lesson can be described in terms of the topics that come up, and designing a lesson around a topic or theme is one way of making a lesson cohesive. Research has shown that most topics in classrooms are initiated by the teacher and only a few by the learners. Interestingly, though, the learner-initiated topics are those that other learners remember best after the lesson (→ **uptake**).

topic sentence → **paragraph**

Total Physical Response METHODOLOGY

Total Physical Response (TPR) is a language-teaching method that was developed by James Asher in the early 1970s. Like the **natural approach**, it is a *comprehension approach*, based on the belief that learners need only understand **input**, and should not be required to speak until they are ready to (→ **silent period**). TPR is modelled on the way that young children receive comprehensible input in their first language. Learners are exposed to input in the form of commands that require a physical response, such as *Stand up, turn around, pick up the orange, hand it to me*, etc. Hence, teaching sequences consist of a series of such commands that learners first see being demonstrated, and then act out themselves. In combining both the physical and mental aspects of learning, its holistic approach situates TPR firmly in the **humanistic** camp.

TPR as a method has had only marginal impact, but as a classroom technique it is particularly suited to the teaching of young learners, or to those beginner adults who have no inhibitions about getting up and moving around the classroom. But for more intellectually-inclined learners, and at more advanced levels, it is difficult to see how a methodology based on acting out commands can be sustained over the long term.

transfer SLA

Language transfer is the effect that one language – particularly the **first language** – has on another. Transfer can occur at all levels: pronunciation, vocabulary, grammar and discourse. It used to be known as *interference*, since, according to the **behaviourist** view, all transfer was seen as being *negative*. Thus, learners' **errors** were attributed to the effect of first language habits transferred into the second. **Contrastive analysis** of the L1 and the L2 attempted to predict and pre-empt such errors. When it failed to do either with any degree of reliability, the role of L1 transfer was re-assessed. For a start, it became clear that transfer could also be *positive* as well as negative. Where forms in the L1 match L2 forms, they can be borrowed successfully. In fact, deliberate transfer from the L1 has been identified as a useful **communication strategy**, especially if the L1 and the L2 share many features in common. Nowadays, transfer is seen as just one of many factors that influence the learner's **interlanguage**, others being developmental factors (→ **order of acquisition**), innate dispositions (→ **universal grammar**), cognitive factors, such as overgeneralizaton (→ **error**), as well as exposure and instruction. This more benign attitude to transfer has influenced classroom practice to the extent that it is no longer felt necessary to keep the L1 and L2 apart at all costs. This has led to the re-instatement of **translation** as a valid classroom activity.

transitivity GRAMMAR

Transitivity refers to the capacity of a verb to take an **object**: such verbs are called *transitive verbs*: *I come to <u>bury</u> Caesar, not to <u>praise</u> him. How dearly he <u>adores</u> Mark Antony!* Transitive verbs can be used in **passive** constructions: *She shall <u>be buried</u> by her Antony. I <u>was adored</u> once too.*

Intransitive verbs, on the other hand, have subjects but do not take objects: *Look, my lord, it <u>comes</u>! To <u>die</u> – to sleep. To <u>sleep</u> – perchance to <u>dream</u>. My words <u>fly up</u>, my thoughts <u>remain</u> below.* Intransitive verbs cannot be made passive.

Some verbs can take two objects: a *direct* and *indirect* object. These verbs are called *ditransitive*: *<u>Lend</u> me your ears. You should <u>read</u> us the will. <u>Give</u> me some light!*

Some verbs can be used both transitively and intransitively, as in *I'll <u>break</u> my staff* and *What light through yonder window <u>breaks</u>?* Or *In winter with warm tears I'll <u>melt</u> the snow* and *O, that this too too solid flesh would <u>melt</u>.* These verbs are sometimes called *ergative verbs*.

Linking verbs, such as the verbs *be*, *feel* and *seem*, take **complements**, not objects, so they are not transitive: *Brutus <u>is</u> an honourable man. Did this in Caesar <u>seem</u> ambitious?* (→ **verb pattern**)

translation METHODOLOGY

If you translate a written text, you produce a version of it in another language. (If it is a spoken text, the term *interpret* is more commonly used.) Translation as practised by translators and interpreters is a skill in its own right. Some learners of English will have translation as an objective. Both learning and teaching this skill require a high level of proficiency in at least two languages, the *source language* and the *target language*. Translating also requires extensive cultural and subject matter knowledge. The latter is particularly important when translating specialized texts, such as medical or legal documents. Successful translators avoid the extremes of a linear, word-for-word approach on the one hand, and an excessively free translation on the other. They are sensitive to features such as the **style** and **register** of the text they are translating (the source text). This includes being able to find suitable equivalents for **metaphors**, **formulaic language**, **collocations**, and words with particular **connotations**, as well as any technical terms in the target text. Finally, they need to be able to write text that is not only an accurate rendering of the source text, but is also coherent for the target audience. Access to reference works such as dictionaries and encyclopedias is clearly an advantage.

Apart from being a skill in its own right, translation is also an aid to teaching and learning a second language. In this sense, translation has been central to some teaching methods, such as **grammar–translation**, and frowned upon by others, such as the **direct method**. The reasons for *not* using translation in teaching include the following:

- Translation encourages a dependence on the L1, at the expense of the learner constructing an independent L2 system.
- Translation encourages the notion of equivalence between languages, yet no two languages are exactly alike (although languages from the same language family may be similar in lots of respects).
- The L1 system interferes with the development of the L2 system.
- Translation is the 'easy' approach to conveying meaning, and is therefore less memorable than approaches that require more mental effort, such as working out meaning from context.
- The 'natural' way of acquiring a language is through direct experience and exposure, not through translation.
- Translation is simply not feasible in classes of mixed nationalities, or where the teacher does not speak the learners' L1.

On the other hand, the arguments *for* using translation in the classroom include:

- New knowledge (eg of the L2) is constructed on the basis of existing knowledge (eg of the L1), and to ignore that is to deny learners a valuable resource.
- Languages have more similarities than differences, and translation encourages the positive **transfer** of the similarities, as well as alerting learners to significant differences.
- Translation is a time-efficient means of conveying meaning, compared, say, to demonstration, explanation, or working out meaning from context.
- The skill of translation is an integral part of being a proficient L2 user, and contributes to overall *plurilingualism* (→ **bilingualism**).
- Translation is a natural way of exploiting the inherent bilingualism of language classes, especially where the teacher is herself bilingual.

In the end, the case for or against translation will depend on contextual factors, including the expectations of the learners, the local educational culture, and the skills of the teacher. The fact that published ELT materials tend to be monolingual, however, does not favour teachers who wish to incorporate translation into their lessons.

uncountable noun → **noun**

universal grammar (UG) LINGUISTICS

Universal grammar is the name given to the theory that all languages share certain fundamental principles. The term was adopted by Noam Chomsky in order to argue that we are genetically 'programmed' with an innate language learning faculty (sometimes called the *language acquisition device* or *LAD*) (→ **mentalism**). UG describes the basic set of abstract principles that this biological mechanism is thought to contain. These universal principles are adjusted for individual languages according to choices that are governed by what are called **parameters**. A parameter is a narrow range of options, the choice of one of which determines a whole proliferation of grammatical features. Parameters are 'switched' on or off in response to cues in the input, and learning a language means applying the correct 'setting' for each parameter.

UG theory aims to account for first language acquisition (FLA), and in particular the fact that FLA is always a hundred per cent successful, despite the widely different exposure that children have. Proponents of this view argue that only UG can explain the highly sophisticated rule systems that children develop in a relatively short time. The role of UG in second language acquisition is much less clear. Some theorists claim that second language learners have *complete access* to their UG and that therefore the parameters can be re-set for a second language, suggesting that native-like proficiency is achievable. At the opposite extreme, others claim that learners have *no access*, ie that, after a certain age, UG is no longer available. They must therefore rely on general learning strategies to learn a second language, hence native-like proficiency is impossible.

UG provides an attractive solution to some of the basic conundrums of language acquisition. But its critics argue that it has done so by resorting to an elusive, even 'magical' faculty, the existence of which has not been proved.

uptake SLA

Uptake is what learners report to have learnt from a language lesson. Typically, what learners say they have learnt does not necessarily match what the teacher intended to teach. Moreover, uptake can vary from learner to learner. Factors that appear to enhance uptake are *salience*, ie, how much emphasis was given to an item or topic, and *source*, ie, whether the item or topic originated in the teacher or in another learner. Research suggests that, although the majority of the topics that occur in lessons are raised by the teacher, the topics that learners remember best (ie, their uptake) are those raised by other learners (→ **topic**).

usage and use LINGUISTICS

Usage refers to the way a community actually uses a language, as described in *descriptive grammars* of the language, or in books of language *usage*. For example, the usage of the verb *have* differs in American English from its usage in British English.

> The present form of *have* with *got* used for possession is more than twice as frequent in spoken BrE as in AmE:
> *I've got one sister and one brother. (BrE)*
> *I have a cousin who never married. (AmE)*[1]

[1] Carter, R. and McCarthy, M. 2006 *Cambridge Grammar of English* (CUP) p.883

Somewhat confusingly, however, the term *usage* is also used by some linguists to make a contrast with language in *use*. *Usage*, in this sense, refers to a person's abstract knowledge of the rules of grammar (what is also called their **competence**). This contrasts with their *use* of that knowledge to achieve some communicative purpose. This distinction, originally formulated by Henry Widdowson, was fundamental to the development of the **communicative approach**, since it lent support to the view that simply teaching the rules of grammar (ie *usage*) was insufficient in the absence of opportunities to put these rules to communicative *use*.

usage-based acquisition SLA

Usage-based is a way of describing those theories of **second language acquisition (SLA)** that argue that acquisition occurs primarily through engaging in communication, ie, through usage. According to this view, language development results from the billions of associations which are made while language is being used. The bulk of learning is implicit, therefore, and is a direct effect of the **frequency** of encounters with an item. From these accumulated encounters the learner abstracts those regularities we call grammar. Because the learner's grammar is derived from frequent encounters with individual instances (or *exemplars*), this theory is sometimes known as *exemplar theory*. And because the learner's grammar 'emerges' as patterns are identified and extracted from the data, it is also known as *emergentism*.

Usage-based theories reject the **mentalist** view that language acquisition can be explained only by reference to some innate language learning faculty (→ **universal grammar**). Instead, they appeal to general learning processes, which include:

- *pattern extraction*: the tendency of the human mind to impose patterns upon disparate pieces of evidence
- '*tallying*': the tendency to note statistical frequencies and sequential probabilities of occurrence (here relating to phonological, lexical and grammatical features of the L2)
- *association learning*: the tendency to note associations between co-occurring elements (→ **priming**)
- '*chunking*': whereby sets of already formed associations that have been stored in memory are welded into larger units
- *rehearsal*: the turning over of items of information in working memory until they become more robust and therefore more likely to be retained (→ **memory**)

All of these processes are optimized where there is maximum exposure and use. This in turn suggests that language teaching that is consistent with a **communicative approach** will serve learners well.

Usage-based theories are associated with **connectionist** models of learning, and with research into the acquisition of expertise: brain imaging evidence has shown differences between the brain functions of novices and experts. More recently, these mental processes have been replicated by researchers in computational linguistics: computer programs have been designed that search for overlapping patterns in naturally-occurring sentences. From these patterns the programs are able to 'work out' the rules of grammar, and use these rules to create original sentences.

utterance → **sentence**; **spoken grammar**

V

vague language DISCOURSE

Vagueness is a common feature of spoken language (→ **spoken grammar**). It performs an important interpersonal **function** in that it allows speakers to avoid either committing themselves to a proposal, or sounding too assertive. In this extract of authentic talk, in which two women are talking about weddings, the vagueness expressions have been labelled:[1]

> **Di** I'd like to just go out and find <u>something</u>[1] <u>a bit</u>[2] unusual that wasn't off the rack of <u>sixty</u>[3] of the same dress and do like my sister did the dress that she wore, <u>something like that</u>[4], and um standing out in a field <u>or something</u>[5], you know? Just a nice setting, you know?
>
> **Jess** Mmm.
>
> **Di** And go back to <u>somebody's</u>[6] place and have a cup of tea or scones <u>or something</u>.[7]
>
> **Jess** Right, yes.
>
> **Di** You know? None of this <u>hooha</u>[8]…
>
> **Jess** Quite <u>sort of</u>[9] simple and …

1, 6	indefinite pronoun
2	vague quantifier
3	round number (approximate number)
4, 5, 7	vague tag
8	general term
9	hedge

Other common ways of expressing vague quantities include *loads of, a lot of, a bit of, umpteen, some, several, a few*. Numbers can be made vague by adding *-ish*, or *or so*: *fortyish, forty or so*. Other vague tags include: *and things*; *and all that sort of thing*; *or what have you*. Other general terms include words like *stuff* and *thing*: these are highly productive in that they can substitute for almost anything. Another vagueness device is the use of *placeholder words* such as *thingy, thingummy, whatsisname* and *whatsit*, which are used to substitute for more specific terms that the speaker either has forgotten or doesn't want to mention.

For language learners vague language – such as the use of words like *stuff* and *whatsit* – has an obvious attraction, as it allows them to compensate for gaps in their lexical knowledge. In this sense, vagueness devices are a useful **communication strategy**.

validity → testing

variability SLA

Variability is a characteristic of learners' **interlanguage**. Learners often use more than one way of expressing the same idea, more or less interchangeably, such as

> **I no understand.*
> **I not understand.*

The variability may be *systematic* or it may be *free*. Systematic variability occurs when one choice is preferred to another in certain conditions, such as when the learner is being more careful. However, some variability appears to be random and unsystematic, ie, *free*. This supports the belief that the learner's interlanguage is inherently unstable and in a constant state of flux.

[1] Thornbury, S. and Slade, D 2006 *Conversation: From Description to Pedagogy* (CUP).

There is also variability *across* learners: different learners, starting from the same point, and exposed to the same conditions, exhibit significant differences in terms of the rate and the outcomes of learning. Factors that might account for inter-learner variability may be internal, such as the learner's first language, **attitudes**, **motivation** and **learning style**. Or they may be external to the learner, such as the amount and type of exposure, the availability of practice opportunities, and whether or not the learner is receiving instruction.

Accounting for both the variable nature of second language acquisition, and its *systematicity* (eg the fact that there is an **order of acquisition**) are the main aims of SLA research.

verb GRAMMAR

Verbs are members of the **word class** that typically express a process or state: *It happened one night. Some like it hot.* Verbs have different forms to indicate contrasts of **tense**, **aspect**, **person** and **number**. The four forms of *regular* verbs in English are the following:

- *base form*: the form that is listed in a dictionary; with *to* this forms the **infinitive**: *(to) happen, (to) like*
- the -*s* form: used for the third person singular in the present: *It happens … She likes you.*
- the **-*ing* form**, also called present **participle**: *What's happening? Liking Paris as much as I do …*
- the -*ed* form: used for the past tense and the past participle: *Whatever happened? I've never really liked oysters.*

Irregular verbs differ in the way they form the past tense, and many have a different past participle form (called either the -*ed form* or the -*en form*): *When Harry met Sally; It's been a hard day's night.* Only one verb has more than five forms in English – the verb *to be*: *be, am, is, are, was, were, being, been.*

Verbs can be classified into two groups: **auxiliary verbs**, including the *primary* and *modal* auxiliaries (→ **modal verb**), and **lexical verbs**. Auxiliary verbs have a mainly grammatical function. Lexical verbs can act as main verbs in clauses and have 'dictionary meaning'. Auxiliaries combine with lexical verbs to make distinctions of **aspect** and voice (→ **passive**). They also function in the formation of **questions** and negatives (→ **negation**):

The Russians are coming. = present progressive

The Eagle has landed. = present perfect

Are you being served? = present progressive passive

How the west was won = past passive

They shoot horses, don't they? = (tag) question

Alice doesn't live here anymore. = negative

Lexical verbs can also be classified according to whether they are *stative* or *dynamic* (→ **stative verb**).

Reflexive verbs are verbs that take a *reflexive pronoun* (→ **pronoun**), so that the subject and the object refer to the same person or thing: *Did you hurt yourself? Behave yourselves!*

Verbs, especially in the form of what are known as '**tenses**', make up a large proportion of standard language-teaching syllabuses and coursebooks. There are good reasons for this, since verbs are an obligatory component of sentences, and, more importantly, they carry an important burden of meaning. There are also historical reasons for the emphasis on verbs. The teaching of highly inflected classical and foreign languages has often been organized according to their different tenses and *conjugations*. Since English is hardly inflected at all, this kind of organization may be somewhat redundant, especially if it occurs at the expense of a focus on other important features of grammar, such as **syntax**.

verb pattern GRAMMAR

Verbs can be classified according to the patterns that they take. Some verbs can stand on their own, without an object, as in *Come back, Shane!* (symbolized as V). Others have to have an object, as in *We rob banks* (V n), while still others take two objects: *Show me the money* (V n n) (→ **transitivity**). Some verbs take an object with an obligatory **adverbial**: *Nobody puts Baby in a corner* (V n adv). Knowing a verb means knowing the pattern that it takes.

Verbs that are followed by other verbs, either the **infinitive** or the **-*ing* form**, are called *catenative verbs*, or verbs *in phase*, as in *I want to be alone. Stop messing about*.

More complex patterns include:

- verb + *that*-clause: *Say (that) it isn't true.*
- verb + object + *to*-infinitive: *Tell them to go out there with all they got …*
- verb + *wh*-clause: *You never know what you're going to get.*

Verbs that take the same pattern often share similar meanings. Thus the pattern *verb + object + to-infinitive* is common for verbs that are concerned with communicating something to someone, such as *tell, warn, request, remind, recommend*. It is also a common pattern for verbs that are concerned with helping or enabling, such as *assist, prepare, equip, train* and *teach*. Many verbs can take more than one pattern, but with differences of meaning. For example, *tell* can take the following patterns:

> verb: *Don't tell.*
> verb + *that*-clause: *I could tell (that) she was lying.*
> verb + indirect object + direct object: *I told them a story.*
> verb + object + *that*-clause: *Did she tell you that she was a tennis champion?*
> verb + object + *to*-infinitive: *Tell the children to go to bed.*

Knowing the patterns associated with verbs is crucial for accuracy, and many learner errors can be attributed to weaknesses in this area.

verb phrase GRAMMAR

Also called the *verb group*, the verb phrase consists of the main verb and any auxiliaries that precede it. The elements of a finite verb phrase are sequenced in this order: *(modal) (have) (be) (be) main verb*.

For example:

(subject)	modal	have	be	be	main verb
					watches
				is	*watching*
		has			*watched*
Sheila			*is*	*being*	*watched*
		has	*been*		*watched*
	must				*watch*
	will	*have*			*watched*
	could	*have*	*been*	*being*	*watched*

The first modal is called the *operator*. It is the operator that changes position with the subject to form questions (→ **inversion**): *Have you watched it? Could Sheila have been being watched?* It is also the operator which takes the negative particle *not*: *They aren't watching the tennis. She won't have been watching the time.* In the absence of an *operator*, the *dummy operator do* is used: *Did you watch the news? I don't watch TV.*

video METHODOLOGY

The use of video in language classrooms is well-established. It is a natural extension of the use of projected images, such as the slide projections and film strips used in some forms of the **audiolingual** approach. It is also a logical development of the now universal use of audio recordings, and compensates for many of the disadvantages of these, notably their lack of visual information. Classroom video use has kept pace with developments in technology, notably the shift from video tape to DVDs (*digital video discs*). Video is also a standard component of most computer and internet-mediated courses. And, in the form of *videoconferencing* software, it allows learners and teachers to interact at a distance, and thus create virtual learning environments (→ **computer–assisted language learning**).

For classroom purposes, teachers can choose between using authentic video material, such as films, advertising material and programmes recorded off air, or using specially prepared video material for language teaching. Video recordings can be used in much the same way as audio recordings, including the use of pre-viewing, while-viewing, and post-viewing tasks (→ **listening**). However, they also lend themselves to tasks that focus exclusively on their visual content. One approach to using films is first to select a short, but key, sequence and to play it with the volume off. The learners try to work out what is happening, the relationship of the characters, and what they might be saying. They then hear it with the volume on, and note down any words or phrases that they hear. Finally, they are given a transcript of the sequence (perhaps with some gaps in it), and they view the sequence again, following it on the transcript.

Video is also useful for focusing on background cultural information, which is often an aid to **comprehension**, as well as being interesting in its own right and a useful tool for raising intercultural awareness. Finally, the widespread availability of video cameras allows teachers to film their learners, with their permission, of course, eg performing drama-based activities, or simply being interviewed. It also allows learners to film each other, and to make short 'documentaries', eg about their local neighbourhood, in English. These can then be exchanged with learners in other settings.

visual aid → **aids**

vocabulary teaching METHODOLOGY

Vocabulary describes that area of language learning that is concerned with word knowledge. Vocabulary learning is a major goal in most teaching programmes. It hasn't always been so. In methods such as **audiolingualism**, vocabulary was subordinated to the teaching of grammar structures. Words were simply there to fill the slots in the sentence patterns. The move towards *semantic* (ie, meaning-based) **syllabuses** in the 1970s, along with the use of **authentic** materials, saw a revival of interest in vocabulary teaching. Subsequently, developments in **corpus** linguistics and **discourse analysis** started to blur the distinction between vocabulary and grammar. In the 1990s the **lexical approach** ushered in a major re-think regarding the role of vocabulary. This concerned both the *selection* of items (**frequency** being a deciding factor) and the *type* of items: **formulaic language** (or lexical chunks) were recognized as being essential for both **fluency** and **idiomaticity**. These developments have influenced the design of teaching materials. Most contemporary coursebooks incorporate a lexical syllabus alongside the grammar one. Recent developments in lexicography have complemented this trend. There is now a wide range of **dictionaries** available for learners, many of which come with sophisticated software for accessing databases of examples and collocations.

It is now generally agreed that, in terms of goals, learners need a receptive vocabulary of around 3000 high-frequency words (or, better, **word families**) in order to achieve independent user status. This will give them around ninety per cent coverage of normal text. For a productive vocabulary, especially for speaking, they may only need half this number.

Classroom approaches to achieving these goals include dedicated vocabulary lessons. Typically these take the form of teaching *lexical sets* of words (ie, groups of thematically linked words) using a variety of means, including visual **aids**, demonstration, situations, texts and dictionary work. As well as the **meaning** of the items, the **form**, both spoken (ie, **pronunciation**) and written (ie, **spelling**), needs to be dealt with, especially if the words are being taught for productive use. Other aspects of word knowledge that may need to be highlighted include **connotation** and **style**, **collocation**, derived forms, and grammatical features, such as the word's **word class**. Vocabulary is also taught as preparation for listening or reading (*pre-teaching vocabulary*) or as a by-product of these skills.

It would be impossible, in class, to teach all the words that learners need. Learners therefore need opportunities for *incidental* learning, eg through *extensive reading*. They may also benefit from training in how to make the most of these opportunities, eg by means of dictionary use, note-keeping, etc. Some strategies for deducing the meaning of unfamiliar words will also help.

Amassing a fully-functioning vocabulary is essentially a **memory** task, and techniques to help in the memorizing of words can be usefully taught, too (→ **memorization**). It also helps to provide learners with repeated encounters with new words, eg through the re-reading of texts, or by reading several texts about the same topic. Constant recycling of newly learned words is essential. One simple way of doing this is to have a *word box* (or word bag) in the classroom. New words are written on to small cards and added to the word box. At the beginning of the next lesson, these words can be used as the basis for a review activity. For example, the teacher can take words out of the box and ask learners to define them, provide a translation or put them into a sentence. The words can also form the basis for peer-testing activities, in which learners take a number of word cards and test each other in pairs or small groups.

vocal cords → **articulator**

voice → **passive**

voice quality → **paralinguistics**

voiced sound PHONOLOGY

A voiced sound is one which is produced while the vocal cords are vibrating (→ **articulator**). A *non-voiced* (or *voiceless*) *sound* is one where there is no vocal cord vibration. To feel if a sound is voiced or not, place the palm of the hand on the throat area and utter the sound in isolation. The phenomenon is called *voicing* and accounts for many phonemic contrasts in English. For example, the only difference between /p/ and /b/ is that the first is non-voiced while the second is voiced (→ **phoneme**). Other consonant pairs distinguished by voicing (with the non-voiced sound in the first of each pair) are /t/ and /d/, /f/ and /v/, /θ/ and /ð/, /tʃ/ and /dʒ/, /ʃ/ and /ʒ/, /s/ and /z/, /k/ and /g/. *All* English vowels are voiced (except when whispering).

vowel PHONOLOGY

Vowels and **consonants** make up the speech sounds (or **phonemes**) of English. Vowels, unlike consonants, are produced without any significant obstruction or constriction of the airflow from the lungs to the lips and beyond (→ **articulator**). What shapes the vowels – and distinguishes them from one another – are the position of the tongue and the shape of the lips. With regard to the tongue, the significant features are the part of it that is raised, and the height that it is raised to. If the front is raised, the vowels that are produced are called *front vowels*; if the back is raised, the vowels are called *back vowels*. *Central vowels* fall somewhere in between. Vowels that are produced with the tongue close to the top of the mouth are called *close vowels* (or *high vowels*). *Mid vowels* and *open* (or *low vowels*) correspond to increasingly lower tongue positions. The various combinations are often portrayed in the form of the *vowel chart*. Here is the vowel chart for the twelve English **RP** (**Received Pronunciation**) vowels (excluding the *diphthongs*).

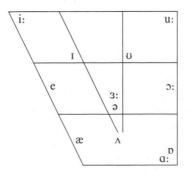

From the chart it can be seen that the sound /iː/ as in *tea*, is a close front vowel, while the sound /ɒ/, as in *pot*, is an open back vowel. The sound written as /ə/, and called *schwa* (/ʃwɑː/), as in the first vowel in *ago*, or the last in *brother*, is a mid central vowel. In fact, this is the neutral, resting position of the tongue, so not surprisingly this is the vowel that is most commonly produced in unstressed syllables (→ **weak form**).

Some vowels are marked with a diacritic (ː), /iː/, /uː/, /ɔː /, /ɜː/ and /ɑː/, as in *see, sue, saw, sir* and *star*, respectively. These are the so-called *long vowels*, all the others being *short*. In fact, the difference is less in terms of length than in what is called *vowel quality*.

The shape of the lips – whether they are rounded or unrounded – also affects vowel production: compare *she* and *shoe*. In some languages lip rounding is a way of distinguishing between vowels, but in English it is not as important a factor as tongue position.

As well as the twelve *monophthongs* in English RP, there are eight *diphthongs*. A *diphthong* is less a combination of two individual vowels sounds than a *glide* from one in the direction of another. This sentence includes all eight diphthongs: *I fear no boy may cure their cow*. For a full list of vowel sounds, see **phoneme**.

The fact that there are twenty vowel sounds in RP (although one or two fewer in different regional varieties) suggests that learning to pronounce them correctly will be a challenge to most learners. Not only do most languages have fewer vowel sounds, but there may not be a close match between the ones that they do have and their English 'equivalents'. For example, the sound represented by the letter 'o' in Spanish *no* and English *no* are pronounced quite differently. Approaches to **pronunciation** teaching that are aimed at replacing the learner's **accent** with an English one attempt to reconstruct the learner's vowel system from scratch. They do this by relocating existing vowels and importing the ones that the learner lacks. This 'elocution' approach is not dissimilar to the way Eliza Doolittle's cockney accent was replaced by an RP one in Shaw's *Pygmalion*.

More recently, the wisdom of this approach has been questioned on a number of grounds. For a start, native speakers display enormous regional and social variation in their vowel pronunciation – much more so than in consonant pronunciation. Vowels are strongly implicated in marking **accent**. But they are less important in terms of **intelligibility**. Native speakers of two different accents are usually mutually intelligible, despite sharing few if any equivalent vowels. Moreover, research has shown that vowel differences do not impede intelligibility between non-native speakers either – except where vowel *length* is involved (→ **phonological core**). This news should come as a relief to both teachers and learners. For many learners an 'elocution' approach is simply not feasible, given both the time available and the physical difficulty (for adults) of restructuring the whole system. And many learners – consciously or unconsciously – may resist changing their accent, since accent is a significant marker of identity.

Nevertheless, a range of techniques has been developed in order to focus on vowel pronunciation, the most well known being **minimal pair** discrimination and production.

wall chart → **aids**

warning FUNCTION

Like *giving advice* and *suggesting*, warning is an interpersonal **function** directed at influencing another person's behaviour. Therefore it is accompanied by a degree of risk to face (→ **politeness**). This risk may be overridden by the urgency of the situation, so that bald **imperatives** can be used: *Watch out! Mind your head! Be careful!* Written warnings are often similarly brief and to the point: *Mind the gap. Danger! Caution: slippery surface.*

Often warnings are accompanied by some condition, and warning is a common function of the first **conditional**: *If you're not careful, you'll fall. If we don't leave soon, we'll miss the last train.* Another way of expressing the same idea is to use two clauses co-ordinated by *or*: *Be careful or you'll fall. We'd better leave or we'll miss the last train.*

Explicit warnings use the verb *warn*: *I'm warning you: the curry is really hot. Don't say I didn't warn you. Warn* is also used to report warnings: *They warned us not to take photos at the border.*

More formal, specially written, warnings are made less threatening by the use of **modal verbs** and **passive** constructions: *In the event of a failure to comply with these terms, you are advised that your account may be terminated without further notice.*

Situations that provide useful contexts for practising warning language include: preparing for a difficult journey or examination, or for taking part in a high-risk sport; giving tourists advice about avoiding crime or illness; roleplays involving negotiations, eg between management and workers.

washback effect → **testing**

weak form PHONOLOGY

The weak form of some words is their pronunciation when they are not stressed. Most **function words** in English, such as *of, at, to, can, must, was, have, and,* etc. have two possible pronunciations, depending on whether they are stressed or not (→ **stress**). Compare, for example:

> *I got to work late.* (to = /tə/)
> *Who were you talking to?* (to = /tuː/)

In the weak form of *to*, the vowel is the neutral unstressed *schwa* sound (→ **vowel**), whereas in its strong form the vowel is given its full value. There are around fifty English words that have both weak and strong forms, the majority being prepositions, pronouns, auxiliary verbs, conjunctions and determiners. Most weak forms involve replacement of the vowel by *schwa*, although some consonant deletion can also occur, as in *must*: strong form = /mʌst/; weak form = /məs/. It's debatable whether learners need to be able to produce weak forms, although their use helps in achieving an English-sounding **rhythm**. At times the use of a strong form where a weak form would be more appropriate can lead to misunderstanding, especially with the modal verb *can*: *I CAN read it* may be interpreted as *I can't read it.* But learners will certainly need to recognize weak forms. Asking learners to count the number of words in a sentence that is read to them at natural speed is one way of sensitizing them to the existence of weak forms.

webquest METHODOLOGY

Webquest is the term that has been coined to refer to an educational task that is carried out by means of the internet. The aim of a webquest is to focus on processing information rather than simply copying it, and thereby to encourage analytic and critical thinking, especially among school-age learners. The model was developed in 1995 at San Diego State University by Bernie Dodge with Tom March. Typically, learners in groups are set a staged task which involves having to evaluate and synthesize information that has been found using the resources of the internet. They then have to present the results to their peers in the form of an oral, written, or web-based presentation. The webquest concept fits neatly into the framework of both **project** work and **task-based learning**, and so has been adapted for the purposes of second language teaching. The basic model that has been used in first language education can be easily adapted for the purposes of ELT, so long as language-focused stages are incorporated at strategic points. These might involve brainstorming vocabulary relevant to the topic, or analysing the structure of a text-type associated with the task.

whole language learning METHODOLOGY

Whole language learning is an educational approach to the teaching of **literacy**. Its guiding principle is that language skills are best learned in authentic, meaningful situations. This contrasts with approaches which break language up into *discrete items* or which separate it into different skills or competencies. In focusing on language in its entirety, whole language learning is a *holistic* approach, and adopts an integrated approach to the teaching of **skills**. It defines the role of the teacher as one of facilitator (→ **facilitation**), and the role of the student as an active participant in a community of learners. The whole language movement originated in North America, and it has strong parallels with **task-based learning**, **content-based learning**, **immersion** teaching and **critical pedagogy**. Some core principles of the whole language movement are that:

- Learning goes from whole to part.
- Reading, writing, speaking and listening all develop together.
- Lessons should be learner-centred because learning is the active construction of knowledge.
- Learning takes place in social interaction.

The whole language approach emphasizes the social and cultural dimension of education. It also aims to promote the learner's self-realization through learning, a feature that distinguishes it from task-based learning, which tends to be more instrumental in its objectives. So far, whole language learning has not had a major effect on second language teaching, although its influence can be detected in the arguments in support of a *process approach* to the teaching of **writing**, and in an *activity-based approach* to teaching **young learners**.

word VOCABULARY

A word is defined as the smallest language item that can occur on its own. The definition is problematic though, as a glance at any text confirms. For example:

> *Wallpaper* lifts the tarpaulin to take a look at three of the best new structures currently taking shape on the world's skylines, as well as taking a whistle-stop tour of some of tomorrow's architectural gems.[1]

[1] *Wallpaper*, 64, December 2003, p 72.

While there may be no argument about *tarpaulin* being a word, is *to* (in *to take*) a word? Can it stand on its own, or is it inextricably part of the infinitive form? Can *a* (in *take a look*) stand on its own? For that matter, can *whistle-stop* stand on its own, or is it part of the larger unit *whistle-stop tour*, from which it is never normally detached? And are *to take (a look)* and *taking (shape)* two words, or two grammatical forms of the single word *take*? Because of these problems, the concept of *word* has been refined, to distinguish between:

- *word forms*: the written or spoken words, that are spelled or pronounced as single units, so that *tarpaulin, to, a, take, taking, whistle-stop* and *skyline* are all different words, even if some of them, like *whistle-stop* and *skyline*, originated in the combining of two words.

- **lexical items**, or *lexemes*: that is, the way words are represented in a dictionary. Thus, *take* is the lexeme of which *to take* and *taking* are variants; and *world* is the lexeme of which *world's* is a variant. In these terms, *whistle-stop tour* is also a lexeme. By extension, it is difficult to argue that *take a look* and *take shape* are not also lexemes. This also means that two words that have the same form, but totally different meanings, are not the same lexeme, but **homonyms**. Thus, *lifts* (in *Wallpaper lifts the tarpaulin …*) is a different lexeme from *lifts*, in *We took one of the lifts to the 32ⁿᵈ floor*. On the other hand, *gems* (in *architectural gems*) could be considered to be an extension of the meaning of *gem* (a *precious stone*), and therefore a **polyseme**.

Defining a word in terms of its meaning has to take into account not just its *denotation*, ie, the literal meaning of a word (*gem = precious stone*) but its **connotations** as well (eg *gem = something to be admired*). Part of the meaning of a word is the associations that are triggered by the words that it commonly co-occurs with, ie, its **collocations**. The word *gem* – in its metaphoric sense – is 'primed' to trigger associations with architecture. *Whistle-stop* and *tour* are even more tightly associated (→ **priming**).

These issues clearly have implications for **vocabulary teaching**. To be sure that learners can appreciate how a word differs from other words of similar meaning, it is not enough to simply give a definition (or a synonym or translation) of the word. Studying words in context, and encouraging learners to record words along with their collocations in the form of a 'spidergram', are alternative approaches.

word class GRAMMAR

A word class is a group of words that, from a grammatical point of view, behave in the same way. For example, in the sentence:

```
1   2         3       4    5   6
I   wandered  lonely  as   a   cloud
```

the words *skipped, danced* and *yodelled* could all substitute for *wandered*, but not for any of the other words. Likewise, *happy, old* and *crazy* fit only into the third slot. *Trombonist, marmot* and *matchbox* fit only into the sixth slot. (Of course, these substitutions ignore the unlikelihood of sentences such as *I yodelled crazy as a matchbox*. But what is not in doubt is that they are grammatical). The slot 2 words are called **verbs**, the slot 3 ones are **adjectives**, and the slot 6 words are

nouns. These are their *word classes* – what were once called *parts of speech*. The other word classes represented by slots in the sentence above are (1) **pronouns** (such as *we, someone, who*), (4) **prepositions** (*like, on, under,* etc), and (5) **determiners** (*some, any, one, this,* etc). The two other word classes not represented here are **adverbs** (*slowly, well, often,* etc) and **conjunctions** (*and, so, because,* etc). (*Interjections,* such as *Wow! Cor! Alas!* are sometimes granted a category of their own, as well.) The classes of pronoun, determiner, preposition, and conjunction are called *closed classes* because they cannot readily be added to. Nouns, verbs, adjectives and adverbs, on the other hand, are *open classes*, as new members are being added almost on a daily basis.

It is important to remember that words can belong to more than one class. *As,* for example, which was a preposition in the example sentence, can also fill the conjunction slot: *As Wordsworth famously wrote .... Cloud* can also be a verb: *Laudanum clouded his judgment.* Some words are very versatile in this respect. *Well,* for example, can function as a noun, verb, adverb, and adjective. It is also worth noting that the form of a word is not always a reliable guide to its word class. *Lonely,* for example, like *friendly, lovely* and *lowly,* looks like an adverb, but it is in fact an adjective. On the other hand, *hard* and *fast* are adverbs even though they do not take the *-ly* suffix.

Finally, the division into word classes is not as neat as it may look. Language is inherently fuzzy, and there are many 'slippery' words that defy tight categorization. For example, the following (invented) sentence contains some word class conundrums:

Her	singing	of	the	pop	song	unaccompanied	made	the	bored	sit	up
deter-miner or adjec-tive?	noun or verb?	prepos-ition or a grammar word in a class of its own?		noun or adjec-tive?		adjective, verb, or adverb?			adjec-tive or noun?		pre-position or adverb?

word family VOCABULARY

A word family is a group of words that share the same root but have different **affixes**, as in *care, careful, careless, carefree, uncaring, carer. Mothercare* and *caretaker* however, do not belong to this family, as they incorporate words from other roots. *Careful, careless,* etc are all *derivatives* of *care*, in that, through the process of *affixation* (→ **word formation**), new lexical words are formed. These new words often belong to different **word classes**: *care* = verb, noun, *careful* = adjective, *carer* = noun. By contrast, grammatical forms of *care*, such as *cares, caring* and *cared*, are called *inflections. Inflections* all belong to the same word class. A *word family*, then, is a base word plus its inflections and its most common derivatives. The concept of word family is useful for compiling vocabulary lists and in estimating the vocabulary needs of learners. For example, rather than calculate that learners need to know 3000 individual words to achieve independent user status, it is more accurate to say that they need 3000 *word families.*

word formation VOCABULARY

Word formation is the process by which new words are created out of elements of existing ones. The study of word formation is one branch of **morphology**. (The other is the study of *inflections* → **word family**). In English, there are two main word-formation processes: *affixation* and *compounding*. **Affixation** is the process of adding **affixes** (either prefixes or suffixes) to the word root. It is an extremely productive way of forming new words. The following relatively recent words were formed by affixation (the affixes are underlined): *cybercrime*, *ecolinguistics*, *superbug*, *shareware*, *globalization*. Compounding is the joining together of two or more words, written either as one word, or hyphenated, or as separate words. Some recent compounds are *airbag, downsize, morning-after pill, asylum seeker, home page*.

Other ways of forming words include:

- *conversion*, when a word changes its **word class** without any change of form, as in *to text someone* (from the noun *text*), *a rave* (from the verb *to rave*), *to out somebody* (from the adverb *out*).
- *clipping*, when a word is shortened: *fridge, nuke, telly*.
- *blends*, when two words merge to form one: *Eurocrat* (= *European + bureaucrat*); *biopic* (= *biography + picture*); *glitterati* (= *glitter + literati*)
- *abbreviations* and *acronyms*: *CD, SARS, SMS*.

In the following text,[2] examples of different word formation principles have been identified:

> The acknowledged father of techno[1], DJ[2] Sven Väth, has masterminded[3] Europe's latest dance venue, CocoonClub. Housed[4] in the appropriately named UFO[5] Building in Frankfurt's Ostend district, this 2,664 sq m über-complex[6] was designed by architects 3deluxe. It includes two restaurants and a main dance floor, which is surrounded by a honeycomb-like[7] membrane wall and dotted with apple-green[8], cocoon-like[9] chill-out[10] areas, three of which come with a private steward, a mini-bar[11] and web-cams.[12]

1. clipping (from *technological*, presumably)
2. abbreviation (*disc jockey*)
3. conversion (from the noun *mastermind*, itself a compound)
4. conversion (from the noun *house*)
5. abbreviation (*unidentified flying object*)
6. affixation, borrowing the German prefix *über* (= super)
7. compounding (*honey + comb*) plus affixation using the suffix *-like*
8. compounding
9. affixation
10. conversion of phrasal verb *to chill out* into a noun
11. affixation
12. compounding (*web + camera*) plus clipping

word order GRAMMAR

'Word order' refers to the way words are sequenced, particularly with regard to the sequencing of elements in a clause or sentence. Thus, the prototypical word order of a sentence in English is subject–verb–object (SVO) (→ **syntax**), as in

---

[2] *Wallpaper*, 73, November 2004, p 162.

Man bites dog, or SVO + **adverbial**, as in *Man bites dog in Ukraine*. But variations on this order are possible for reasons of grammar, discourse, and style. Thus, questions cause **inversion** of subject and verb (or *operator*): *Did the man bite the dog?* Likewise, some negative adverbials in initial position require inversion: *Seldom do men bite dogs*. The **passive** reverses the order of elements: *The dog was bitten by the man*, and both *fronting* and *clefting* (→ **cleft sentence**) involve changing the order so as to *topicalize* elements: *Did you hear? That dog that belongs to the woman who lives on the corner, a man bit it. It was the dog that the man bit. What the man did was bite the dog.* (→ **topic**). Many adverbials can be placed in initial, medial, or final position, according to emphasis: *In Ukraine a man bit a dog. A man in Ukraine bit a dog. A man bit a dog in Ukraine.* But other adverbials are more tightly constrained in terms of where they can go: *Men are always biting dogs*, but not *★Always men are biting dogs*, or *★Men always are biting dogs*. Word order also refers to the way words are sequenced in **phrases**. Thus, there is a conventional way of ordering the adjectives in a **noun phrase**, where the general tends to precede the particular: *a friendly little wire-haired terrier; an aging black British bulldog* (→ **adjective**). Likewise, **determiners** obey a fixed order before nouns.

Word order is a frequent source of learner error, as different languages vary in the way that words can be sequenced. Moreover, being an uninflected language, English word order is generally less flexible than that of many languages. This means that the subject and object elements of a sentence like *The bulldog bit the terrier* cannot be reversed without a complete change of meaning.

word stress → **stress**

world Englishes SOCIOLINGUISTICS

World Englishes are varieties of English (also called *nativized varieties*) that are spoken in countries such as India, Nigeria and Singapore, where, for historical reasons, English plays an important second language role. The widespread use of English in these multilingual settings has led to the development of particular standards of usage: *Singlish* (or Singapore English) is a good example. It has developed a distinctive vocabulary and pronunciation, as well as some unique grammatical and pragmatic features.

The use of the plural (*World Englishes*) deliberately challenges the notion that English is still 'owned' by its native speakers, or that there is a uniform *World Standard English*, ie, a single model whose standards are universally accepted and adopted. Experts predict that World Englishes are likely to flourish, but will co-exist with **English as an international language**, which will be spoken as a *lingua franca* amongst speakers who do not share a nativized variety.

writing METHODOLOGY

Like speaking, writing is a productive **skill**, and, like other skills, writing involves a hierarchy of *sub-skills*. These range from the most mechanical (such as handwriting or typing legibly) through to the ability to organize the written text and lay it out according to the conventions of the particular text type (→ **text**). Along the way, writers also need to be able to:

- produce grammatically accurate sentences
- connect and punctuate these sentences

- select and maintain an appropriate style
- signal the direction that the message is taking
- anticipate the reader's likely questions so as to be able to structure the message accordingly

In order to enable these skills, writers need an extensive knowledge base, not only at the level of vocabulary and grammar, but at the level of connected discourse (→ **discourse analysis**). This includes familiarity with a range of different text types, such as *informal letters, instructions, product descriptions,* etc. It follows that if classroom writing is mainly spelling- or grammar-focused, many of the sub-skills of writing will be neglected.

Nevertheless, the teaching of writing has tended to focus on the 'lower-level' features of the skill, such as being able to write sentences that are both accurate and complex, that demonstrate internal cohesion, and that are connected to the sentences next to them (→ **linker**). This language-based approach is justified on the grounds that stricter standards of accuracy are usually required in writing than in speaking. Also, writing demands a greater degree of explicitness than speaking, since writers and their readers are separated in time and space. They therefore can't rely on immediate feedback in order to clear up mis-understandings.

By contrast, a text-based approach to teaching writing takes a more 'top-down' view. This approach finds support in **discourse analysis**, which shows that a **text** is more than a series of sentences, however neatly linked. Instead, texts are organized according to larger *macrostructures,* such as problem-solution, or definition-examples. Hence, learners need explicit guidance in how texts are structured. This typically involves analysing and imitating models of particular text types. For example, a business letter might be analysed in terms of its overall layout, the purpose of each of its paragraphs, the grammatical and lexical choices within each paragraph, and the punctuation. Each of these features is then practised in isolation. They are then recombined in tasks aimed first at reproducing the original text and then at producing similar texts incorporating different content.

This approach is called a *product approach* to the teaching of writing, since the focus is exclusively on producing a text (the product) that reproduces the model. By contrast, a *process approach* argues that writers do not in fact start with a clear idea of the finished product. Rather, the text emerges out of a creative process. This process includes: *planning* (*generating ideas, goal setting* and *organizing*), *drafting* and *re-drafting; reviewing,* including *editing* and *proofreading,* and, finally, '*publishing*'. Advocates of a process approach argue for a more organic sequence of classroom activities, beginning with the brainstorming of ideas, writing preliminary drafts, comparing drafts, re-drafting, and *conferencing,* that is, talking through their draft with the teacher, in order to fine-tune their ideas.

The process approach to writing has a lot in common with the **communicative approach** to language teaching, and each has drawn support from the other. The communicative approach views writing as an act of communication in which the writer interacts with a reader or readers for a particular purpose. The purpose might be to ask for information about a language course, to relay personal news, to complain about being overcharged at a hotel, or simply to entertain and amuse. Thus, advocates of a communicative approach argue that classroom writing tasks should be motivated by a clear purpose and that writers should have their reader(s) in mind at all stages of the writing process. Such principles are now reflected in the design of writing tasks in public examinations, such as this one, from the Cambridge ESOL First Certificate in English (FCE) paper:[3]

> You have had a class discussion on how to keep healthy and your teacher has now asked you to write a report for new students in your college giving them advice on places to go in the area. You should include information on sports facilities and healthy places to eat locally.
>
> Write your report.

The social purposes of writing are also foregrounded by proponents of a *genre-based approach*. **Genre** analysis attempts to show how the structure of particular text-types are shaped by the purposes they serve in specific social and cultural contexts. Put simply, a business letter is the way it is because of what it does. Advocates of genre-based teaching reject a process approach to teaching writing. They argue that to emphasize self-expression at the expense of teaching the generic structures of texts may in fact disempower learners. Many learners, especially those who are learning English as a *second* language, need a command of those genres – such as writing a CV, or requesting a bank loan – that permit access to the host community. A genre approach to teaching writing is not unlike a product approach, therefore. It starts with model texts that are subjected to analysis and replication. The difference is that these models are closely associated with their contexts of use, and they are analysed in functional terms as much as in linguistic ones (→ **systemic functional linguistics**). The genre approach has been particularly influential in the teaching of academic writing (→ **English for specific purposes**).

In reality, none of these approaches is entirely incompatible with any other. Resourceful teachers tend to blend elements of each. For example, they may encourage learners to 'discover' what they want to write, using a process approach. They may then give them a model text, both as a source of useful language items, and as a template for the final product. They may also provide exercises in specific sub-skills, such as linking sentences, or using a formal style.

young learners, teaching METHODOLOGY

The term *young learners* is used to describe children of pre-primary and **primary** school age, although it is sometimes used to include **adolescents** as well. Teaching English to young learners has a long history: in many multilingual countries, primary school children are taught English as preparation for secondary school, where it is the medium of instruction. In recent years there has been a phenomenal increase in the teaching of English to young learners, in EFL contexts as well as in ESL, and in state schools as well as in private ones. In many countries the obligatory starting age for learning English is as young as eight, and there is an ongoing tendency to lower it even further. Research into the optimal **age** for learning a second (or third, etc) language is still inconclusive. While some researchers argue that the sooner the learner starts the better, others are of the

[3] from Cambridge ESOL website:
http://www.cambridgeesol.org/support/handbooks.htm

opinion that the disadvantages outweigh the benefits. Moreover, learners who start later soon catch up. In some **bilingual** contexts, one way of addressing the need for second language learning has been early **immersion**, whether total or partial. Partial immersion involves the teaching of certain school subjects in the target language. In the form of *content and language integrated learning* (CLIL) (→ **content-based teaching**), it is a model that is being enthusiastically promoted in many European countries. However, many institutions, both public and private, will continue to provide English-as-subject classes, often just a few hours a week. Such classes demand a methodology that meets the special characteristics and needs of young learners.

The special characteristics of young learners, and those that distinguish them from adult learners, can be grouped under the headings *cognitive*, *affective* and *social*. The most relevant cognitive factors are: children's relatively limited world knowledge; the fact that they are still developing concepts and language simultaneously and that their memory is still developing; their inability – particularly at a very young age – to conceive of language as an abstract system, which means they have a limited understanding of **metalanguage**, and do not recognize error correction as such; a difficulty in sustaining attention for extended periods of time; a preference for holistic as opposed to analytic learning, and a related preference for remembering 'episodes' (ie, things that happened) rather than facts; a greater tolerance for ambiguity – in the sense that children don't have to know what every word means: they are predisposed to understand messages, even when they don't recognize the 'code'.

Affective factors include a lack of self-consciousness about expressing themselves inaccurately or through minimal means, and the need for encouragement and support. Also, young learners are more likely to be motivated by intrinsic factors, such as the inherent interest of an engaging task or game, than by extrinsic factors, such as the need to pass a test (→ **motivation**). They are particularly predisposed to learning through play. Social differences include a lack of social skills, especially where peer collaboration is required, and consequently a greater dependency on the teacher for direction and support. Their socialization into classroom life is helped when they can recognize and rely on regular routines (→ **socialization**).

These differences suggest a number of rules of thumb when teaching young learners, including:

- Provide opportunities for learning through doing, rather than through formal study of the system, eg, grammar.
- Situate the content of lessons in the world of the learners (→ **personalization**).
- Plan short, varied activity cycles.
- Systematically recycle language in different contexts.
- Incorporate activities which engage learners in using language for reasons and purposes which they can relate to, such as **games**, stories and **songs**.
- Do activities, including physical activities, which involve all the senses (→ **multiple intelligences**).
- Provide opportunities for divergent responses and for experimenting and being creative with language.

- Provide plenty of 'comprehensible **input**', eg in the form of teacher talk that is supported by actions, pictures, etc (→ **Total Physical Response**).
- 'Scaffold' the learners' talk, to provide them with a conversational framework within which they can express themselves (→ **scaffolding**).
- Establish regular routines in class, such as calling the roll, beginning or ending each lesson with a song, etc (→ **routine**).
- Train young learners in how to learn, by, for example, setting learning goals, explaining reasons for doing things and asking learners to reflect on their learning (→ **learner training**).
- Don't over-rely on **pairwork** and **groupwork**, but include plenty of teacher-fronted activities as well.
- When doing pairwork and groupwork, monitor to make sure learners are 'on task', and intervene if necessary to ensure learners are collaborating with one another (→ **monitoring**).

Many of these principles are, in fact, perfectly consistent with a **communicative approach**, especially the emphasis on learning through doing rather than through formal study. These are principles that are also shared by **task-based learning** and **whole language learning**. Finally, the theoretical model that perhaps offers the most support for the above principles is that of **sociocultural learning theory**, with its emphasis on the formative role of social interaction.

Z

zero article → **article**

zone of proximal development (ZPD) → **sociocultural learning theory**

Index

These terms and people are referred to within the entries, but are not included as headwords.

Further Reading

Discourse analysis and pragmatics

Thornbury, S. 2005. *Beyond the Sentence: An Introduction to Discourse Analysis.* Oxford: Macmillan.

Yule, G. 1996. *Pragmatics.* Oxford: Oxford University Press.

Functions and notions

Leech, G., & J. Svartvik. 1994. *A Communicative Grammar of English* (2nd edition). Harlow: Longman.

Grammar

Collins COBUILD English Grammar. 1990. Glasgow: HarperCollins.

Swan, M. 2005. *Practical English Usage* (3rd edition). Oxford: Oxford University Press.

Thornbury, S. 1999. *How to Teach Grammar.* Harlow: Pearson Education.

Thornbury, S. 2001. *Uncovering Grammar.* Oxford: Macmillan.

Linguistics

Cook, G. 2003. *Applied Linguistics.* Oxford: Oxford University Press.

Crystal, D. (ed.) 1997. *The Cambridge Encyclopedia of Language* (2nd edition). Cambridge: Cambridge University Press.

Phonology

Dalton, C., & B. Seidlhofer. 1994. *Pronunciation.* Oxford: Oxford University Press.

Underhill, A. 2005. *Sound Foundations* (new edition with audio CD). Oxford: Macmillan.

Sociolinguistics

Spolsky, B. 1998. *Sociolinguistics.* Oxford: Oxford University Press.

Vocabulary

Cobb, T. *The Compleat Lexical Tutor:* www.lextutor.ca

Lewis, M. 1993. *The Lexical Approach.* Hove: Language Teaching Publications.

Macmillan English Dictionary for Advanced Learners. 2002. Oxford: Macmillan.

Schmitt, N. 2000. *Vocabulary in Language Teaching.* Cambridge: Cambridge University Press.

Thornbury, S. 2002. *How to Teach Vocabulary.* Harlow: Pearson Education.

Psychology and psycholinguistics

Stevick, E.W., 1996. *Memory, Meaning and Method* (2nd edition). Boston: Heinle & Heinle.

Williams, M., & R.L. Burden. 1997. *Psychology for Language Teachers.* Cambridge: Cambridge University Press.

SLA (second language acquisition)

Ellis, R. 1997. *Second Language Acquisition.* Oxford: Oxford University Press.

Lightbown, P., & N. Spada. 2006. *How Languages are Learned* (3rd edition) Oxford: Oxford University Press.

Methodology

Harmer, J. 2001. *The Practice of English Language Teaching* (3rd edition). Harlow: Pearson Education.

Larsen-Freeman, D. 2000. *Techniques and Principles in Language Teaching* (2nd edition) Oxford: Oxford University Press.

Nunan, D. (ed.) 2003. *Practical English Language Teaching.* New York: McGraw Hill.

Scrivener, J. 2005. *Learning Teaching* (2nd edition). Oxford: Macmillan.

Onestop English: www.onestopenglish.com

Professional development

Bailey, K., A. Curtis, D. Nunan. 2001. *Pursuing Professional Development: The Self as Source.* Boston: Heinle & Heinle.

Richards, J., and T. Farrell. 2005. *Professional Development for Language Teachers.* Cambridge: Cambridge University Press.

Websites of teachers' associations:
TESOL: www.tesol.edu
IATEFL: www.iatefl.org
English Australia: www.englishaustralia.com.au
TESL Canada: www.tesl.ca
JALT (Japan): www.jalt.org

Testing

Council of Europe. 2001. *Common European Framework of Reference for Languages: Learning, Teaching, Assessment.* Cambridge: Cambridge University Press.

Hughes, A. 2003. *Testing for Language Teachers* (2nd edition). Cambridge: Cambridge University Press.

University of Cambridge ESOL Examinations www.cambridgeesol.org

Trinity College, London, ESOL Examinations: www.trinitycollege.co.uk

City & Guilds Pitmans Qualifications, ESOL Examinations: www.pitmanqualifications.com

TOEFL (Test of English as a Foreign Language): www.toefl.org